# Citizen of the World

## Critical Insurgencies

*A Book Series of the Critical Ethnic Studies Association*

Series Editors: Jodi A. Byrd and Michelle M. Wright

Critical Insurgencies features activists and scholars, as well as artists and other media makers, who forge new theoretical and political practices that unsettle the nation-state, neoliberalism, carcerality, settler colonialism, Western hegemony, legacies of slavery, colonial racial formations, gender binaries, and ableism, and challenge all forms of oppression and state violence through generative future imaginings.

**About CESA**  The Critical Ethnic Studies Association organizes projects and programs that engage ethnic studies while reimagining its futures. Grounded in multiple activist formations within and outside institutional spaces, CESA aims to develop an approach to intellectual and political projects animated by the spirit of decolonial, antiracist, antisexist, and other global liberationist movements. These movements enabled the creation of ethnic studies and continue to inform its political and intellectual projects.

www.criticalethnicstudies.org

# Citizen of the World

## The Late Career and Legacy of W. E. B. Du Bois

EDITED BY

## Phillip Luke Sinitiere

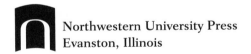

Northwestern University Press
Evanston, Illinois

Northwestern University Press
www.nupress.northwestern.edu

Printed in the United States of America

10   9   8   7   6   5   4   3   2   1

Library of Congress Cataloging-in-Publication Data

Names: Sinitiere, Phillip Luke, editor, author.
Title: Citizen of the world : the late career and legacy of W. E. B. Du Bois /
    edited by Phillip Luke Sinitiere.
Other titles: Critical insurgencies.
Description: Evanston : Northwestern University Press, 2019. | Series:
    Critical insurgencies | Includes index.
Identifiers: LCCN 2019007706 | ISBN 9780810140325 (paper text :
    alk. paper) | ISBN 9780810140332 (cloth text : alk. paper) | ISBN
    9780810140349 (e-book)
Subjects: LCSH: Du Bois, W. E. B. (William Edward Burghardt), 1868–
    1963—Political and social views. | Du Bois, W. E. B. (William Edward
    Burghardt), 1868–1963—Criticism and interpretation. | Du Bois,
    W. E. B. (William Edward Burghardt), 1868–1963—Influence. | African
    Americans—Politics and government—Philosophy. | African Americans—
    Intellectual life—20th century.
Classification: LCC E185.97.D73 C58 2019 | DDC 303.484—dc23
LC record available at https://lccn.loc.gov/2019007706

# CONTENTS

## The Politics of Memory and Meaning

# Acknowledgments

Books are always collective efforts, and this volume is no exception. It materialized after a panel on Du Bois's late career that I organized for the 2011 Organization of American Historians annual meeting in Houston. I thank the participants, Lauren Louise Anderson, Jodi Melamed, and Eric Porter, as well as the audience who offered probing questions and useful insights, especially Shawn Leigh Alexander. In an earlier incarnation of this project, I received feedback from Robert Sloan, formerly of Indiana University Press, and Duke University Press's Gisela Fosado. I'm grateful for their suggestions.

My friend and colleague Keisha Blain introduced me to the fantastic folks at Northwestern University Press, all of whom were wonderful to work with: Gianna Mosser, Nathan MacBrien, JD Wilson, Greta Bennion, Marianne Jankowski, Greta Polo, and Anne Gendler. Gianna, thank you for believing in this book, for giving it a chance, and for your vision in reshaping it. Similarly, I'm thrilled that Michelle M. Wright and Jodi A. Byrd welcomed this volume into Northwestern University Press's Critical Insurgencies series. I'm also very thankful for copyeditor Judith Hoover's skillful work. The manuscript's anonymous readers strengthened the project as well.

A large measure of gratitude goes to Rob Cox, Head of Special Collections at UMass Amherst, for the image of Du Bois that graces the cover. Thanks also to Duke University Press, the University of Massachusetts Press, and the CPUSA, publisher of *Political Affairs*, for permission to reprint revised versions of several essays that appear in this book. I also offer heartfelt gratitude to Whitney Battle-Baptiste, Director of the W. E. B. Du Bois Center at UMass Amherst. I finished edits and updates for this book at the Du Bois Center as a 2018–19 W. E. B. Du Bois Visiting Scholar, a fellowship funded by the Andrew W. Mellon Foundation.

Finally, I salute the contributors to this volume for their excellent and engaging work, and for their patience and forbearance as the book came into being over many years. I am grateful to collaborate with so many brilliant scholars in the larger Du Bois studies family. As always, Jenni, Matt, Alex, Maddie, Nate, and Eli provide inspiration.

# Citizen of the World

# "To Know and Think and Tell the Truth as I See It"

*Phillip Luke Sinitiere*

As, then, a citizen of the world as well as of the United States of America, I claim the right to know and think and tell the truth as I see it. I believe in Socialism as well as Democracy. I believe in Communism. . . . I despise men and nations which judge human beings by their color, religious beliefs or income. I believe in free enterprise among free men and individual initiative under physical, biological and social law. I hate War.
—W. E. B. Du Bois, *In Battle for Peace* (1952)

As part of his West Coast spring lecture tour, on February 14, 1953, W. E. B. Du Bois addressed the Southern California Peace Crusade (SCPC) with a speech titled "World Peace and Revolt in Africa." The Korean American cultural activist and communist Peter Hyun introduced the eighty-four-year-old scholar to his Los Angeles audience. In praise of Du Bois, he quoted Madame Sun Yat-sen's definition of a hero: "The hero in any age is one who carries out with a surpassing degree of devotion, determination, courage and skill the main tasks with which his times challenge every man. Today these tasks are worldwide, and the contemporary hero—whether he works at home or in a foreign land—is a world hero, not only in historical retrospect but now." Hyun's description of Du Bois as a world hero was not empty praise. In 1951 U.S. authorities arrested Du Bois on suspicion of communist activities, the kind of anticommunist political persecution with which Hyun was also intimately familiar. It was quite meaningful, therefore, to have Du Bois stand before a sympathetic southern California

audience to speak on peace. Hyun's invitation to the Los Angeles event
unveiled plans for a testimonial dinner in Du Bois's honor during
which the SCPC would "pay tribute not only to the person but also to
the symbol of Peace and Equality." Unified by leftist political commitments, Hyun's introduction of Du Bois also signified global dimensions
of a shared freedom struggle for peace: a Korean American communist
quoted a Chinese communist in support of a black radical intellectual
and would-be communist whose speech on postcolonial Africa called
for international solidarity of the working class.[1]

Du Bois's speech centered the "negro problem" on economic equality in global perspective. He rehearsed a short history of black political
advancement in the United States from the mid-nineteenth to the
mid-twentieth century, but cautioned his audience not to translate
political achievements into bourgeois comfort and a life of leisure. Too
often, he stated, everyday concerns centered on "how large an income
we can get, how much money we can control. . . . The object of our
ambition is rising to higher and higher income brackets." By contrast,
Du Bois expressed a critical philosophy of economic equality rooted
in communal-mindedness: "Work is service not gain. The object of
work is life, not income. The reward of production is plenty, not private property. We should measure the prosperity of a nation not by
the number of millionaires, but by the absence of poverty, the preva-
lence of health, the efficiency of the public schools, and the number
of people who can do read worthwhile books. . . . All for one and one
for all is an axiom of life." He pointed out that the future of freedom
for black people in the United States was bound to the fate of freedom movements abroad, especially decolonization struggles in Africa.
Freedom, he emphasized, privileged liberation "to think and believe,
and to express our thoughts and to dream our dreams. And to maintain our rights against secret police, witch hunters, or any other sort
of modern fool or tyrant." Freedom's future, Du Bois continued, would
come "not by slavery to corporations, and monopoly of press, cinema,
radio and television, but by united social effort for the common good so
that decently fed, healthy, and intelligent people can be sure of work,
not afraid of old age, and hold high their heads to think and say what
they damn please without fear of liars, informers, or a sneaking FBI."
The SCPC's testimonial dinner for Du Bois recognized his efforts in
the modern black freedom struggle, while it also offered a platform on
which he explained the global intersections of economic, racial, and
political work for justice and democracy.[2]

The preceding episode samples one year in Du Bois's final decades to illustrate the international dimensions of his leftist political orientation. It also demonstrates—especially in his personalized references to "secret police" and "liars, informers, or a sneaking FBI"—a rebellious awareness of the U.S. government's surveillance of his activities. About his southern California lecture tour, for example, Du Bois's FBI file richly documents that informants fed the Bureau intelligence about his travels. The content of his 1953 speech about economic exploitation in Africa received particular attention.[3] Perhaps more important than the FBI's surveillance of Du Bois—and of course he was not the only leftist on which the U.S. government set its investigative crosshairs—was his response to this kind of anticommunist scrutiny: it steeled his moral resolve to more fastidiously support peace, freedom, and liberation for oppressed peoples both at home and abroad.

Observation of Du Bois's resolve in such circumstances means a rejection of the alienation thesis, a prevailing perspective that assumes his leftist political convictions in his later years resulted from anger and bitterness, a helplessness that spawned a bitter retreat to Ghana in 1961. If the anticommunist persecution Du Bois underwent bolstered his commitments to socialism and peace, then his later decades deserve considerably more attention, a core scholarly conviction on which *Citizen of the World* focuses.

This volume defines his late career from the 1930s to the 1960s. Longitudinally it starts with the historical moment in which he left the NAACP, a juncture during which he argued for black collective power in the face of the Great Depression's economic disaster, and runs to his death in 1963. However, matters of historical legacy and intellectual heritage, topics this volume also addresses, constitute one meaning of Du Bois's late career.

*Citizen of the World* chronicles selected chapters of Du Bois's final three decades by orienting his extraordinarily active and productive later years to social, cultural, and political changes across the globe. In concert with a growing body of scholarship this collection asserts the fundamental importance of considering his later decades not as a life that descended into blind ideological allegiance—a conviction that inhabits the alienation thesis—but as the life of a productive, generative intellectual who, responding rationally, imaginatively, and radically to massive midcentury political, cultural, and social changes around the world, remained committed to freedom's realization until his last hour. This volume offers selective snapshots of the closing thoughts, political ideas, commentary, social analysis, and legacy of one of America's most important citizens of the world.

The opening cluster of essays, "A Global History of Race and Revolution," examines questions of political change, global revolution, and Du Bois's intellectual engagement with international civil rights. Yuichiro Onishi and Toru Shinoda center Japan in Du Bois's political imagination in the 1930s. The authors document how Toyohiko Kagawa's philosophy of cooperative practice inspired and influenced Du Bois's proposals for African American cooperative activities in response to upheavals the Great Depression unleashed. Examining an overlooked collection of Du Bois's political thought, Derek Catsam's essay uses Du Bois's writings in *Phylon* published between 1940 and 1944 to explain how the intrepid intellectual produced insightful engagement about South Africa from a Pan-African perspective. With the New Deal era in view from the perspective of the cold war, Bill Mullen captures Du Bois's thinking about political revolution in light of his developing grasp of Marx's writings, most specifically found in his unpublished manuscript "Russia and America." Erik McDuffie considers Du Bois's final *Autobiography* as a text of black radical possibility that shows his incisive analysis of global affairs through a commitment to political equality and economic democracy. These essays innovatively read further and wider into Du Bois's archive by examining his unpublished writings, journalistic publications, and autobiographical reflections to unveil even more clearly, in contrast to prevailing opinion, the intellectual vitality of the black radical internationalist conception of civil rights and political revolution expressed during his life's closing decades.

The volume's second segment of essays, "Gender and the Politics of Freedom," uses a feminist lens to investigate Du Bois's political thought both in his theoretical reflections and through his everyday life. Lauren Louise Anderson analyzes the pseudonymous "Anne Du Bignon" stories from *The Crisis* magazine to speculate why in the 1930s Du Bois pronounced his philosophy on cooperative economics in a female voice at a key moment in his life and career, when he exited the NAACP. On the related question of labor and gender, Alys Eve Weinbaum probes another publication from the same era, *Black Reconstruction*, to spell out a feminist reading of Du Bois's magnum opus that connects women's plantation labor, domestic work, and biocapitalism to grapple with the contemporary mechanisms of slavery's afterlife. Bettina Aptheker presents some of her own personal memories of Du Bois and his second wife, Shirley Graham—including recollections of her parents, Herbert and Fay, and their work on Du Bois's archive—to underscore the black scholar's human dimension. She connects his everyday dispositions to the rigor of his ideas and the impact of his activism and scholarship on generations of artists and activists. The cumulative benefit of these essays shows that despite the overarching masculinist framework in which he saw the world, Du Bois's investment in gender equity, however checkered it was, fundamentally shaped his intellectual artistry in *The Crisis*, his clear grasp through a Marxist lens of slavery's sexual exploitation of black women, and the everyday politics he expressed in his collaboration and friendship with the Aptheker family.

"The Politics of Memory and Meaning," the book's third section, considers the cultural significance of Du Bois as a cold war–era black radical in concert with matters of legacy and intellectual heritage. David Levering Lewis illuminates Du Bois's years in Brooklyn—the same era during which Bettina Aptheker knew him—to explain how the broad arc of his long political and intellectual life animated the friendships and relationships he had while living in New York City under federal surveillance. Moving beyond 1963, when Du Bois died, Gary Murrell narrates Herbert Aptheker's storied struggle with academia, university presses, federal funding, independent presses, and cold war anticommunism in getting Du Bois's work published. Phillip Luke Sinitiere widens the lens of publishing Du Bois's archive to account for historical and cultural developments that shaped and reshaped Du Bois scholarship over the past five decades, during which time his work has become much more accessible. Finally, Robert Williams picks up the theme of accessibility from the perspective of a scholar and a website creator to analyze the digital availability of Du Bois materials and how digitization opens new avenues of inquiry, political formation, and pedagogy through which scholars will carry out future work. These essays collectively account for Du Bois's cultural significance during his late career and beyond. And while they show how antiblack anticommunism hampered his twilight years and how its residual presence has in part shaped his legacy into the present day, due to the ongoing efforts within the black radical tradition and the ways that modern technology make his work more widely available than ever, the memory and meaning of Du Bois's life portend possibility for years to come.

The origins of this book stem from a panel on Du Bois's late career I organized for the 2011 Organization of American Historians annual meeting in Houston. In preparing the volume contributors developed essays in relation to the international shape of Du Bois's closing decades, from the 1930s to the 1960s, as well as the significance of his legacy. Essays in *Citizen of the World* selectively analyze Du Bois's political thought and social activism in connection with themes germane to Northwestern University Press's Critical Insurgencies series, such as white supremacy, feminist methodologies and practices, privatization, social movements, resistance, and protest, as well as the politics of autonomy and economic inequality.

Oriented around selected topics from Du Bois's late career, the essays in *Citizen of the World* do not offer a comprehensive picture of his life's closing seasons but rather anthologize particular moments and their specific relationship to social, political, and cultural history that spanned the 1930s through the 1960s and beyond. Collectively the essays aim to effectuate much-needed scholarly nuance to understanding Du Bois's twilight period, years that emboldened his commitment to democracy's realization in a world whose structural inequalities imperiled freedom's presence at nearly every historical turn. Du Bois devoted his life to this realization, and although he had many reasons to feel defeated or deterred, he possessed a measured hope through his final days. His outlook as a citizen of the world demonstrates that the very act of remembering his late career and legacy catalyzes a rigorous reception and critical application of his enduring intellectual achievements for a new century.

## Notes

1. W. E. B. Du Bois, "World Peace and Revolt in Africa," February 20, 1953, Pacifica Radio Archives, Archive #KZ2230. For the Madame Sun Yat-sen quote, see Ted Allan and Sydney Gordon, foreword, in *The Scalpel, the Sword: The Story of Doctor Norman Bethune* (1952; Tonawanda, NY: Dundurn Press, 2009), 9–12. On Peter Hyun's career and political work, see Marn J. Cha, *Koreans in Central California (1903–1957): A Study of Settlement and Transnational Politics* (Lanham, MD: University Press of America, 2010), 121–56; Nikolas Huot, "Peter Hyun (1906–1993)," in *Asian American Autobiographers: A Bio-Bibliographical Critical Sourcebook*, ed. Guiyou Huang (Westport, CT: Greenwood Press, 2001), 135–38. Du Bois's spring 1953 West Coast lecture tour included stops north in Oakland and San Francisco. See "Southern California Peace Crusade to W. E. B. Du Bois," November 18, 1952, W. E. B. Du Bois Papers

Digital Archive, mums312-b138-i163; "Southern California Peace Crusade to W. E. B. Du Bois," December 4, 1952, W. E. B. Du Bois Papers Digital Archive, mums312-b138-i166; "Southern California Peace Crusade to W. E. B. Du Bois," December 16, 1952, W. E. B. Du Bois Papers Digital Archive, mums312-b138-i169.

2. Du Bois, "World Peace and Revolt in Africa."

3. Federal Bureau of Investigation, "E. B. (William) Du Bois (Part 2)," *FBI Records: The Vault*, https://vault.fbi.gov/E.%20B.%20(William)%20Dubois.

# A Global History of Race and Revolution

# The Paradigm of Refusal

## W. E. B. Du Bois's Transpacific Political Imagination in the 1930s

*Yuichiro Onishi and Toru Shinoda*

In February 1935 Alain Locke invited W. E. B. Du Bois to submit a manuscript for the Associates in Negro Folk Education booklet series, where he served as a series editor, only to halt, after a little over a year, an effort to publish it. Locke called Du Bois's manuscript "direct propaganda"; he judged the contents far too political. In "The Negro and Social Reconstruction," Du Bois chronicled the past and present struggles of peoples of African descent—from slavery to the New Deal—to resist the persistence of racism and economic exploitation, unending violence, de jure and de facto segregation, and political disenfranchisement. And the deepening crisis of global capitalism in the mid-1930s, he reasoned, put African America, a population of twelve million, at the crossroads. From our vantage point in the present, Du Bois engaged in theoretical and political practices. The rejected manuscript that ultimately remained unpublished, surely was not a mere short history written for a general readership. Framed as an essay toward a history of the present, this history was written to make generative the very process of imagining a new future within the unfinished African American struggle for democracy.[1]

The core of Du Bois's history-making project was to give meaning to the capacity for black autonomy within the American nation. He emphasized the assertion of black sovereignty through economic cooperation among ordinary African Americans in segregated rural and urban communities across the United States. He called it a "cooperative State" forged out of "voluntary self-grouping."[2] Rather than waiting for a higher power of sorts, be it God or the federal government, to fulfill the promise of freedom, Du Bois insisted on black self-emancipation. In

13

the 1935 essay titled "A Negro Nation within the Nation," he explained
the program of racial action in this way:

> With the use of their political power, their power as consumers,
> and their brain power, added to that chance of personal appeal
> which proximity and neighborhood always give to human
> beings, Negroes can develop in the United States an economic
> nation within a nation, able to work through inner cooperation,
> to found its own institutions, to educate its genius, and at the
> same time, without mob violence or extremes of race hatred,
> to keep in helpful touch and cooperate with the mass of the
> nation. This has happened more often than most people realize,
> in the case of groups not so obviously separated from the mass
> of people as are American Negroes. It must happen in our case,
> or there is no hope for the Negro in America.[3]

Du Bois made it clear that the proposed program was not a mere
compilation of myriad traditions of historical black struggles. Neither
Booker T. Washington's program of racial uplift through self-reliance
nor the back-to-Africa nationalism of Marcus Garvey, he stressed his
program's specificity. It was grounded in mobilizing the power of self-
determined ordinary African Americans, particularly as consumers
and producers, to build an economic nation of their own. Moreover
this racial action had nothing to do with the Communist Party of the
U.S.A.'s call for black national self-determination in the Deep South,
although the title, "A Negro Nation within the Nation," certainly
evoked such an orientation. It did, however, represent a repudiation
of racial integration, the cornerstone of black advocacy for which he
played a principle role.

   The merit of this program for black self-emancipation, he reasoned,
was that it would proceed from the basic assumption concerning black
humanity, or what he called "free, self-assertive modern manhood."
This ontological and epistemological thrust was the key, given that
New Deal reform did not acknowledge this very fact. In the midst of
Franklin D. Roosevelt's broad agenda to transform the federal government into an agent of change responsible for the nation's economic
and social planning, Du Bois found very little optimism. Tersely he
wrote: "The colored people of America are coming to face the fact
quite calmly that most white Americans do not like them, and are planning neither for their survival, nor for the definite future if it involves

free, self-assertive modern manhood."[4] Du Bois was at odds with the majority of black leaders and intellectuals, who approached New Deal reform with some level of acceptance and engagement; in contrast, he maintained a critical distance, refusing to enter into a contract with this emergent socially democratic state. Such was what we call the paradigm of refusal, so central to his effort to fashion a distinct theory of black politics in the 1930s.

This essay theorizes Du Bois's conceptual politics that he articulated at a time of great upheaval to advance black internationalism. The 1930s was a period when the existing system of inequality based on race and class created out of the ascent and expansion of imperialism, colonialism, New World slavery, and aggressive militarism called "racial capitalism" plunged into a deep crisis of political and economic legitimacy.[5] Far from weakening at a critical turning point in the movement of world history, white supremacy underwent renewal. Intervening in this space, Du Bois sought to embolden the black ethos of cooperation to fight the curse of the modern world caused and heightened by rapacious greed and rampant prejudices that furthered the damnation of the already impoverished. He demanded careful social planning, combined with self-organization, no matter how much segregation would be required, "to secure a place for ourselves." "Our first business in the midst of the great economic revolution," he explained, was "to realize that race segregation is the white man's loss and not the black man's damnation."[6] Du Bois chose the position of "self-defense alloyed with self-preservation," to borrow from Stefano Harney and Fred Moten, as a strategy to articulate a new kind of politics within the black public sphere, but also lift up this historically specific black politics to a degree much greater than the politics of race within the United States.[7]

Then too Du Bois was monitoring the many social planning experiments based on cooperative economics that were gaining ground in smaller countries, especially Japan's cooperative movement. He believed in consumers' and producers' cooperatives within African America and an "economic alliance with the industrial powers of the country."[8] In his thinking specifically about black internationalism, "Du Bois's Japan" had a specific place in his political imagination since the turn of the twentieth century. His transpacific comparative outlook, for instance, appeared in two essays written for the American Negro Academy's sessions, "The Conservation of Races" (1897) and "The Present Outlook for the Dark Races of Mankind" (1900), and it continued to crop up throughout the early 1900s, as Nahum Dimitri

Chandler finds in Du Bois's early writings.[9] What Du Bois's sustained
interest in Japan reveals is a strategy to engage with "the problem of the
color line."[10] Japan had a conceptual function.

Amid the concerted efforts by African American intellectual elites to
proclaim the fact of black humanity, for which he was a key architect at
the turn of the twentieth century, Du Bois looked to the rise of modern
Japan as a reference point. His "remarkably steady and singular eye for
the assertions of Japan," Chandler observes, had much to do with his
response to the shifting configurations of race and power that under-
wrote the expansion of imperial sovereignty and colonial governance in
the United States and the international system, particularly in a wider
Asia. In the years surrounding the First Universal Race Congress, held
in July 1911 in London, and throughout the interwar period, Du Bois
began shaping imperatives for black ontology and epistemology, so central to the articulation of black politics, that could at once move in
various scales and operate in productive ways in relation to not just
Japan but also Sun Yat-sen's China and Mohandas Gandhi and Rabin-
dranath Tagore's India. Chandler explains that these years led Du Bois
to cultivate "a whole possible epistemic-political path for an intervention beyond national- and regional-level presumptions."[11] The essay
published in 1925, "Worlds of Color," and the novel *Dark Princess: A
Romance* (1928) are two results of his internationalist interest.

Yet "Du Bois's Japan" was far from static. It underwent reworking
in crises over race and global capitalism in the 1930s. At the time,
Du Bois's primary preoccupation was to translate the imperative of
black self-determination as an essential frame of reference with which
to make political judgments about the future direction of the world. For
him, this was a time to make a bold and creative move in thought and
action. In this regard, "Du Bois's Japan" was a method to communicate
the need for an independent conceptual politics that could help set up
the African American ethics of engagement to fulfill the goal of the second emancipation.[12] His goal was to convey what it would take to strive
toward a committed human life in all its fullness, richness, and complexity without feeling the brunt of the corruption of the concept of
race. Du Bois mobilized black history against the whole edifice of modern thought. Chandler offers the concept of "modern global historicity"
to get to the core of Du Bois's politics, how Du Bois sought in the
1930s to activate global and local manifestations of "race contact" and
make them become generative for "persistent parallaxes" to have shaping power. Myriad race contacts across multiple color lines engendered

"a kind of 'second sight' within and beyond the historicity in which it is produced," Chandler argues about Du Bois's politics, which helped to rework the movement of world history in service of the advancement and liberation of the Darker World.[13]

Du Bois was indeed seeking a way of making the ethical process of engagement with the highly uneven and unjust world productive for new formations, especially in terms of the shaping of a strong political subjectivity and collectivity in African America. Such was the Du Boisian moral law. He referred to his effort to construct a distinct moral law to engage with and arrest the philosophical challenge of his time as "the Problem of the future world," a conceptual framing that Eric Porter has recently analyzed to chart Du Bois's midcentury intellectual trajectory in the last phase of his life.[14] In what follows, we discuss political contexts that influenced the construction of Du Boisian moral law as a conceptual tool to apprehend the directions of reform initiatives coming out of the New Deal state and the deep crisis of this era. Specifically, we recast Du Bois's political imagination in a transpacific direction by locating the appeal of the world's leading spokesperson of the modern cooperative movement, Toyohiko Kagawa.[15]

## 1936: World Tours

On January 24, 1936, Toyohiko Kagawa lectured at Atlanta University (AU), where Du Bois was teaching. Du Bois's close friend John Hope, AU's president, presided and shared the stage with Kagawa, but Du Bois was not with them. Just a few weeks earlier, Kagawa had appeared at Spelman College in the course of meeting and interacting with black and white leaders of local colleges and universities and church leaders in the Atlanta area. Then, too, Du Bois was absent. American Christians revered Kagawa, a leading Japanese Christian leader who adhered to the principles of socialism and pacifism, as a saintly social reformer. In early 1936 he embarked on a six-month tour across the United States, supported by the Federal Council of the Churches of Christ. Highly publicized, both in newspapers and via airwaves, his tour put Kagawa center stage within the American Social Gospel movement.[16]

Although Du Bois had missed meeting Kagawa in person, he too held him in high esteem, often placing him next to Mahatma Gandhi for explicit praise. As many other American Christians did, he highlighted Kagawa's principal role and success in the building of producers' and consumers' cooperatives in Japan. Then, as now, observers commonly regarded Kagawa as the father of the modern cooperative movement. He was instrumental in helping to expand various types of cooperatives in Japan throughout the first half of the twentieth century, from producer-owned to consumer-owned enterprises to credit unions and mutual aid and beneficial societies. American Christians flocked to him because of his contributions to large-scale cooperative movement mobilization. They propagated his philosophy of cooperative economics suffused with Christian messages by translating his writings into English and publishing them. Du Bois, however, placed Kagawa's significance elsewhere. It had little to do with his stature as a spiritual leader of the world, much less a progressive reformer.[17] The appeal of Kagawa, according to Du Bois, was all about politics.

In 1936 Toyohiko Kagawa (1888–1960) and W. E. B. Du Bois (1868–1963) were two "progressive travelers," both literally and in terms of their philosophy and faith in cooperatives.[18] They both embarked on world tours that year. Kagawa conducted his missionary tour in the United States from December 1935 to July 1936. This was part of a new movement he launched in Japan in 1928–32 called the Kingdom of God Movement ("Kami no kuni" Undo). During those years, the onset of the Great Depression, he visited all over Japan, including rural and impoverished areas, and stayed in the homes of common people. The movement's goal was to mobilize thousands of converted Japanese Christians around the power of God's redeeming love to respond to the pressing problems of poverty and injustice. For Kagawa, the ontological concern resided deep within. In his notes and comments on various local places he toured in Japan, which were published in *Wandering and Pilgrimage* (*Hoko to Junrei*), Kagawa showed eagerness to seek his own soul, as well as the souls of ordinary people. Along the way, he searchingly carved out the sense of peoplehood among converted Japanese Christians as a source of redemptive love. He committed himself to this work of salvation and was trying to expand the cause globally.[19]

Orphaned at a young age, Kagawa understood cruelty. Throughout much of his childhood, he lived in poverty and abandonment. His conversion to Christianity as a teenager changed his life. He found a supportive community in the Southern Presbyterian Church when he met Reverend Harry Myers, a missionary living and working in Japan. Kagawa made up his mind to devote his life to the work of serving the poor, the despised, and the unemployed. He lived among the poorest of the poor, including Burakumin, a racialized outcast group in the slums of Kobe called Shinkawa, until he left to study at Princeton Theological Seminary. Upon his return from the United States in 1916, he immersed himself in both the Japanese labor movement and the farmers' struggle and by the early 1920s emerged as a leading Christian socialist leader spreading the message of the Social Gospel. By the mid-1930s he had become the face of the cooperative movement in Japan, which represented nearly "six million people, almost a tenth of the nation's population," as the historian Robert Shaffer emphasizes.[20]

According to Shaffer, Kagawa's 1936 U.S. tour drew large crowds at every major city, particularly in Chicago, Boston, New York, and Seattle. American Christians knew of his achievements and status. Some of these gatherings, particularly in the southern states, were interracial in character. He visited Birmingham, Atlanta, New Orleans, Nashville, Knoxville, and several cities and towns in North Carolina and Virginia. Overall Kagawa visited 150 cities and towns in six months and encountered thousands of Americans (nearly 750,000). The radio broadcast of his lectures reached thousands more. The enthusiasm around him appeared most explicitly in how the mainstream media often characterized him as "a symbol of Christ-living in the twentieth century."[21] He spoke with validity and vitality.

Du Bois set out on a six-month world tour starting in June 1936, during which he visited Germany, the Soviet Union, China, and Japan. In part funded by the Oberlaender Trust, his travel abroad was to conduct comparative research on the European model of industrial education in Germany and Austria and Booker T. Washington's program of racial uplift centered on vocational training, industrial education, and agricultural studies. But Du Bois had something else in mind. He turned this opportunity for international research into his own search for breakthroughs—to see the wider world beyond Europe with his own eyes and observe the reality of darker nations and peoples rising. In the midst of change and uncertainty resulting from the collapse of unfettered capitalism and competing systems of governance vying for legitimacy (e.g., liberal democracy, communism, and fascism), he made a case for independent African American political action grounded in the theory and practice of cooperative economics. He worked out his own ideas about cooperativism as a strategy for development and empowerment within African America as a columnist for the *Pittsburgh Courier* from February 1936 to January 1938.[22]

The following assumptions grounded Du Bois's turn to cooperative economics in the 1930s. Given that economic and racial injustices against African Americans intensified in times of racial capitalism's crises, he proposed that African Americans would need to engage in a qualitatively different kind of development and empowerment project, something other than those based on Keynesianism and Marxism and certainly not capitalism founded on classical liberalism tied to individualism or self-possession. He regarded the mobilization of a highly organized and segregated consuming public within the African American community as an important first step, similar to ideas Lauren Louise Anderson's essay in this volume identifies. He relied, in part, on the Rochdale model of cooperative enterprise as a blueprint for black social planning.

The Rochdale principles of cooperation originated in England in 1844, when the members of the Rochdale Society of Equitable Pioneers began building alternative economic arrangements founded upon the values of cooperation for mutual gains and benefits, shared governance, equality, and democratic control and participation. These principles had become, by the late 1800s and early 1900s, foundational to the modern cooperative movement, as they were adapted by a number of cooperative associations and initiatives, both local and international, led by sellers, buyers, consumers, and owners who sought to work together to help each other achieve their shared economic and social goals rather than succumbing to capitalist practices that contributed to overproduction and business instabilities resulting from competition and rising costs.[23]

Du Bois, in his characteristically succinct prose, described cooperative economic practice founded on Rochdale principles in this way:

> It is an organization of people, membership [in] which is open to everybody. It is democratic: one member, one vote. That means that the members do not have votes according to the money that they invest or according to the amount of goods which they buy. The rule is, one member one vote. On capital invested limited interest is paid, but dividends on purchases are paid to each purchaser according to the amount he has purchased during the year. The goods in a co-operative store sell for cash at regular market price. The co-operative store does not sell cheaper than other stores. It makes every effort to sell at the same price. On the other hand, while the profits of other stores go to the owner, the profits of a cooperative are divided at the end of the year among the people who purchased goods in proportion to

the amount of goods which they purchased. Co-operative stores are neutral in that they recognize neither race, religion, nor politics. Above all, they educate their members continuously and constantly in the meaning and object of co-operatives; and finally and of the greatest importance, they expand continuously, knowing that one co-operative cannot maintain itself long. It can hope to be perpetual if it helps quickly in organizing other co-operatives so that these co-operatives standing together can become producing co-operatives.[24]

Du Bois was an early supporter of the Rochdale model of cooperative enterprise. It was never tangential in his thinking. In his early career as a scholar, he took seriously cooperative economics as a strategy for racial uplift. Just a few years after earning a Ph.D. from Harvard University, for instance, he published the book *Some Efforts of American Negroes for Their Own Social Betterment* (1898). A decade later, while building the Niagara movement, he published another book, *Economic Co-operation among Negro Americans* (1907). According to Jessica Gordon Nembhard, Du Bois chronicled variations of African American cooperative economic practice in these books, including "mutual-aid and beneficial societies, mutual insurance organizations, fraternal organizations and secret societies, buying clubs, joint-stock ownership among African Americans, and collective farming."[25] Also throughout the early twentieth century, he corresponded with the nation's leading promoters of cooperatives, such as the Co-operative League of America and its leader, James P. Warbasse. In 1918 he helped found the Negro Cooperative Guild to create a forum to study cooperative economics. Through this study group he sought to help educate and train future leaders capable of putting Rochdale principles into practice. He also kept abreast of the international cooperative movement.[26]

All the while following the general trends of cooperativism within Europe and mainstream America, Du Bois argued that the cooperative movement was not entirely the product and property of European social struggles and experiments. Well before the introduction and institutionalization of Rochdale principles, this tradition of mutuality, cooperation, and collective resistance was constructed and cultivated over centuries of struggles for black liberation. It enabled African Americans to survive enslavement and systematic racial oppression throughout the post–Civil War era. Such was his sharp critique of Eurocentric assumptions surrounding cooperative economics and its influence in the wider world that Du Bois asserted in his newspaper column, "Economic co-operation has been a main occupation of [the] American Negro from the beginning."[27]

Indeed Du Bois's interest in Kagawa had much to do with his effort to radically shift the terms of discussing and propagating the imperative of economic cooperation as a strategy to overcome the crisis of racial capitalism. What he wanted to convey was that darker nations and people, including African America and Japan, understood the essence of cooperative economics grounded in Rochdale principles far better than its proponents in the West did. They had always utilized the principles of mutuality and cooperation as essential resources for their survival and renewal. His focus and framing were always global and often Afro-Asian in perspective.[28]

When Du Bois appeared alongside William Patterson and Harry H. Pace, his close acquaintances, at the forum on consumers' cooperatives held at the Church of the Good Shepherd on Chicago's South Side in the spring of 1939, he made his position clear. Expounding on the "value of consumers cooperatives for Negroes," he delved deep into the philosophical and historical contributions of African-descended people to the advancement and promotion of cooperative thought and practice rather than simply locating the beginning of the modern cooperative movement in the Rochdale Society of Equitable Pioneers in 1844. His periodization started with the transatlantic slave trade. As the reporter for the *Chicago Defender* explained, the theme of Du Bois's talk was, in essence, the sweeping history of African-descended people's roles in the "rise of the world co-op system." Writing against despair, powerlessness, self-denigration, and nihilism, he offered a grand counternarrative.[29] The key for him was historical and political consciousness-raising, which would enable moral imperatives to action toward cooperative economic practice.

## Keeping Faith in Cooperatives

Throughout the 1930s Du Bois kept faith in cooperatives. On this, he and Kagawa agreed. Beyond that, they relied on idioms of their own to talk about the imperative of liberation. Their trajectories are more like concentric circles. While Du Bois, as Bill Mullen analyzes in this volume, grappled with the concept of world revolution to respond to the local and global demands of darker people, the Christian language of the power of redemptive love suffused Kagawa's preaching on the matter of transforming existing society.[30] After all, he was a proselytizer and a preacher. Kagawa built his conviction upon the principle that the deep understanding of Christianity, or its faith, could lead to the creation of alternative economics that are capable of overcoming the curse of industrial imperialism, or what he called "the poverty of plenty," perpetuated by greed, individualism, private property rights, labor exploitation, and materialism.[31] He called this new form of economics "brotherhood economics" and considered it vital to the creation of a truly cooperative, just, and egalitarian society. Kagawa first presented this concept to an American audience at Colgate-Rochester Divinity School in 1936, where he delivered the Walter Rauschenbusch lectures during his U.S. tour. Shortly afterward, Harper and Brothers published these lectures as a book.[32]

In *Brotherhood Economics*, Kagawa contended that orthodox Marxists so often looked solely at something concrete, such as income and wealth and workers' control of the means of production, and neglected to consider deep human needs and desires to create a society built upon love, cooperation, human dignity, and individual creativity. He explained:

> If the economic life were fundamentally materialistic, its problem might be solved in a materialistic way. But, in the last analysis, the economic life is a movement in the realm of values. . . . It has other phases that touch man's conscious moral and ethical life. Materialistic economics goes over into the realms of psychological economics.[33]

He believed that to revolutionize existing economic life governed by the capitalist and communist states, "there must take place a fundamental revolution of ideas concerning wealth and professions in their relation to property rights, inheritance, and rights of contract." He continued, "Only as a revolution of these conceptions is based on religious consciousness, progressing until it is organized into social consciousness, can economic revolution be completely realized."[34] Kagawa scrutinized the whole category of materialism to redefine what it would take to achieve human happiness.

Kagawa also considered the cooperative movement a more effective path to elevating the well-being of workers and farmers than the revolutionary proletarian struggle. Missing from efforts to mobilize the masses

based on class consciousness, according to Kagawa, was "a sense of
social solidarity grounded in a consciousness of redemptive love."[35] He
generally detested the strain of syndicalism within labor radicalism in
Japan and elsewhere. For Kagawa, concrete engagement in the cause of
social and economic justice involved Christian brotherhood and love in
action, not workers' direct action to take over the means of production.
He wrote, "Violent revolution, though temporarily successful, is never
permanently so. . . . The only good that may be said of it is that it may
abolish a powerful exploiting class."[36]

Du Bois probably would have agreed with Kagawa's point that the
advancement of economic cooperation required "a fundamental revolution of ideas concerning wealth and professions in their relation to
property rights, inheritance, and rights of contract."[37] Kagawa's assertion was that material reality would never be transformed without
considering the metaphysical, or such cognitive dimensions of human
experience as greed and deep desire (or spiritual need) on the part of
labor to pursue a committed human life to grow and evolve with purpose
through collaborations with and love and care toward others. According to Kagawa, adherents of both capitalism and communism had yet
to probe in depth "the fact that economic want is psychological."[38]

Du Bois possessed a similar sentiment in his effort to mobilize the
African American cooperative movement. If not Christian brotherhood
and love, or the power of redemptive love, Du Bois embraced "race
consciousness." His thinking was guided by the following dictum, so
central to the challenge of "being black" in a society built upon racial
subordination and exploitation, which he expressed in "Of Our Spiritual Strivings," an essay collected in *The Souls of Black Folk* (1903):
"To attain his place in the world, he must be himself, not another."[39]
Given the entrenchment of white supremacy within the struggles of
labor, he argued, "race consciousness, [or] race solidarity . . . becomes
not the enemy of labor solidarity but the only path to it." He elaborated, "They form a perfect Hegelian category: the thesis of Negro
race consciousness; the antithesis: the union of all labor across racial,
national, and color lines; and the synthesis: a universal labor solidarity arising through the expansion of race consciousness in the most
exploited labor class to all labor."[40] For Du Bois, the cooperative movement represented "race consciousness in action," closely linked to
dialectical materialism, capable of turning despair, powerlessness, and
self-denigration into what he called "vigorous and decisive action." It
was a motivating and dialectical force: "Let us not affront our own

self-respect by accepting a proffered equality which is not equality, or submitting to discrimination simply because it does not involve actual and open segregation; and above all let us not sit down and do nothing for self-defense and self-organization just because we are too stupid or too distrustful of ourselves to take vigorous and decisive action."[41]

## A Mirror of the Possible

This kernel of Du Boisian moral law in the 1930s was stored in his commitment to economic cooperation, and the appeal of Kagawa enabled its sowing. Specifically, it helped Du Bois articulate the type of African American leadership capable of advancing cooperative economics to transform the existing world, not just locally but, most important, through the expansion of global race consciousness. As he often reiterated, "To doubt that this is possible is to doubt the essential humanity and the quality of brains of the American Negro."[42] Indeed Du Bois became interested in referencing the successful case of Japan's cooperative movement to validate his call for independent political action within African America founded on the scheme of "voluntary self-grouping" among African Americans. The following outline, presented in "A Negro Nation within the Nation," makes clear the manner in which he formulated black solidarity in the context of cooperativism:

> There exists today a chance for the Negroes to organize a cooperative State within their own group. By letting Negro farmers feed Negro artisans, and Negro technicians guide Negro home industries, and Negro thinkers plan this integration of cooperation, while Negro artists dramatize and beautify the struggle, economic independence can be achieved.[43]

For instance, upon his return from the world tour, during which he visited Kagawa's cooperative projects in Tokyo, Du Bois heralded the ethics of commitment he witnessed among workers and neighborhood activists at the local level. Japanese cooperatives led by the vision of Kagawa, according to Du Bois, were "self-supporting" and were "feeding thousands of poor people three meals a day at a cost of eight cents." Similarly he regarded cooperatives involving sellers, buyers, consumers, and owners working together through voluntary self-segregation as the best strategy to build the African American economy and reduce economic hardships experienced by the people. Echoing Kagawa's proclamation that "the poverty of to-day is not the poverty of want but the poverty of plenty," Du Bois, speaking to a large crowd in the Harlem YWCA auditorium, said the key to "being happy was not to want so much."[44]

Not surprisingly, a call "to organize a cooperative State" within African America elicited criticisms from his peers. To be sure, Du Bois understood their skepticism. During the 1930s, while the civic nationalist ethos and the growing strength of organized labor to buoy the fight for racial integration swept up many moderate and left-leaning African American leaders, Du Bois rejected this commonplace aim. He also repudiated mainstream social planning and economic development that laid the groundwork for welfare state formations. He did not see the U.S. nation-state, let alone nation-states of Europe, as the arbiter of black freedom. These were not entities capable of validating the value of darker people. The racial polity, he was convinced, would not uphold the fact of black humanity because its survival in the moment of a deep crisis in the existing economic system required the subordination of darker people through continued colonialism, imperialism, and aggressive militarism.

In short, the appeal of Kagawa was that his work allowed Du Bois to articulate an entirely different path to organize—from the bottom up—overlapping spheres of independent political action and economic engagement through self-propelled activity and cooperation, all the while maintaining a critical distance from the racial state that maintained the mechanism of impoverishment. In the iconic significance of Kagawa, Du Bois found the language to articulate the moral authority of darker people under colonial and racial domination to pursue another world. To his naysayers on the matter of creating a cooperative state through black economic cooperation, he proclaimed, "[It] has already been accomplished in the organization of the Negro church, the Negro school and Negro retail business, and despite all the justly due criticism, the result has been astonishing."[45]

To dramatize his point about a new black politics guided by the principles of self-organization and self-activity, Du Bois used the case of the Spanish Civil War (1936–39), then raging on the other side of the Atlantic Ocean. In Spain the destiny of progressive, left-leaning democracy was on the line as the fascist force of General Francisco Franco assaulted the Popular Front government of the Spanish Republic under siege in the capital city of Madrid. The cause of antifascism in Spain drew support from around the globe. Du Bois was cognizant of the concern that ordinary black Americans, the readership of his weekly *Pittsburgh Courier* column, expressed toward the Spanish Republic.[46] Although he assured his readers that he hoped never to see Madrid fall into the hands of fascists, he did find it useful to recall a similar kind of political energy to complete the work of besieging what he called the "city of Privilege and Prejudice." Using the notion of the siege to draw a comparison between the impoverishment of African America within the system of white supremacy and the Spanish Republic under siege by fascist power, he tried to make his point in a measured yet optimistic tone. He assigned tremendous moral and political authority to independent African American political action:

> We Negroes are besieging a city. It has been a long, hard, desperate fight. We have not won. No one living is likely to see the final victory, and yet the success we have had, the ground we have covered, the extraordinary things that have happened in this long warfare ought to hearten us all and leave no doubt as to the final outcome. But a siege does not consist in forging continually forward in one line for victory after victory. Tactics change. One attacks now here, now there. We stop for consultation. We rearrange our forces. We even give ground. But always the objective stands: We are fighting for universal equality; for the right of black men in America and every part of the world to be considered as men; to have equal income, equal opportunity for education; equal chance to develop in every direction according to our ability.[47]

Always historically attuned in thinking about the immediate challenges of African America, Du Bois described in this column the following three cases of the black assault on this "city of Privilege and Prejudice" since the Reconstruction period that decisively informed the present struggles and future developments. The focus of the first assault was the right to education, how the drama of black self-emancipation in the immediate aftermath of the Civil War spurred "the drive for the right to know." Here he had in mind the black working-class, ex-slaves, buoying the work of the Freedmen's Bureau, the crown jewel of federal Reconstruction policy that steered a new nation toward universal equality through the creation and expansion of the system of free public education.

The second assault involved the campaign to use newly gained political rights to make significant headway into American democracy during
Reconstruction. Such was the nucleus of the struggle for black Reconstruction. But the white polity stifled this effort. In response, the self-help
movement led by Booker T. Washington, which Du Bois referred to as "a
shrewd turning movement," enabled some segments of black labor and
the black middle class to gain some ground (i.e., achieve upward social
mobility), despite the rising tide of segregation and white terror.

The third assault was the one carried out by the black intelligentsia.
According to Du Bois, this work of black political advocacy, although
still not far-reaching, had become "more widely recognized" by the
mainstream during the first two decades of the twentieth century and
tested the legitimacy of the American polity founded on the principle of
equal protection under the law.[48]

Deeply enmeshed in much of these efforts throughout the first two
decades of the twentieth century as the cornerstone of the black intelligentsia, Du Bois, being self-reflective, had come to the conclusion
that the kind of transformation that could usher in a truly just and
egalitarian society demanded what Martin Luther King Jr. articulated
four decades later, in April 1967, as "the radical revolution of values."
One had to make radical alterations to one's outlook on modern life
and progress. Du Bois thus conceived the new strategy of assault on
the "city of Privilege and Prejudice." He argued that the goal of racial
justice, or universal equality, as well as economic justice, could not be
achieved as long as the general welfare of "the vast majority of mankind," darker peoples of the world, did not receive attention.[49] He
reserved the harshest criticism for the black petite bourgeoisie.

> The average educated American Negro wants to become a rich
> capitalist with an "independent" income, separated from the
> poor black, white and brown, and recognized as a part of the
> ruling world aristocracy. This old ideal of American and Euro-
> pean life is being taught in our schools and colleges. Most of
> the teachers of economics in colored institutions are more or
> less unconsciously reactionary. They regard poverty as a crime
> and crime as deliberate sin. They look upon sickness as mere
> weakness. They depend upon exploitation and thrift to estab-
> lish us in business, help us accumulate property, and thereby
> bomb our way into the inner circles of power. Right here our
> whole conception and outlook must change.[50]

This commentary, published shortly after his return from the world tour in April 1937, was a self-criticism of his own theory of black leadership, called "the Talented Tenth," the concept he aspired to cultivate and forge among the trained few in the early twentieth century. But as he reminded his readers, "The job of the 'Talented Tenth' is not ended when they become intelligent; it has simply begun."[51] In the 1930s Du Bois's focus was now on the creation of the "nucleus of a conscious dictatorship of intelligence" to engage in "the uplift of the mass."[52]

In his reconceptualization of black leadership informed by the idioms of Karl Marx, the key phrase was "a conscious dictatorship of intelligence." To become *conscious* entailed knowing the history of black self-emancipation, from slavery to freedom, and the very import of this past in the present. Specifically, Du Bois saw in "a history of the part which Black folk played in the attempt to reconstruct democracy in America," the long subtitle to the book *Black Reconstruction in America, 1860–1880*, the historical moment of a black nation-in-the-making, the cooperative state, within the American nation:

> Can we imagine this spectacular revolution? Not, of course, unless we think of these people as human beings like ourselves. Not unless, assuming this common humanity, we conceive ourselves in a position where we are chattels and real estate, and then suddenly in a night become "thenceforward and forever free." Unless we do this, there is, of course, no point in thinking of this central figure in emancipation.[53]

Du Bois explained why he characterized this history in the way he did: "I have emphasized in my book, 'Black Reconstruction,' the tendency among Negroes after the Civil War to begin an economic reconstruction which was quite different from the dominant American idea and which foreshadowed a conduct of the State for the benefit of the masses by wide democratic control."[54] He considered this thrust, "critical reason and the capacity for autonomy and self-governance," to borrow from Nikhil Pal Singh's framing, that he found in black history was indeed a guiding light for black liberation in the 1930s. Du Bois was self-consciously engaged in history writing to make history in the present. He approached the writing of *Black Reconstruction* as the history of the present.[55]

In the mid-1930s Du Bois communicated the same message: African Americans ought to work on the creation of more cooperative

arrangements within their own segregated economic and social realities with hopes that such a more just and egalitarian state would
replace the existing racial polity. The objective in times of uncertainty
and precariousness was to take the position of self-organization deliberately. Du Bois described the creation of this distance from the New
Deal state as a "far-fetched dream," but, as he wrote, "it is worth the
contemplation."[56]

Specifically Du Bois issued the following two directives, particularly
to African American intellectuals and leaders: (1) to immerse themselves in the study of key tenets of the Rochdale cooperative movement
and (2) to *consciously* turn to African Americans' past attempts to
engage in economic cooperation and use this history as a springboard
to "rehearse the future" in the present.[57]

> When after the [Civil] war Negro education was set on its
> feet, it was through tremendous and persistent efforts in co-
> operation on the part of the Negroes themselves. While the
> United States government helped somewhat, and missionary
> societies, it must be remembered that the freedmen themselves
> out of their poverty contributed, from 1866 to 1870, $785,000
> toward their schools and that much of the money that came
> from the Freedmen's Bureau came through work and taxes laid
> on the freedmen.[58]

This history was important to him because he was interested in making
palpable what Manu Goswami calls "the historical category of the possible" in the present.[59] "We do not realize what the small group can do,"
Du Bois wrote in his weekly column for the *Pittsburgh Courier*.[60] The
small group, albeit despised, could forge a nation within the nation, as
it had done in the past during the period of Reconstruction.

Du Bois was quite serious about the power of cooperativism as a
lever with which to consolidate what he called "inner-organization
for self-defense."[61] It would hinge on the principle of profit sharing
rather than the policy and attitude of laissez faire. As long as African
American producers operated with the capitalist mode of producing
wealth through self-aggrandizement, possessive individualism, and
manipulation, the whole effort was doomed to failure. Emphasizing the
socialization of wealth as foundational to the development of the "cooperative State" within African American communities, he demanded "a
complete revolution" in thought. He insisted that African Americans

must decisively break away from the operating principles of market and political liberalism.[62]

Du Bois's investment in the cooperative movement intensified during the 1930s because he regarded African Americans' serious engagement with cooperative economics as the best method of self-defense and self-organization against the relentless assaults on their dignity and humanity. For him, it was a political challenge, to be sure. But he also approached the realization of a new society based on cooperative economics as a philosophical challenge, for he considered the growing strength of the cooperative movement in times of crisis as part and parcel of the movement of world history. For Du Bois, the appeal of Kagawa was such that it possessed the capacity to bring together the African American struggles of the past and the present and, through this important synthesis, move forward with strong conviction to achieve the goal of human liberation. In other words, Kagawa was not just a figure to be revered; he represented what we call a "mirror of the possible" to help sow the African American ethos of self-determination into the future. Writing in April 1937 for the *Pittsburgh Courier*, Du Bois so aptly translated this perspective into the following clear-cut dictum: "Not to become white men; not to become yellow men; but to become ourselves and to hold ourselves the equal of any."[63]

## Notes

1. W. E. B. Du Bois, "The Negro and Social Reconstruction," in *Against Racism: Unpublished Essays, Papers, Addresses, 1887–1961*, edited by Herbert Aptheker (Amherst: University of Massachusetts Press, 1985), 103–4; Nikhil Pal Singh, *Black Is a Country: Race and Unfinished Struggle for Democracy* (Cambridge, MA: Harvard University Press, 2004), 58–100; Yuichiro Onishi, *Transpacific Antiracism: Twentieth-Century Afro-Asian Solidarity in Black America, Japan, and Okinawa* (New York: NYU Press, 2013), 54–93.

2. W. E. B. Du Bois, "Forum of Fact and Opinion," *Pittsburgh Courier*, May 1, 1937, in *Newspaper Columns, 1883–1944, Volume 1*, edited by Herbert Aptheker (White Plains, NY: Kraus-Thompson Organization, 1982), 196–97; W. E. B. Du Bois, "A Negro Nation within the Nation," in *Writings by W. E. B. Du Bois in Periodicals Edited by Others, 1910–1934*, vol. 2 (Millwood, N.Y.: Kraus-Thompson Organization, 1982), 5.

3. Du Bois, "A Negro Nation within the Nation," 5.

4. Du Bois, "A Negro Nation within the Nation," 2.

5. Cedric J. Robinson, *Black Marxism: The Making of the Black Radical Tradition* (London: Zed Press, 1983).

6. W. E. B. Du Bois, "Social Planning for the Negro, Past and Present," *Journal of Negro Education* 5:1 (1936), 122, 125.

7. Stefano Harney and Fred Moten, *The Undercommons: Fugitive Planning & Black Study* (Brooklyn: Autonomedia, 2013), 19.

8. Du Bois, *Newspaper Columns*, 204. He explained, "The economic program of American Negroes divides itself into two main parts. First, a nationwide organization of their power as consumers, which is large; and also an organization of their power as producers, which is at present small; and secondary, alliance with the economic organization of the nation."

9. W. E. B. Du Bois, *The Problem of the Color Line at the Turn of the Twentieth Century*, edited by Nahum Dimitri Chandler (New York: Fordham University Press, 2015), 56, 113–14; Nahum Dimitri Chandler, "A Persistent Parallax: On the Writings of W. E. Burghardt Du Bois on Japan and China, 1936–1937," *CR: The New Centennial Review* 12:1 (2012): 291–96.

10. Du Bois, *The Problem of the Color Line at the Turn of the Twentieth Century*, 6–11.

11. Chandler, "A Persistent Parallax," 296–97. Also see Nahum Dimitri Chandler's annotations in W. E. B. Du Bois, "Chapter 17—Jones Looks Back on China," *CR: The New Centennial Review* 12:1 (2012), 284–87.

12. Du Bois, *Newspaper Columns*, 203–4.

13. Nahum Dimitri Chandler, "Introduction: On the Virtues of Being—At Least, but Never Only—Double," *CR: The New Centennial Review* 12:1 (2012), 14; Chandler, "A Persistent Parallax," 291, 298.

14. Eric Porter, *The Problem of the Future World: W. E. B. Du Bois and the Race Concept at Midcentury* (Durham, NC: Duke University Press, 2010). Singh, *Black Is a Country*, 119.

15. W. E. B. Du Bois, "Chapter 16—Jones in Japan," *CR: The New Centennial Review* 12:1 (2012), 262. Also see Nahum Dimitri Chandler's annotations in the same essay, 270–71.

16. "A.U. Students Hear Japanese Leader in Talk," *Chicago Defender*, January 25, 1936; "Dr. Kagawa Heard at Spellman," *Atlanta (GA) Daily World*, January 6, 1935; Robert Shaffer, "'A Missionary from the East to Western Pagans': Kagawa Toyohiko's 1936 World Tour," *Journal of World History* 24:3 (2013), 590.

17. On Du Bois's interest in Gandhi, see Vijay Prashad, "Waiting for the Black Gandhi," in *From Toussaint to Tupac* (Chapel Hill: University of North Carolina Press, 2009), 179–96.

18. Daniel Rogers, *Atlantic Crossings: Social Politics in a Progressive Age* (Cambridge, MA: Harvard University Press, 1998), 87.

19. Shaffer, "'A Missionary from the East to Western Pagans,'" 590; Toyohiko Kagawa, *Hoko to Junrei* (Tokyo: Tokyo Shunju-sha, 1933).

20. Shaffer, "'A Missionary from the East to Western Pagans,'" 588–89; Mikio Sumiya, *Kagawa Toyohiko* (Tokyo: Iwanami Shoten, 2011).

21. Shaffer, "'A Missionary from the East to Western Pagans,'" 585–96, 591.

22. David Levering Lewis, *W. E. B. Du Bois, 1919-1963: The Fight for Equality and the American Century* (New York, NY: Henry Holt and Company, 2000), 388–421.

23. Jessica Gordon Nembhard, *Collective Courage: A History of African American Cooperative Economic Thought and Practice* (University Park, PA: The Penn State University Press, 2014), 1–15, 21–22.

24. Du Bois, *Newspaper Columns*, 214.

25. Nembhard, *Collective Courage*, 32.

26. Committee on Cooperation, "Proposed Scheme of Co-operation among American Negroes," ca. 1918, W. E. B. Du Bois Papers (MS 312), Special Collections and University Archives, University of Massachusetts Amherst Libraries; Du Bois, W. E. B. (William Edward Burghardt), 1868–1963, letter from W. E. B. Du Bois to the Cooperative League of America, August 20, 1918, W. E. B. Du Bois Papers (MS 312), Special Collections and University Archives, University of Massachusetts Amherst Libraries; Warbasse, James Peter, 1866–1957, letter from James P. Warbasse to W. E. B. Du Bois, March 17, 1930, W. E. B. Du Bois Papers (MS 312), Special Collections and University Archives, University of Massachusetts Amherst Libraries.

27. Du Bois, *Newspaper Columns*, 210.

28. On the framing of historicity in global terms, see Chandler, "A Persistent Parallax," 294–96.

29. "Du Bois Traces Rise of World Co-op System," *Chicago Defender*, March 4, 1939; Simon Critchley, *Infinitely Demanding: Ethics of Commitment, Politics of Resistance* (New York, NY: Verso, 2007), 6–8.

30. Bill Mullen, *Un-American: W. E. B. Du Bois and the Century of World Revolution* (Philadelphia: Temple University Press, 2015).

31. Toyohiko Kagawa, *Brotherhood Economics* (New York: Harper & Brothers,1936), 3.

32. Shaffer, "'A Missionary from the East to Western Pagans,'" 586.

33. Victor Edward Marriott, ed., *Kagawa and Cooperatives* (Chicago: Kingdom of God Fellowship, 1935), 7.

34. Kagawa, *Brotherhood Economics*, 76–77.

35. Marriott, *Kagawa and Cooperatives*, 9.

36. Kagawa, *Brotherhood Economics*, 75.

37. Kagawa, *Brotherhood Economics*, 76–77.

38. Kagawa, *Brotherhood Economics*, 26, 56.

39. Quoted in Sterling Stuckey, *Slave Culture: Nationalist Theory and the Foundations of Black America* (New York: Oxford University Press, 1988), 289.

40. Du Bois, *Newspaper Columns*, 207.

41. *The Crisis*, March 1934, 85.

42. Du Bois, "A Negro Nation within the Nation," 6.

43. Du Bois, "A Negro Nation within the Nation," 5.

44. W. E. B. Du Bois, "Forum of Fact and Opinion," *Pittsburgh Courier*, August 21, 1937; Roy Wilkins, "Watchtower," *New York Amsterdam News*, January 30, 1937.

45. Du Bois, "A Negro Nation within the Nation," 6.

46. Penny M. Von Eschen, *Race against Empire: Black Americans and Anticolonialism, 1937–1957* (Ithaca, NY: Cornell University Press, 1997).

47. Du Bois, *Newspaper Columns*, 189.

48. Du Bois, *Newspaper Columns*, 191.

49. W. E. B. Du Bois, *Dusk of Dawn: An Essay toward An Autobiography of a Race Concept*, in *Writings*, edited by Nathan Irvin Huggins (New York: Library of America, 1986), 320.

50. Du Bois, *Newspaper Columns*, 189–90.

51. Du Bois, *Newspaper Columns*, 204.

52. Du Bois, *Newspaper Columns*, 195.

53. W. E. B. Du Bois, *Black Reconstruction in America: An Essay toward a History of the Part Which Black Folk Played in the Attempt to Reconstruct Democracy in America, 1860–1880* (New York: Atheneum, 1935), 121.

54. Du Bois, *Newspaper Columns*, 211.

55. Singh, *Black Is a Country*, 95–96. Of Du Bois's intellectual formations of the 1930s, Singh wrote, "This was the most pressing question for Du Bois, and one he believed needed to be posed for the difficult times ahead."

56. Du Bois, "The Negro and Social Reconstruction," 156.

57. Bunyan Bryant, "Rehearsing the Future," *In Context* 40 (Spring 1995), http://www.context.org/iclib/ic40/bryant/.

58. Du Bois, *Newspaper Columns*, 213.

59. Manu Goswami, "Colonial Internationalisms and Imaginary Futures," *American Historical Review* 117:5 (2012), 1467.

60. Du Bois, *Newspaper Columns*, 193.
61. Du Bois, "The Negro and Social Reconstruction," 146.
62. Du Bois, "The Negro and Social Reconstruction," 151.
63. Du Bois, *Newspaper Columns*, 189.

# W. E. B. Du Bois, South Africa, and *Phylon*'s "A Chronicle of Race Relations," 1940–1944

*Derek Charles Catsam*

Of all of William Edward Burghardt Du Bois's contributions to global intellectual life, one of the most significant yet perhaps underappreciated is his conceptualization of and advocacy for a Pan-African world in which the "color line" was the defining challenge. He first introduced this global concept in a 1900 essay, "The Present Day Outlook for the Dark Races of Mankind," which appeared in the *A.M.E. Church Review* in October of that year and has only rarely been republished.[1] In that essay he wrote:

> It is but natural for us to think that our race question is a purely national and local affair, confined to nine millions Americans and settled when their rights and opportunities are assured, and yet a glance over the world at the dawn of the new century will convince us that this is but the beginning of the problem— that the color line belts the world and that the social problem of the twentieth century is to be the relation of the civilized world to the dark races of mankind.[2]

Later in that paragraph Du Bois proposed, "Outside of America the greatest field of contrast between whites and Negroes to-day is South Africa, and the situation there should be watched with great interest." He argued, for example, that "in the Free State," one of the Boer-settled states of South Africa, "no Negro has to-day a third of the rights which he enjoys in Georgia—he cannot hold land, cannot live in town, has practically no civil status, and is in all but name a slave."[3]

The theme of the color line as a global phenomenon would be a consistent thread throughout Du Bois's long, storied career as a scholar, thinker, writer, advocate, propagandist, teacher, speaker, agitator, and leader. And naturally this thread would continue to lead him to South Africa. One of the periods in Du Bois's life when these Pan-Africanist trends merged was in his editorship of and contributions to the journal *Phylon*.

He compiled and wrote a recurring feature, "A Chronicle of Race Relations," for every issue of *Phylon* that he edited, from the first issue of that vital journal in 1940 to 1944, when he stepped down from his position as editor. His editorship of *Phylon* represented a continuation of the editorial work he had done for much of his career. Most famously he was the founding editor of the NAACP's *The Crisis*, a role he maintained from 1910 until his break with the NAACP over his increasingly confrontational politics in 1934. But prior to his pioneering work with *The Crisis* Du Bois had served as founding editor of the short-lived *Moon Illustrated Weekly* from its founding in December 1905 until its closing in the summer of 1906 and *The Horizon: A Journal of the Color Line*, which he edited for its entire run, from 1907 to 1910. Each of these journals (and many of his opinion pieces in myriad newspapers and magazines, such as *Amsterdam News*, *Chicago Defender*, and *National Guardian*) revealed Du Bois's deep commitment to Pan-Africanism, as his focus was never solely on the race question in America, as his many publications, including several of his books, makes clear.[4]

Du Bois spearheaded *Phylon*'s founding in 1940. A wryly named editorial, "Apology," in *Phylon*'s first issue laid out the justification for the new publication. The new quarterly "proposes to study and survey the field of race and culture and of racial and cultural relations" with an eye toward "emphasiz[ing] that view of race which regards it as cultural and historical in essence, rather than primarily biological and psychological."[5] Du Bois and his cohort took the idea of *Phylon* as a "quarterly review" quite seriously. "We wish to establish ourselves as a place of Re-Views;—that is, as an organ for considering again and after the event, the happenings and opinions which have to do with the cultural advance and inter-cultural relations of men, in order to reach more final and definite judgments." The main goal was not to "attempt to present happenings as news but rather to submit both recent and past occurrences and opinions to more careful scrutiny and interpretation."[6]

It is within this larger understanding of the journal's mission that we can understand "A Chronicle of Race Relations." The journal intended to pursue its mission "humbly by means of original research both direct and indirect, by essays on analogous but widely separated subjects," and "by a careful chronicle of events and an intelligent review of opinion." This was clearly an ambitious intellectual agenda. Yet it is worth noting that the editorial staff wanted as broad an audience as possible, and so they set a subscription price of one dollar, "well within reach of every one; not because our enterprise is going to be cheap and merely popular, but because we do not want to let any reasonable obstacle stand between us and a wide and intelligent audience."

A passing observation about South Africa in the very first installment of *Phylon*'s "Chronicle of Race Relations" revealed all of Du Bois's strengths as a Pan-Africanist: "In South Africa the recrudescence of the old split between Dutch and English threatened for a while to keep South Africa out of the war; but economic and social pressure were too strong and the Union entered the war on the side of England. No new methods of oppressing the black majority have been heard of."[7]

Du Bois combined insight: the split between English-speaking South Africans and Afrikaners being second in significance only to that between whites and blacks in that country; foresight: the division that led to the narrow vote to enter World War II on the side of the Allies revealed tensions that directly fueled the rise of the National Party and their subsequent victories in the country's 1948 elections; and a caustic wit: "No new methods of oppressing the black majority have been heard of," which represents an elegant twist of the dagger while bringing to the forefront white South Africa's racism, which only got worse in the years to come.

Du Bois penned eighteen editions of "A Chronicle of Race Relations." Almost all of these were journal-length pieces in their own right. Each provided a roundup of events related to race relations across the globe. Du Bois divided his global coverage into sections on Europe, the West Indies, Asia, and India, as well as a catchall category of "racism." And of course Du Bois, the apodictic Pan-Africanist, gave special attention to Africa in nearly every "Chronicle," occasionally breaking his coverage into regions. He also, not surprisingly, given its increasing prominence, its parallels with American history and politics, and its economic clout, gave South Africa independent coverage.

Although it might be easy to dismiss Du Bois's "Chronicles" as little more than news aggregation, a sort of proto-blog in which he compiled the work of others into a readable, accessible summary, the reality is far different. As Du Bois explained in the second of his "Chronicles":

> Not only are facts concerning racial and cultural groups, unless
> they are sensational, seldom regarded as "news" by distribut-
> ing agencies, but there is a distinct tendency to suppress such
> information under the mistaken assumption that publication of
> the facts aggregates difficulties; when of course, in race prob-
> lems as in other problems the exact opposite is true. It is today,
> therefore, difficult to obtain real news concerning race prob-
> lems in West Africa and East Africa and largely in South Africa.[8]

Anyone who has begun a research project on South Africa during the
time that Du Bois wrote these overviews is well aware of the absences
in the era's American periodicals. It is Du Bois's emphasis on South
Africa that will be the focus of this essay both because of the explicit
nature of the racist regime in South Africa and because it helps to
elucidate Du Bois's brilliance in assessing and commitment to Pan-
Africanism. When the Afrikaner National Party won the 1948 elections
on an explicit policy of apartheid, the world slowly turned its attention
to that regime. Tellingly, however, Du Bois wrote "Chronicles" during
the World War II era, when South Africa's two major white populations
struggled for political dominance. English speakers largely controlled
South African politics in the Commonwealth nation up until 1948.
However, Afrikaners (sometimes known as Boers, the Dutch/Afrikaans
word for "farmers") oftentimes resented the English population in no
small part because of long-ranging historical tensions, including but not
limited to British brutality against the Boers during the South African
War (or Boer War) of 1899–1902. The onset of apartheid was a difference of degree, not of kind, however, as South Africa before 1948 was a
deeply segregated country by law and by custom. South Africa's various
black cultures—the so-called Native Africans, sometimes referred to as
"Bantu," mixed-race "Coloured" South Africans, and Asians, primarily Indians—dominated numerically but found themselves increasingly
excluded from all aspects of the public sphere. White South Africans
disagreed over many issues, including the intensity that white supremacy should take. They did not, however, disagree that white supremacy
should prevail.

The range of Du Bois's coverage on South African issues is rather
astonishing and perspicacious. In the second "Chronicle" he reminds
readers that "most of the crime[s] in South Africa are crimes against
arbitrary statutory offenses," such as taxation laws, the onerous pass
laws, labor offenses, and "various segregation and servant acts," in

addition to violations of liquor laws and "various municipal offenses."[9] He sometimes foreshadowed issues that emerged as salient in the future. For example, he acknowledged the white split in entering World War II whereby English-speaking South Africans wanted to intervene on the part of the Allies but Afrikaner Nationalists either wanted to remain neutral or in some cases were sympathetic to the Nazis. Du Bois also showed deep foresight in observations about the difficulty of land reform to "supply natives with necessary land by giving back to them some of the vast amount that has been sequestered by the whites."[10] Land would continue to vex South Africa, and solutions to the problem Du Bois identified ranged from the emergence of Bantustans under apartheid to the current stalemate over land reform programs today.[11]

Du Bois pointed out hypocrisies aplenty. He noted that 215,000 "natives" held what amounted to bank accounts in the country's post offices in 1940 (a significant increase from a decade earlier), yet they were still prohibited from working as clerks in those same post offices.[12]

In addition to identifying the ongoing (and indeed rising) discrimination in pre-apartheid South Africa, Du Bois occasionally illustrated important studies. One such work was "South Africa Native Policy and the Liberal Spirit," by a liberal English-speaking professor, R. F. A. Hoernle, which asked the following question: "What have the two liberty-loving white groups made, what are they making of their historical task of governing a multi-racial community?" Hoernle's too generous attitude and paternalistic outlook led him to three possibilities: "Parallelism," which amounted to a policy of "separate but equal" that Hoernle rejected as "impracticable"; "Total Assimilation," which was also, of course, "impracticable" in light of the fact that the overwhelming majority of the white population rejected it out of hand; and "Total Separation." Du Bois summed up Hoernle's conclusion: "None of these, he admits, at present seem possible. But he regards total separation as the long run goal." Both Hoernle and Du Bois, as so often was the case, prove prescient on this point nearly a decade before the National Party's rise on a platform of explicit apartheid.[13]

White South Africa was especially interested in the control of both influx and labor, with the two intimately connected. Cheap labor was at the heart of South Africa's most prosperous industry. The country's white population thus looked with alarm at riots of workers in the copper mines of Northern Rhodesia (Zambia).[14]

World War II served as a vital backdrop to Du Bois's writing in this forum. And it is clear that elsewhere in the world winds of change might have been blowing, but South Africa was countercyclical to these trends. Within two decades African nations would begin to claim and receive—however reluctantly—independence in no small part because of the claims both implicit and explicit in the cause of the Second World War. White South Africa, on the other hand, would tighten its grip. Where Du Bois occasionally showed glimmers of hope about what the war might mean for the postwar world, at the same time he stridently revealed the hypocrisies and cynicism of countries putatively fighting for democracy and freedom while denying that freedom to citizens in their countries and ignoring violations of rights in the colonies of allies. He showed few such illusions about South Africa. This context also serves as a useful reminder that while 1948 is a crucial year in South African history because of the National Party's shock victory in the general elections, it hardly represented a radical transformation within the country so much as the logical culmination of generations of white supremacy that descendants of both the English and the Dutch settlers imposed.

Indeed, even where observers could identify modest improvements in the lot of South Africa's native population, Du Bois quickly tempered any optimism. He turned again to Hoernle, who had noted in *Race Relations* six "improvements in the attitudes of whites toward natives in South Africa." These improvements included the University of the Witwatersrand opening up medical and dental training opportunities to "Negro students," an eventuality made possible due to "the development of native hospitals"; the establishment of the Hofmeyer School of Social Work in Johannesburg for the purpose of training Africans; the provision of better water and sanitation services and "to some extent" better schools, hospitals, and libraries; the abolishment of school fees in native primary schools (which "still leaves native education severely in need of attention but is a step forward"); the development of native trade unions in newly industrializing areas; and the increased influence of the Native Representative Council. To these things Du Bois concluded rather succinctly, "This does not mean any visible settlement of the race problems in South Africa. The white population is still unmoved and unimpressed and the body of law and restriction, discrimination and segregation is large."[15] His conclusions may strike one as pessimistic, even cynical. But history proved them correct.

Nonetheless there were moments when Du Bois revealed his hidden optimism. He was pessimistic and cynical but realistic, and perhaps not unremittingly so. In the second quarter issue of 1942, he excerpted an address from Jan Smuts in Cape Town:

Of Race Relations there had formerly appeared only two possible courses in Native policy—either complete equality or
permanent European "top-doggism." The principle of trusteeship had emerged in recent years. Trusteeship implied that the
trustee regarded the rights of his ward as sacred. South Africa
had tried segregation, which had failed, and the provision for
Native health, housing and nutrition had been shamefully
deficient. These problems had to be tackled. . . . We want to
take a holiday from old ideas which have brought nothing but
bitterness and strife to our country and try to the best of our
ability to fashion a variegated but harmonious race pattern in
South Africa.[16]

It may or may not be telling that Du Bois excerpted this speech without
providing additional commentary. Perhaps his own view became clearer
about a year later, when he wrote in the "Chronicle":

Marshall Jan Christian Smuts, Prime Minister of the Union of
South Africa, where two million white people rule seven million
colored folk without allowing them any real voice in government and industry said: "At the bottom, therefore, this war is
a new crusade, a new fight to the death for man's rights and
liberties and for the personal ideals of man's ethical and spiritual life."

Du Bois responded tartly, "Just what Mr. Smuts meant by 'Man' in this
case is not clear, probably even in his own mind. In the mind of his
late colleague and rival, Hertzog, there never was the slightest question.
He meant white men and even here he discriminated against English."
Du Bois pulled no punches in his conclusion to this section of the
"Chronicle": "Fortunately, James Barry Munik (sic) Hertzog third Prime
Minister of South Africa, is dead at Capetown (sic)."[17] To underscore
his point, a few pages later Du Bois prefaced an excerpt from an N. N.
Franklin article in the September 1942 *African Studies* that cites a
report on the economic plight of Africans (and a tiny minority of whites)
in South Africa. For Du Bois the report from the Agricultural Commission of South Africa served as a reminder that "while Smuts is preaching
democracy in Europe, in his own South Africa" things are not so great.[18]
    Similarly, a few months later Du Bois excerpted writing from *Race
Relations News* to undercut optimistic news that South Africa might

be coming to embrace a form of social security that was allegedly to apply to "all races." "It is not reassuring," the excerpt notes, "that the social security code, proposed at Durban, is divided according to racial groups in a wider sense, viz. Europeans, Coloureds, Asiatics, Africans." It was similarly "not reassuring that the range of the proposed benefits is graded steeply downwards from a maximum for Europeans, to a minimum for Africans, as if insecurity, poverty, ill health, etc., were at their greater among Europeans and at their lowest among Africans!"[19] Du Bois cited such studies and reports not because he did not think social security was a good idea but rather because he simply did not believe the government as then constituted truly would move forward with such policies. His "Chronicle" two issues later again quoted economic data from *Race Relations News* exploring employment disparities. He continued to illustrate how crime data in the Witwatersrand served more as an indictment of poverty and segregation than native criminality. He would also explain the debate over arming Africans for the war and how it was "agitating the Union," and he provided hopeful news about meetings from the newly established South African Institute of Race Relations.[20] In the same issue he also reminded readers of the difficulties Indian South Africans experienced in an era of racial division.[21]

Du Bois clearly thought comparatively and transnationally—such thinking was, indeed, at the heart of the "Chronicle of Race Relations" during its truncated run. In looking at President Franklin Roosevelt's addresses in the months preceding the U.S. entry into the Second World War Du Bois could not help but think of the implications outside of the intended American audience: "In his Labor Day message of September 1941, it is certain that 'free labor' did not apply to South Africa nor did 'interdependence of rights' envisage India. . . . He speaks of the right of people 'immediately interested' to organize labor, but he is evidently not thinking of labor unions in South Africa."[22]

In the fourth-quarter "Chronicle" from 1943 Du Bois published a letter from "an African from the Gold Coast to Senator Rheinallt Jones," who represented African voters from the Transvaal and Orange Free State from 1937 until he was defeated in 1942. In his letter the correspondent compared the race situation, especially labor conditions for Africans, in South Africa and his native West Africa. He detailed the indignities of segregation that he experienced from the moment he boarded the ship to South Africa until he returned to Gold Coast. "I was not able to penetrate into the hinterland of the Union, where I understood the colour bar is intensely strong," he wrote, "but I found from my four weeks in Cape Town that the South African native or the coloured man for that matter is in a most deplorable state." This from a black man from a West African colony of Britain not destined to gain independence for well more than a decade. He was "surprised" to discover in Cape Town "such jobs as office messengers, train guards, railway engine drivers, police constables, prison warders, clerical jobs, railway ticket sellers, porters, stationmasters, carpenters, masons and other jobs too many to mention being done by white men." He added, "In West Africa all these jobs are done by Africans, and not only these."[23] Du Bois had no illusions about life in colonial Africa, and so once again he reminds readers that even within the framework of African race relations during a pre-independence era South Africa's were especially onerous.

Labor was rarely far from Du Bois's musings. In the same "Chronicle" that contains the rejoinder to FDR, Du Bois illustrates the plight of workers through the story of "a black milkman's eighty-four hour week in Johannesburg." After laying out a day that begins at 1:00 a.m., Du Bois throws in his characteristically dry and succinct conclusion: "For this the employers wanted a wage of $22 a month with unlimited hours while the employees ask for $40 a month which has not yet been granted." Similarly he outlined the limits of black South African workers to strike despite lousy pay and no rights and the denial of even basic political rights. Du Bois did not shrink from the occasional improvement in the lot of black South Africans, such as modest relaxations of the onerous pass laws and promising developments such as the formation of the National Union of South African Students (NUSAS). In the case of the latter, however, he points out that once the prospect of admitting students from the Native College at Fort Hare came to the agenda, the putatively liberal NUSAS shrank and its "Boer" members "seceded" and formed the perhaps ironically named "African National Student Body," which "excludes all Non-Europeans, Roman Catholics, Jews and English South Africans." Even after the departure of the presumably more conservative Afrikaners, however, a proposal to include native students failed by a two-thirds majority "for fear of further secessions."[24]

In Du Bois's penultimate "Chronicle" he discusses how "for the first time in history the Department of State and the United States Government has made a statement concerning the relations between America and Africa." The statement came on August 19, 1943, from Henry S. Villard, "great-grandson of William Lloyd Garrison and Assistant Chief

of the Division of Near Eastern Affairs." And while Du Bois was heart-
ened, he remained wary, and his characteristic irony came through:

> There is much commendable in this carefully considered
> statement of the State Department; but there is also an illog-
> ical mixture of the Open Door (equal right to exploit servile
> labor and cheap materials); God-bless-England (whose colonial
> record is perfect); Isolation (power without responsibility); Mis-
> sions (opening wedge for trade and obedience); and Self-rule
> (for the few who want it and can use it).[25]

This represented Du Bois's last engagement with South Africa in
the too short-lived "Chronicle of Race Relations" series in *Phylon*. "A
Note by the Associate Editors" announced that he had been elected to
the National Institute of Arts and Letters, "a society founded in 1898
for the furtherance of literature and fine arts in the United States and
composed of not more than 250 American citizens 'qualified by notable
achievements in Art, Music and Literature.'"[26] South Africa would not
feature in the final installment of the "Chronicle" in the second-quarter
issue of *Phylon* in 1944, his last with the journal.[27] The celebration
from the associate editors masked Du Bois's ugly separation from
Atlanta University, the result of the machinations of an invasive university president, Rufus Clement.[28] Outrage led the university to grant
Du Bois professor emeritus status, and the seventy-six-year-old still had
a vital phase of his career ahead. But his too brief period of stewardship
over *Phylon*, and especially his "Chronicle of Race Relations" series,
embodied so many of Du Bois's strengths and serves as a reminder, like
his books on Africa published in the same period (*Color and Democracy: Colonies and Peace* [1945] and *The World and Africa* [1947]), of
his status as arguably the single most vital force in the Pan-African
movement of the mid-twentieth century.

## Notes

1. The original appeared in *A.M.E. Church Review* 17, no. 2 (October
1900): 95–110. For the most recent and most fully annotated version, see
Nahum Dmitri Chandler, ed., *W. E. B. Du Bois: The Problem of the Color
Line at the Turn of the Twentieth Century. The Essential Early Essays* (New
York: Fordham University Press, 2015), 111–37.

2. W. E. B. Du Bois, "The Present Day Outlook for the Dark Races of Mankind," in *The Problem of the Color Line*, 111–12.

3. See ibid., 112 for the quotation and 112–13 for more discussion on South Africa. Du Bois gets some things right, a few things muddled, but on the whole his analysis of South Africa (and its relationship with the situation in the United States South) is generally insightful.

4. Among Du Bois's many books are *Africa, Its Geography, People and Products* (1930); *Africa: Its Place in Modern History* (1930); *Color and Democracy: Colonies and Peace* (1945); *The World and Africa, an Inquiry into the Part Which Africa Has Played in World History* (1947); and the twelve-page pamphlet *Africa in Battle against Colonialism, Racialism, Imperialism* (Chicago: Afro-American Heritage Association, 1960). See also Eugene F. Provenzo Jr. and Edmund Abaka, eds., *W. E. B. Du Bois on Africa* (Walnut Creek, CA: Left Coast Press, 2012); Anthony J. Ratcliff, "The Radical Evolution of Du Boisian Pan-Africanism," *Journal of Pan African Studies* vol. 5, no. 9 (March 2013): 151–70; Nahum Dmitri Chandler, *Toward an African Future—of the Limit of the World* (London: Living Commons Collective, 2013); Carol Anderson, *Bourgeois Radicals: The NAACP and the Struggle for Colonial Liberation, 1941–1960* (Cambridge, UK: Cambridge University Press, 2014). And of course, as with anything Du Bois–related, see David Levering Lewis, *W. E. B. Du Bois: Biography of a Race, 1868–1919* (New York: Henry Holt, 1993) and *W. E. B. Du Bois: The Fight for Equality and the American Century, 1919–1963* (New York: Henry Holt, 2000).

5. Du Bois, "Apology," *Phylon*, first quarter, 1, no. 1 (1940): 1. On the "Apology" see also Phillip Luke Sinitiere and Amy Helene Kirschke, "W. E. B. Du Bois as Print Propagandist," in *Protest and Propaganda: W. E. B. Du Bois, The Crisis, and American History*, ed. Amy Helene Kirschke and Phillip Luke Sinitiere (Columbia: University of Missouri Press, 2014), 43–44.

6. Du Bois, "Apology," 1–2.

7. W. E. B. Du Bois, "A Chronicle of Race Relations, 1939," *Phylon*, first quarter, 1, no. 1 (1940): 93. [Hereafter I will refer to the "Chronicle" with issue information when citing these installments.]

8. Du Bois, "Chronicle," *Phylon*, second quarter, 1, no. 2 (1940): 175.

9. Ibid.,178–79.

10. Ibid., 179.

11. See, for example, Edward Lahiff, "'Willing Buyer, Willing Seller': South Africa's Failed Experiment in Market-Led Agrarian Reform," *Third World Quarterly* 28, no. 8 (2007): 1577–97.

12. Du Bois, "Chronicle," *Phylon*, third quarter, 1, no. 3 (1940): 277.

13. Du Bois, "Chronicle," *Phylon*, fourth quarter, 1, no. 4 (1940): 380. See also *South African Native Policy and the Liberal Spirit: Being the Phelps-Stokes Lectures, Delivered before the University of Cape Town, May, 1939* (University of Cape Town, 1939); William Sweet, "R. F. A. Hoernlé and Idealist Liberalism in South Africa," *South African Journal of Philosophy* 29, no. 2 (2010): 178–94.

14. Du Bois, "Chronicle," *Phylon*, second quarter, 2, no. 2 (1941): 183–84.

15. Du Bois, "Chronicle," *Phylon*, third quarter, 2, no. 3 (1941): 290.

16. Du Bois, "Chronicle," *Phylon*, second quarter, 3, no. 2 (1942): 215.

17. Du Bois, "Chronicle," *Phylon*, first quarter, 4, no. 1 (1943): 74. Hertzog died November 21, 1942, in Pretoria at the age of seventy-six.

18. Ibid., 84.

19. Quoted in Du Bois, "Chronicle," *Phylon*, second quarter, 4, no. 2 (1943): 176.

20. Du Bois, "Chronicle," *Phylon*, fourth quarter, 4, no. 4 (1943): 382–83.

21. Ibid., 384–85.

22. Du Bois, "Chronicle," *Phylon*, fourth quarter, 2, no. 4 (1941): 389.

23. Du Bois, "Chronicle," *Phylon*, fourth quarter, 4, no. 4 (1943): 381–82.

24. Du Bois, "Chronicle," *Phylon*, fourth quarter, 2, no. 4 (1941): 397–98.

25. Du Bois, "Chronicle," *Phylon*, first quarter, 5, no. 1 (1944): 76–77.

26. Ibid., 89.

27. Du Bois, "Chronicle," *Phylon*, second quarter, 5, no. 2 (1944): 101–2, 165–88.

28. Atlanta University later became Clark Atlanta University.

# Russia and America

## An Interpretation of the Late W. E. B. Du Bois and the Case for World Revolution

### Bill V. Mullen

As some of the essays in this volume make clear, inattention to the "late" Du Bois corresponds to inattention to the "global" Du Bois. A strident domestication of Du Bois's life and career depended for too long upon a conception of Du Bois as an American (and African American) race man tethered to a scholarly praxis of American exceptionalism. This conception confined interest in Du Bois's early work to U.S.-centric definitions of race, racial uplift, and the fate of the U.S. nation-state, evidencing what Du Bois himself once called, disparagingly, a "racial provincialism." Even his two most famous critical formulations from early in his career—"the color line" and "double consciousness"—intended as commentary on the black *worldly* subject, have often been reduced to parables of American Jim Crow, segregation, or assimilation of the American races. Indeed these exceptionalist formulations were constitutive of, predictive of practices of exclusion that obtained around Du Bois during the cold war. Critical consensus that Du Bois was either American or un-American helped propel and legitimate ignorance of his extensive writings on the non-U.S. world—China, Japan, and the Soviet Union most prominently—while tacitly reinforcing the anticommunist bias that refused to think of Du Bois's open attachment to socialism as itself a form of globality. In short, by freezing much of Du Bois's work and reputation around its earliest canonizing moments, most particularly around *The Souls of Black Folk*, history and scholarship have stood still in refusing to name the Du Bois who was always already a citizen of the world.[1]

This line of demarcation in Du Bois scholarship arguably began to erode with the end of the cold war, as Phillip Luke Sinitiere's comments in this volume further elucidate. More broadly, what Alan Wald has called the "polarizing thinking" of cold war scholarship—West and non-West, communist and capitalist, First and Third World—began to winnow after the "formal" end of state capitalist regimes in the Soviet Union, China, and Eastern Europe.[2] The Prague Spring enabled a temporospatial renaissance in Du Bois scholarship coincident with the "transnationalization" of Western research, global geopolitical realignment, and a serious reconsideration of the legacy of communism and socialism on American writing and culture. Eric Porter's 2010 book, *The Problem of the Future World: W. E. B. Du Bois and the Race Concept at Midcentury*, may be emblematic here of this shift. Motivated by a desire to cross and tear down conceptual borders and walls constructed by cold war ideology, Porter's careful attention to late work in Du Bois's oeuvre begins with his 1940 book, *Dusk of Dawn*. Porter's observation, for instance, that "Du Bois might have praised Stalin, . . . but he was not a Stalinist in any systematic way,"[3] helped enable a reclassification process in Du Bois scholarship that was also a historical reconsideration. Porter's book was coincident with other waves of appraisal in both African American studies and U.S. cultural studies: for the former, a more pliant model of "diasporic" scholarship giving serious attention to the non-U.S. world; for the latter a return of repressed questions of political internationalism, globalization, and empire.[4]

To any reconsideration of Du Bois's late career and his global citizenship now, his 1950 unpublished manuscript, "Russia and America: An Interpretation," must be central. This is the only book-length manuscript Du Bois completed that to this day remains unpublished. Publisher Henry Giroux responded to the manuscript, finished in New York in June 1950, with a rejection letter stating the book was "an uncritical *apologia* for Soviet Russia and an excessive condemnation of the United States."[5] Until recently, Du Bois scholars, with few exceptions,[6] have ignored the manuscript or argued that its unpublished status is a gift to Du Bois's reputation. David Levering Lewis's magisterial biography, for example, says Harcourt Brace "rendered Du Bois's legacy a favor by declining to publish."[7] Lewis decries the "venom and bad taste" of Du Bois's characterization of Trotsky in the manuscript, and his "adjusted . . . Russian casualty tables" as an unforgiveable downplaying of the calamities of the Soviet Union under Stalin's rule. His five-sentence reflection on page 317 of the manuscript concludes, "To Du Bois, the degradation of the communist ideal in Soviet Russia was philosophically irrelevant to the expiation of the sins of American democracy, whose very possibility he now deeply doubted."[8]

Lewis codifies in one fell swoop "Russia and America" as a metonym for Du Bois's late career as a dupe or demagogue on behalf of Soviet communism. Most damagingly for Du Bois scholars, readers take Lewis's judgment as self-explanatory, with little attention given, for example, to the particular and peculiar brand of Marxism Du Bois's manuscript conveys. Critical to understanding Du Bois's developing ideas is its dedication to what he called in the manuscript "world revolution," the Bolshevik program for advancing socialist parties and socialist revolutions around the world after 1917. First articulated at the Communist International in 1919 by Lenin and Trotsky (with support from Stalin), the program drew Du Bois to sympathy with the Revolution, inspired him to visit the Soviet Union in 1926, and impelled his support for Indian and Chinese independence movements. As much as any other aspect of twentieth-century communism, the "world revolution" idea explains Du Bois's gradual conversion to and open identification with communist politics. Indeed the "world revolution" idea is a key to understanding what we mean, politically, by a "global" W. E. B. Du Bois.[9]

It is therefore significant that in recent years "Russia and America" has begun to earn the attention of scholars unwedded to earlier cold war paradigms of scholarship, and who are thus sensitive to the book's own ambitions of global and geopolitical realignment. Etusko Taketani, for example, has paid careful attention to the book's representation of Du Bois's travels in Manchuria under Japanese occupation in 1936, and his own short-lived dreams of Japan as a "champion of the darker world."[10] More recently Vaughn Rasberry's 2016 *Race and the Totalitarian Century: Geopolitics in the Black Literary Imagination* perceptively interprets Du Bois's manuscript as a deliberate meditation on the scales of authoritarianism during the cold war. Du Bois, Rasberry notes, carefully evaluates the history of the Russian Revolution and its Stalinist crimes against a history of hyperviolent and genocidal Western imperialism and colonialism, while also positing a truly global framework free of cold war binarisms by which to evaluate emancipatory struggles for human freedom. As Rasberry puts it, Du Bois's "Russia and America" manuscript seeks "to develop a global history of modern nation states entwined in an emergent world system marked by continuous war and revolution. In addition, to the United States and the Soviet Union, the other national actors in this drama include Germany and Italy, Britain and France, China and Japan."[11]

Indeed "Russia and America" is arguably Du Bois's most singularly *global* text. He assembled the text based on multiple trips to the Soviet

Union in 1928, 1936, and 1949, and it replicates portions of published essays about his visits to China and Japan in 1936 and 1937. In telling the story of U.S. and Soviet history, Du Bois draws on sources from the British communists Beatrice and Sydney Webb. The manuscript also considers the entire history of the modern West within its scope, from the Protestant Reformation to the French Revolution. A global perspective therefore shapes its analysis of U.S. history. "Russia and America" begins where Du Bois ends his magisterial 1935 *Black Reconstruction*, with a meditation on the contours of global capitalism and imperialism—from Africa to Asia—as consequences of the end of the U.S. Reconstruction project in the American South. The manuscript is in fact a retrospective, updated interpretation of that event, a sequel as it were, compelled by insights and analogical and comparative thinking about global capitalist history as it determines the conditions of African Americans living in the wake of the 1917 Russian Revolution and in the midst of an intensely global event: the cold war.

To make this thematic clear, I will argue that the "Russia and America" manuscript, along with Du Bois's late, revised commentary on the 1962 reissue of his book on John Brown, is in fact part of his global revisionist "trilogy" on the U.S. Civil War and Reconstruction. This simple theme unites the trilogy: "If American Negroes had been given the chance that the Russian peasant has had since 1917 his contribution to the uplift of the world might easily have been startling."[12] In "Russia and America," Du Bois updates and broadens this thesis to include all citizens of Russia and the United States living in the era of the cold war. American freedmen (and the white working class) from the Reconstruction era become in "Russia and America" a prototypic revolutionary group whose tactics of self-emancipation are offered as examples for modern-day Americans and Russians to follow. Du Bois conceives of the stalemate between the Soviet Union and the U.S. as a braided chain of modern capitalist history, a "world counterrevolution." The threat of atomic war between the states and the economic catastrophe that could follow require an alliance between the peoples of the Soviet Union and of the U.S. to avert a repeat of historical tragedy. Thus Du Bois works to develop a parallel history of "revolution from below" in both countries as an antidote to the present.

By the time Du Bois sat down to compile "Russia and America: An Interpretation" the spirit of what he called in *Black Reconstruction* "counterrevolution" was everywhere. With its victory in World War II, the United States had entered a period of political lockdown.

Stalin and the Soviet Union had flipped from ally to mortal political and military enemy; Roosevelt's New Deal—once a bright hope of progressive reform for Du Bois and African Americans—had given way to unfettered capitalist boom, consumption, and backlash against labor; Russia's Revolution had itself reached a bureaucratic apex manifest in its incapacity, outside of China, to generate prospects for communist revolutions elsewhere in the world. Du Bois underscored this stalemate to highlight the deeply repressive domestic atmosphere. As he wrote "Russia and America," anticommunists attacked his close friend Paul Robeson at Peekskill, New York, for proclaiming at the Paris Peace Conference that African Americans would never take up arms against the Soviet Union. The comment had such a potent political afterlife that it pulled Robeson down permanently into the blacklist, soon to take Du Bois as well. Completed less than a year after news of the Soviet Union's first testing of its atomic bombs on August 29, 1949, an event that challenged his adoration of the Soviet regime, the book implicates both superpowers in a global race to the bottom destined to inflict violence and poverty on citizens of both nations. To write a book of revolutionary *hope* in such a climate was to write against the grain of history. Thus in his final chapter of the book, Du Bois endeavors to interweave the national histories of his adversaries into a "third" way, toward renewed revolution.

The framing argument of Du Bois's historiographic project comes midway through the manuscript of "Russia and America." Chapter 5, titled "The Reign of Roosevelt," commences the second, comparative half of the manuscript, wherein Du Bois endeavors to weigh U.S. history between the start of the Depression in 1929 to the present, a framing roughly congruent with the years of the Russian Revolution. The comparative structure and timeline in which he fashions the book suggest parallels of Russian and U.S. history. He ponders the possibility of transposing the two, dialectically, into a single, unitary trajectory. The fifth chapter also commences the American section of the book's odd autobiographical frame: the first four chapters describe Du Bois's first, second, and third entrees into Russia, in 1926, 1936, and 1949; the second half begins with the declaration "I am an American":

> I can thus at once look on the United States as an outsider and
> continuous visitor, integrated into this culture and yet knowing
> and sharing it. I can see as few others can, the way in which
> the presence of a depressed class of human beings has distorted

and still distorts our social development. . . . Meanwhile my full
and unstinting loyalty and service went to my fellows of Negro
descent, not simply in the United States, but in the West Indies
and in Africa. Thence by logic I gave my friendship to all colored folk, in Asia and in the South Seas, hoping that in some
way the dark world would unite forces and thrust itself across
the color bar.[13]

Du Bois's "outside in" perspective on the U.S. indexes his position as
a correspondent for world revolution—a rapporteur, à la John Reed,
from a Bolshevik present back onto his native U.S. He thus offers to
interpret American history, including the history of the Civil War, by
comparison with his Russian experience. He recounts the rise of "economic power" in the U.S. on the backs of slave labor and an "organized
anti-slavery movement, helped by fugitive slaves and by white laborers
who sought to get rid of slave competition"—his joint protagonists of
the "general strike" of *Black Reconstruction*.[14] Then ensued the war,
and emancipation. "What was to be done?" Du Bois writes, channeling
the Lenin of 1902 to the U.S. of 1863. Following was an "attempt" at
adequate employment, civil rights, and minimum land, then a Freedmen's Bureau—the edifice of Reconstruction. "This," Du Bois writes,
"was a great start toward incipient socialism in the United States, without color caste and with full economic opportunity."[15] Yet as in the
original *Black Reconstruction*, a counterrevolution of property resists
progress. "By 1885, the United States had adopted its basic philosophy: Life was Business and Business was Life; Civilization was the
product of Industry and Industry was seed and product of Human Culture. . . . The United States entered upon its fabulous modern career as
the greatest industrial nation on earth."[16]

Du Bois has come to Russia thrice, it turns out, to *reverse history*: to
see if he could find in the Soviet Union the consummation of "incipient socialism" that would change the course of events in the U.S. He
structures "Russia and America" as an interrogation of the historical conditions that enable or disable political and social revolutions,
an interrogation overlaid with anxiety and threats of counterrevolution both without and within. It begins with "The Apology," in which
Du Bois confesses that he composed the book based on three brief
visits to the Soviet Union, though "four-fifths" of his allotted hundred
years have been lived in the U.S. He even anticipates in his foreword a
counterrevolution against his own account—"may men have mercy on

my word"—before plunging into a first chapter titled, confessionally again, "A Quest for Clarity." The chapter recounts his earlier fleeting glimpses and near misses with both the 1917 Revolution and Marxism leading to his decision to visit Russia to learn "at first hand just what has taken place in Russia and just what the development is at present."[17] A priori perceptions and arguments about the Revolution appear in his analysis. "We had made essays towards socialism" before 1917, he writes, "but when the Socialistic state appeared full-fledged, most of us called it by other names and refused to judge it by its socialism, but rather we insisted on investigation of the ethics of the methods underlaying its establishment"[18]—an allusion to his hesitations dating to his Fabian socialism of the pre–World War I period over workers' takeover of state power. By comparison, in order to achieve socialism, Du Bois writes, the Soviets had first nationalized the land, a far cry from the betrayed promise of forty acres for every freedman. The state also nationalized industry and, more important, invested heavily in education so that peasants would slowly rise from ignorance and poverty. Investment in peasant education combined with liquidation of the kulaks is for Du Bois a key to their simultaneous uplift with the working classes:

> We must remember that this problem of the farmer in modern life has been neglected to our cost. Here are folk who in every land have been physically by-passed by science, education and technique; they have in all lands been natural victims of exploitation and propaganda and in the automatic world market have been deprived of a decent income. . . . This has stopped democracy in France, Germany, Britain, and the United States.[19]

Du Bois justifies this claim by arguing that the Farm Security Administration has squeezed black farmers out of relief programs, thus deterring their historical progress and the progress of the U.S. working classes as a whole. He turns with ocular evidence from Soviet agriculture to a historic comparison of nineteenth-century Russian peasants and black American freedmen to demonstrate how the former have leaped over the latter in a "Reconstruction" fulfilled. Yet it is in his accounting for the peasant's place in the Soviet Revolution that Du Bois also exhibits important qualms about the most reactionary aspects of the Revolution. He describes as "savage" Stalin's January 1933 attacks on the kulaks who resisted liquidation, some of whom "had to be dealt with summarily."[20] "Something like a million out of 2.5 million peasant families were removed," he writes, penciling in the larger figure above the smaller. "Those who refused to cooperate were removed to distant places and put to work at road building, cutting timber or mining. It was hard, poorly paid work, and caused much suffering."[21] Du Bois then writes in and crosses out by hand this paragraph, obviously never intended for publication in the final manuscript:

> There were a million kulak families in Russia in 1928, but of 25,000,000 peasant families, and the State proceeded to break their power. The proceedings involved force and cruelty. The kulaks reduced agricultural output, stirred up revolt, and slaughtered animals, so as to bring a crisis in 1929 to 1932. But the state persisted. Large numbers were banished to Siberia and the struggle was won by 1934.[22]

This excised passage indexes several important dimensions of Du Bois's relationship to the Revolution. His clear distaste for violence and brutality in Russia echoes his long-standing anxieties about what he sometimes called Marxist "dogma." It kindles memories of his anxieties about how the Communist Party in Alabama used African Americans as "shock troops" during the Scottsboro Boys case. The passage is also a reminder that throughout the 1920s and 1930s Du Bois described himself generally or specifically as a "pacifist" ill at ease with political violence of any kind,[23] a politics codified by his work on the Stockholm Agreement after World War II. At the same time, Du Bois's reports on Soviet agriculture confirm that his primary sources for analysis of events between 1926 and 1936 in the Soviet Union were Sidney and Beatrice Webb's *Soviet Russia: A New Civilisation?* and articles by British trade unions, both soaked in Stalinist hagiography. Du Bois's inflated statistical summaries of Soviet economic and agricultural production were drawn from the Webbs, as were his glowing reports of industrial productivity.[24] He was also heavily influenced in his account by a book he favorably cites in "Russia and America": Albert Kahn and Michael Sayer's *The Great Conspiracy: The Secret War against Soviet Russia*. Kahn was an American journalist who joined the Communist Party in 1938 and during World War II published two widely selling books suffused with Popular Front adulation for Stalin and the Soviet role in World War II. Sayers was an Irish-born poet and communist blacklisted during the McCarthy period. Du Bois reproduced wholesale in his manuscript their aggressive defense of three key aspects of Stalin's Soviet Union: First, the Soviet economic miracle: "Stalin's first Five-Year Plan was galvanizing Old Russia into unprecedented feats of creative labor."[25] Second, an emphasis on the Russian Revolution as under constant siege after 1917 to German, Japanese, and capitalist countries—an argument Du Bois inflects to account for the tenacious grip of the cold war after 1945. And third, their unidimensional account of the Soviet "show trials" for treason in the 1930s—"The trials were fair and the testimony overwhelming."[26]—and Du Bois's virulent vilification of Trotsky. Book 3 of *The Great Conspiracy*, titled "Russia's Fifth Column," provided the template for Du Bois's acidic representation of Trotsky as one-man counterrevolution.[27] Du Bois reproduces uncritically Sayer and Kahn's claims that Trotsky collaborated with German fascists to overthrow Stalin and ordered the assassination of Stalin, Voroshilo, and Kirov.[28] He denies Soviet responsibility for Trotsky's murder in Mexico and concludes that Trotsky was "one of the great traitors of history."[29]

Foundational to Du Bois's negative dialectics in "Russia and America" is his contradictory response to violence in the Russian Revolution. He defends the deeply flawed Revolution because it inhabits archetypally the idea, or *typology*, of world revolution, which, in the depths of cold war hostilities, he is not willing to let die:

> We may ask whether or not the Russian Revolution might not have been carried through with less blood and cruelty, with less appeal to brute force. We may believe that with all the gain from the efforts of Lenin and Stalin, most of it might not have been accomplished at lower cost to the decent instincts of mankind. But Russia answers and has right to answer, that this revolution cost less in life and decency than the French Revolution, than the Protestant Reformation, and than the English Civil War; that the chief guilt for the high cost of communism was not the fault of Russia but of America which silently condoned the slavery of Russians for centuries and then at fabulous cost tried for ten years to reinslave them to the degenerate Czars and filthy priesthood. If the cost of revolution was excessive and revolting, the fault is certainly not to rest on Russia alone.[30]

Du Bois here revisits the *Black Reconstruction* conception borrowed from Marx that an agrarian and industrial workers' revolution "from

below" during the Civil War constituted an advance in the world revolution typology over its bourgeois revolution antecedents: these historical
echoes redound in Du Bois's doubling use of the word "slavery" to
describe Russian life under the czars. Consistent with this analysis,
he revisits and reasserts the "right of self-determination" thesis first
developed at the 1919, 1922, and 1928 Cominterns in relationship to
the colonies (and applied by Du Bois to African Americans in *Black
Reconstruction*) as an inalienable "right" of the Soviet Union, a fledg-
ling communist nation-state itself still coming up from czarist rule.[31]
Too, Du Bois, as he did in his retrospective revisions to John Brown,
here accepts late-in-life violence as part of the course of revolution.
Where he had argued about Brown's raid on Harpers Ferry in 1909 that
revolution is "always a loss and a lowering of ideals," in his revisions
for the 1962 reissue of the book he would write, "If it is a true revolution it repays all losses and results in the uplift of the human race."[32]
Du Bois's struggle to accept Brown's attack on Harpers Ferry as an
advance on human freedom is an entangled subtext of his struggle to
understand the Russian Revolution as a template for black (and white)
freedom. His revisionist account of Brown's life in the 1962 edition
of the book relocates the famous armed rebellion in a revolutionary
"typology" similar to the one that included the French Revolution and
Protestant Reformation. Thus Du Bois's meditations in "Russia and
America" anticipate his 1962 revisions to that text.

Beyond that, the Communist International's "world revolution" idea
also necessitated that Du Bois develop an interlocking conception of
world history, what Trotsky called "combined and uneven development,"
and what Marx, Engels, and Lenin referred to as capitalism's tendency
to unite the world in its predatory grasp. This is another significance of
the "comparative" framework of Du Bois's study. His rationalization of
the "high cost" of communism attempts to recognize the immense task
the working class faces in reversing the course of capitalist history that
long predates the cold war and the appearance of communism on the
world stage. It was this process he referred to in his 1951 declaration:
"I believe in Communism wherever and whenever men are wise and
good enough to achieve it; but I do not believe all nations will achieve
it in the same way or at the same time." The book's historiographic
method thus seeks to revisit nineteenth-century American and Soviet
peasantries in order to argue for U.S. and Soviet history as a singular,
not binary strand of capitalist history, as what Marxists call a "totality,"
a premise already established for the reader in Du Bois's interpretation

of Russia 1917 as a "second" Reconstruction. Du Bois again: "I can interpret the Soviet Union today through my experience with two million American Negroes in the last half of the nineteenth century." The book's second half and conclusion spell out explicitly the resolution of this interpretive method and its conclusions.

Du Bois's revolutionary narrative casts the challenges of the Depression that brought Roosevelt to power in the U.S. as analogous to crises in economic conditions that the Bolsheviks sought to overcome in 1917 and the U.S. government after the Civil War: "restoration of industry; relief distress and reform of the social organization."[33] Du Bois describes the initial stages and steps of the New Deal as "naked socialism"—government relief, welfare, the "dole," come undone by both a failed education in Leninist and Soviet method and by "the most reactionary defenders of wealth and monopoly,"[34] that is, congressional opponents to New Deal legislation. By analogy, Du Bois casts the New Deal as a second effort at "incipient socialism," which, like Reconstruction, has come up against the "counterrevolution of property." Now, as then, Du Bois turns his attention to African Americans as the historic group for whom counterrevolution is the most significant betrayal. After emancipation, he writes, "the plight of the Negroes themselves aggravated the unemployment situation by furnishing a mass of labor which had to accept wage at any level offered."[35] World War I brought black workers into industry for the first time, and the Depression into conditions of super exploitation; all workers lost jobs, "but in the case of the Negro worker, everything was worse in larger or smaller degree."[36] Du Bois thus measures the New Deal's betrayal by its effects on black workers:

> The first blow to Negroes came when farm laborers and domestics were not included under the protection of the N.R.A. [National Recovery Administration] codes for industry. Thus three million Negro workers, more than half of the total number who must work for their livelihood, were not covered by the industrial codes. These three million were the backbone of the Negro consumer market. For them an immediate rise in prices meant additional insecurity and suffering. Furthermore, in certain areas where uniform minimum wages were established for black and white workers, employers replaced Negroes with whites rather than pay the same wages. Thus the New Deal not only met opposition of concentrated wealth based on

Negro disenfranchisement, but also increased the opposition of white labor by increasing or failing greatly to decrease the number of poor and unemployed Negroes whose plight threatened the white standard of living. The result was violence and race riots.[37]

To observe the historical pattern Du Bois wants us to see repeated, we can simply turn back to the pages of *Black Reconstruction*:

> It must be remembered and never forgotten that the Civil War in the South which overthrew Reconstruction was a determined effort to reduce black labor as nearly as possible to a condition of unlimited exploitation and build a new class of capitalists on this foundation. . . . The lawlessness in the South since the Civil War has varied in its phases. First, it was that kind of disregard for law which follows all war. Then it became a labor war, an attempt on the part of impoverished capitalists and landholders to force laborers to work on the capitalist's own terms. From this, it changed to a war between laborers, white and black men fighting for the same jobs. Afterward, the white laborer joined the white landholder and capitalist and beat the black laborer into subjection through secret organizations and the rise of a new doctrine of race hatred.[38]

Read dialectically, the 1943 riots in Harlem and Detroit, postwar lynchings, New Deal disenfranchisement, and attacks on returning black soldiers after the war reiterate the "Thermidor" of post–Civil War counterrevolution: white backlash, the rise of the Klan, lynchings, what in *Black Reconstruction* Du Bois called the Negro's backward movement toward slavery after a moment in the sun of freedom. Typologically, then, the 1877 end of Reconstruction which helped launch the modern capitalist-colonial system—a central argument of Du Bois's 1935 book, as we have seen—remains held fast in place now in 1950 by the specter of permanent cold war:

> We know well that the main hindrance to security and democracy has been the fact that the attempt to raise the status of labor in civilized lands has for centuries been accompanied by the deliberate degradation of the laboring masses in colonial regions. The greatest insurance against future wars, which will

continue to masquerade as national expansion and self-defense, will be the clear recognition of the right of colonial peoples to a living wage, education, and self-government.[39]

It is *this* conjuncture Du Bois seeks to illuminate by the "experiment in Marxism" which is the book "Russia and America: An Interpretation." In his own "midnight hour" of the cold war, Du Bois creates from a seeming historical impasse a new theory of world revolution that can reanimate its core premise that capitalism will eventually produce the "gravediggers" of its demise. To this end, he asserts that it is the *populaces* of the Soviet Union and U.S., not its states or leaders, that will be the final arbiters of the present. The chapter "World Peace" carries forward the argument from the penultimate chapter of the manuscript, describing Du Bois's attendance at the 1949 Moscow Peace Conference, a continuation of his anti–nuclear proliferation work initiated by the U.S. dropping of atomic bombs on Hiroshima and Nagasaki. This macrocosmic urge to resist the global effects of nuclear proliferation leads directly to a cautionary parable that both the Soviet and U.S. nation-states have abandoned their own histories of revolution:

> It was revolution in the United States against exploitation of colonial labor that led to echoing revolution in France and Haiti, and resulted in uplift of labor throughout Europe and particularly in the great republic this side of the seas, *where the wage and standard of living among the working masses today leads the whole world*. It was revolution in Russia that founded a nation built on the determination to abolish poverty in the modern world by equitable redistribution of wealth made through the democratic power of an intelligent people; *and to start towards this great end by making the mass of people intelligent*.[40]

Du Bois's concluding "experiment in Marxism" in "Russia and America" is to imagine the democratic masses of the two antagonistic nations, like the freedmen and white laborers of nineteenth-century America, as co-actors and allies in leading a world revolution for the "abolition of war and the abolition of poverty."[41] The argument's logic is historical materialist and typological: from oppressed people's revolutions sprang both nations, toward revolutions they must lead. The book hearkens back to and globalizes anew two lines of political argument from *Black Reconstruction*: the U.S. must "not forget that the

slave system which stifled democracy in the United States for a century
after the first brave effort to declare all men equal, is today denying
under various guises the equal humanity of the majority of mankind,"
and merges the arguments of African American activity in U.S. history (*Black Reconstruction*) and the 1919 Comintern into a resolution
to which "it should be easy for both parties to agree": "That the right
of people anywhere to follow their own line of thought and action, in
accord with the thought of any nation is sacred so far as there is no
attempt to transgress the law."[42]

It is difficult to assess these conclusions merely, as did Henry Giroux,
as an "excessive condemnation of the United States" and "uncritical
apologia" for the Soviet Union. Du Bois not only consecrates the idea
of national self-determination in the name of a *vox populi* in "Russia and America," but also invigorates it with a democratic fervor that
seeks to find its popular and populist essence in both Soviet and U.S.
histories. "Russia and America" in this context invests national self-
determination and "world revolution" with something like a Popular
Front valence: it carries forward the optimistic spirit of alliance of the
U.S. and Soviet Union during the Second World War into a broad if
unrealistic appeal for peace and prosperity after the war's end: "The
American people want Peace. They want to neither conquer the world
nor police it. They have no desire to meddle in other people's affairs,
or censor their thought or control their industry. They want to spend
the billions now wasting in war on human education and uplift for all
men."[43]

At the same time, the idiosyncratic application of national self-
determination to the cold war constituted what Du Bois called in *Black
Reconstruction* an "experiment in Marxism" that was itself rooted in
challenges and contradictions of his time. Du Bois endorsed the Comintern line of self-determination in "Russia and America" seven years
after Stalin disbanded it. In this way, the manuscript functioned as an
attempt to restart and replace a historical dead letter in the world revolution corpus. Du Bois's revolutionary optimism in this endeavor is
partly the result of real political triumphs emerging in the time of his
writing. He composed the manuscript in the aftermath of the successful 1945 Manchester Pan-African Congress, where attendees advanced
anticolonial unity and a conscious Third World perspective as an alternative to Soviet Communism. As Kwame Nkrumah intoned at the
conference, "Colonial and Subject Peoples of the World—Unite!"[44] By
1950 the contours of African and Asian independence were becoming

clear; the Third World was just around the corner. Thus India's independence in 1947 and China's liberation in 1949 each registered to Du Bois as successful national liberation struggles that could rebalance the cold war by extending democracy and uplift to the world's workers and keeping alive Comintern ideals, if not the institution. These examples also superseded stalled results of the United Nations meetings in 1945, where a failure to condemn colonialism stood in stark contrast, and where Du Bois himself was to petition for recognition of U.S. treatment of African Americans as "genocide" on par with Nazi extermination of the Jews. The U.N. failure was for Du Bois also a reminder of the League of Nations and Wilsonian democracy advocating "self-determination" only for the noncolonized. Seen in this light, "Russia and America" was an attempt by Du Bois to blast away much twentieth-century Western imperial history, not only the standstill of U.S.-Soviet relations but the stalemate of ossified cold war polarization. This aspect of the book, too, makes it a clear artifact of Third World politics, also known as the "Bandung Era" of the cold war. Nehru's theory of "nonaligned" politics as a balancing act between communism and capitalist democracy is reminiscent of Du Bois's strained efforts to make the Soviet Union and U.S. coequal partners for world peace.

At the same time, the implausible "optimism of the will" of "Russia and America" marks it as a clear artifact of the Stalin era. Like so many of his contemporaries who began as supporters of the Russian Revolution—Nehru, George Padmore, Agnes Smedley, and others—Du Bois's improvised relationship to Marxism and its application reflects distortions brought about by Soviet Russia's evolution from Bolshevism to authoritarianism and state capitalism. Du Bois's book glosses over the worst violent excesses of the Stalin years, justifying the violent destruction of the kulaks, describing the horrendous 1936 Moscow Trials as "fair," and rationalizes the repression of dissidents to the Soviet states as the price of revolution. In this light, Stalinist bastardizations of Marxism helped to produce bastardized texts like "Russia and America." The zigzagging years of Stalinist policy and the violence that marked it produced numerous rogue species of Marxism across the planet—"experiments"—few of which resembled or resulted in the eight outcomes of socialism Marx and Engels listed in bullet points in section 2 of *The Communist Manifesto*. Workers of the world, despite Du Bois's exhortations and creativity, were still chained to exploitative conditions in both Russia and America. In this way "Russia and America" is an avatar of not only disparate and competing twentieth-century theories of world revolution, but the unevenness and incongruity of world events that shaped them. The manuscript tells us how far Du Bois journeyed as a fellow traveler to Soviet socialism before joining the U.S. Communist Party in 1961, predicts his 1953 hagiographic tribute to Stalin written upon his death, and anticipates the shadow of the blacklist and exile that fell over him just a year after completing the manuscript.

"Russia and America" thus might be considered a crossroads moment in the development of the global Du Bois, looking back nearly a century at his first infatuation with socialist politics, Asian liberation, and Russia, and forward to his final choice of political and geographical exile from America. What is absolutely clear is that no account of Du Bois's life, especially his political life, is possible without attention to "Russia and America." A future full accounting of Du Bois's life must acknowledge its proper place.

## Notes

1. There are exceptions to this trend. Most prominently Gerald Horne's *Black and Red: W. E. B. Du Bois and the Afro-American Response to the Cold War, 1944–1963* (Albany: SUNY Press, 1985); Manning Marable's *W. E. B. Du Bois: Black Radical Democrat* (New York: Routledge, 1985). Also David Levering Lewis's two-volume biography of Du Bois does not shy away from his enthusiasm for socialism. Another important exception is Nahum Dimitri Chandler's work, especially *Toward an African Future—Of the Limit of World* (Newport Beach, CA: Living Commons Collective, 2013). For more on Du Bois's nuanced conception of the "color line," and his own changing conception and use of that idea, see my *Un-American: W. E. B. Du Bois and the Century of World Revolution* (Philadelphia: Temple University Press, 2015). See also Phillip Luke Sinitiere's essay in this volume.

2. Alan Wald, "From 'Triple Oppression' to 'Freedom Dreams,'" *Against the Current* 162 (January–February 2013): 24.

3. Eric Porter, *The Problem of the Future World: W. E. B. Du Bois and the Race Concept at Midcentury* (Durham, NC: Duke University Press, 2010), 202.

4. The most notable book in the former category would be Paul Gilroy's *The Black Atlantic: Modernity and Double Consciousness* (Cambridge, MA: Harvard University Press, 1995). In the latter we can include Michael Denning's *The Cultural Front: The Laboring of American Culture in the*

*Twentieth Century* (New York: Verso, 2011); Alan Wald's trilogy of books on the American literary left, beginning with *Exiles from a Future Time: The Forging of the Mid-Century Literary Left* (Chapel Hill: University of North Carolina Press, 2002) and Barbara Foley's *Radical Representations: Politics and Form in U.S. Proletarian Fiction, 1929–1941* (Durham, NC: Duke University Press, 1993).

5. Kate Baldwin, *Beyond the Color Line and the Iron Curtain: Reading Encounters between Black and Red, 1922–1963* (Durham, NC: Duke University Press, 2002), 367.

6. See Vaughn Rasberry, *Race and the Totalitarian Century: Geopolitics in the Black Literary Imagination* (Cambridge, MA: Harvard University Press, 2016) and Etsuko Taketani, *The Black Pacific Narrative: Geographic Imaginings of Race and Empire between the Wars* (Hanover, NH: Dartmouth University Press, 2014).

7. David Levering Lewis, *W. E. B. Du Bois, 1919–1963: The Fight for Equality and the American Century* (New York: Henry Holt, 2000), 557.

8. Ibid.

9. For elaboration on this idea, see my *Un-American*.

10. In a 1905 essay Du Bois declaimed that Japan's victory over Russia in its territorial war in Manchuria constituted the first time the "color line" had been crossed in history. This was the first of many uses and revisions by Du Bois of the "color line" trope. For more see my *Un-American*; Porter, *The Problem of the Future World*; Chandler, *Toward an African Future*.

11. Rasberry, *Race and the Totalitarian Century*, 203.

12. W. E. B. Du Bois, "Russia and America: An Interpretation," unpublished draft ms., 1950, W. E. B. Du Bois Papers, University of Massachusetts, Amherst, 300.

13. Ibid., 257.

14. Ibid., 158.

15. Ibid., 159.

16. Ibid., 161.

17. Ibid., 16.

18. Ibid., 35.

19. Ibid., 78.

20. Ibid., 76.

21. Ibid., 77.

22. Ibid.

23. W. E. B. Du Bois, "Letter to George Streator," April 24, 1935, in Herbert Aptheker, ed., *The Correspondence of W. E. B. Du Bois*, vol. 2 (Amherst: University of Massachusetts Press, 1997), 163.

24. Du Bois read Sidney and Beatrice Webb's *Soviet Communism: A New Civilization and Russia Today. The Official Report of the British Trade Union Delegation Visiting Soviet Russia and the Caucasus* in preparing the manuscript of "Russia and America."

25. Du Bois, "Russia and America," 169.

26. Ibid., 82.

27. Michael Sayers and Albert Kahn, *The Great Conspiracy* (New York: Little, Brown, 1946).

28. Ibid., 81.

29. Ibid.

30. Ibid., 77–78.

31. The idea that Du Bois would think of the Russian Revolution as a struggle for national self-determination would have comported with his support for Stalin, who wrote one of the earliest Bolshevik treatises on the question, "Marxism and the National Question," Marxists Internet Archive, https://www.marxists.org/reference/archive/stalin/works/1913/03a.htm. A Georgian, Stalin was also hailed by some African American sympathizers with the Soviet Union as a "Black Russian." More generally, Du Bois's notion of the Russian Revolution as self-determination was part of his analogous mode of thought comparing the black self-determination struggle in the U.S. and globally with groups like Russian peasantry. This parallel is a strong, sustaining subtext throughout "Russia and America."

32. W. E. B. Du Bois, *John Brown* (New York: International Publishers, 2014), 296.

33. Du Bois, "Russia and America," 171.

34. Ibid.

35. Ibid., 181.

36. Ibid., 182.

37. Ibid., 183–84.

38. W. E. B. Du Bois, *Black Reconstruction 1860–1880* (New York: Simon and Schuster, 1999), 670.

39. Du Bois, "Russia and America," 301.

40. Ibid., 300. Emphasis added.

41. Ibid.

42. Ibid., 301, 305.

43. Ibid., 314.

44. Hakim Adi and Marika Sherwood, *The 1945 Manchester Pan-African Congress Revisited* (London: New Beacon, 1995), 115.

# "A Soliloquy on Viewing My Life from the Last Decade of Its First Century"

## The Black Radical Vision of *The Autobiography of W. E. B. Du Bois*

*Erik S. McDuffie*

W. E. B. Du Bois was happy. It was a warm and sunny day on August 8, 1958. He was about to board an ocean liner from New York to Europe for his fifteenth trip across the Atlantic. He gleefully recounted this day in the opening of his third memoir, *The Autobiography of W. E. B. Du Bois: A Soliloquy on Viewing My Life from the Last Decade of Its First Century*, published posthumously in 1968, five years after his passing in the West African nation of Ghana. He wrote, "Many friends with flowers and wine were at the dock to bid me and my wife goodbye." There was much to celebrate. "I felt like a released prisoner, because since 1951, I had been refused a passport by my government, on the excuse that it was not considered to be 'to the best interests of the United States' that I go abroad."[1]

Du Bois did not overstate his sense of relief in his memoir. The prior seven years had been extremely difficult for the African American scholar-activist who had been at the front lines in the struggle against the global color line since the early twentieth century. In 1951 the U.S. government stripped Du Bois of his passport and declared him an "unregistered foreign agent" for his involvement in the Peace Information Center (PIC), an antiwar, nuclear nonproliferation group based in New York City. Du Bois chaired the organization.[2] It was the height of the cold war between the United States and the Soviet Union for global supremacy. Domestically the McCarthy period was in full swing.

Named after the U.S. senator Joseph McCarthy (R-Wisconsin), this era saw government officials charge and launch aggressive investigations of thousands of Americans for being communists and communist sympathizers.[3] U.S. cold warriors viewed the PIC as a Soviet-controlled subversive organization. U.S. officials eventually barred Du Bois from traveling overseas. They feared that his outspoken criticisms of Jim Crow, U.S. empire, and colonialism and his vocal support for the Soviet Union, communism, and peace would damage U.S. attempts to win the hearts and minds in newly emergent nations in Africa and Asia against the Soviets.[4] The longtime scholar-activist earned the wrath of U.S. cold warriors and black liberal civil rights spokespersons.

Due to his own efforts and international pressure, the U.S. Supreme Court in August 1958 ruled in his favor, restoring his right to travel. Immediately after the Court's decision, Du Bois along with his wife, the activist and writer Shirley Graham Du Bois, departed the United States. The couple visited Europe, the Eastern Bloc, the Soviet Union, and the People's Republic of China. His time abroad strengthened like never before his commitment to the Soviet Union, China, global decolonization, socialism, peace, and, above all, global black freedom.[5] He vividly recounted the impact of his travels, as well as his life journey, in his final autobiography. He drafted most of the manuscript in his ninetieth year, between 1958 and 1959. The book is organized into three sections. The first part discusses his extended trip overseas in 1958 and 1959 and his enthusiasm for socialism, while the second part moves back in time to recount his earlier years and radicalization during the 1930s and 1940s. The final section returns to the 1950s. He recounts his turn toward the radical left, persecution, frustration with politically mainstream civil rights groups, and hope for a future communist world.[6]

The importance of *The Autobiography of W. E. B. Du Bois*—and other writings from the final ten years of his life—to appreciating the long arc of Du Bois's intellectual and political evolution has yet to be fully assessed by scholars. Scholars have often dismissed his final decade as a period mired in dogmatism, left-wing sectarianism, and blind allegiance to the Soviet Union. This position frames Du Bois's decision to join the U.S. Communist Party (CPUSA), to move to Ghana in 1961, and to renounce his U.S. citizenship shortly before his passing in 1963 as a cynical move of a cranky, old, disillusioned man.[7]

This view is evident in the work of the cultural scholar Eric Porter. In his intellectual biography *The Problem of the Future World:*

*W. E. B. Du Bois and the Race Concept at Midcentury*, Porter argues
that Du Bois formulated some of his most insightful scholarship about
race, geopolitics, and freedom between 1948 and 1952—a period Porter terms the "early late period" of Du Bois's life. According to Porter,
Du Bois's writings from these years anticipated contemporary color-
blind racial ideology, which argues that racial oppression has declined
and no longer constitutes a salient issue in shaping early twentieth-
century U.S. life.[8] Du Bois was keenly aware of the shifting character
of modern racism in the cold war era. U.S. rulers understood that Jim
Crow constituted the Achilles heel of the United States in its efforts
to win the hearts and minds of newly independent nations in Asia and
Africa against the Soviet Union. The exigencies of the U.S.-Soviet
rivalry for global supremacy, an emergent civil rights movement, and
decolonization therefore required the formulation of a new and more
sophisticated U.S. racial ideology. This new ideology disavowed Jim
Crow and scientific racism while maintaining global white supremacy
and colonialism. The emergence of this new form of racism, Du Bois
argued, provided ideological cover for efforts by U.S. rulers to gain the
support of African Americans and the emergent Third World against
the Soviet Union.[9]

While he praises Du Bois's "early late period" writings, Porter is less
enthusiastic about the veteran black scholar-activist's work during the
final years of his life. Porter claims that Du Bois's "criticisms became
significantly less nuanced" after 1952: "His take on communist states
and leaders . . . seems increasingly driven more by hagiography, wishful
thinking, and a refusal to acknowledge disturbing facts than by analysis."[10] Arguably his discomfort with the longtime scholar's turn toward
the radical left after the early 1950s may help explain Porter's dismissal
of Du Bois's last decade.[11]

In this essay I extend and recast Porter's analysis of Du Bois's final
years through an examination of *The Autobiography of W. E. B. Du Bois*.
In contrast to some scholars who dismiss his late writings for their
alleged sectarianism and dogmatism, I argue that his final memoir constitutes an invaluable work for understanding Du Bois's long life journey
and intellectual evolution. In contrast to his first two memoirs, *Darkwater: Voices from Within the Veil* and *Dusk of Dawn: An Essay toward
an Autobiography of a Race*, published in 1920 and 1940, respectively,
Du Bois wrote his final autobiography unapologetically from a black
radical standpoint.[12] Informed by his responses to global decolonization, the cold war, the emergent U.S. black freedom movement, state

persecution, and international travel during the 1950s, *The Autobiography of W. E. B. Du Bois* advances a position that unequivocally opposes capitalism, imperialism, white supremacy, U.S. empire, and liberalism. Arguing that white supremacy, anticommunism, and war are inextricably connected and foundational to U.S. domestic and foreign policy, he criticizes the African American middle class, or what he termed earlier in his life "the Talented Tenth," for its apparent complicity in supporting U.S. cold war foreign and domestic policy with the hope of receiving civil rights reforms at home. Placing his faith in ordinary people as agents of transformative change, he calls for a future world based on the principles of peace, socialism, human rights, Pan-Africanism, and international solidarity. Indeed Du Bois's third autobiography articulates a politics very much in line with what the historian Vijay Prashad has termed "the Third World project" of the 1950s and 1960s. This political vision proffered by newly emerging nations in Asia and Africa called for a new world order based on human rights, decolonization, and the redistribution of global power.[13]

*The Autobiography of W. E. B. Du Bois* is also important because it reveals both the breaks and the continuities within the veteran black scholar-activist's thought and life journey as articulated in his earlier memoirs. On the one hand, his final autobiography shared much in common with his previous life writing. According to Herbert Aptheker, the American Marxist historian, CPUSA leader, and good friend of Du Bois who edited his final memoir, the third autobiography is "an essay on the concept of race as illuminated by his own life." In this sense, *The Autobiography of W. E. B. Du Bois* resembles his previous memoirs where he sought to understand the global contours of the color line through his own lived experiences.[14] On the other hand, his final memoir differs from his previous autobiographies. Writing in the late 1950s allowed Du Bois a unique opportunity to reevaluate the story of his earlier life through a black radical lens.

Meanwhile *The Autobiography of W. E. B. Du Bois* sheds light on the genre of life writing by U.S. radicals—black and white—of the Old Left period. According to the historian James R. Barrett, these memoirs share a similar story line: "The narrative builds to a moment of conversion to socialism and then marches through a process of movement building in which the author is important only insofar as her/his story helps to explain the development of the party and its fate."[15] Although he moved to the far left in his final years, Du Bois's third autobiography differs from those by leading U.S. communists. Granted Du Bois had not joined the CPUSA when he penned his final memoir, but he was very close to the Party from the late 1940s onward. In the third auto-biography, Du Bois is not so much concerned with his conversion to socialism or Party building as he is with using his life as a lens for appre-ciating racial oppression and for imagining a future socialist world.

Although his third autobiography broke new ground on multiple fronts, Du Bois's last memoir frames freedom in highly masculin-ist terms. This stance is a departure from *Darkwater*, where he takes up women's emancipation in his classic essay "The Damnation of Women."[16] The essay was in many respects ahead of its time for its proto-black feminist pronouncements articulated by a black male writer. Drawing from his own lived experiences and expertise as a social commentator, the chapter condemns patriarchy. Du Bois also celebrates the achievements of black women from antiquity to his con-temporary moment. Looking toward the future, he calls for economic independence as well as for the education of and full citizenship rights for all women. The upliftment of women, he believes, would realize full freedom for all humanity.[17] Unlike his first memoir, his final autobiog-raphy does not contain a chapter or significant discussion of women. Du Bois's gendered understanding of freedom affirms what the liter-ary scholar Michelle Ann Stephens has called the "masculine global imaginary" promoted by twentieth-century black Caribbean male intel-lectuals and activists in the United States like Marcus Garvey, C. L. R. James, and Eric Williams. They sought to forge a "global vision of race" and worldwide movement of black people against European colonial-ism and racism. Yet their masculinist global vision of race and discourse for building transnational black formations often paralleled the dis-courses and practices of European empire and colonialism.[18] Du Bois's masculinist global vision of freedom demonstrates how his thinking did not completely break from orthodoxy.[19]

Finally, *The Autobiography of W. E. B. Du Bois* is significant because it contains important lessons for understanding and transforming our contemporary globalized world in which white supremacy remains salient. This is most evident in the election of Donald J. Trump to the U.S. presidency in 2016. Du Bois's final memoir anticipates resurgent white supremacy following the dismantlement of de jure segregation. In addition, his final memoir foresees what the historian Sundiata Keita Cha-Jua refers to as the "New Nadir" in African American life.[20] He coined the term to describe African American life since 1980 charac-terized by increased legal and extralegal state violence and surveillance against African Americans, mass incarceration, growing intraracial class fragmentations, the immiseration of the black American working-class and poor, and the emergence of political conservatism among some African Americans. According to Cha-Jua, the end of de jure segregation in response to the civil rights–black power movement (1954–80) did not end racial oppression; rather desegregation and the suppression of the most radical tendencies within the black freedom movement, together with globalization and deindustrialization, created new forms of structural and ideological racism that have unevenly impacted black America.[21] Decades earlier, *The Autobiography of W. E. B. Du Bois*, especially the last section, predicted the "New Nadir." Arguing that the move to end Jim Crow in response to cold war imperatives introduced a new form of racial oppression and concomitant racial ideology, Du Bois emphasizes the inextricable linkages between racism, anticommunism, the expansion of U.S. empire into Africa and the Global South, class fragmentations within black America, the complicity of some African Americans in U.S. imperialism, and the broadening of state surveillance and violence. On this issue, *The Autobiography of W. E. B. Du Bois* was ahead of its time. Yet the gaps in his thinking, especially around gender, provide opportunities for forging a capacious vision of human freedom. For these reasons, his third autobiography is a must-read book not only for appreciating Du Bois's life and legacy but also for imagining a free and just world.


## Communism and Global Sojournings

Through recounting his travels to Western Europe, the Soviet Union, Eastern Bloc nations, and China in the late 1950s, part 1 of *The Autobiography of W. E. B. Du Bois* makes it undeniably clear that the scholar-activist was now committed to socialism and the Third World project like never before. At the same time, the memoir reveals the limitations of his thinking, namely its masculinist framings of black freedom and human progress. Great Britain was his first stop overseas during his 1958 trip. From there, he visited France, the Netherlands, Belgium, and West Germany, nations he had visited and in some cases had lived in decades earlier. While these nations had established liberal democracies and had rebuilt themselves from the ashes of World War II, Western Europe, the elderly black radical believed, remained stuck in the past. He wrote, "Today, to my mind, Western Europe is not prepared to surrender colonial imperialism." Western Europe in alliance with the United States clung to its desire to maintain global wealth and power through the exploitation of "cheap colonial labor."[22] For Du Bois, the United States and Western European nations were morally bankrupt and standing on the wrong side of human history.[23]

Although he was disappointed with Western Europe, Du Bois's optimism for the future grew as he journeyed through the Soviet-allied communist states of Eastern Europe: East Germany, Czechoslovakia, Hungary, and Poland. Rejecting the claim by U.S. cold warriors that Eastern Europeans were a "captive people" of the Soviet Union, he marveled at the economic growth and cultural vitality of the region under communism. He defended Soviet repression of the Hungarian Revolution of 1956, a popular, nationwide uprising against the Soviet-backed Hungarian government. In his view, a revolt allegedly led by middle-class "reactionaries" warranted Soviet military intervention.[24]

Visiting the Soviet Union was one of the most exciting parts of Du Bois's extended overseas journey. The trip further cemented his belief that socialism was most adequate to achieving racial equality and human freedom. His journey to the Soviet Union in 1958 was not his first to the socialist country. He had previously visited in 1926, 1936, and 1949. These trips were critical in helping him to gradually dispense with the belief that racial equality and human freedom could be achieved under capitalism. *Darkwater* made no reference to the Russian Revolution. However, *Dusk of Dawn* commented on his first Soviet trip. In 1940 he wrote, "It was the Russian Revolution which first illuminated and made clear this change in my basic thought."[25] Noting that his upbringing shaped a belief in liberal democracy, he declared that visiting the Soviet Union prompted him to begin to rethink his previous assumptions, a point Bill Mullen's essay in this volume explicates. Du Bois adds, "Mentally I came to know Karl Marx and Lenin, their critics and defenders. Since that trip my mental outlook and the aspect of the world will never be the same."[26] His second journey to the Soviet Union, during the Depression, further weakened his faith in liberal reform. Still, his second autobiography did not advocate socialism. Instead Du Bois called for "self-segregation," a black nationalist program reminiscent of the economic nationalism of his former adversary Marcus Garvey; it called for African American self-sufficiency and cooperative economics, along with civil rights and education.[27]

Unlike his previous memoirs, *The Autobiography of W. E. B. Du Bois* made it clear in his discussion of the Soviet Union that he was now a hard-core socialist. W. E. B. Du Bois and Shirley Graham Du Bois spent five months in the communist state. They visited Moscow and Leningrad and traveled to Uzbekistan, the heart of Soviet Central Asia, populated by dark-skinned Muslims. Conferring with Soviet premier Nikita Khrushchev was one of the highlights of the couple's trip to the Soviet Union.[28]

Du Bois's final autobiography praises the USSR. He was convinced that "the Soviets are making a new people" by building a socialist society in which the working class produced the country's wealth and knowledge.[29] Du Bois was especially impressed with the Soviets' apparent support for African independence and development, as well as for establishing African studies institutes and recruiting students from the continent to study in the Soviet Union. In Du Bois's estimation, the Soviet Union was far more committed to African liberation than was the United States. He also called attention to the apparent enhanced status of Soviet women: "There is under communism a use of women for more than pleasure and physical reproduction." The Soviet government "released [women] from the household drudgery" and made them key agents in building a new socialist society.[30]

While his travels through the Soviet Union and the Eastern Bloc inspired him, sojourning to the People's Republic of China was the most transformative experience of his extended overseas journey during the late 1950s. Du Bois's excitement about China and Sino-African relations exposed both his exuberance for the Third World project and the limitations of imagining a counterhegemonic new world order. Du Bois and Graham Du Bois spent eight weeks in China, from February to April 1959. Visiting the major cities of Beijing, Shanghai, Nanking, and Guangzhou, as well as rural areas, the couple traveled five thousand miles across this vast nation. Journeying to China was a bold move; the United States did not recognize the communist country and barred its citizens from visiting.[31] Du Bois's trip to China in 1959 was not his first journey to the East Asian nation. He first visited in 1936. At the time, the country was largely controlled by European nations, who openly despised and unapologetically exploited the Chinese people. Looking back twenty years, he marveled at how much China had progressed under communism. China mesmerized Du Bois: "Fifteen times I have crossed the Atlantic and once the Pacific. But never so vast and glorious a miracle as China." He added, "I have never seen a nation which so amazed and touched me as China in 1959."[32]

For Du Bois, China symbolized the victory of a nation of color in which its one billion people had defeated feudalism, European foreign rule, and capitalism under the leadership of Mao Zedong, the leader of the Chinese Communist Party and founder of the People's Republic of China in 1949. Du Bois met twice with Mao. They spent four hours together. Du Bois also conferred with Zhou Enlai, the premier of China.[33]

Du Bois was most impressed with the everyday Chinese people he encountered—factory workers, farmers, and servants—who were building a new China. "I saw a happy people; people with faith that needs no church or priest," he claimed. Personally he felt free of racism in China. "In all my wanderings, I never felt that touch or breath of insult or even dislike—I who for 90 years in America scarcely ever saw a day without some expression of hate for 'niggers.'"[34] The apparent progress made by Chinese women under communism also intrigued Du Bois. "The women of China are becoming free," he wrote. Calling attention to women working in factories and defying traditional gender conventions by wearing pants, he marveled at the improved status of Chinese women.[35]

Traveling to China provided Du Bois with a unique opportunity to critique U.S. empire and to anticipate American participation in the Vietnam War. He asserted that the United States hoped to "supplant France as colonial ruler in Southeast Asia."[36] The veteran black activist-intellectual's predictions would come true: in a few short years the United States would launch a full-scale war in Vietnam, which would lead to the deaths of more than fifty-eight thousand Americans and millions of Vietnamese military personnel and civilians.[37] The darker world was on the move, and China was leading the global charge against capitalism, imperialism, and white supremacy.

There is no question that Du Bois's exuberance for the Soviet Union, China, and communism prompted him to romanticize and overlook the authoritarian side of these nations. His blanket support for the brutal Soviet repression of the Hungarian Revolution of 1956 is but one example. Soviet military intervention left thousands of everyday people dead and precipitated a serious refugee crisis of Hungarians fleeing their country. Hungary deeply divided Western Marxists and communist parties, including in the United States. Du Bois's third memoir made no mention of these developments.[38] While he readily admitted, "China is no utopia," Du Bois did not mention that Mao had already begun to silence and in some cases kill his opponents. Millions of Chinese perished as a result of the Great Leap Forward, a state-initiated economic and social plan launched in 1958 to rapidly industrialize the nation.[39]

And antiblack racism did exist in Communist China. Violence against Africans began soon after the first arrival of African university students to the East Asian nation in the early 1960s.[40] Moreover Du Bois framed Chinese-African friendship in paternalist terms. As Frazier argues, African nations, in Du Bois's thinking, "were never positioned as having something to offer China in terms of knowledge production, cultural exchange, and geopolitical strategizing." Instead Africa was a junior partner in the continent's relationship to China.[41] Even Du Bois could not fully reimagine a world in which Africa would truly emerge as a sovereign continent.

Du Bois read the Soviet Union and China through a masculinist lens. Scholar Robeson Taj Frazier correctly argues, "Du Bois's representation of Chinese communism was . . . gender specific, denoting male activity, male knowledge, and a geopolitics as a site of male struggle."[42] Although he drew some attention to the enhanced status of Soviet and Chinese women under communism, Du Bois overlooked how sexism remained alive and well in these nations.[43] Given the proto-feminism of "Damnation of Women," it is telling that his final autobiography largely neglects black women's struggle for equality and dignity and their instrumental role in precipitating his move toward the left. So while so much of Du Bois's thinking in his last years was revolutionary and prescient, his masculinist articulations of liberation in his final autobiography were very much in line with his times.

Du Bois was hardly the first—or last—U.S. leftist who overlooked the darker sides of Soviet and Chinese communism. However, his apparent naïveté or willful blindness about the realities of the Soviet Union and China should hardly be used to dismiss his political journey in his final years. Du Bois was most concerned with the oppression and freedom of African-descended people globally. It was Western Europe and the United States, not the Soviet Union or China, that had enslaved millions of African people and colonized most of the world. The United States professed to be the freest nation in the world, yet African Americans remained second-class citizens suffering extreme state and extralegal violence in the Jim Crow U.S. In the United States black Americans lived under lynching, rape, and disfranchisement. Du Bois personally had endured years of repression in his own country. Internationally the United States backed ruthless regimes around the world, including apartheid South Africa, and intervened militarily in Vietnam and elsewhere under the guise of defending democracy from communism. Soviet and Chinese officials treated Du Bois with the utmost respect and recognized him as the preeminent scholar of the African-descended. So from this standpoint, Du Bois's support of the Soviet Union and China made sense and was echoed by millions of people globally who looked to the Soviet Union, China, and the emerging Third World as sites for building a new world.

## Reassessing His Earlier Years

While the opening section of *The Autobiography of W. E. B. Du Bois* discusses Du Bois's last decade, part 2, the longest section, moves back in time, tracing his life from his birth in 1868 in Great Barrington, Massachusetts, through the mid-1940s. Like his two previous memoirs, *The Autobiography of W. E. B. Du Bois* recounted his early years growing up in a small New England town in a family that proudly traced its roots to West Africa, Haiti, and France. From there the story shifts to his time at historically black Fisk University in Nashville, Tennessee, Harvard University, and the University of Berlin. The section then discusses his life and activism during the early twentieth century: his emergence as a preeminent African American scholar, his role in founding civil rights formations like the Niagara movement and the National Association for the Advancement of Colored People (NAACP), and his leadership in interwar Pan-African conferences. The final part of the section looks at his nascent radicalism and growing political disputes with NAACP officials during the Depression and World War II. However, the third memoir does not simply rehash his early life, which he told in *Darkwater, Dusk of Dawn*, and other writings. Instead Du Bois in his last autobiography reassesses his first seventy years through a black radical framework.

This position is evident in Du Bois's rereading in his final memoir of the epic rivalry at the turn of the twentieth century between him and Booker T. Washington, the ex-slave and founder of Tuskegee University in Alabama, who emerged as the leading proponent of industrial education and accommodationism to Jim Crow. In his classic 1903 book, *The Souls of Black Folk*, Du Bois includes a chapter that assails Washington for calling for black economic self-improvement at the expense of full citizenship rights. In contrast, Du Bois demands voting rights and a liberal arts education for African Americans. Looking toward the future, he places his faith in what he terms "the Talented Tenth," a group of college-educated black people he believed were best suited for leading the race.[44] *The Souls of Black Folk* positioned Du Bois as Washington's leading adversary.[45]

At the end of his life, the longtime black scholar-activist rethought his rivalry with Washington. Charging that "these two theories of Negro progress were not absolutely contradictory," Du Bois acknowledged, "Neither I nor Booker Washington understood the nature of capitalistic exploitation of labor, and the necessity of a direct attack on the principle of exploitation as the beginning of labor uplift."[46] While he remained opposed to racial accommodation, Du Bois nonetheless acknowledged that both men embraced a pro-capitalist position. This stance failed to understand that capitalism was inherently antithetical to African American freedom. The scholar-activist also conceded that he embraced an elitist perspective. By the end of his life, he identified working people, not the elite, as the vanguard for transformative change.

Du Bois's rereading of his early encounters with Marxism and the Soviet Union constitute another important difference between his last autobiography and his first two memoirs. Late in life he proudly acknowledged that he "believed in the dictum" of Marx's materialist conception of history.[47] But his path to Marxism received little attention in his first autobiographies. *Darkwater* made no reference to his first introduction to Marx while studying at the University of Berlin in the 1890s, brief membership in the Socialist Party of America in 1912, or thoughts about the Russian Revolution of 1917. Instead the first memoir portrays the young Du Bois as a militant race reformer whose politics were forged by the racial pride of his family and the liberal democratic traditions of New England. *Dusk of Dawn* briefly notes that Marx "was hardly mentioned at Harvard."[48] Even more, Du Bois's second memoir unequivocally states his opposition to communism during the 1930s: "I was not and am not a communist. I do not believe in the dogma of inevitable revolution in order to right economic wrong."[49] Du Bois's position on communism and revolution would change.

*The Autobiography of W. E. B. Du Bois* framed the conversation differently from *Dusk of Dawn* about his early encounters with and positions on Marx. The final memoir hardly painted the young Du Bois as a closet Marxist; however, it repeatedly mentions the omission of Marx from his undergraduate and graduate education. Looking back seven decades, Du Bois admits that as a young man he "was blithely European and imperialist in outlook; democratic as democracy was conceived in America."[50] This vision explains his complicated response to the Soviet Union following his first visit to the nation in 1926. Echoing the previous section of the final autobiography, Du Bois admits that his first trip to the Soviet Union convinced him that African Americans would never achieve freedom under capitalism. But he did not embrace the far left following his first Soviet trip. Opposing the U.S. Communist Party and revolution, he believed that racial equality could be won through gradual and peaceful reform.[51] This perspective informed his work for years to come.

The final memoir's discussion of his involvement in and break from the NAACP provides the clearest insight into Du Bois's move toward the hard left by the early 1950s. Unlike in *Dusk of Dawn*, Du Bois pulls no punches in the final memoir in his criticism of what would become the largest U.S. civil rights group, an organization he cofounded in 1909. He served as editor of *The Crisis*, the NAACP's official periodical, which in essence became his mouthpiece in promoting racial equality. More broadly, the NAACP emerged at a moment when "empire; the domination of white Europe over black Africa and yellow Asia . . . [and] industrial imperialism in America" over African Americans was "triumphant," as Du Bois puts it.[52] The NAACP embraced a top-down, legalistic strategy for winning African American civil rights through the courts and public opinion. Looking back from the late 1950s, he writes that "the question as to how far educated Negro opinion was going to have the right and opportunity to guide the Negro group" informed his work and the NAACP's program. He admits that the relation of African Americans to the labor movement constituted "an unasked question" for him and the NAACP in its early years.[53] So while the NAACP called for black voting rights and the end of lynching, its overall program remained within the ideological parameters of liberal democratic reform.

Tensions between Du Bois and NAACP officials over strategies for black freedom existed from the group's very beginning. He pointed to his work in building the Pan-African movement in the 1920s as one example. He took the lead in organizing four Pan-African conferences during the interwar years. Held in Europe and attended by black elites mostly from the United States and the Caribbean, the conferences reflected his belief that the "Negro world [would] be led by American Negroes." In 1923 he traveled to Africa for the first time. In his final autobiography he claims that NAACP officials criticized him for "moving too fast" on the international front and that the board "was not interested in Africa." Instead the NAACP, Du Bois charges, developed "its narrowest program," rejecting an understanding of African American freedom in global terms.[54]

Disagreements mounted between Du Bois and the NAACP by the early 1930s in response to his advocacy of black nationalist and internationalist solutions to racism that challenged the NAACP's unequivocal opposition to racial separatism—black or white—and its ambivalence toward Pan-Africanism. Numerous factors explain his radicalization during these years. Like scores of African American intellectuals, Du Bois moved left in response to the political and economic upheavals of the 1930s: the Great Depression, the Scottsboro case, the New Deal, trade union militancy, the Italo-Ethiopian War, and the rise of fascism in Europe.[55] By the early 1930s he "slowly but surely" had come to believe that most white people in the United States and Europe opposed racial equality.[56] He also came to detest Walter White, the fair-complected NAACP executive secretary, for his alleged egotism and dictatorial leadership style. Sensing growing opposition against him, Du Bois resigned his position from the NAACP in 1934 and returned to a full-time academic career at Atlanta University.[57] Ten years later he rejoined the NAACP as director of special research. From this office he pursued his internationalist work. He drafted in 1947 "An Appeal to the World : A Statement of Denial of Human Rights to Minorities in the Case of Citizens of Negro Descent in the United States of America and an Appeal to the United Nations for Redress." The report called for the United Nations to charge the United States with violating the human rights of African Americans.[58] The NAACP endorsed the "Appeal." However, long-standing disputes between Du Bois and White remained over the direction of the NAACP, namely its advocacy of legalism as the fulcrum for African American equality and the group's nascent anticommunism. He came to believe that the organization struck a Faustian bargain with American rulers for civil rights concessions in return for their support of U.S. cold war domestic and foreign policy. The board fired Du Bois in 1948 from an organization he cofounded.[59]

Ten years after his firing, Du Bois offered more biting criticism of the NAACP's legalistic approach to African American freedom. Framed by a black radical perspective, he argued that the organization failed to understand how cold war politics and international opinion played a crucial role in prompting U.S. rulers to begin dismantling Jim Crow. To make his point he cited the *Brown v. Board of Education* case of 1954, in which the U.S. Supreme Court ruled that separate but equal schools were unconstitutional. Although supportive of the decision, he asserted that the ruling would have been impossible "without the world pressure of communism led by the Soviet Union." Continued legal racial discrimination harmed the global image of the United States as the leader of the "Free World." He added that "legal enactment and decision" was useful, but it did not "ensure action" against white supremacy. Noting that the white South was in open "rebellion" against the Supreme Court, Du Bois castigated the NAACP for its hierarchal, undemocratic leadership structure and unwillingness to ally itself with U.S. workers, the socialist world, and global Africa.[60] The elder black radical was through with liberalism and reform.

Despite his break from the NAACP, Du Bois found new sites to fight against white supremacy, colonialism, and capitalism during and immediately after World War II. Internationally the Fifth Pan-African Congress in Manchester, England, in October 1945 deeply impacted his work. He cochaired the conference organized by the longtime Pan-Africanists Amy Jacques Garvey of Jamaica and George Padmore of Trinidad. A milestone in African decolonization, the gathering marked the first time a large contingent of African and Caribbean students, trade unionists, and activists attended a Pan-African conference. Many of those in attendance, such as Kwame Nkrumah of the Gold Coast and Jomo Kenyatta of Kenya, would later emerge as leaders of independent African states.[61]

The final autobiography identified the Southern Negro Youth Congress (SNYC) as a key site for radicalizing Du Bois and providing him with new political allies. Formed in 1937, the SNYC was a pioneering progressive civil rights group that came to be headquartered in Birmingham, Alabama. Appreciating African American freedom in global terms, the Youth Congress supported trade unionism, antifascism, internationalism, and decolonization. Many of the group's key leaders—the radical married couples James E. Jackson Jr. and Esther Cooper Jackson, Louis and Dorothy Burnham, and Ed and Augusta Strong—were brilliant thinkers and tireless activists who had joined the Communist Party during the 1930s.[62]

The SNYC provided a platform for Du Bois to move toward the radical left. He was the keynote speaker at the Youth Congress's famous Sixth All-Southern Negro Youth Legislature held in Columbia, South Carolina, on October 20, 1946. The three-day conference was the largest in the group's history. More than 850 delegates—black and white—from across the South representing trade unions, fraternities, sororities, fraternal organizations, and political organizations attended the gathering held in Antisdel Chapel at the historically black Benedict College.[63] His address, "Behold the Land," eloquently linked the struggle against Jim Crow with global struggles against imperialism, capitalism, war, and white supremacy. The third autobiography published excerpts of his address, in which he exclaimed, "[The South] is the firing line not simply for the emancipation of the American Negro but for the emancipation of the African Negro and the Negroes of the West Indies; for the emancipation of the colored races; and for the emancipation of the white slaves of modern capitalistic monopoly."[64] Instantly becoming a classic, Du Bois's speech signaled his turn toward the radical left, which Esther Cooper Jackson, James Jackson, and their SNYC colleagues helped to initiate. These young militants idolized Du Bois. The respect was mutual. In the final autobiography, he noted that he "admired" James Jackson and Louis Burnham "for their hard work and sacrifice."[65] Following the conference, James Jackson and Esther Cooper Jackson and their black comrades grew closer to Du Bois and frequently conversed with him about race, socialism, and the future world.[66]

Curiously *The Autobiography of W. E. B. Du Bois* erased the importance of Esther Cooper Jackson in moving Du Bois left during and immediately after World War II. An astute thinker and effective leader, Cooper Jackson was born in 1917 in Richmond, Virginia. She graduated from Oberlin College and attended graduate school at Fisk University, where she joined the Communist Party and wrote a pioneering study of African American women domestics in relation to trade unionism.[67] In 1942 she came to lead the SNYC. Her position reflected the group's commitment to fighting sexism and to promoting women in the group's leadership. In addition to Cooper Jackson, Dorothy Burnham, Augusta Strong, Mildred McAdory, and Sallye Bell Davis occupied prominent leadership roles in the SNYC.[68] Cooper Jackson first met Du Bois in November 1945 at the left-leaning World Youth Congress in London. Through her, he met young radicals of color from around the globe who came to the conference inspired to build a new world. Cooper Jackson and Du Bois kept in touch after they returned to the United States. She introduced Du Bois to her husband, James Jackson, and Louis Burnham.[69] Above all, it was Cooper Jackson who invited the veteran scholar-activist to deliver the keynote address and who gave the opening remarks before his famous speech at the SNYC's Sixth All-Southern Negro Youth Legislature in Columbia, South Carolina. *The Autobiography of W. E. B. Du Bois* made no reference to her, although Du Bois briefly mentioned James Jackson and Louis Burnham, crediting these two young black men for spearheading the conference.[70]

So as the clouds of war and reaction gathered in the United States against communism and the Soviet Union in the years immediately after World War II, Du Bois found politically progressive allies at home and abroad committed to building a new world following his break from the NAACP and liberalism. However, his last memoir reveals how masculinism prevented him from breaking with from all aspects of conventional thought.

## The Cold War, Persecution, Radical Pan-Africanism, and Imagining a Socialist World

Part 3 of the final memoir returns to where the book begins, in Du Bois's discussion of his turn toward the radical left, persecution, and vision of a future socialist world. Through focusing on his political persecution during the McCarthy period, Du Bois understood how the dismantlement of Jim Crow in response to cold war exigencies introduced new forms of racial oppression and signaled the expansion of U.S. empire. Anticipating the New Nadir, he observed growing class fragmentations within black America in response to the emergence of the cold war order.[71]

Du Bois's legal troubles began in 1950 following efforts by the U.S. Justice Department to shut down the Peace Information Center. The PIC endorsed the Stockholm Appeal, a global initiative that called for nuclear nonproliferation and peaceful coexistence between the United States and the Soviet Union. Given the PIC's stance and U.S. cold war anxieties, the State Department targeted the organization and Du Bois. In February 1951 the government briefly jailed him. Later that year he stood trial in Federal Court in New York for his leadership of the PIC. According to the longtime black scholar-activist, "the real object" of the trial was to silence and punish any person who dared to speak out against U.S. racism and imperialism.[72] The indictment and trial infuriated him. Ultimately he was found innocent due to the lack of credible evidence. However, significant damage had been done. This attention tarnished his name, and the State Department stripped Du Bois of his passport.[73]

While he framed his persecution as a broad attack against opponents of the cold war order, Du Bois also discussed his trial to highlight growing political and class fragmentations within black America. The most painful aspect of his persecution was the lack of support during his trial from black liberal middle-class intellectuals and professionals. He wrote that as a group the "'Talented Tenth' . . . was [mostly] either silent or actually antagonistic" at his defense. Du Bois felt betrayed and abandoned by a group he had helped to create. Their stance signaled the moral bankruptcy and complicity of black liberals in the racist and imperialist U.S. cold war project.[74] Arguing that segments of the black middle class "had become American in their acceptance of exploitation as defensible and in their imitation of American 'conspicuous expenditure,'" he charged that many African Americans "hated 'communism' and 'socialism' as much as any white American."[75] Looking toward the future, he predicted that the "dichotomy in the Negro group" in regard to class divisions would sharpen as legal racial discrimination against African Americans decreased.[76] He predicted that some black Americans would become politically conservative as they gained wealth and incorporation into the U.S. ruling elite. What these Negroes failed to realize, Du Bois argued, was that their modicum of wealth and power would not protect them from white supremacy and capitalism. He pointed again to *Brown v. Board of Education*. Although the Supreme Court had ruled that de jure segregation in U.S public schools was unconstitutional, Du Bois asserted that white Americans had a "long habit of ignoring and breaking the law," especially in the South. Simply put, the battle against Jim Crow was not over. In the book's most ominous prediction, Du Bois warned that African Americans might one day find themselves in the same position as the Jews in Nazi Germany during the 1930s. He warned, "It only took a psychopathic criminal like Hitler to show them their tragic mistake. American Negroes may yet face a similar tragedy. They should prepare for such an eventuality."[77] According to Du Bois, the future for African Americans was bleak if they embraced liberal anticommunism and consumerism while the bulk of humanity pursued socialism and decolonization.

Despite his experiences with state persecution and abandonment by black liberals, Du Bois remained confident and excited about the possibilities of a future world. Circling back to the beginning of the third memoir, he looked to Africa, global decolonization, and the communist world as fulcrums for transformative change. He was especially intrigued with Ghana. The former British colony known as Gold Coast gained its independence on March 6, 1957. Led by the militant Pan-Africanist Kwame Nkrumah, Ghana electrified the black world and emerged as a symbol of radical Pan-Africanism.[78] Du Bois met

The W. E. B. Du Bois Memorial Centre for Pan African Culture (Accra, Ghana), 2019. Photo by the author.

Nkrumah at the Fifth Pan-African Congress at Manchester, England, in 1945. Nkrumah invited Du Bois to attend the independence ceremonies in the West African nation's capital, Accra. However, the U.S. government's travel ban prevented Du Bois from journeying to Ghana.[79]

Du Bois's absence from the Ghanaian independence ceremonies did not prevent him from appreciating the significance of the new West African nation to global Africa and the world. In his reply to Nkrumah's invitation, he expressed his disappointment that he could not travel to Accra, and he offered his advice to the prime minister: "Today, when Ghana arises from the dead and faces this modern world, it must no longer be merely a part of the British Commonwealth or a representative of West Europe, Canada, and the United States. Ghana must on the contrary be the representative of Africa."[80] For Du Bois, Ghana represented the success of Pan-Africanism, global decolonization, peace, and socialism. He urged Nkrumah to promote "Pan-African socialism" for the economic, political, and cultural development of the entire continent and black world.[81] In an address by the black scholar-activist penned in the Soviet Union in 1958 and read by Shirley Graham Du Bois in Accra that same year, Du Bois asserted, "Today Africa has no choice between Capitalism and Socialism. The whole world, including Capitalist countries, is moving toward Socialism, inevitably, inexorably."[82] As prime minister, Nkrumah pursued a national and foreign policy that resembled Du Bois's vision for a future world. Committed to socialism, decolonization, peace, and nonalignment, Nkrumah called for a United States of Africa, a federation of all sovereign nations on the African continent.[83]

African decolonization and the independence of Ghana also transformed Du Bois's thinking about the relationship of Africa and the diaspora to global black freedom. Through the Fifth Pan-African Congress and Ghanaian independence, he came to realize that Africa, not the diaspora, would take the lead in the worldwide struggle for black liberation: "American Negroes had too often assumed that their leadership in Africa was natural."[84] Rejecting the elitist Pan-Africanism he espoused earlier in life, Du Bois's thinking was increasingly in line with the Third World project.

Beyond Ghana, part 3 of *The Autobiography of W. E. B. Du Bois* concluded with an endorsement of Communist China and a clarion call for Sino-African unity. This position was most evident in a speech he delivered in Beijing on his ninety-first birthday, in February 1959. Broadcast nationwide and reprinted in his final memoir, the veteran black scholar-activist's address began with a humble acknowledgment:

> I speak with no authority; no assumption of age nor rank; I hold
> no position, I have no wealth. One thing alone I own and that
> is my own soul. Ownership of that I have even while in my own
> country for nearly a century I have been nothing but a "nigger."
> On this basis and this alone I dare speak, I dare advise.[85]

Although he felt like a second-class citizen in the land of his birth, Du Bois felt free in Communist China. Witnessing firsthand a nation he believed had thrown off the shackles of colonialism and white supremacy, he called on African-descended people around the world to look to the East Asian nation. "Speak, China, tell your truth to Africa and the world," he declared. Envisioning China as an alternative to the United States and the West and a sincere ally to people of color globally, he urged the Chinese government to invite Africans to the communist nation. Once there, they would learn from a formerly colonized people technical training, the art of modern state-building, and a new sense of freedom.[86] Du Bois saw in China a symbol and model of liberation for the African-descended and people of color globally.

The Autobiography of W. E. B. Du Bois discusses neither the veteran black radical's decision in October 1961 to enlist in the U.S. Communist Party nor his decision to move to Ghana. In his letter of application for membership in the CPUSA, he expressed his belief that "capitalism cannot reform itself; it is doomed to self-destruction. No universal selfishness can bring social good to all."[87] Tracing his long and gradual radicalization from studying Marx at the University of Berlin in the 1890s to his brief membership in the Socialist Party in 1912 to his four trips to the Soviet Union, Du Bois concluded that the U.S. Communist Party provided the United States "with a real Third Party and thus [could] restore democracy to this land."[88] Joining the Communist Party was a bold move given that anticommunist repression remained alive and well in the United States. However, Gerald Horne correctly notes that Du Bois's decision to enlist in the CPUSA "was contrary to the opinion of many—not a radical departure from his past praxis and, in actuality, a logical continuation" of his work since the mid-1940s.[89] Similarly, just as Bettina Aptheker's essay in this volume suggests, we should not read his decision to move to Ghana and to renounce his U.S. citizenship in 1963 as a cynical move by a tired and cranky old man. Instead his emigration to Ghana illustrates his excitement in helping to build a nation dedicated to Pan-African liberation and socialism.[90]

While part 3 of The Autobiography of W. E. B. Du Bois provides a road map for understanding his political evolution in the 1950s, Du Bois's account of his turn toward the radical left omits the importance of black women radicals in prompting his political transformation during his final years. This is most apparent in the cursory discussion in his third memoir of his second wife, Shirley Graham Du Bois. Forty years his junior, Graham Du Bois was a brilliant black radical thinker and activist in her own right. Born in 1896 in Indianapolis to a preacher and a devoted mother, Graham Du Bois was an accomplished author, playwright, world traveler, and activist who may have joined the Communist Party *before* her marriage to Du Bois in February 1951. Internationally minded, she was deeply committed to Pan-Africanism, civil rights, peace, trade unionism, and women's equality. She played a critical role in radicalizing Du Bois, building a global amnesty movement to defend him from cold warriors, and providing physical care for her husband. As Horne notes, Du Bois was "lucky to have Shirley Graham Du Bois by his side. Though her years with Du Bois were not the most productive" in terms of advancing her professional ambitions, "her talents in so many different areas helped to extend and enrich his life."[91] Following his death, Graham Du Bois remained in Ghana, where she became a close adviser to Nkrumah and befriended Malcolm X when he visited the West African republic in June 1964. Following the overthrow of Nkrumah in 1966, she eventually made her way to China. Once there, she became close to Mao and Zhou Enlai and emerged as a leader in the African American exile community in this communist nation. She died in China in March 1977.[92] Yet *The Autobiography of W. E. B. Du Bois* treats her largely as a minor figure in the veteran black radical's life.

While he provided cursory discussion of Graham Du Bois, Du Bois's final autobiography also erased the importance of a community of black women radicals who rallied in his defense against McCarthyite repression. Shirley Graham Du Bois, CPUSA leader and theorist Claudia Jones, Harlem Renaissance luminary and veteran communist organizer Louise Thompson Patterson, poet Beulah Richardson, artist Margaret Burroughs, journalist and world traveler Eslanda Robeson, and Esther Cooper Jackson were at the front lines of the black left after World War II.[93] Collectively these women in 1951 agitated in the Sojourners for Truth and Justice, a short-lived, all-black women's progressive social protest group based in Harlem. The Sojourners espoused black left feminism, a politics that understood the status of African American women in intersectional and transnational terms and that framed black women in the United States and across the African diaspora as the vanguard of transformative social change globally. The organization publicized Du Bois's case and spoke out against government persecution of him. At the same time, many of these women, like Graham Du Bois, Robeson, Thompson Patterson, Cooper Jackson, and Jones, experienced state repression because of their black left feminist politics.[94] Yet despite their importance to his life and the black left, *The Autobiography of W. E. B.*

*Du Bois* includes only passing references to black women radicals like
Graham Du Bois, Robeson, and Burroughs and makes no reference to
the Sojourners. For a man whose thought was so ahead of its time on
so many fronts, his masculinist global vision prevented him from completely breaking free from the hegemonic order.

## Conclusions: The Legacy of Du Bois in the Age of Trump and Global Crisis

In the postlude to *The Autobiography of W. E. B. Du Bois*, the black sage
concludes, "I know the United States. It is my country and the land of
my fathers." Looking toward the future, Du Bois asserts, "It is still a
land of magnificent possibilities. It is still the home of noble souls and
generous people." Yet the United States was "selling its birthright . . .
and betraying its mighty destiny."[95] For him, the nation's permanent
war footing against the Soviet Union, morbid fear of socialism, and
intractable racial inequalities symbolized a growing existential crisis for
the United States and the world. Despite the state persecution he had
endured and the possibilities of nuclear war, Du Bois remained cau-
tiously optimistic about the future, writing, "Our dreams seek Heaven,
our deeds plumb Hell." This hell could be found in the "evil" of the
Jim Crow South and apartheid South Africa, as well as the "evil of evil
which is what [the United States] hope[s] to hold in Asia and Africa,
in the southern Americas and the islands of the Seven Seas." Calling
on Americans to remember their ancestors who dreamed of freedom,
Du Bois concludes his third memoir by asking, "Teach us, Forever
Dead, there is no Dream but Deed, there is no Deed but Memory."[96]
The past and ongoing struggle for freedom, international solidarity, and
peace would provide a road map for creating a future world.

Certainly the future has not unfolded as Du Bois probably would have
imagined. The Soviet Union and the Eastern Bloc collapsed due in part
to their own authoritarianism.[97] China abandoned socialism decades
ago, emerging as the most dynamic capitalist economy on the planet.
Nkrumah was overthrown in 1966. His dream of a socialist United
States of Africa has yet to be achieved. And other Third World militant
states, such as Cuba and Vietnam, have embraced neoliberalism.[98] The
United States has tightened its military grip on Africa, ironically under
the first black American president, Barack Obama. Curiously, a large
segment of the African American political class has remained silent

W. E. B. Du Bois's Tomb at the W. E. B. Du Bois Memorial Centre for Pan African Culture (Accra, Ghana), 2019. Photo by the author.

about this development.[99] In addition, *The Autobiography of W. E. B. Du Bois* often fails to appreciate the gendered contours of racial oppression and understands human freedom in masculinist terms.

Despite the gaps in *The Autobiography of W. E. B. Du Bois*, the elderly black radical was not mistaken in his claim that white supremacy would remain a potent force in American life for decades to come. Since 1980 a white backlash, together with globalization, has reversed many of the political and economic gains won by African Americans during the civil rights–Black Power era.[100] Black Americans remain second-class citizens and targets of state and extralegal violence, as evidenced in the widely publicized deaths of Michael Brown, Eric Garner, Rekia Boyd, Trayvon Martin, Aiyana Mo'Nay Stanley-Jones, Sandra Bland, Philando Castile, Tanisha Anderson, and Laquan McDonald at the hands of police and white vigilantes. Black people make up nearly half of those incarcerated in the United States.[101]

The election of Donald Trump as the forty-fifth U.S. president confirmed Du Bois's warning that white America could turn toward fascism. Winning the majority of white American voters, Trump unapologetically campaigned on racism, misogyny, ultranationalism, Islamophobia, and xenophobia. Playing on the genuine fears of white Americans, especially working-class people in the "Rust Belt," of economic vulnerability caused by deindustrialization and globalization, Trump scapegoated Mexicans, other people of color, and "elites" for immiserating segments of white America. His continued call for building a wall along the U.S.-Mexico border and ongoing efforts to ban travelers from predominantly Muslim nations through executive orders illustrates that Trump has showed no signs of moderating his extremist stance following his inauguration.[102]

Globally, far right, antiestablishment movements have gained traction in France, Germany, Italy, the Netherlands, and elsewhere. Brexit, the national referendum on whether the United Kingdom should leave the European Union, won due in no small part to racism and xenophobia. The African-descended across the diaspora increasingly face mass incarceration, police terror, and immiseration. In Africa globally linked political, economic, environmental, social, and health crises are destabilizing nations and devastating millions of people. African-descended women and children around the world disproportionately bear the brunt of these crises.[103]

Du Bois foresaw much of the contemporary existential crisis that would face African-descended people. His final memoir is especially sharp in its denunciation of white supremacy, war, imperialism, misery, and liberalism. Still searching for solutions to the global color line, his late writings illustrate his ability to reevaluate his previous positions, underscoring his continued intellectual growth. Above all, his final work reveals how he unapologetically took the position that the role of the scholar was not simply to interpret world but to change it. Humanity is standing on the abyss of an existential crisis. Du Bois was willing to sacrifice his professional career and to endure state persecution for his beliefs. What an inspiring legacy for those of us committed to building a more just and democratic future world.

## Notes

1. W. E. B. Du Bois, *The Autobiography of W. E. B. Du Bois: A Soliloquy on Viewing My Life from the Last Decade of Its First Century* (New York: International Publishers, 1968), 11.

2. Quoted in ibid., 439; Gerald Horne, *Black and Red: W. E. B. Du Bois and the Afro-American Response to the Cold War, 1944–1963* (Albany: State University Press of New York, 1986), 151–82.

3. For a discussion of McCarthyism, see Ellen Schrecker, *Many Are the Crimes: McCarthyism in America* (Princeton, NJ: Princeton University Press, 1998).

4. For a detailed study of the global dimensions of the U.S.-Soviet rivalry, see Odd Arne Westad, *The Global Cold War* (Cambridge, UK: Cambridge University Press, 2007); Horne, *Black and Red*.

5. Du Bois, *Autobiography of W. E. B. Du Bois*, 183–221.

6. Ibid., 5.

7. Biographer David Levering Lewis subscribes to this line of reasoning about Du Bois's alleged irritability, sectarianism, and dogmatism in his final years. Lewis asserts, "An eloquent grumpiness seemed to overtake [Du Bois] more often than not as the fifties ran down, a rutted readiness to pontificate apocalyptically that was less due to advanced age than ideological predilections in need of updating and fine tuning." David Levering Lewis, *W. E. B. Du Bois: The Fight for Equality and the American Century, 1919–1963* (New York: Henry Holt, 2000), 558. In contrast to Lewis's dismissive take on the late Du Bois, literary scholar Jodi Melamed emphasizes *The Autobiography of W. E. B. Du Bois* "as an important intervention into the global politics of race in the period." Jodi Melamed, "W. E. B. Du Bois's UnAmerican End," *African American Review* 40.3 (Fall 2006), 534.

8. For discussions of color-blind racism, see Sundiata Keita Cha-Jua, "The Changing Same: Black Racial Formation and Transformation as a Theory of the African American Experience," in *Race Struggles*, ed. Theodore Koditscheck, Sundiata Keita Cha-Jua, and Helen A. Neville (Urbana: University of Illinois Press, 2009), 9–47; Eduardo Bonilla-Silva, *Racism without Racists: Color-Blind Racism and the Persistence of Racial Inequality in America*, 3rd ed. (Lanham, MD: Rowman & Littlefield, 2010).

9. Eric Porter, *The Problem of the Future World: W. E. B. Du Bois and the Race Concept at Midcentury* (Durham, NC: Duke University Press, 2010).

10. Porter, *The Problem of the Future World*, 3. Similarly, historian Carol Anderson downplays the importance of Du Bois to shaping post-war African American anticolonial politics. Carol Anderson, *Bourgeois Radicals: The NAACP and the Struggle for Colonial Liberation, 1941-1960* (Cambridge: Cambridge University Press, 2015).

11. In fairness to Porter, he does acknowledge that some scholars "have often erred in overemphasizing the extent to which his post-1948 . . . work

was defined by the limitations brought by advancing age and political dogmatism."

12. W. E. B. Du Bois, *Darkwater: Voices from Within the Veil* (New York: Harcourt, Brace, and Howe, 1920); W. E. B. Du Bois, *Dusk of Dawn* (Millwood, NY: Kraus-Thomson Organization, 1975). My understanding of black radicalism is informed by Cedric J. Robinson. He understands the black radical tradition as a shared revolutionary consciousness and vision rooted in African-descended people's ontological opposition to racial capitalism, slavery, and imperialism. In addition, he frames black radicalism and Marxism as "two programs for revolutionary change," appreciating the latter, despite its universalist claims, as "a Western construction—a conceptualization of human affairs and historical experiences of European peoples mediated, in turn, through their civilization, their social orders, and their cultures." Marxism, in Robinson's view, remains grounded to its own detriment in the racialism deeply embedded within Western civilization. For these reasons, Marxism fails to understand the histories of black resistance and complexities of black life. Although the late Du Bois embraced Marxism, he nonetheless acknowledged the centrality of race to the making of the modern world. Cedric J. Robinson, *Black Marxism: The Making of the Black Radical Tradition* (Chapel Hill: University of North Carolina Press, 2000), 1–2.

13. Vijay Prashad, *The Darker Nations: A People's History of the Third World* (New York: New Press, 2007).

14. Aptheker claims that he made only minor changes to the final manuscript, published first in shorter versions in 1964 and 1965 in China, the Soviet Union, and East Germany. Du Bois, *Autobiography of W. E. B. Du Bois*, 5.

15. James R. Barrett, "Was the Personal Political? Reading the Autobiography of American Communism," *International Review of Social History* 53.2 (December 2008), 404.

16. Du Bois, *Darkwater*, 163–86; Lewis, *W. E. B. Du Bois*, 11–12, 16, 18–19.

17. For Du Bois, women's equality was critical to human freedom. He wrote, "The uplift of women is, next to the problem of the color line and the peace movement, our greatest cause." The chapter focused special attention on black women from the dawn of humanity to the contemporary moment. Appreciating the intersections among gender, race, and class, Du Bois emphasized that all humans descended from an African woman; celebrated Cleopatra, Candace, Sojourner Truth, and Harriet Tubman; and decried the economic and sexual oppression of black women under

slavery, Jim Crow, and urban industrial capitalism. Above all, he acknowledged the importance of African American women to leading the charge for racial uplift: "To no modern race does its women mean so much as to the Negro nor come so near to the fulfillment of its meaning." Du Bois, *Darkwater*, 173, 181.

18. Michelle Ann Stephens, *Black Empire: The Masculine Global Imaginary of Caribbean Intellectuals in the United States, 1914–1962* (Durham, NC: Duke University Press, 2005).

19. *Dusk of Dawn* also framed African American history and the black freedom movement in highly masculinist terms. The second biography contains neither a chapter on nor a significant discussion of African American women.

20. Sundiata Cha-Jua, "The New Nadir: The Contemporary Black Racial Formation," *Black Scholar* 40.1 (2010), 38–58.

21. Ibid., 39–47.

22. Du Bois, *Autobiography of W. E. B. Du Bois*, 20–21.

23. Ibid. Du Bois was hardly the only black radical of the 1950s who viewed the Western world as morally bankrupt. The poet, writer, and politician Aimé Césaire drew similar conclusions in his classic study *Discourse on Colonialism* (New York: Monthly Review Press, 1970).

24. Du Bois, *Autobiography of W. E. B. Du Bois*, 24; Victor Sebestyen, *Twelve Days: The Story of the 1956 Hungarian Revolution* (New York: Pantheon Books, 2006).

25. Du Bois, *Dusk of Dawn*, 286.

26. Ibid., 287.

27. Ibid., 268–326.

28. Du Bois, *Autobiography of W. E. B. Du Bois*, 32.

29. Ibid., 34.

30. Ibid., 38–39.

31. Robeson Taj Frazier, *The East Is Black: Cold War China in the Black Radical Imagination* (Durham, NC: Duke University Press, 2015); Du Bois, *Autobiography of W. E. B. Du Bois*, 47.

32. Du Bois, *Autobiography of W. E. B. Du Bois*, 53, 47. For further discussion of Du Bois's visits to and writings on China in 1936, see Nahum Dimitri Chandler, "A Persistent Parallax: On the Writings of W. E. Burghardt Du Bois on Japan and China, 1936–1937," *CR: The New Centennial Review* 12.1 (2012), 291–316.

33. Du Bois, *Autobiography of W. E. B. Du Bois*, 48.

34. Ibid., 49.

35. Ibid., 52.

36. Ibid., 48. Du Bois anticipated positions held by Malcolm X and Martin Luther King on U.S. military involvement in Southeast Asia. Both leaders denounced the Vietnam War—although Malcolm X came out against the conflict in 1964, while King did not unequivocally oppose the war until 1967. Framing the war as a racist and imperialist U.S. venture, they argued that American rulers sought to exploit Vietnamese resources and to thwart the Vietnamese people's right to self-determination. Malcolm X, *By Any Means Necessary* (New York: Pathfinder Books, 1970), 194; Michael Eric Dyson, *I May Not Get There with You: The True Martin Luther King Jr.* (New York: Free Press, 2000), 51–77.

37. Marilyn B. Young, *The Vietnam Wars: 1945–1990* (New York: HarperCollins, 1991).

38. Sebestyen, *Twelve Days*; Maurice Isserman, *If I Had a Hammer: The Death of the Old Left and the Birth of the New Left* (Urbana: University of Illinois Press, 1987), 29–31.

39. Quoted in Du Bois, *Autobiography of W. E. B. Du Bois*, 51; Frazier, *The East Is Black*, 49–50.

40. Berry Sautman, "Anti-Black Racism in Post-Mao China," *China Quarterly* 138 (1994): 413.

41. Frazier, *The East Is Black*, 49.

42. Ibid., 53.

43. For discussions of sexism in the Soviet Union and China under communism, see Elizabeth A. Wood, *The Baba and the Comrade: Gender and Politics in Revolutionary Russia* (Bloomington: Indiana University Press, 1997); Wang Zheng, *Finding Women in the State: A Socialist Feminist Revolution in the People's Republic of China, 1949–1964* (Berkeley: University of California Press, 2017).

44. W. E. B. Du Bois, *The Souls of Black Folk* (New York: Norton, 1999), 34–45, 62–74.

45. Lewis, *W. E. B. Du Bois*, 238–342.

46. Du Bois, *The Autobiography of W. E. B. Du Bois*, 236.

47. Ibid., 290.

48. Du Bois, *Dusk of Dawn*, 40.

49. Ibid., 302.

50. Du Bois, *Autobiography of W. E. B. Du Bois*, 126.

51. Ibid., 291.

52. Ibid., 255.

53. Ibid., 254–55.

54. Ibid., 291.

55. For discussions of growing African American militancy and internationalism during the mid-twentieth century, see Nikhal Pal Singh, *Black Is a Country: Race and the Unfinished Struggle for Democracy* (Cambridge, MA: Harvard University Press, 2004); Penny Von Eschen, *Race against Empire: Black Americans and Anticolonialism, 1937–1957* (Ithaca, NY: Cornell University Press, 1997).

56. Du Bois, *Autobiography of W. E. B. Du Bois*, 295.

57. Ibid., 293. At Atlanta University, Du Bois penned his magnum opus, *Black Reconstruction in America, 1860–1880* (New York: Atheneum, 1992). Published in 1935, the book signaled the growing significance of Marxism on his thought. Refuting prevailing racist narratives of the alleged failure of Reconstruction due to black corruption and ignorance, Du Bois argued that African Americans played a crucial role in bringing democracy to the post–Civil War South and that state violence, white terrorism, and the complicity of northern industrialists and workers led to the overthrow of the country's first experiment in multiracial democracy. The final autobiography did not discuss *Black Reconstruction*.

58. Du Bois, *Autobiography of W. E. B. Du Bois*, 332–33. The final memoir did not explicitly discuss the "Appeal to the World." Lewis, *W. E. B. Du Bois: A Biography*, 666–67.

59. Du Bois, *Autobiography of W. E. B. Du Bois*, 326–35.

60. Ibid., 333–34.

61. Kwame Nkrumah, *Ghana: The Autobiography of Kwame Nkrumah* (New York: International Publishers, 1957), 52, 53; Hakim Adi and Marika Sherwood, *The 1945 Manchester Pan-African Congress Revisited* (London: New Beacon Books, 1995); Du Bois, *Autobiography of W. E. B. Du Bois*, 330.

62. Erik S. McDuffie, *Sojourning for Freedom: Black Women, American Communism, and the Making of Black Left Feminism* (Durham, NC: Duke University Press, 2011), 102, 126–27, 141–42; Johnetta Richards, "The Southern Negro Youth Congress: A History," PhD diss., University of Cincinnati, 1987.

63. For a detailed account of the Southern Youth Legislature, see Peter Lau, *Democracy Rising: South Carolina and the Fight for Racial Equality since 1865* (Lexington: University of Kentucky Press, 2006), 156–73. For an insightful discussion of the anticolonial politics of the SNYC and other southern civil rights groups during the mid-twentieth century, see Lindsey R. Swindall, *The Path to the Greater, Freer, Truer World: Southern Civil*

*Rights and Anticolonialism, 1937–1955* (Gainesville: University Press of Florida, 2014).

64. Quoted in Du Bois, *The Autobiography of W. E. B. Du Bois,* 332. For the full text of his speech see, W. E. B. Du Bois, *Behold the Land* (Birmingham, Al.: Southern Negro Youth Congress, 1946), 7.

65. Du Bois, *Autobiography of W. E. B. Du Bois,* 332.

66. McDuffie, *Sojourning for Freedom,* 156.

67. Ibid., 100–103, 115–16.

68. Sallye Bell Davis was a Birmingham-based teacher and SNYC organizer who is best known as the mother of activist, scholar, and former political prisoner Angela Y. Davis. McDuffie, *Sojourning for Freedom,* 144.

69. Ibid., 141–47, 153–59; Richards, "The Southern Negro Youth Congress."

70. Du Bois, *Autobiography of W. E. B. Du Bois,* 332.

71. Du Bois was not the only black leftist the U.S. state targeted and who had his passport stripped. The U.S. government also stripped the passport of his good friend, the actor and spokesperson Paul Robeson. Cold warriors deported Claudia Jones, a Trinidad-born activist and theorist who emerged as the most visible black woman in the CPUSA during the 1940s and 1950s. Gerald Horne, *Paul Robeson: The Artist as Revolutionary* (London: Pluto Press, 2016), 121–42; Carole Boyce Davies, *Left of Karl Marx: The Political Life of Black Communist Claudia Jones* (Durham, NC: Duke University Press, 2008), 99–166.

72. Du Bois, *Autobiography of W. E. B. Du Bois,* 388.

73. Ibid., 343–60.

74. Ibid., 370.

75. Ibid.

76. Ibid., 371.

77. Ibid., 392–93.

78. Kevin G. Gaines, *American Africans in Ghana: Black Expatriates and the Civil Rights Era* (Chapel Hill: University of North Carolina Press, 2006), 1–26.

79. Du Bois, *Autobiography of W. E. B. Du Bois,* 401.

80. Du Bois reprinted the letter in his final memoir (ibid., 400–401).

81. Ibid., 400.

82. Ibid., 402.

83. Kwame Nkrumah, *Neocolonialism: The Last Stage of Imperialism* (New York: International Publishers, 1965).

84. Du Bois, *Autobiography of W. E. B. Du Bois,* 401.

85. Ibid., 405.

86. Ibid., 407–8.

87. W. E. B. Du Bois, "Application for Membership in the Communist Party of the United States of America," in *W. E. B. Du Bois: A Reader*, ed. David Levering Lewis (New York: Henry Holt, 1995), 632.

88. Ibid.

89. Horne, *Black and Red*, 289.

90. Ibid., 344.

91. Gerald Horne, *Race Woman: The Lives of Shirley Graham Du Bois* (New York: New York University Press, 2000), 133. Historian Yunxiang Gao emphasizes the crucial role Graham Du Bois played in her husband's radicalization in his final years and to the couple's visit to China. Gao also stresses how living in China during the Cultural Revolution transformed and further radicalized Graham Du Bois. Yunxiang Gao, "W. E. B. and Shirley Graham Du Bois in Maoist China," *Du Bois Review* 10.1 (2013), 59–85.

92. Gao, "W. E. B. Du Bois and Shirley Graham Du Bois in Maoist China," 80.

93. McDuffie, *Sojourning for Freedom*, 160–92.

94. Erik S. McDuffie, "New Freedom Movement of Negro Women: Sojourning for Truth, Justice, and Human Rights during the Early Cold War," *Radical History Review* 101 (Spring 2008), 81–106.

95. Du Bois, *Autobiography of W. E. B. Du Bois*, 419.

96. Ibid., 422–23.

97. Stephen Kotkin, *Armageddon Averted: The Soviet Collapse*, updated ed. (Oxford: Oxford University Press, 2008); Ronald Coase and Ning Want, *How China Became Capitalist* (New York: Palgrave Macmillan, 2012).

98. Vijay Prashad, *The Poorer Nations: A Possible History of the Global South* (London: Verso, 2012), 143–230.

99. The apparent disinterest among African Americans in the growing U.S. military presence in Africa was most evident in the ambivalence toward and support from black elected officials for the overthrow Muammar Qaddafi in October 2011. This U.S.-led action played a key role in destabilizing Libya and West Africa, as well as in triggering the migration crisis to Europe beginning in 2015. Erik S. McDuffie, "Obama, the World, and Africa," *Souls: A Critical Journal of Black Politics, Culture, and Society* 14.1–2 (2012), 28–37; Dan Murphy, "How the Fall of Qaddafi Gave Rise to Europe's Migrant Crisis, *Christian Science Monitor*, April 21, 2015, http://www.csmonitor.com/World/Security-Watch/Backchannels/2015 /0421/How-the-fall-of-Qaddafi-gave-rise-to-Europe-s-migrant-crisis-video (accessed March 19, 2017).

100. Cha-Jua, "The New Nadir," 40–50.

101. Keeanga-Yamahtta Taylor, *From #BlackLivesMatter to Black Liberation* (Chicago: Haymarket, 2016); Angela Y. Davis, *Freedom Is a Constant Struggle: Ferguson, Palestine, and the Foundations of a Movement* (Chicago: Haymarket, 2016).

102. *New York Times*, March 18, 2017; "In Stinging Blow to President, Hawaii and Maryland Judges Block Trump's Second Muslim Ban," *Democracy Now*, March 16, 2017, https://www.democracynow.org/2017/3/16/in_stinging_blow_to_president_hawaii (accessed March 16, 2017).

103. Shafik Mandhai, "Protests in UK against Post-Brexit Racism," *Al Jazeera*, March 18, 2017, http://www.aljazeera.com/news/2017/03/protests-uk-post-brexit-racism-170318140636538.html (accessed March 19, 2017); *New York Times*, March 14, 2017.

# Gender and the Politics
of Freedom

# Du Bois in Drag

## Prevailing Women, Flailing Men, and the "Anne Du Bignon" Pseudonym

*Lauren Louise Anderson*

This essay suggests a startlingly new way to understand W. E. B. Du Bois's late career. A famously heterosexual masculine man, Du Bois was willing to have a woman proclaim his ideas and model his life. In 1933 he introduced his ideas of economic self-segregation in *The Crisis* in what appears to be feminist fiction under the female pseudonym Anne Du Bignon, "The Three Mosquitoes: A Story of Marriage and Birth" (January 1933), "The Doctor's Dilemma: A Story of Tuberculosis" (February 1933), and "The Farm on the Eastern Shore: A Story of Work" (serially published in March and April 1933).[1] These three stories use vibrant fictional scenarios to convince audiences that black people must unify despite phenotypical differences and internalized racism. The stories also show that a communal arrangement offers strength and protection, even if that means giving up the fight to integrate.

This essay suggests several possible interpretations for Du Bois's surprising gender play, some in support of prior Du Bois scholarship, but most suggesting new interpretations that will require future analysis alongside additional works by Du Bois. The first builds on those scholars who focus on Du Bois's belief that black women's experiences at the intersections of oppressions gave them the most potential to enact radical change.[2] It may be that Du Bois believed that readers would more readily accept his own ideas of a race-based economic cooperative when expressed by two feminist women (the pseudonymous author and the main character) or that he was nervous to articulate feminist ideas under his own byline in *The Crisis*. It may also be that Du Bois's extramarital appreciation for many intelligent women inspired the feminism in the stories and influenced his decision to write under Anne Du

Bignon's name. If there is strength in the interpretation of Du Bois's use of the Du Bignon pen name, then it necessitates a reconsideration of his affairs as something more than (just) salacious. Most intriguing, this episode suggests that we must ask if Du Bois could identify himself in a female mind and body. The Jean Du Bignon character in *The Black Flame Trilogy* gives credence to this last interpretation. Du Bois's ability to identify so completely with a woman, first through a pseudonym and much later in autobiographical fiction, demands a reanalysis of his career, for which this essay is a beginning, not a conclusion.

When Du Bois wrote under the name Anne Du Bignon he joined a small group of men who wrote under female pseudonyms, which the literary scholar Lorrayne Carroll calls "rhetorical drag." She argues that instances of "rhetorical drag" indicate "that gender is the key to signify a speaking subject, because gender so profoundly signals the subject's disposition in the world."[3] It is therefore essential to take seriously the gendered aspect of Du Bois using a female pseudonym to introduce his belief that black leaders must accept segregation and build a black-only economic cooperative. Because the gender of an author signals so much cultural capital, this essay reimagines the well-documented end of Du Bois's term with the NAACP and *The Crisis* through a gendered analysis and suggests that he possessed much more flexibility in his gender thinking than scholars have previously recognized.

This essay sketches some of the implications of this greater flexibility; in particular, we discover that Du Bois did not always adhere to the gendered norm that literary scholar Vilashini Cooppan identifies. She argues that "ravaged women, rising men" dominate Du Bois's writings, a trope that appears across the "extraordinary breadth of Du Bois's career."[4] Cooppan contends that the repetition of this trope shows that Du Bois had a "remarkably fixed ideology of gender."[5] In stark contrast, the Anne Du Bignon stories and the Jean Du Bignon character show prevailing women and flailing men. Not only does the content of these stories challenge Cooppan's argument; so does Du Bois's placing himself within a feminine mind-set and within a female character. What other transformations of Du Boisian scholarship will this new lens reveal?

## Du Bois in Drag?

A year before his notorious break with the National Association for the Advancement of Colored People (NAACP) in 1934, W. E. B. Du Bois inhabited a woman's voice to articulate his new philosophy of racial self-segregation. To the casual observer it would seem that Anne Du Bignon wrote the three short stories as part of the *The Crisis*'s year-long series "Toward a New Racial Philosophy." However, the obvious assumption, that the publication of the Du Bignon stories reflected the editor's choice to rely upon another's fiction to promote his ideology, is insufficient. Why insufficient? Simply because Anne Du Bignon does not exist in census records. The only place an Anne Du Bignon appears in the historical record is as the stage name of Du Bois's Atlanta par-amour, Adrienne Herndon, who had died in 1910, twenty-three years before Anne Du Bignon's byline appeared in *The Crisis*.[6]

Herndon had had a brief theater career before it became known that the light-skinned actress was an African American, a discovery that forced her off the stage.[7] Du Bois had befriended her and her husband, Alonzo Herndon, while he was a professor at Atlanta University in the early 1900s. Historian David Levering Lewis describes Herndon, the daughter of a former slave, as "a Giselle-like beauty with raven hair and ivory skin who taught French at Atlanta University." It was there that "a lively friendship with Du Bois had blossomed."[8] Du Bois found in her the intellectual companionship that his wife Nina, who preferred the nursery to the literary salon, lacked. Lewis suggests the significance of the friendship by explaining, "Will and Adrienne frequently attended the closed campus community's social affairs together. Whether or not there was ever more than friendship with Du Bois, it was widely noticed that she delighted in his urbanity."[9] This means that almost thirty years later, in 1933, Du Bois wrote two short stories and attributed them to the stage name of Adrienne Herndon, his long-dead friend, and perhaps lover.

There is no direct documentary proof that Du Bois wrote the Du Big-non stories. No letter in which he tells a friend about the decision has come to light, for example. However, there are at least five factors that suggest that this was the case. First, he was an editor who "maintained complete control in his position as editor, despite attempts to place lim-itations on him," as Shawn Leigh Alexander elucidates.[10] Indeed one of the main reasons Du Bois subsequently left the NAACP in 1934 was because Executive Secretary Walter White tried to assert some rules about what Du Bois could and could not publish. Du Bois had financed the magazine independently since its founding, which had meant he resolutely maintained editorial independence. The magazine was, as Amy Helene Kirschke and Phillip Luke Sinitiere show, Du Bois's "per-sonal organ and the 'expression of myself.'"[11]

The second reason it makes sense to believe that Du Bois wrote the Du Bignon stories is that there is evidence he used pseudonyms for other short stories in the 1920s and 1950s. Both pseudonyms were anagrams of his name. In the 1920s he kept a list of story title ideas for "Bew Siobud" to write. In the 1950s he submitted over thirty short stories under the name "Bud Weisob" to publishers, who never published them. Robert McDonnell first brought attention to these stories' existence in a 1980 article for *The Crisis* describing their inclusion in the new microfilm version of the *W. E. B. Du Bois's Papers* published by the University of Massachusetts–Amherst. He suggests Du Bois used the pseudonym at that time to avoid the blacklisting that might cause stories with his own name to be rejected.[12]

A third reason Du Bois was likely the author of the Du Bignon stories is that he was a close personal friend of Adrienne Herndon (and perhaps more) and so knew her stage name. Who else at *The Crisis* would encapsulate Du Bois's new philosophy in fiction and give that fiction the stage name of the first woman with whom he (probably) had an affair? As perhaps one of the first women with whom he engaged as an intellectual peer, Du Bois would have had reason to remember her in tribute. Fourth, the philosophy in the stories closely mirrors the ideas of self-segregation evident in his 1933 and 1934 *Crisis* editorials. And fifth, he invoked the Du Bignon name twenty-five years later in the *Black Flame*, when he imbued the fictional Jean Du Bignon with autobiographical characteristics. Several scholars discuss similarities between Du Bois and Jean Du Bignon, but none makes the connection to the 1933 Anne Du Bignon stories or to Adrienne Herndon's stage name.

For the past fifty years, scholars have debated whether Du Bois was being consistent with his earlier philosophies or whether he was embarking on a new viewpoint when he advocated segregation.[13] Yet few have analyzed Du Bois's 1933 series, "Toward a New Racial Philosophy," used to lay the groundwork for his 1934 editorials on segregation. Scholars' focus on Du Bois's 1934 editorial about segregation and his economic thought thereafter may be one reason no one seems to have written about the Du Bignon stories.

**January–April 1933: "Toward a New Racial Philosophy"**

The three Anne Du Bignon stories appeared as part of Du Bois's plan to engage black college graduates in a "new racial philosophy," because he believed the existing paradigms were no longer working. His frustration stemmed, like that of his friend and colleague, NAACP president J. E. Spingarn, from the lack of support from the younger generation for his ideas, and the stress upon the organization from the Great Depression frustrated him. Unlike Spingarn, who introduced the Second Amenia Conference to revitalize the NAACP, Du Bois did not necessarily think this new paradigm of resistance had to be developed through *The Crisis*'s mother organization.[14] He decided to devote 1933 to see if the NAACP would withstand the test of radical ideas offered on the pages of that journal.[15]

Du Bois introduced his new endeavor in the January 1933 editorial, "Toward a New Racial Philosophy." He started the passage with the troubling declaration that the NAACP offered "nothing" to a young college graduate who had come to Du Bois and asked, "What has the NAACP published concerning the present problems of the Negro, and especially of young Negroes just out of college?"[16] Du Bois suggested that the NAACP, which had begun with "a clear-cut and definite program," had lost its way in recent years, due to the way the Great Depression had transformed "what is called the Negro problem."[17] In order to guide black America toward a new set of solutions to that "problem," Du Bois explained that *The Crisis* would in 1933 examine the difficulties faced by black Americans in twelve distinct areas, including work, family life, housing, education, religion, and discrimination.[18]

Du Bois encouraged readers to get involved in this effort by writing fiction to reimagine and address social, economic, and racial justice, a creative capacity his own work had occupied and supported during the Harlem Renaissance.[19] He recommended they model their submissions on the first Du Bignon story, "The Three Mosquitoes." And he outlined the requirements for short story submissions: "They must not be 'defeatist'; we want them to be artistic; we want them true; but we do not propose to have every story end in a lynching or a suicide, for the simple reason that we do not believe that death is the necessary answer to any of these situations."[20] He argued that fiction, rather than philosophical and programmatic essays alone, was essential to the endeavor of creating a new racial philosophy because fiction cemented the humanity of ideas. Du Bois's reliance in this instance upon fiction to express his ideas was not unusual in his life. As the scholars Michelle Elam and Paul Taylor argue, Du Bois's fiction "makes extant a political reality in and for the imagination, and thereby offers a vision for, if not yet of, the real 'world' in which he lived."[21] His fiction was an essential

element in his overall work as a "print propagandist."[22] By introducing
the full scale of his plan for a race-based cooperative economy first in
a fictional setting; as he does in the third Du Bignon story, he did not
undermine the potential for the scheme to work in real life—that is,
by suggesting that his vision could be realized only in a fictional world.
Rather he used the fiction to emphasize that his plan could work in the
lives of real people by setting the story among the kinds of educated
black people he targeted. In this case, he painted fiction as more "real"
and "possible" than nonfiction (although he also relied on the latter to
explicate his points).

### "The Three Mosquitoes"

The first of the Du Bignon stories, "The Three Mosquitoes," exemplifies the type of fiction Du Bois imagined as particularly effective.[23] The
story about three childhood friends growing up in a difficult Jim Crow
world does not yet advance economic cooperation because Du Bois
needed first to convince a black audience that race could be the organizing principle of a community, even if they had experiences of colorism
and internalized racism that generated skepticism.

Mary, Pinkie, and Sally grow up together in Harlem and dub themselves "the Three Musketeers" when they discover Alexandre Dumas's
African ancestry in English class. Their male peers call them "the Three
Mosquitoes" and they accept the new designation. One day in 1910,
walking home, they discuss the basketball game they had just won. It
was their first game after integrating the team; all their white class-
mates, except the new Spanish and Italian immigrants, had quit the
team because of their presence. The subsequent conversation of the
three friends—"a tall white girl, a chunky, pretty mulatto and a small
lithe black"— reveals they are not as united as their nickname suggests.[24] Mary hates to be associated with Sally's childhood friend Jack
because his dark color makes people who assume she is white look at
her with new skepticism. She declares she will marry a rich white man
and have no children because they "might show [her] other blood."[25]
Pinkie, the teenager with mid-tone skin, proclaims she will never marry
so she can pursue writing for a living. Though she cannot join Mary in
the white world because of her appearance, she rejects living in a black
one by proclaiming, "I'm not going to write about Negroes or about
'races' at all. I don't care what the professor advises. I'm just going to

write about people."[26] Only Sally is willing to stay within a black community, and not just tolerate it but embrace it. When her friends warn
her away from marrying Jack because their babies will be too dark, she
says, "I hadn't really thought of that. And what of it? So am I and I like
his color. He's handsome."[27]

The story fast-forwards a decade to 1920, when Pinkie gets back in
touch with Sally and Jack. She has recognized on her own that her
prior assumption that she could write characters without race was
immature. Every time she started to write about "people," they became
"colored people" like those she knew and loved. She tells her friend
she is going to have to marry for the meal ticket, not for love, because
publishers refuse to publish books with the kinds of black characters
she wants to write. Sally and Jack have a good life and love their three
children but still have to fight against the constant assaults of northern
racism. For example, their oldest son is one of the brightest in his kin-
dergarten class, but because of systemic racism they struggled to find
an elementary school that would enroll him. Neither Sally nor Pinkie
has much knowledge of Mary's life other than hearing that she did
marry a rich white man, but they had a child who revealed Mary's color.
Her husband stayed with her until he died, but his family rejected her
immediately. She is living in Europe, where her son is rumored to have
Spanish ancestry.

The final section begins in 1930, when a devastated Mary returns to
New York City from Europe. She absent-mindedly leaves her jewelry
case on the backseat of her cab. The next day a police officer brings
the cab driver to her apartment. The boy confesses he was planning
to steal the jewels in part to save his family because his father is quite
ill and in part out of anger because the college explicitly denied him
a scholarship becasue of his race. Mary is drawn to the young man,
Jackie, and declares she will fund his college and that he must bring
his mother to meet her. When the mother arrives the next day, Mary
recognizes and runs to her. It is Sally, and the sick father is her Jack.
Sally reveals that Jack has lost his job at United Electric (UE); the subtext is that during the Great Depression black men lost positions first
regardless of merit. Mary promises Sally she will use her shares of UE
to work behind the scenes to get his job back, while saying nothing to
protect his sense of masculine pride. In exchange, Mary asks if she can
become Jackie's benefactor to replace her own lost son; rejected when
she revealed that his father's family wanted him to become their heir,

but only if he rejected his mother and her race.[28] Finding her Harlem
friends soothes Mary's sadness and loneliness at her son's rejection.
When the elder Jack worries he is losing his son to Mary and his daughter to Pinkie, Mary declares, "Don't you know that these three children
belong to us three women?—each for all and all for each—The Three
Mosquitoes!"[29]

Like all three Du Bignon stories, this story promotes solidarity along
racial lines. Like the third story, it also has a feminist perspective and
challenges Cooppan's argument that Du Bois relied throughout his
career on "an unchanging set of gendered tropes—ravaged women,
rising men" to discuss "the problem of the color line."[30] "Three Mosquitos" reveals that solidarity within the race across color differences
is the only way to create a protected community within a Jim Crow
world. The common experience of persecution is more important than
physical identification. As the light-skinned character in "The Three
Mosquitos" realizes, she cannot, and does not want to, escape her
racial identity, not because of the physical "reality" of her race (she has
easily passed) but because she feels most at home and most understood
by other people of color, who comprehend the reality of persecution
and oppression. Moreover, it is female solidarity that forges together
this community of prevailing women, including at the end that odd line
that almost shoves Jack out of his family and certainly shoves him out
of his "ownership" of his children (a noun Du Bignon repeats).

### "The Doctor's Dilemma"

Unlike the first and third stories, the second Du Bignon story, "The
Doctor's Dilemma: A Story of Tuberculosis," in the February 1933
issue, has no substantive women characters.[31] It questions the rein-
ing assumption among many middle and upperclass black families that
segregation must be opposed no matter the personal cost and regardless if there is a valid black alternative to support. In "The Doctor's
Dilemma," Dr. Brown's daughter Margaret has tuberculosis. Dr. Taylor,
a successful and influential black colleague, convinces Brown to use
Margaret as a test case to desegregate a New York sanatorium. Taylor
is angry that the beautiful sanatorium that taxpayers fund refuses to
admit black patients. But the father worries that his daughter is too
delicate and sensitive to serve as a "battering rod" against racism.[32]
Taylor convinces him by arguing that there is nowhere else to send
Margaret to recover. He implies that the new Abyssinian Sanatorium,

the only alternative, would surely be inadequate *because* it was funded and run by black people.

When Taylor checks on Margaret a month into her stay at the white sanatorium, he finds she has received inadequate care and worsened. He scoops her up and, rather than doing what he intended—fighting the doctors and nurses until she received the best care—he walks out the door with her in his arms. After Taylor wonders aloud where to go with the quickly fading Margaret, the taxi driver suggests a small black sanatorium over the hill. There she receives excellent care and recovers fully, at the place run by the Abyssinian Baptist Church that Taylor had previously dismissed sight unseen. Months later, when Taylor is criticized at a meeting of black doctors for giving up his principles and joining the staff of the "Jim Crow" sanatorium, Taylor happily reports that it was "'Jim Crow' or death" for Margaret, and given that he intends to marry her he is happy with his decision.[33] His accuser curses him for giving up his principled fight against segregation and letting whites continue to use black tax dollars to discriminate. The final line of the story is this doctor damning Taylor as "one hell of a race leader."[34]

In this short story, Du Bois defends voluntary segregation and criticizes the sort of "race leader" who would fight all instances of segregation even if it led to indignity and death. This was not a new idea for Du Bois, the consistent defender of HBCUs like Fisk and Howard, schools that some black people condemned as giving in to "Jim Crow."[35] However, telling the story of voluntary segregation through a "doctor's dilemma" was particularly poignant in February 1933. That month black newspapers revealed that the most influential black doctor in Harlem and Du Bois's friend, Dr. Louis T. Wright, was under investigation for how he had hired black physicians. The NAACP created the committee investigating him. In the mid-1920s the Bellevue Hospital group that oversaw the Harlem Hospital finally agreed to allow black physicians to serve in all capacities in the hospital and gave Dr. Wright permission to hire fifty black doctors. The white doctors who would be dismissed as part of this decision unsurprisingly condemned it.[36] However, a group of black doctors also ended up condemning Wright's actions when he hired only black doctors who had graduated from northern, majority-white medical schools and not the Meharry or Howard medical schools.[37] In the same February issue in which "The Doctor's Dilemma" appears, Du Bois supported Wright by explaining that Wright was just being very careful to select only the most qualified black doctors rather than filling the hospital with "dead

weight" and thus playing "directly into the hand of every 'Nigger hater'
in the land and 'prov[ing]' the inability of the Negro physician to measure up to modern, exacting standards."[38] *Crisis* subscribers who read
both "The Doctor's Dilemma" and Du Bois's editorial on the Harlem
Hospital would come away with a much more nuanced perspective on
voluntary segregation than if they read only Du Bois's bold defense of
Wright, which also condemned his critics as inferior physicians. With
only the editorial, the reader would connect Du Bois's condemnations
with the *Chicago Defender*'s explanation that Wright was accused of
not hiring any HBCU grads and assume that Du Bois thought segregated institutions were inferior. Reading "The Doctor's Dilemma"
alongside the editorial may have suggested to subscribers that it was
possible to prefer all black spaces when they contained superior quality and not patronize them when their quality was not as high as that
of white hospitals or universities. The case Du Bois built throughout
1933 in the Du Bignon stories and stated directly in 1934 was, after all,
for *voluntary* segregation.

### "The Farm on the Eastern Shore"

The third Du Bignon story, "The Farm on the Eastern Shore: A Story of
Work," published in two parts in March and April 1933, connects the
female solidarity and powerful women characters of the first Du Bignon story to the support for independent black institutions evident in
the second.[39] The story revolves around life after graduation for three
Howard University roommates, Frank, Harry, and Jim, as they face the
difficult transition from the Roaring Twenties to the Great Depression.
Realtor Frank Farley and Dr. Harry Forbes succeeded in the 1920s by
taking economic risks, only to lose all their funds in the stock market crash. Jim Holmes withstood the early Depression because he had
returned to his family farm after graduation, something the others had
mocked him for. With the onset of the Depression, Frank, his wife,
Anne, and Harriet, a single friend, join Jim on the farm. Frank had not
learned prudence; rather than accept a simple existence on black-owned
land, he wanted to mortgage the farm and invest all of the money in
equipment and seed to expand their operation. Jim reluctantly took out
a mortgage, against the explicit dying wish of his father and against the
vocal opposition of Anne and Harriet. Just when a bountiful crop makes
it seem as though the men's gamble has succeeded, the white banker
demands an early repayment, precisely because surrounding whites do

not like to see the black people's farm expanding. When the men can't repay the loan, the banker comes to repossess the farm, accompanied by an angry white mob, but at the last moment, Anne and Harriet reveal that they have surreptitiously saved the mortgage money and spent only money they raised themselves. Thus the women are able to buy back the farm, free and clear, and save the day. The white mob that came to strip the successful black people of their farm goes away in disappointment.

The story does not end on this triumphant note, however. Frank, the most hotheaded and imprudent of the men, decides to sell the remaining harvested crop in the city in order to recoup his losses and thus soothe his masculine ego by retaining his economic self-sufficiency over the women. Anne, his wife, tries to keep him from going, fearing that his presence in the city will throw the day's success in the face of the angry white mob. As Anne predicted, Frank never makes it to the city to sell the crop; the mob catches and lynches him. But this tragedy does not end the story, either. As Du Bois had instructed in his initial editorial introducing "the new racial philosophy," death cannot be the final statement of this philosophy of economic cooperation.[40]

The white mob's lynching of Frank links this third Du Bignon story to the first. In each, a man's attempt to succeed within a white world by directly attacking racial norms leads to tragedy, to firing in "The Three Mosquitos" and death in "The Farm on the Eastern Shore." In the latter, Du Bignon/Du Bois does not criticize the wife for urging her husband to obey racial norms, but rather mourns the husband's refusal to understand racial reality, which illustrates Du Bois's own acceptance of the reality of segregation. Throughout the story, the women speak the words of wisdom, while the men are ignorant, hot-headed, sodden with drink, and/or intemperate with shared money.

At the end of the story, the most capable of all the women, Harriet— the leader of those who saved the joint farm from the hands of the greedy (and desperate) white banker—explains Du Bois's program of a self-segregated cooperative economy. Just as her friend Frank lost his life by trying to flout racial norms, she argues, "There's no use of our trying to win this bread and butter game by bucking the white competitive market. They control credit, markets, prices and all the tricks of trade. They've got us beaten before we start." The only way they can hope to succeed is to find black buyers, brought together "not by law and police but by a new religion of race salvation. We'll buy black because we must or starve."[41] Harriet also argues that it is necessary to become as ascetic as possible, to "regiment and stabilize and systematize our wants along simple, primary lines which we can supply with our own hands, our own brains, our own unmortgaged land."[42] This asceticism will lead to a "community not of exploited serfs but of friends and neighbors," who will work together to educate themselves, stay healthy, and work "like the devil or get out."[43] Du Bois would repeat this theme, that the benefits of racial solidarity belong only to those who worked for it in his 1934 essays advocating self-segregation.

Harriet then lays out the steps those remaining on the farm need to take. First they will take care of their own physical needs: food, hygiene, housing, clothing. Then they will expand their production to make goods for other black people to buy. Racial solidarity means that there will be consumers for their goods, even if they are not of the latest style and even if they are more expensive than goods produced by white people. She argues, "They'll buy because black hands made the goods and black wants to support black work." Their work will get better each year and their circle of production and consumption will expand. Those black people who do not buy black will find punishment "with pitiless ostracism and social death."[44]

Harriet denies that white people will succeed in their inevitable attempts to sabotage this cooperative. She argues "If we stand firm they can't stop us. We'll be impervious to retaliation or boycott." Indeed it is even possible to try to work with white labor, but only once African Americans have established their cooperative and only so far as white labor is willing to "follow our rules and yield to our leadership." The advantage of a racial cooperative like this is that African Americans will be empowered to "bargain as trained and independent leaders and not sue as ignorant and blind beggars." Jim, the original owner of the farm and now Harriet's fiancé, agrees with her description and adds that his father had suggested the moral guidelines with which to proceed. His father

> was silent and worked hard. He did not boast nor crawl. He did good for evil but he never called evil good. He forgave his enemies, but he neither loved nor forgot them and wasted no precious time in hate. He knew no color in pain and turned no beggar, white or black, away. He was long-suffering but he had two shot guns always in his home. They were loaded and his neighbors knew it. He died poor but rich in friends.

Jim tells her that they will indeed build her vision of a cooperative, but that they will be careful to go to the market "by daylight and ride with a rifle in our hand," unlike poor Frank, who had gone at night without a rifle.[45]

This final emphasis upon self-defense brings a black nationalist dimension to Harriet's race-based economic cooperative. Du Bois kept a loaded shotgun in his house, as he had ever since the Atlanta riot in 1905, but to urge armed self-defense in print publicly challenged NAACP standards.[46] Not only does Du Bignon act as Du Bois's mouthpiece, but Harriet lives out Du Bois's "new racial philosophy." Through the Harriet character, Du Bois uses fiction to explain how the philosophy of economic cooperation works in an individual's life. This adds another layer of Du Bois placing himself and his ideas into a woman's life.

### "Postscript: The Right to Work"

In his April "Postscript," located just a few pages after fictional Harriet describes her ideal race-based economic cooperative, Du Bois adds further explanation of her program without actually referencing Du Bignon or Harriet.[47] In this editorial, Du Bois argues that black people have to recognize the inevitability of segregation and racial hatred. Despite the incredible difficulties they face, African Americans are strong, albeit with an untapped strength. The only way that African Americans will be kept "in continued industrial slavery" is if "we continue to enslave ourselves, and remain content to work as servants for white folk and dumb driven laborers for nothing." In this last sentiment, Du Bois leans heavily upon the black nationalist idea of self-help and breaking the bonds of mental slavery. It was not enough to recognize the persistence of racial oppression and fight against it. Black people had to scourge mental slavery, so eloquently described by Carter G. Woodson in *The Mis-education of the Negro,* published the same year, 1933.[48]

In this editorial, Du Bois offered the economic cooperative as the solution to racism's imperviousness to change as well as the key to unlock the prison that growing up surrounded by racism built in black people's own minds. He intended for black people to consume what they produced and produce as much as possible to meet the needs of black consumers. To those who would say that worker cooperatives had always failed in the past, he explained that these previous failures lacked the cohesion that race brought to African Americans. He argued, "We have a motive such as they [the failed cooperatives] never had. We are fleeing, not simply from poverty, but from insult and murder and social death. We have an instinct of race and a bond of color, in place of a protective tariff for our infant industry."[49] This directly parallels the plan Harriet defines for the future of her friends in "The Farm on the Eastern Shore."[50]

Du Bois recognized the difficulties he was asking African Americans to go through for this cooperative; he demanded rigid discipline, subordination of desire to need, and an acceptance of years of poverty. But it would give black people a great purpose in life. Success would mean "no nation, here or elsewhere, can oppress us. No capital can enslave us." Black Americans would join Afro-Caribbeans, black South Americans, and black Africans and as a whole, people of African descent would "stretch hands and hands of strength and sinew and understanding to India and China and all Asia. We become in truth, free."[51] For African Americans and for people of color across the world, Du Bois believed that economic independence would remove the possibility of political and social oppression by taking away the primary weapons of the powerful and by gaining power themselves. Du Bois's argument here is connected to ideas surrounding Du Bois's philosophy of world revolution, which Bill Mullen's essay in this volume addresses. And yet nowhere in this editorial does he mention that black women might have different needs or desires around labor and management of capital than black men.

Without recognizing that Du Bois was behind the Du Bignon stories, one would be left only with this editorial, assuming he did not believe black women had anything to contribute to this new economic cooperative he envisioned. Collectively the three Du Bignon stories explain how black people must unify across color differences and must identify with black people no matter what skin tone they themselves are. The three stories show how integration is a painful and often unfulfilling goal that encourages prejudice rather than defeating it. And they show that together black people can protect themselves from the onslaughts of slavery, but only by voluntarily accepting segregation and creating their own economic system. And yet seeing Du Bois sign Du Bignon's name raises as many questions as it opens new avenues of interpretation.

## Analysis of Du Bois's Use of the Du Bignon Pseudonym

Why did Du Bois first introduce his ideas of a race-based economic cooperative in the mouth of a strong fictional woman and within a fictional story with a woman's byline? What did he think a woman's byline could achieve that the awe-inspiring name Du Bois could not? This essay considers the interrelation of five possibilities: (1) that he thought the more people who articulated his points, the better; (2) that he believed women were more progressive and able to make greater societal transformations than men; (3) that he was unwilling to articulate strong feminism under his own byline; (4) that he was offering a tribute to Adrienne Herndon and through her to other intelligent women with whom he had had affairs; and (5) that he could imagine himself with a female mind and name. These are five possibilities rather than five solid interpretations because the potential of Du Bois assuming a female identity requires more research to determine which of the five would be most likely. Raising these five possibilities opens up intriguing new options in the active argument over Du Bois's commitment to feminism.

Characterizing these stories as "Du Bois in drag" does not suggest that Du Bois emulated the part of drag performances that mock gendered styles and heighten femininity in an outlandish way. None of the female characters in the stories exhibits heightened femininity in personality or appearance; indeed the hypermasculine men who refuse to listen to sage female advice receive the most ridicule. Du Bois seems genuine in his appropriation of female voices, in part because they so completely articulate his own positions. Carroll argues that one of the primary hallmarks of men writing in rhetorical drag in captivity narratives of the eighteenth and nineteenth centuries was the use of a simplistic style that seemed to evoke what "any" woman might say, rather than attempting to develop the style of a specific individual woman. In contrast, Du Bois does not alter his fictional voice significantly to write in the guise of Du Bignon. Though he is more aggressive in his assertion of the capability of women (and the failures of men), his voice is similar to that in other pieces of fiction that he wrote around the same time.[52]

### The More the Merrier

By letting his authorial voice appear in what Carroll calls "rhetorical drag," Du Bois showed that he believed his ideas would have greater credence articulated by both himself and a feminist woman in the same issue.[53] By writing the story through a pseudonym, Du Bois may have been trying to indicate that his ideas had greater currency among other

African Americans than they did. Or perhaps Du Bois chose to write in the voice of Du Bignon because he believed that a woman's point of view would sway more (female) readers than his ideas alone. And yet it would be striking for the time if he believed a woman's voice gave added credence to his ideas. It is a powerful instance of gender subversion if he was inferring in 1933 that a woman's voice had a power to command ideological adherence that his own famous male name alone could not.

### Women's Potential as "Agents of Social Transformation"

Du Bois's use of Harriet to introduce his economic cooperative, particularly as a contrast to Frank's wrongheaded masculine bravado that results in his death, can be seen as a way Du Bois believed black women were better suited to be the leaders of the economic revolution. The scholar Reiland Rabaka explains that only a "few scholars have pointed out that in many instances in his writings, Du Bois placed black women's socio-political theory and praxis on par and, at certain intervals, *over* that of black men."[54] Rabaka comes to this conclusion by analyzing Du Bois's essay "The Damnation of Women" in the 1920 *Darkwater* collection, which is the first point of departure for anyone asking to what extent Du Bois supported women's rights and female autonomy.[55]

In this essay Du Bois traces how black women had been at the center of three great oppressions and had survived with resiliency and strength. They were even at that moment pursuing a moral and economic revolution as they reenvisioned marriage and motherhood so that they could have economic independence and authority. Du Bois recognized that black women working outside the home disrupted traditional labor relations within it, but rather than suggesting they force black women out of the workforce, he argues that marriage had to change to adapt to women's economic independence. He explains, "We cannot abolish the new economic freedom of women. We cannot imprison women again in a home or require them all on pain of death to be nurses and housekeepers."[56] He also argues that black women are the most likely to be leaders of the revolution because of the way they survived slavery, rape, and Jim Crow with strength and dignity.

Despite his praise for black women's economic leadership and his praise for their minds as well as their beauty, he does not give much named recognition to specific intellectuals. Reading his essay, one would assume Du Bois did not recognize contemporary black women intellectuals. Farah Jasmine Griffin explains, "Du Bois focuses his attention on black women as mothers, workers, and activists but not as intellectuals. This is why contemporary black feminist intellectuals continue to claim him as an important ancestor even as they critique some of his failures around gender."[57]

Hazel Carby asserts that Du Bois completely failed "to imagine black women as intellectuals and race leaders."[58] Ironically, Harriet's powerful rescue of the cooperative farm and recovery of her fiancé Jim's esteem for his father's advice shows Du Bois could indeed *imagine* a woman as both things Carby describes. But with a different verb such as "recognize," Carby's point stands because rather than ask a contemporary black woman to write her own true or fictional story, Du Bois wrote his own. And then rather than claim the ideas as his own, Du Bois put Harriet under the signature of Du Bignon. This reluctance to claim her words suggests that he may have had a less laudatory reason for his pseudonym than the subsequent two points suggest.

### Potential Unwillingness to Publish Feminist Ideas under His Own Byline

Nowhere in the April 1933 postscript, mere pages after Harriet's call to action in "The Farm on the Eastern Shore," did Du Bois mention the particular problems faced by black women as something different from those experienced by black men, nor did he state that black women were the ones succeeding over men in the new climate of the Great Depression, as the Du Bignon stories had. This suggests that in spite of the feminism on display in the Du Bignon stories, he was unwilling to address under his own byline the issues faced by black women in particular. Du Bois may have felt uncomfortable expressing the strong feminism in the stories in his own voice. He could appear as the editor of the stories and be considered magnanimous to include such fervent feminism in the pages of *The Crisis*, but perhaps he was unwilling to go so far as to claim the feminist part of the stories as his own. Maybe he believed only a woman could or should write about men flailing and failing to such a degree.[59] In many ways, these two suppositions are not at odds. He could both believe that his ideas would have greater currency articulated in more voices and also hide behind the Du Bignon pseudonym. This hiding lends credence to those scholars who argue that Du Bois was a weak feminist, if a feminist at all.[60] However, his reluctance to claim Du Bignon's feminism for himself does not erase "her" stories printed in black and white in the pages of *The Crisis*.

Under the Du Bignon name, Du Bois critiques black men for not protecting black women (economically in this case, but with a subtext of the violence that could happen without economic independence). But he also shows prevailing black women protecting themselves and their sisters through agency and intelligent pragmatism. He succumbs to something akin to a stereotype—that of dreaming, risk-taking men and pragmatic women and mothers (which Lorraine Hansberry evoked twenty years later to great effect in *A Raisin in the Sun*). The man in the story puts himself in danger because he cannot accept the protection of a woman or the better decision of a woman. This is a clear feminist critique of patriarchy and masculine ego. It could also be a functionalist use of a female character to point out Du Bois's concern with masculine development. The lynching of the excessively masculine, risk-taking character is followed by a proposal of black collectivism that doesn't presuppose patriarchy (in the way that black nationalist thinkers have often done).

If one were to read only Du Bois's postscript, without the context of the Du Bignon stories, it would seem that the "new racial philosophy" had no place for the particular problems or leadership of black women. By placing the Du Bois postscript into conversation with the Du Bignon stories, it seems that Du Bois intended for his readers to discuss feminism but that he was unwilling to place that conversation under his own name.

### Tribute to Intelligent Women

How do we understand this newly revealed evidence that Du Bois created strong fictional feminist women under a pseudonym alongside his repeated dismissal or ignorance of real-life black women intellectuals? In addition to recognizing Du Bois's failure to include black women intellectuals in "The Damnation of Women," Griffin also decries his failure to cite any black women in *Black Reconstruction* by writing, "Once again, he ignores the work of black women as intellectuals."[61] Du Bois's repeated failure to acknowledge by name black women's intellectual work is odd given his friendships and physical relationships with many of the most intelligent women in his circle, a point Erik McDuffie's chapter makes about Du Bois's final *Autobiography*. If one were to analyze only how his personal life affected his feminism through his role as father and husband, Du Bois appears exceedingly patriarchal.[62] But when we open the analysis to his lovers and female friends, the picture becomes more complicated, though no less problematic.

Perhaps he wrote the stories (and later created the *Black Flame* character of Jean Du Bignon) as a tribute to Adrienne Herndon, his long-dead friend and, possibly, first extramarital affair (as Lewis implies).[63] It would not be the only time Du Bois paid tribute to one of the women widely known in Harlem social circles to be his lover. Mere pages before the February Du Bignon story is a profile of the Philadelphia physician Virginia Alexander, Du Bois's lover during the early 1930s.[64] In 1935 he dedicated the very book Griffin criticized—his momentous history *Black Reconstruction*—to Alexander.[65] Few scholars who have written about the nuances of Du Bois's feminism have included in their analysis his serial affairs with intelligent women.[66] Lewis chronicles them assiduously in his two-volume Du Bois biography, placing responsibility for the affairs on the "intelligent women" attracted to Du Bois's "considerable and tested appeal," but he does not analyze what they meant about Du Bois himself beyond documenting Du Bois's private chauvinism.[67] Even Lewis's chronicling is inappropriate scholarship for some; Rabaka describes Lewis's description of Du Bois's affairs as "shocking," scandalous, "sordid," and an attempt to create a "cause celebre."[68]

Rather than ignoring these affairs, as Rabaka seems to suggest, scholars must consider what they reveal about Du Bois and his gender politics. To what extent did he use his power "to leverage physical and sexual intimacy with female members of the office staff as well as women . . . with literary aspirations, for whom Du Bois was a key professional gatekeeper," as the literary scholar Mark Van Wienen asks?[69] This is an essential question at any time, but particularly in the post-#MeToo world. All of the women that Du Bois had affairs with were women well-regarded in their circles as intelligent, influential leaders. Why did Du Bois choose the women he did? Did Du Bois adore their minds as well as their bodies? Was his disinterest in his wife Nina not just because of her prudish sexuality (Du Bois wrote that she had been too well trained in abstinence) but also because she disinterested him intellectually?[70] What does it mean that he often failed to recognize black women intellectuals in print while pursuing them in the bedroom? His behavior must have been very hurtful to Nina and surely had a wide array of effects on the women with whom he slept. Du Bois could have written the Du Bignon stories as a tribute to Herndon and her dream of shining in the footlights; he placed what he believed intelligent women could accomplish under her stage name. Because he used her name so many years after her death, Du Bignon/Herndon could have been one of Du Bois's greatest loves, among many great loves. And yet, the fact remains that he only imagined gender equality in his 1933–34 writings under a pseudonym.

## Du Bois's Gender Flexibility

While these stories capture Du Bois's ability to imagine successful intelligent women and perhaps were meant as a tribute to Herndon, they could also represent a greater flexibility of gender within Du Bois himself than has been previously noted. Perhaps the correlation of Du Bois with Du Bignon was not just a romance, as Brent Hayes Edwards describes it in reference to Jean Du Bignon in the *Black Flame* Trilogy, but also an identification, a drag, a way in which Du Bois took on the character of a woman to express his ideas, hopes, and goals, almost a kind of self-romance, a union of male and female in one body.[71] Perhaps his taking on of the Du Bignon name suggests greater gender malleability than heretofore recognized in the very masculine Du Bois, who frequently urged black men to become "men" in all the fullness of their masculinity.[72]

Jean Du Bignon's character in *The Black Flame* trilogy encourages us to take the question of Du Bois's gender flexibility more seriously than we might with only the Anne Du Bignon stories as evidence. In his final novel, published in three segments from 1957 to 1961, Du Bois created a vast historical narrative describing the swath of African American public and private life through which he had lived for the past eight decades. Several scholars have noted that many of the characters in *Black Flame* parallel Du Bois's life, including, most obviously, James Burghardt, a founder of the NAACP.[73] But another close parallel is the almost-white woman Jean Du Bignon. Scholar Keith E. Byerman explains that Jean and Du Bois are both sociologists "planning a revival of the *Atlanta Studies* in the 1940s." There is a legal action taken against both of them because they are peace activists. The government charges them with being "the agent of a foreign power; these patently false charges are easily disproved and the defendants are released." These biographical similarities are not as significant as "the spiritual associations," according to Byerman. Both Jean and Du Bois are light-skinned enough that they must choose whether or not to affiliate with black culture and people. Byerman explains, "For both of them, the element of choice introduces moral possibilities in what for others is simply genetic fate. By taking the more difficult path in insisting on her blackness, Jean becomes a saintly figure who willingly identifies with the suffering of others."[74] Though he traces the spiritual connections between female Jean and male Du Bois, Byerman leaves it there, without exploring the gendered implications of this identification.[75]

The literary scholar Brent Hayes Edwards brings a gendered analysis to the same similarities, but treats this coupling as a romance rather than an instance of gender play or drag. Rather than revealing something about Du Bois's own identity, Edwards suggests the difference it makes is in explaining Du Bois's original subtitle to the trilogy: "The Romance of History." Edwards interprets the common characteristics between Du Bignon and Du Bois as a sort of romance between a fictional woman and a living man rather than a self-identification of that man with the fictional female character he created. First, Edwards shows how Du Bignon, and not "the novels' titular protagonist, Mansart," is the one whose political sensibility "so clearly" parallels Du Bois's own. Du Bignon creates a "tentative plan for cooperative, continuous sociological investigation in each state as a scientific beginning."[76] Federal authorities accuse Du Bignon of the same cold war treachery, and acquit her, exactly as Du Bois was acquitted in real life. She uses her light skin to pursue "a sort of underground activism" that the omniscient narrator explains because Du Bignon felt she was "bone of their bone and flesh of their flesh," a phrase echoing *The Souls of Black Folk*'s "Forethought." Edwards transitions from these biographical similarities between Du Bignon and Du Bois to explain it via the "December-May" romances of Du Bignon and Mansart and Du Bois and Shirley Graham's own. Edwards explains, "In the novel, 'late romance' has everything to do with an erotics of deferral, duty, and long term devotion." Du Bois's praise for Du Bignon's devotion to her elderly spouse becomes a "commemoration" of Graham Du Bois's devotion to himself.

Not only does Edwards move to romance and marriage to explain Du Bois and Du Bignon, he explicitly rejects the idea that the "constant parallels" between Du Bignon and Du Bois would make the trilogy act as "autobiographical fiction."[77] He raises these parallels only to caution readers away from a simple equation between the elderly dying Mansart and the octogenarian author, not to suggest a blurring of male/female lines. Yet that warning seems to use gender as an analytic tool in only one binary way: a male author putting his own identifying features into a female character must be romance or spousal tribute, but not self-knowledge. Why could the trilogy not be a collective autobiographical fiction, with gender switches between the author and the identifying character revealing new interpretative vistas?

The literary scholar Celena Simpson agrees that Du Bois created Jean Du Bignon as a "representation of . . . himself" and sees in that identification not gender fluidity on Du Bois's part, but rather support for James and Carby's argument that Du Bois was interested only in masculinist development.[78] She argues that Jean Du Bignon succeeds more than any other character in the book because, as Du Bois himself describes her, she was "not quite a woman."[79] Simpson shows that Du Bignon succeeds because she is able to distance herself from her femininity. This distance is precisely because of the identification between Du Bois and Du Bignon. Du Bois tried to create a strong female character, Simpson argues, but instead created only a masculinist imitation of one.

Putting Anne Du Bignon alongside Jean Du Bignon challenges Simpson's categorical dismissal of Du Bois's potential self-identification with a fictional woman of his own creation. Instead it suggests that Du Bois was much more at ease with seeing himself through female eyes than other scholars have argued. This self-identification with women, coupled with his problematic power-tainted affairs with intelligent women, suggests that Du Bois wanted to stay in a world where he benefited from his male privilege, even while sometimes trying to understand the world through a female gaze.

W. E. B. Du Bois advocated self-segregation in 1933 and 1934, a move that shocked many and seemed utterly deviant from the earlier views made famous in his critiques of the black nationalists Booker T. Washington and Marcus Garvey. Du Bois chose to first articulate his ideas about self-segregation in a feminist short story written under a female pseudonym, a startling bit of gender play that indicates his trust in feminism as an idea that would sway his audience toward his philosophy, as well as his willingness to experiment with gender. Du Bois's ideas about self-segregation in 1933 and 1934 allowed him to express gender in a new way, one that was not about "ravaged women, rising men," but rather about women at the center of the struggle for an improvement in the lives of African Americans. He followed up this 1930 invocation of the Du Bignon name over twenty years later with the Jean Du Bignon character in *The Black Flame*. In that character he charted his own anxiety with being light-skinned and considered the moral implications of choosing a black community, culture, and affiliation that also meant choosing to fight to make African American lives matter. This reflects a new way of analyzing Du Bois's publications after 1934 and calls for further scholarship to see if these two instances of "Du Bois in drag," the former illustrating prevailing women and flailing men and the latter placing a black man's life within a black-by-choice woman's body, were persistent themes throughout his late career, and if so what that means for how we interpret Du Bois's feminism and personal ideas of gender.

## Notes

Acknowledgments: I would like to thank my Luther College research assistants Emily England and Hannah Butler for their diligent help on this article. Several colleagues provided invaluable insight into different drafts, including Keisha Blain, Emma Cassabaum, Marie Drews, Zebulon Hurst, Alison Mandaville, Michelle Moravec, and Clarie Potter.

1. Anne Du Bignon, "The Three Mosquitos: A Story of Marriage and Birth," *The Crisis*, January 1933, 10–12; Anne Du Bignon, "The Doctor's Dilemma: A Story of Tuberculosis," *The Crisis*, February 1933, 36–37; Anne Du Bignon, "The Farm on the Eastern Shore: A Story of Work," *The Crisis*, March 1933, 61–62, 70, and April 1933, 85–87.

2. Reiland Rabaka, "W. E. B. Du Bois and 'The Damnation of Women': An Essay on Africana Anti-Sexist Critical Social Theory," *Journal of African American Studies* 7, no. 2 (Fall 2003): 37–60; Farah Jasmine Griffin, "Black Feminists and Du Bois: Respectability, Protection, and Beyond," *Annals of the American Academy of Political and Social Science* 568 (March 1, 2000): 28–40, doi:10.2307/1049470.

3. Lorrayne Carroll, *Rhetorical Drag: Gender Impersonation, Captivity, and the Writing of History* (Kent, OH: Kent State University Press, 2007), 185.

4. Vilashini Cooppan, "Move On Down the Line: Domestic Science, Transnational Politics, and Gendered Allegory in Du Bois," in *Next to the Color Line: Gender, Sexuality, and W. E. B. Du Bois*, ed. Susan Gillman and Alys Eve Weinbaum (Minneapolis: University of Minnesota Press, 2007), 37.

5. Ibid.

6. I base this claim on a thorough search in the census records housed at Ancestry.com. The Du Bignon stories have been anthologized in at least one collection of black women's writing without biographical details. Judith Musser, ed., *"Girl, Colored" and Other Stories: A Complete Short Fiction Anthology of African American Women Writers in* The Crisis *Magazine, 1910–2010* (Jefferson, NC: McFarland, 2011).

7. Carole Merritt, *The Herndons: An Atlanta Family* (Athens: University of Georgia Press, 2002).

8. David Levering Lewis, *W. E. B. Du Bois: Biography of a Race, 1868–1919* (New York: Henry Holt, 1993), 320–21.

9. Ibid.

10. Shawn Leigh Alexander, "*The Crisis*: A Record of the Darker Races. An Introduction," in *Protest and Propaganda: W. E. B. Du Bois*, The Crisis, *and American History*, ed. Amy Helene Kirschke and Phillip Luke Sinitiere (Columbia: University of Missouri Press, 2014), 4.

11. Amy Helene Kirschke and Phillip Luke Sinitiere, "W. E. B. Du Bois as Print Propagandist," in Kirschke and Sinitiere, *Protest and Propaganda*, 38.

12. There is a list from around 1920 of works and publications by "Bew Siobud." W. E. B. Du Bois Papers (MS 312), Special Collections and University Archives, University of Massachusetts–Amherst Libraries. Robert McDonnell, "The W. E. B. Du Bois Papers," *The Crisis*, November 1980, 364; letter from *Elks Magazine* to unidentified correspondent, September 1951, W. E. B. Du Bois Papers (MS 312), Special Collections and University Archives, University of Massachusetts–Amherst Libraries; letter from Grosset & Dunlap, Inc., to Bud Weisob, December 18, 1952, W. E. B. Du Bois Papers (MS 312), Special Collections and University Archives, University of Massachusetts–Amherst Libraries.

13. Those who argued that Du Bois was consistent in his views before and after 1934 include Mark Van Wienen and Julie Kraft, "How the Socialism of W. E. B. Du Bois Still Matters: Black Socialism in 'The Quest of the Silver Fleece'—and Beyond," *African American Review* 41, no. 1 (April 1, 2007): 67–85, doi:10.2307/40033766; Mark Tushnet, "The Politics of Equality in Constitutional Law: The Equal Protection Clause, Dr. Du Bois, and Charles Hamilton Houston," *Journal of American History* 74, no. 3 (December 1, 1987): 884–903, doi:10.2307/1902158. Raymond Wolters argues for both sides, writing that Du Bois had been articulating socialism for many years, but not with the intensity or forcefulness of the 1933–34 era. He says that the 1934 editorial caused the bang, but also mentions the buildup of the earlier editorials. Raymond Wolters, *Du Bois and His Rivals* (Columbia: University of Missouri Press, 2003). Those who argue that 1934 represented a break from Du Bois's earlier ideas tend to appear before the above. They include Kenneth Mostern, "Three Theories of the Race of W. E. B. Du Bois," *Cultural Critique* 34 (Autumn 1996): 27–63; Thomas C. Holt, "The Political Uses of Alienation: W. E. B. Du Bois on Politics, Race, and Culture, 1903–1940," *American Quarterly* 42, no. 2 (June

1, 1990): 301–23, doi:10.2307/2713019; Elliott M. Rudwick, "Du Bois's Last Year as *Crisis* Editor," *Journal of Negro Education* 27, no. 4 (October 1, 1958): 526–33, doi:10.2307/2293801; Zhang Juguo, *W. E. B. Du Bois: The Quest for the Abolition of the Color Line* (New York: Routledge, 2001). Also important to this discussion is Jessica Gordon Nembhard, *Collective Courage: A History of African American Cooperative Economic Thought and Practice* (State College: Penn State University Press, 2014), who documents Du Bois's thinking on cooperatives through the Atlanta Studies and some of his economic commentary in the 1930s in *The Crisis*. She does not address the Du Bignon stories.

14. The August 1933 Second Amenia Conference was a significant event in the life of the NAACP. Spingarn, Du Bois, and Walter White collaborated to bring together those whom they considered the best black minds in the country to discuss the future of race relations. For more information, see W. E. B. Du Bois, "Youth and Age at Amenia," *The Crisis*, October 1933, 226–27; Jonathan Scott Holloway, *Confronting the Veil: Abram Harris Jr., E. Franklin Frazier, and Ralph Bunche, 1919–1941* (Chapel Hill: University of North Carolina Press, 2002); Lauren Kientz, "Untrammeled Thinking: The Promise and Peril of the Second Amenia Conference, 1920–1940," PhD diss., Michigan State University, 2010; Eben Miller, *Born along the Color Line: The 1933 Amenia Conference and the Rise of a National Civil Rights Movement* (New York: Oxford University Press, 2012).

15. Du Bois first advocated "consumers' co-operation for Negroes" in an editorial series in 1918. Nembhard, 102. However, this new series included a more stringent racial separatism that would raise considerably harsher criticism than his prior work.

16. W. E. B. Du Bois, "Postscript: Toward a New Racial Philosophy," *The Crisis*, January 1933, 20.

17. Ibid.

18. Ibid.

19. For many years, scholars dismissed Du Bois's fiction for how didactic it was. However, "recently scholars have begun to reverse this disparagement while excavating how Du Bois used fiction to test out and amplify his developing philosophical and sociological positions over the many decades of his career." Adrienne Brown and Britt Rusert, "Introduction to The Princess Steel," *PMLA* 130, no. 3 (May 2015): 819–29.

20. Du Bois, "Postscript: Toward a New Racial Philosophy."

21. Michele Elam and Paul C. Taylor, "Du Bois's Erotics," in Gillman and Weinbaum, *Next to the Color Line*, 224.

22. In "W. E. B. Du Bois as Print Propagandist," Kirschke and Sinitiere explain Du Bois's role as "print propagandist" in *The Crisis* particularly well. They examine it specifically through Du Bois's creation of historical memory and identity in its pages.

23. Du Bignon, "The Three Mosquitos."

24. Ibid., 10.

25. Ibid.

26. Ibid.

27. Ibid.

28. Ibid., 12.

29. Ibid.

30. Cooppan, "Move On Down the Line," 37.

31. Du Bignon, "The Doctor's Dilemma." Though this story has no substantive women characters, the same issue of *The Crisis* contains an editorial that reveals volumes about Du Bois's feminism. Titled "It Is a Girl," it provides parents with a script to say to anyone who would greet their new baby girl with "Too bad it wasn't a boy." Parents should explain that the desire for a male child was a "relic of barbarism" and needed to be ended forever. They could also explain, however, that daughters were even better than sons in many highly gendered ways: they helped more around the house, did not run wild, and were more subject to the parents' influence. This defense of womanhood rooted in essentialism reflects the kind of feminism black women scholars have challenged Du Bois on. Those who make this argument include Joy James, "The Profeminist Politics of W. E. B. Du Bois with Respects to Anna Julia Cooper and Ida B. Wells Barnett," in *W. E. B. Du Bois on Race and Culture: Philosophy, Politics, and Poetics*, ed. Bernard W. Bell, Emily R. Grosholz, and James Benjamin Stewart (London: Routledge Taylor & Francis), 141–60; Hazel V. Carby, *Race Men* (Cambridge, MA: Harvard University Press, 2000); Celena Simpson, "Du Bois's Dubious Feminism: Evaluating through *The Black Flame* Trilogy," *Pluralist* 10, no. 1 (2015), 48–63, http://www.american-philosophy .org/saap2014/openconf/modules/request.php?module=oc_program& action=view.php&id=112.

32. Du Bignon, "The Doctor's Dilemma," 36.

33. Ibid., 37.

34. Ibid.

35. Lauren Kientz Anderson, "A Nauseating Sentiment, a Magical Device, or a Real Insight? Interracialism at Fisk University in 1930," in special issue on The African American Experience in Higher Education Before the Civil Rights Era ed. Roger L. Geiger, Christian Anderson, and

Marybeth Gasman, *Perspectives on the History of Higher Education* 29 (August 2012): 105–6.

36. "Chicago Doctors Get Real Facts on Harlem Hospital," *Chicago Defender*, December 31, 1927; W. E. B. Du Bois, "Postscript: Harlem Hospital," *The Crisis*, February 1933, 44–45.

37. Vanessa Northington Gamble, *Making a Place for Ourselves: The Black Hospital Movement, 1920–1945* (New York: Oxford University Press, 1995), 57–59.

38. Du Bois, "Postscript: Harlem Hospital," 45.

39. Du Bignon, "The Farm on the Eastern Shore."

40. Du Bois, "Postscript: Toward a New Racial Philosophy."

41. Du Bignon, "The Farm on the Eastern Shore," April 1933, 87. The publication of this story preceded the New Negro Alliance's "Don't Buy Where You Can't Work" movement in DC by mere months. Michele F. Pacifico, "'Don't Buy Where You Can't Work': The New Negro Alliance of Washington," *Washington History* 6, no. 1 (1994): 66–88.

42. Du Bignon, "The Farm on the Eastern Shore," April 1933, 87.

43. Ibid.

44. Ibid., 37.

45. Ibid., 87.

46. W. E. B. Du Bois, "Postscript: Dodging the Issue," *The Crisis*, February 1933, 46; Shannon King, "'Ready to Shoot and Do Shoot': Black Working-Class Self-Defense and Community Politics in Harlem, New York, during the 1920s," *Journal of Urban History* 37, no. 5 (September 1, 2011): 757–74, doi:10.1177/0096144211413234; Sundiata Keita Cha-Jua and Clarence Lang, "The 'Long Movement' as Vampire: Temporal and Spatial Fallacies in Recent Black Freedom Studies," *Journal of African American History* 92, no. 2 (Spring 2007): 265–88.

47. W. E. B. Du Bois, "Postscript: The Right to Work," *The Crisis*, April 1933, 93.

48. Carter G. Woodson, *The Mis-education of the Negro* (Trenton, NJ: Africa World Press, 1998).

49. Du Bois, "Postscript: The Right to Work," 94.

50. Du Bignon, "The Farm on the Eastern Shore," April 1933, 87.

51. Du Bois, "Postscript: The Right to Work," 94.

52. See, for example, the Mary character in Du Bois's short story "The Son of God," published in *The Crisis* in December 1933. For more on this story, see Phillip Luke Sinitiere, "W. E. B. Du Bois's Prophetic Propaganda: Religion and *The Crisis*, 1910–1934," in Kirschke and Sinitiere, *Protest and Propaganda*, 4.

53. Carroll, *Rhetorical Drag.*

54. Rabaka, "W. E. B. Du Bois and 'The Damnation of Women,'" 39.

55. W. E. B. Du Bois, "The Damnation of Women," in *Darkwater*, in *W. E. B. Du Bois: Writings*, ed. Nathan Huggins (New York: Library of America, 1986), 953–68.

56. Ibid., 963–64.

57. Griffin, "Black Feminists and Du Bois," 28.

58. Carby, *Race Men*, 10.

59. He often condemned black men who were not living up to his expectations for the Talented Tenth, but he did not systematically charge black men with imprudence in the way that this story does. For example, in his discussion of Louis T. Wright's campaign to bring black doctors into Harlem Hospital, discussed above, he made a distinction between the well-qualified and those who rested on their laurels and refused to continue to improve in their craft; his pointed critique condemned the type of men who chose shortcuts over standards but was directed at peers rather than the way patriarchy leads men to make shortsighted and risky decisions liable to hurt everyone in the family, like this story. Du Bois, "Postscript: Harlem Hospital," 44–45.

60. See note 31 for a list of those who make this argument.

61. Ibid., 37.

62. Griffin explains, "For the most part, black feminist intellectuals acknowledge Du Bois's sexism in his personal life (specifically his treatment of his daughter), but many of them also applaud his effort on behalf of black women and claim him as an intellectual ancestor." Ibid., 29.

63. Lewis, *W. E. B. Du Bois: Biography of a Race, 1868–1919*, 320–21.

64. "Can a Colored Woman Be a Physician?," *Crisis*, February 1933. Alice Dunbar-Nelson describes one time Du Bois and Alexander sat next to each other at an economic conference and "were inseparable and horribly obvious all day." Alice Dunbar Nelson, *Give Us Each Day: The Diary of Alice Dunbar-Nelson*, ed. Gloria T. Hull (New York: Norton, 1984), 426. Julia Bond, in an interview with David Levering Lewis, said that Du Bois's affairs were an accepted reality in Harlem. "Everybody accepted it. [Du Bois] had always been like that. It was just sort of his personality, and people knew that he liked young women, and he always liked to be in their company." David Levering Lewis, *W. E. B. Du Bois, The Fight for Equality and the American Century* (New York: Henry Holt, 2000), 274.

65. W. E. B. Du Bois, *Black Reconstruction, 1860–1880* (New York: Harcourt Brace, 1935).

66. Some of those who have written about Du Bois as a feminist, whether a complicated one or not, include Bettina Aptheker, "On 'The Damnation

of Women': W. E. B. Du Bois and a Theory for Woman's Emancipation,"
in *Woman's Legacy: Essays on Race, Sex, and Class in American History*,
ed. Bettina Aptheker (Amherst: University of Massachusetts Press, 1982);
Joy James, "The Profeminist Politics of W. E. B. Du Bois with Respects
to Anna Julia Cooper and Ida B. Wells Barnett," in Bell et al., *W. E. B.
Du Bois on Race and Culture*; Griffin, "Black Feminists and Du Bois"; Reiland Rabaka, "W. E. B. Du Bois and 'The Damnation of Women': An Essay
on Africana Anti-Sexist Critical Social Theory," *Journal of African American
Studies* 7, no. 2 (Fall 2003): 37–60; Joy James, "Profeminism and Gender
Elites: W. E. B. Du Bois, Anna Julia Cooper, and Ida B. Wells-Barnett,"
in Gillman and Weinbaum, *Next to the Color Line*, 69–95.

67. Lewis, *W. E. B Du Bois: Biography of a Race*, 350, 449–65. Lewis
supports his claim that Du Bois was a chauvinist with evidence of his tendency to rule at home as a patriarch over his wife and daughter.

68. Reiland Rabaka, *Against Epistemic Apartheid: W. E. B. Du Bois and
the Disciplinary Decadence of Sociology* (Lanham, MD: Lexington Books,
2010), 221n 8.

69. Mark Van Wienen, *American Socialist Triptych: The Literary-Political
Work of Charlotte Perkins Gilman, Upton Sinclair, and W. E. B. Du Bois*
(Ann Arbor: University of Michigan Press, 2012).

70. Du Bois wrote Nina throughout his life, updating her about his
activities, but they often arranged to live separately. In his tribute to her
upon her death, he wrote, "Sometimes I felt burdened under it; our home
seemed a bit too clean and too carefully kept. I wanted many times to have
her forget her housework and throw away her careful plans for daily life
and romp and laugh. She seldom did this, because she could not; it was
not in her nature. She was always serious and yet a good companion."
W. E. B. Du Bois, "I Bury My Wife," in *W. E. B. Du Bois: A Reader*, ed.
David Levering Lewis (New York: Henry Holt, 1995), 142.

71. Brent Hayes Edwards, "Late Romance," in Gillman and Weinbaum,
*Next to the Color Line*, 133.

72. For example, Herman Beavers argues, "Although Du Bois's intellectual prowess with respect to the discourses of race and class was ahead of
its time in the 1920s, his attitude regarding gender, while tending toward
progressivism, was highly reflective of the historical moment." Herman
Beavers, "Romancing the Body Politic: Du Bois's Propaganda of the Dark
World," *Annals of the American Academy of Political and Social Science* 568
(March 1, 2000): 262–63, doi:10.2307/1049484. Carby argues, "The conceptual structure of Du Bois's genealogy of race and nation has, at its center,
the dilemma of the formation of black manhood." Carby, *Race Men*, 31.

73. These include Keith E. Byerman, *Seizing the Word: History, Art, and Self in the Work of W. E. B. Du Bois* (Athens: University of Georgia Press, 2010); Lily Wiatrowski Phillips, "*The Black Flame* Revisited: Recursion and Return in the Reading of W. E. B. Du Bois's Trilogy," *CR: The New Centennial Review* 15, no. 2 (Fall 2015), Project Muse; Edwards, "Late Romance"; Simpson, "Du Bois's Dubious Feminism."

74. Byerman, *Seizing the Word*, 155.

75. Another scholar to raise the connection between Du Bois and Du Bignon, recognizing the gendered implications but without analyzing them, is Lily Wiatrowski Phillips. She writes, "Finally we can see Du Bois in the figure of Jean Du Bignon, who shares his racially 'impure' heritage, his early interest in socialism, and his proclivity for indictment for failing to register as a foreign agent. Even her French name, with its masculine spelling, connects her to Du Bois (she is Jean, not Jeanne, after all). (Although I will mention that Du Bignon is also, in my opinion, a stand-in for Shirley Graham, Du Bois's wife, in her position as assistant to the great man Manuel Mansart and the way she leads Mansart closer to the Left)." Phillips, "*The Black Flame* Revisited."

76. Edwards, "Late Romance," 133.

77. Ibid., 141.

78. Simpson, "Du Bois's Dubious Feminism."

79. Ibid., 14.

# The Gender of the General Strike

## W. E. B. Du Bois's *Black Reconstruction* and Black Feminism's Philosophy of History

*Alys Eve Weinbaum*

This investigation into the general strike, and my proposal that it has been and ought to be recognized as gendered, begins with a perhaps contentious observation: there are only two periods in the history of racial capitalism during which women's in vivo reproductive labor power and reproductive products have been engineered for profit. First, during the four hundred years of chattel slavery in the Americas and the Caribbean; second, over the past four decades. To be clear on the scope of this observation from the outset, I do not mean to imply that women's reproductive labor, broadly construed as the reproduction of workers and the relations of production, has not been exploited at other times and in other places. Relatedly, I do not wish to suggest that contemporary forms of reproductive extraction are identical to those that took place in the slave past. Rather my observation is specific, if also less familiar: over the past four decades, the human reproductive body, in a robust material sense, has been exploited in a manner that has *epistemic* precedent in Atlantic chattel slavery and the culture of enslaved reproduction on which it relied. And this is so even though the reproductive afterlife of what I call *the slave episteme* has gone unacknowledged by scholars of reproductive labor in contemporary capitalism—that is, save by the black feminists who are the focus of the present essay who have implicitly taken up the question of the gender of the general strike in the slave past, effectively clearing space for consideration of the endurance of the slave episteme in the biocapitalist moment during which these same feminists produced reflections on sexual and reproductive extraction and slave women's refusal of it.[1]

This is no surprise. "Biocapital" and "biocapitalism" were not terms that black feminists used when they wrote in the 1970s, 1980s, and 1990s because neither term was yet in circulation. And yet it was precisely during these three decades that the biocapitalist economy that is today dominant first emerged and began to solidify.[2] This biocapitalist economy, in which in vivo reproductive labor enters the exchange relationship (often in the form of surrogacy), encompasses the commodification of a full range of biological processes and raw materials that women reproduce, including eggs, embryonic stem cells, cord blood, and, not least, human beings. Taken together, the forms of reproductive extraction that exist today suggest the urgency of examining the epistemic connections between the contemporary reproductive scene and that of slavery. After all, slavery is the principal economic system historically predicated on women's productive and reproductive labor, on women's work in the fields and in plantation households, and on their in vivo reproductive labor and its biological, human products.[3]

Although a range of thinkers has attended to the intersection of racism, sexism, and capitalism in the context of the long history of racial capitalism, only black feminism—by which I here encompass black feminist theory, history, and literary fiction—constitutes *a philosophy of history* that is adequate to the task of comprehending the work of the slave episteme as it manifests as an uncanny feature of racial capitalism's global expansion.[4] In limning the ongoing work of the slave episteme, in accounting for what might be thought of as the afterlife of reproductive slavery in contemporary biocapitalism, black feminism makes visible the thought system that haunts as it actively enables the material exploitation of human reproductive labor and its products. And as important, black feminism dares to imagine what the refusal of such exploitation might have looked like in the past, what it could look like in the present, and how it might yet play a role in shaping the future. For this reason, black feminism is as relevant to an understanding of contemporary biocapitalism and of our individual and collective responses to it, as it is to an understanding of the slave past. Indeed, black feminism ought to be recognized as *the* philosophy of history that allows the reproductive history of the present to be excavated and then to be set to work in the interest of a more liberated future.

Through examination of the scale and scope, material and psychic, of slave women's sexual and reproductive exploitation, black feminism enables an understanding of contemporary reproductive extraction and, simultaneously, reveals the relevance of recalling the struggles

THE GENDER OF THE GENERAL STRIKE                                            135

for freedom from sexual and reproductive bondage that slave women fought. Black feminism, expressed in and across the multiple idioms ought, therefore, to be understood as expressive of what the historian Robin D. G. Kelley has labeled "freedom dreams." Such dreams are unapologetically utopian. Though they may not be readily materialized in situations of ongoing extractive violence, such dreams nonetheless demand transformation of conventional understandings of human "agency" and "resistance" and the connections of both to Marxist conceptual mainstays such as "work," "the worker," and "class consciousness." As Kelley elaborates, to conceive of freedom dreams is to "recover ideas—visions fashioned mainly by those marginalized black activists who proposed a different way out of our contradictions." However, the point of engaging in the process of recovery of the dreamer's dreams is not to "wholly embrace their ideas or strategies as the foundation for new movements." Rather it is to allow such ideas or strategies to "tap the well of our own collective imaginations" so that we may dream (again) of forms of freedom that are unbound from free enterprise.[5]

In suggesting the significance of black feminism of the 1970s, 1980s, and 1990s to analysis of and response to the rise of contemporary biocapitalism, I suggest the existence of a relationship of complex historical reciprocity (as opposed to a relationship of either continuity or epochal distinction) between slave racial capitalism and contemporary biocapitalism that has not elsewhere been fully acknowledged or explored. Contrary to other theorists who regard biocapitalism as the "new face" of capitalism, I suggest that it behooves us to conceptualize slavery as itself an early biocapitalist formation.[6] Relatedly, in contrast to historians of black feminism who place this political and intellectual formation in the context of the long civil rights movement, the rise of black power, and the ascendance of racially dominant forms of feminism, here I suggest that black feminism can be contextualized otherwise.[7] It is certainly imperative to recognize, as others have, that black feminism negotiated the sexism, masculinism, and heterosexism of black nationalism and the racism and classism of second wave feminism, and, too, to discern how, beginning in the 1970s, black feminists (alongside other antiracist feminists) shifted the mainstream reproductive rights movement away from its narrow focus on access to abortion to focus on the entire range of reproductive "freedoms" (as opposed to "rights"), including the freedom to refuse sterilization abuse and related forms of racist, sexist, and eugenic reproductive coercion, and the economic freedom to bear, raise, and care for one's children.[8] The present argument could not be advanced without prior scholarship on biocapitalism, prior histories of black feminism, and prior accounts of black feminists contributions to the range of civil rights movements in the past century. And yet here I depart from existing approaches by situating slavery as an early biocapitalist formation and by placing black feminist production within the context of an emergent biocapitalist hegemony epistemically rooted in slavery. In this way, I bring black feminism of the '70s, '80s, and '90s into view as part and parcel of a long black radical tradition invested in full-scale critique of slave racial capitalism *and* biocapitalism. And, I recognize it as *a philosophy of history*—a theory of historical transformation that is attentive to the slave past, and, simultaneously, responsive to the biocapitalist present—which is fitting since contemporary biocapitalism is the material context in which black feminism was brewed up, and thus that to which it was by necessity (if not always expressly) responsive.

As should be apparent, the present argument shares much with scholarship on women of color feminism that reads it as a critique of late capitalism and neoliberalism.[9] So too it builds on the work of literary scholars writing in the 1980s and 1990s such as Hazel Carby, Anne DuCille, Deborah McDowell, and Valerie Smith (to name only a few) who offered watershed analyses of representations of enslaved motherhood in black women's fiction, and drew our attention to the importance of centering slave women's sexual and reproductive lives. Where I depart is in expressly keying black feminism to the rise of biocapitalism, in examining the importance of the fact that black feminists took up the history of sex and reproduction in slavery as biocapitalism and the modes of (re)production that it entails began to take hold, and in offering a reading of black feminism that examines the conjunctural significance of its simultaneous movement back to slavery and forward into the present and future.

## The Gender of the General Strike

In treating black feminism as a philosophy of history that grabs hold of the afterlife of reproductive slavery as it flashes up in our present moment of danger, I have found it both necessary and useful to read it as a profound polyvocal response to a question first posed in 1935 by W. E. B. Du Bois in his tome on the American Civil War and its foreclosed horizons, *Black Reconstruction*.[10] In this book of nearly eight hundred pages, Du Bois argues that slaves ought to be cast as "black workers" and the war that ended in the abolition of slavery as a "general strike" against the conditions of slave work that had not only national but global impact. As important, though not heretofore acknowledged, in *Black Reconstruction*'s opening chapter Du Bois considers the possibility that the general strike comprised a range of specifically gendered acts of resistance and refusal. Indeed, it is possible to read *Black Reconstruction* as the text that opens up what I will henceforth call *the question of the gender of the general strike*. For even though Du Bois did not (and perhaps could not) sustain his fleeting insights into the sexualized and gendered nature of slave work, he cleared space for consideration of enslaved women as members of a revolutionary group of black workers whose insurgency against sexual and reproductive extraction changed the course of history and transformed the shape of racial capitalism globally.

Of course, it may at first seem counterintuitive to some readers to situate *Black Reconstruction* thus. As has been demonstrated by others, Du Bois's writings and deeds were neither consistently pro-feminist nor even proto-feminist. His biographers and feminist critics together concur that he was a "retrograde rake" who played the role of "priapic adulterer" throughout several decades in an unhappy first marriage. He had a notoriously poor track record of publicly crediting women antilynching crusaders, civil rights activists, literary muses, and editors—that is those women with whom he routinely collaborated on a range of projects, and on whose brilliance and dedication to their work he often relied. Moreover, when he wrote on issues of gender and sexuality, as he did not only in *Black Reconstruction* but throughout his corpus, his contributions were often contradictory and rarely, if ever, sustained.[11] To be clear, what follows is not an argument for recognition of Du Bois as a black feminist thinker. Rather it is an argument about how *Black Reconstruction* locates the conceptual site where black feminist excavation and analysis of slave women's participation in a revolutionary war against slavery will eventually take place roughly half a century later. It is therefore also a call to prioritize analysis of Du Bois's contradictory and unsustained work on gender and sexuality, lest the opportunity to recognize this work as a black feminist touchstone be missed. And, not least, it is a reminder that black feminism constitutes a major if not always recognized contribution to the black radical tradition of which Du Bois is often regarded as a progenitor—and more

specifically still as a contribution to the black Marxist tradition that has
consistently been construed by male scholars as male and as originat-
ing with Du Bois and C. L. R. James, among others.

Although black feminist texts treated here do not directly cite *Black
Reconstruction*, each robustly engages the central concepts that animate Du Bois's story of the implosion of slavery, the outbreak of the
Civil War, and the unfinished project of emancipation. Each implicitly
develops the idea of the general strike of slaves against slavery as the
motor of modern history, while in the process recalibrating to expressly
feminist ends Du Boisian insights about gendered insurgency and historical methodology. Like Du Bois, black feminists recognized that
how one tells the story of the past transforms what counts as historical
agency and what constitutes historical "truth." Indeed, black feminist
texts collectively proffer a counterhistory or to use Du Bois's term, a
"propaganda of history," that constellates past and present, and, in
the process, expresses a dream about a truly substantive freedom yet
to come.

In reading *Black Reconstruction* in order to raise the question of the
gender of the general strike and, in turn, reading black feminism to
envision a response to this question, I highlight how and why wom-
en's removal of sexual and in vivo reproductive labor and products
(children) from circulation was at one time, and today remains, a revolutionary act that has not been but ought to be understood as part of a
general strike against slavery. For even though Du Bois only fleetingly
casts female slaves as workers who elected to take sexual and reproductive labor power and products out of circulation, when placing *Black
Reconstruction* and black feminism into sustained dialogue, it becomes
clear that slave women's refusal of rape and the work of slave breeding
was central not only to the struggle against slavery in the nineteenth
century but also to conceptualization of struggles against sexual and
reproductive extraction in what Walter Benjamin would call "the time
of the now"—the time of writing and the time of reception.

Given the compendious nature of the story of the transition from
slavery to Civil War and from Civil War to the failures of Reconstruction, it is instructive that Du Bois's discussion of gender and sexuality
almost exclusively appears in the opening chapters of *Black Reconstruction*. These are foundational chapters as they set the stage for Du Bois's
argument about the general strike, and explicitly subtend one of the
book's central claims: the conflicts that erupted under the pressure
of slavery's internal contradictions emerged as a full-blown historical

crisis—the Civil War—a fact that had not been acknowledged by previous historians or, for that matter, by those whom, Du Bois argued,
exploited a falsified history in order to silence the true history of black
revolutionary force. As Cedric Robinson has observed, Du Bois's
recasting of the slave as "the black worker" caught up in the decisive
eruptive moment is a Marxist move, a major innovation on Marxism,
and thus a foundational contribution to black Marxism.[12] In casting
the slave as "the worker," Du Bois retooled the idea of the paid laborer
as the model proletariat and rendered the unpaid, hyperexploited slave
the centerpiece of an expressly black proletariat.[13] In this way, he positioned slavery as key to the operations of global capitalism, and the
Civil War and the crushing of the black revolutionary impulses that
animated it, as the two world historical events that set the stage for
the development of a violent capitalist modernity grounded in human
slavery and the racialized division of the global labor force that we have
today inherited.

And yet, even as he beautifully captures the enormity of Du Bois's
conceptual shift away from traditional Marxist conceptions of history
and historical agency, Robinson is not alert to questions about the
black worker's gender and the reproductive and sexualized aspects of
slave work that *Black Reconstruction* poses in the same opening chapters that he regards as foundational. Despite Du Bois's discussion of
women slaves and their gender specific refusal of slave work, Robinson
describes the black worker about whom Du Bois writes as presump-
tively ungendered, or, perhaps more aptly, he reifies the implicit
masculinity of the traditional Marxist category by omitting discussion
of Du Bois's gendering of the category in the opening chapters of *Black
Reconstruction*. Thus, while I necessarily build on Robinson's insights
into Du Bois's contributions to black Marxism, I also find it necessary
to bring into view that which Robinson does not: Du Bois's inconsistent and unsustained, but, nonetheless, enormously consequential
attention to slave women's sexual and reproductive work and the significance of slave women's refusal of this work to the outbreak of the Civil
War and the revolution in the relations of production that it catalyzed.

In Du Bois's opening sally, the chapter boldly entitled "The Black
Worker," he acknowledges the centrality of the self-production of
"real-estate" to the system of slavery, and the varied ways in which
forced sex and reproduction subtended the reproduction of the relations of production within slavery. He explains, "Human slavery in the
South pointed and led in two singularly contradictory and paradoxical

directions—toward the deliberate commercial breeding and sale of
human labor for profit and toward the intermingling of black and white
blood. The slaveholders shrank from acknowledging either set of facts
but they were clear and undeniable" (11). When Du Bois goes on to
discuss the role of rape in the "deliberate commercial breeding" of
new slaves, he emphasizes the instrumental value of sexual violence
in the perpetuation of the slave economy. Finally, when he discusses
runaways as historical agents protesting the conditions of their labor
(and thus as figures that prefigure the revolutionary agency he will subsequently discuss in his pivotal chapter on the general strike), two of
the three fugitives whom he identifies are female. This singling out
of slave women who ran away is noteworthy. As Du Bois knew, historical consensus was (and remains) that slave men were more able
and likely to run. Slave women, uniquely constrained by familial duties
and ties to children, were compelled to consider their actions in view
of motherhood—electing whom to leave behind or take along—and
thus to negotiate maternity as the condition of and context for action.
Apparently Du Bois regarded slave women, even when operating under
conditions of constricted mobility, as active insurgents.

The chapter entitled "The Planter" follows shortly after "The Black
Worker," and together with the latter sets up the opposition of forces that
animate the overarching narrative that conveys the book's argument as a
whole.[14] In this chapter focused on white plantation owners, Du Bois's
consideration of the gendered and sexualized dynamics of enslavement
intensifies. In a passage on the slave home, for instance, he examines
the impact on the structure of slave families of slave women's labor in
the fields and thus away from young children, imagining the destabili-
zation of family bonds and the insecurity and vulnerability of children
that women's separation from children produced (40). Relatedly, he considers the emotional toll on women of being forced to birth and raise
"slaves . . . for systematic sale on the commercialized cotton plantations"
(41), those on which, he argues, reproductive exploitation was especially
intensive and forced separation of families most pervasive.

While in each of these instances Du Bois expressly attends to the
gender-specific conditions of work and the impact of women's work
on slaves' intimate, familial, and psychic lives, it is ultimately when he
imagines the toll that was taken by planter violence *on planter men*
that he finally conceptualizes the gendered and sexualized violence
to which slave women were subjected as the catalyst of the crisis that
brought down the system of slavery tout court. When planters sought to

increase surplus by further exploiting workers, Du Bois observes, they routinely employed productive *and* reproductive forms of exploitation. They increased crops and profits by acquiring land, and they took up the lash to force all workers to increase their productivity. Simultaneously they increased surplus by engineering enslaved women's rate of reproduction of human commodities through explicit orchestration of sexual and reproductive violence. As Du Bois makes plain, the planter's "only effective economic movement . . . could take place against the slave. He was forced, unless willing to take lower profits, continually to beat down the cost of slave labor. . . . One method called for more land and the other for more slaves" (41). While planters "surrounded it with certain secrecy, and it was exceedingly bad taste for any . . . planter to have it indicated that he was deliberately raising slaves for sale . . . that was a fact. . . . A laboring stock was deliberately bred for legal sale" (42–43). Du Bois concludes by noting that these "plain facts" were "persistently denied" by planters. Because planters "could not face the fact of Negro women as brood mares and of black children as puppies"—because the system they had created "so affronted the moral sense of the planters themselves that they tried to hide from it" (43)—they shamefacedly responded to their intimate involvement and speculative investment in slave breeding with forms of disavowal that found expression in the violence that they directed toward enslaved women and toward the children whom these women bore for and often to them.

Du Bois's subsequent lament about the "sexual chaos that arose from [the] economic motives" (44) that characterized plantation life exhibits his understanding of slave women's particular exploitation and his all-too-familiar bourgeois concern with what he calls here and elsewhere in his writings the lack of a "bar to illegitimacy" (44), which was, in his view, the slave breeding system's correlate.[15] As his moral ire surfaces, in other words, it undercuts the feminist possibility that is embedded within the analysis that precedes it. And yet, undercutting duly noted, what comes before—Du Bois's account of sexual and reproductive exploitation as the foundation of the interstate slave trade—remains of utmost importance. The fact remains, Du Bois's argument in his book's foundational chapter on planter-slave relations is built on an account of the sexual and reproductive exploitation that enslaved women endured at the hands of planters. The upshot: through its implicit teleological movement Du Bois's historical narrative emphasizes, even as it forecloses, sexual and reproductive exploitation's centrality to the profitability of slavery. It underscores, even as it undercuts, the fact that the antagonism between planters and enslaved women was part and parcel of the antagonism between black workers and planters that led to the eruption of the internal contradictions of slavery and, in turn, to the Civil War. And although Du Bois never expresses it thus, when taken to its logical conclusion his narrative suggests that when the slave system's internal contradictions reached their breaking point, the crisis precipitated ought to be understood, at least in part, as a consequence of enslaved women's revolt against planters' gendered and sexualized violence—as a strike against the world that the planters created with and through their female slaves, through their exploitation of enslaved women's sexuality and in vivo reproductive labor, and through commodification of the children born to slave women and thus, following the law of *partus sequitur ventrem*, born into slavery.

In the recursive historical rhythm of Du Bois's book (it moves from antagonism to revolt, from revolt to crisis, from crisis to entrenchment, and then again to antagonism), the gendered and sexualized reproductive conflicts and contradictions that are constitutive of the narrative at the outset go missing from the story of the Civil War and Reconstruction that eventually unfolds. The unfortunate consequence of this is that Du Bois's pivotal chapter, "The General Strike" (which immediately follows that on the planter), evacuates the account of reproductive and sexual work and the account of gendered and sexualized conflict that he initially offered in the preceding chapters that I have discussed, those on the black worker and the planter. When discussing the general strike, slaves emerge as black workers, but these workers are no longer differentiated by gender. Likewise slaves who are variously described throughout this chapter as "swelling," "flooding," and "swarming" Union troops (64–65), as withdrawing their labor from plantations, as sabotaging the production of surplus value through labor stoppages, and as stanching the supply of food to plantations and Union troops, are virtually all characterized as male.[16] Consequently when Du Bois arrives at the apex of his argument and asserts that the black worker, now fully transformed into an insurgent member of a black proletariat, was not "merely . . . . [expressing] the desire to stop work," but rather that "*it* [the Civil War] was a strike on a wide basis against the conditions of work" (67), these conditions are unselfconsciously stripped of the gender-differentiated labor processes and of the reproductive and sexualized forms of exploitation that Du Bois had, up until this crucial point in his argument, vividly if fleetingly remarked upon.

For readers immersed in the story the gendered and sexualized antagonism between the black worker and the planter, Du Bois's discussion
of the general strike signals an abrupt narrative break. It also marks
the presence of a profound conceptual aporia. Suddenly slave work
has been reduced to the slave's production of agricultural commodities. But what about the production of those other, fleshy raw materials
that Du Bois had posited as essential to the reproduction and thus the
continued existence of the slave economy? What of the black workers
whom he had, until this crucial point in his argument, recognized as
those who reproduced human commodities for sale on the interstate
market? In short, how can we account for the disappearance of reproductive workers, in vivo reproductive labor, and its products (human
chattel) from the discussion of the general strike? In unselfconsciously
foreclosing on an answer to these queries, Du Bois's account of the general strike inaugurates an exquisite experience of the narrative opening
and, simultaneously, of narrative deferral. The question of slave wom-
en's reproductive and sexual labor infuses the story that precedes that
on the strike—those chapters that are devoted to the gendered crisis
that produces the general strike. And yet when Du Bois treats the strike
itself, the female slave as a singular figure, and reproductive and sexual
work as part of the general work that was performed by black workers
as a collectivity, is no longer anywhere in evidence. Where a gender-
differentiated black mass once momentarily stood, a masculinized
labor force assumes its place. Where sexual and reproductive labor was
previously acknowledged as gendered labor, it is subsumed within the
exclusively "productive" category of slave work.

The textual aporia that remains results from unexamined textual jux-
tapositions and interrupted narrative momentum. And it necessarily
begs a series of essential but too often unasked questions about the
gendered historiography of slavery and about historical epistemology
more generally: How might our understanding of the history of slavery,
the Civil War, and Reconstruction be transformed by consideration of
slave women as participants in a general strike against slavery? How
might slave women's protest of the conditions of their reproductive and
sexual work and the forms that such protest took be more fully imagined? What alternative genres and narrative idioms lend themselves to
exploration of slave women's membership in the mass of black workers that took their labor out of circulation in the process of waging
war? What alternative narrative and historiographic approaches would
enable imagination of slave women's withdrawal of their sexual and

reproductive labor, and thus of their contribution to "wide scale protest against the conditions of work"? And, finally, how should concepts such as "work," "worker," and "class consciousness" be reconceived and thus rendered responsive to the question of the gender of the general strike?

As I have argued thus far, the general strike is an invaluable heuristic device that can be used to study enslaved reproduction and the impact of slave women's refusal of sexual and reproductive extraction. However, as already suggested at the outset, in the present moment, historical intervention into the account of the slave past is neither the only nor the most pressing reason to excavate and reprise the question of the gender of the general strike. Today we must write the intellectual genealogy of this question and attempt to answer it because this question not only compels constellation of past and present and it also enables us to *imagine* a relationship between slave women's protest of the conditions of their sexual and reproductive work in the past and the struggle against contemporary biocapitalism that might yet take place were reproductive laborers, individually and collectively, to refuse the extraction of their reproductive labor and products. Put otherwise, the challenge posed by my return to *Black Reconstruction* is not solely about creation of a gendered supplement to dominant historiography. In the spirit of *Black Reconstruction*, the challenge also lies in reconceptualization of the slave past in the present and for a future that lies in the balance. Though new "facts" about women in slavery are always welcome, it is incorporation of counterhistories and unverifiable truths that recalibrate received understandings of the relationship between past and present that are urgently needed.[17] While it may be impossible to know with absolute empirical certainty what a general strike inclusive of women's refusal of sexual and reproductive extraction looked like in, say, 1861, we can nonetheless grasp the political urgency of being able to imagine such a strike in the present. Better yet, we can grasp the importance of imagining such a strike when we seek to respond to a yet-to-arrive crisis in the mode of reproduction that is being ushered in by contemporary iterations of both racial capitalism and biocapitalism.

## "The Propaganda of History" and the Rise of Black Feminism

"The Propaganda of History" is perhaps the only chapter of *Black Reconstruction* that is as often cited by scholars as "The General Strike." In this treatise on the politics of the Civil War and Reconstruction historiography, Du Bois offers a searing two-pronged critique of how "the facts of American history have in the last half century been falsified because the nation was ashamed" (711), and of how such falsified "facts" have contributed to the perpetuation of both a racist national formation and a racist global division of labor.[18] In producing this critique, Du Bois crystalizes *Black Reconstruction*'s twinned agendas: (1) refutation of the long history of the "scandalous white historiography" of the Civil War and its aftermath, and (2) demonstration, through analysis of both the promise and the failure of Reconstruction, of historiography's role in the legitimation of Jim Crow, American imperialism, colonial domination, and a corresponding racial division of the global labor force predicated on exploitation of those whom Du Bois had, for several decades, taken to describing as "the darker peoples of the world."[19]

In not only casting white historiography as propaganda but also in suggesting that all historians are implicated in a contest over historical "truth," Du Bois situated historical narratives, his own included, as necessarily presentist.[20] As he explained, the historian must not only correct the record, but ideally, he (*sic*) ought to ring changes on the meaning of "propaganda" through the production of accounts of the past that have the capacity to catalyze a more liberated future. To this end, *Black Reconstruction* exemplifies the methodology it proposes, demonstrating what its title announces. It is a *black (re)construction* of white supremacist history that is also a form of counterhistory or a "propaganda of history" to use Du Bois's own turn of phrase. Black Reconstruction produces the "truth" of the historical narrative that it adumbrates as it mobilizes this narrative in and for the project of black liberation from racial capitalism and white racial nationalism in its moment of writing. As already discussed, one of the central "truths" *Black Reconstruction* proffers is that slaves were black workers and slaves en masse agents of human emancipation. But what of the other historical truths that press for a hearing when the question of the gender of the general strike is raised to the fore?

It is here that black feminism enters. Black feminism elaborates a unique, future-oriented response to the question of the gender of the general strike. In so doing it approaches the aporia that Du Bois's attenuated discussion of the gender-specific contributions of female slaves leaves in its wake. It treats this aporia not only as a textual absence but also as an imaginative possibility—as a call for feminist counterhistory, for a *feminist* propaganda of history that insistently imagines enslaved women's agency as well as the epistemological and political significance of slave women's past insurgency in the context of the present moment of black feminist writing and the transformations in the reproduction of the relations of production to which the contemporary reader bears witness. Though I might draw upon numerous texts in limning the cultural, political, and activist horizon that I short-hand "black feminism," I turn first to two written in the 1970s that explicitly treat slave women's protest of reproductive and sexual exploitation while simultaneously imagining the importance of slave women's insurgency in and for women in the present moment of writing. As we shall see, these early historiographical interventions set the stage for the outpouring of black feminist fiction that constitutes the apogee of the black feminist response to the question of the gender of the general strike and to the rise of biocapitalism.

"Reflections on the Black Woman's Role in the Community of Slaves" (1971) is, to my knowledge, the first publication to argue expressly for the centrality of slave women's day-to-day resistance to slavery. In this polemical article, which first appeared in the *Black Scholar*, Angela Davis posits domestic life in the slave quarters as the primary site of sustained slave insurgency against the system of slavery. Originally written while Davis was in prison as part of an unfinished exchange with fellow Black Panther, George Jackson, Davis's article takes aim at the neglected history of slave women and at the figure of the so-called black matriarch that, at the time of her writing, formed the basis for negative public perception and punitive policy on the black family, especially in the wake of Senator Daniel Patrick Moynihan's infamous report.[21]

Building on *Black Reconstruction*'s revisionist project, Davis corrects the historical record somewhat unconventionally. Making clear to the reader that her concern is excavation of the slave past in the interest of illumination of the present, she observes, "The matriarchal black woman has repeatedly been invoked as one of the fatal by-products of slavery. . . . An accurate portrait of the African woman in bondage must debunk the myth of the matriarchate. Such a portrait must simultaneously attempt to illuminate the historical matrix of her oppression and must evoke her varied, often heroic response to the slaveholder's domination" (4). In refuting the myth of the black matriarch "at its presumed historical inception" (3), Davis first moves to defamiliarize the dominant historical account of slave rebellion and resistance. On the one hand, she unsettles the notion (which, she observes, male scholars, black and white alike, too often hold) that black women "actively assented" to slavery and related to "the slave holding class as collaborators" (4).[22] On the other hand, she submits the unprecedented thesis that it was, "by virtue of the brutal force of circumstances . . . [that] the black woman," as opposed to the black man, "was assigned the mission of promoting the consciousness and practice of [slave] resistance" (5).

Davis offers two interrelated arguments for the black woman's exceptional centrality to slave resistance. Domestic space was the site of resistance because it was at the greatest distance from slaveholders' reach: "Of necessity . . . [the slave] community would revolve around the realm which was furthermost removed from the immediate arena of domination. It could only be located in and around the living quarters, the area where the basic needs of physical life were met" (6). In ministering to the needs of men and children, she continues, slave women performed "the *only* labor of the slave community which could not be directly and immediately claimed by the oppressor." It was thus "only in domestic life . . . away from the eyes and whip of the overseer . . . [that] slaves could . . . assert . . . freedom" (6). Whereas previous accounts of slave resistance had focused on documented rebellions and revolts, Davis (following in the footsteps of social historians such as Herbert Gutman and John Blassingame) highlights the quotidian: "if domestic labor was the only meaningful labor for the slave community as a whole" (7), she reasons, then slave women's labor not only "increased the total incidence of anti-slavery assaults" but ought to be viewed as the "barometer indicating the overall potential for [slave] resistance" (15). Contra Du Bois, who had lamented slave women's inability to do the care work involved in social and cultural reproduction, Davis expressly regards slave women's "domestic work" as the source of not only individual but also of community sustenance and resistance.

Davis's arguments have been challenged. Some have queried her ideas about the existence of "domestic space" on plantations and her emphasis on women's role within it. Others have taken issue with a perhaps misplaced attribution of "agency" to those whose ability to act was so heavily circumscribed. Yet in creating a dialogue between *Black Reconstruction* and black feminism that integrates both into the long history of black Marxist critique of racial capitalism, it is ultimately unnecessary to adjudicate whether Davis got it "right" or "wrong." Rather, in the spirit of Davis's project, I suggest that we instead historicize it, effectively reading her article as a context-specific response to the question of the gender of the general strike, and, more important

still, as a specifically black Marxist *feminist* response to the question
of the gender of the general strike that insists on *imagining* the importance of slave women's role in this strike in the present moment of
Davis's writing.[23]

Davis pushes readers toward recognition of her *imaginative* project by acknowledging her scholarly shortcomings, engaging potential
objections to her argument, and delineating the political gains that may
be obtained by electing to forge ahead despite both. She notes, "No
extensive and systematic study of the role of black women in resisting slavery has come to my attention," and yet there is great "urgency
to undertake a thorough study of the black woman as anti-slavery
rebel" (9). In prison, without ready access to archives and sources, she
knows she can offer neither an in-depth nor a complete study. Instead,
she explains, she has decided to provide "a portrait of the *potential
and possibilities* inherent in the situation to which slave women were
anchored" (14, emphasis added). In prying a story of the gender of the
general strike from available sources, in other words, in working with
and against the few historiographical works at her disposal, Davis does
not seek to prove but rather to *imagine* that slave women's resistance
was central to the downfall of slavery. By imagining slave women's
resistance she frees herself to explore how knowledge of past insurgency and agency might impact black women's liberation and the black
liberation movement's engagement with the question of black women's
freedom present and future.

Given Davis's strategy, it is unsurprising when she rapidly exhausts
her discussion of women's participation in slave revolts as these were
documented in the existing scholarship to which she had access (her
discussion is almost entirely gleaned from an against-the-grain reading
of Herbert Aptheker's 1943 classic, *American Negro Slave Revolts*) and
concedes that in order to show that slave women's insurgent response
to "counter-insurgency [is] not as extravagant as it might seem" (8), it
is necessary for her to build the argument for existence of slave wom-
en's insurgency from a new starting place.[24] In order to reveal "the
black woman as anti-slavery rebel" (9), she will not restrict herself to
the project of mining available historiographical accounts but will also
imagine the gendered "insurgency" that evoked the principal form of
"counter-insurgency" to which slave women were routinely subjected
by planters: rape.

Davis's argument that rape is *counterinsurgency* and that women's
resistance to rape is a major form of *insurgency* transforms her essay

into counterhistory—indeed, not just a propaganda of history but rather *the* propaganda of history that paves the way for future black feminist responses to the Du Boisian question of the gender of the general strike. Turning her attention away from "open battles," from organized acts of rebellion, Davis focuses instead on individual, intimate acts of resistance that might not be evident in available archives and the scholarship based on them. Such quotidian acts, Davis *imagines*, were the resistant reality lived by the majority of enslaved women. As she explains, "The oppression of slave women had to assume dimensions of open counter-insurgency" (12). In rape and forced reproduction, "the slave woman" must have "felt the edge of this counter-insurgency [the master's] as a fact of her daily existence" (12). Routine acts of sexual aggression are for Davis "terrorist methods designed to dissuade other black women from following the examples of their [insurgent] sisters" (12). Making recourse to the conditional tense—and thus calling attention to the politically imperative (as opposed to factually grounded) nature of her conclusions—Davis specifies, "The act of copulation, reduced by the white man to an animal-like act *would* be symbolic of the effort to conquer the resistance the black woman *could* unloose. In confronting the black woman as adversary in a sexual contest, the master *would* be subjecting her to the most elemental form of terrorism distinctively suited for the female" (13, emphasis added). Having introduced the idea of slave women's insurgency as a self-evident historical "truth" (as opposed to "fact"), and having predicated the existence of this "truth" on the then controversial claim that planters routinely raped slaves, Davis brilliantly concludes that slave women routinely *provoked* and *countered* planters' counterinsurgency.

The power of Davis's argument resides in its ability to fold the reader's knowledge of the "truth" in on itself and then to convert this knowledge into felt (as opposed to documented) evidence of women's resistance to slavery. From one perspective, Davis argues, women's and men's productive labor was exploited; from another perspective (one that prefigures subsequent work on the paradoxical ungendering of slave women),[25] women's resistance to exploitation must be understood as a response to sexual and reproductive exploitation. By "reestablish[ing] her femaleness by reducing her to the level of her *biological* being," the master directly "attack[ed] . . . the black female as a potential insurgent" whose resistance to domination ought thus to be simultaneously recognized as specifically female and as part and parcel of the general strike against slavery (13). Davis concludes, "Countless black women did not passively submit to these abuses, as the slaves in general refused to passively accept their bondage. The struggles of the slave woman . . . were a continuation of the resistance interlaced in the slaves' daily existence" (14).

Whereas Du Bois had positioned *Black Reconstruction* as a critique of white supremacist historiography, as counterhistory or propaganda possessing the power to restore agency to black workers and to their descendants struggling to live in and live through Jim Crow, Davis positions her contribution as a critique of the prevailing masculinist historiography of slavery possessing the power to restore agency to slave women and their descendants in the early 1970s. Davis's slave woman is not the emasculating matriarch of the *Moynihan Report*; she is a sexually and reproductively oppressed black worker whose gendering by the master class is meted out as sexualized violence against her (re) productive body. Neither victim nor aggressor in any simple sense, she is an activated member of a striking collectivity whose contribution to the larger struggle against slavery is expressed through individual, often intimate acts of rebellion that directly target the sexualized and reproductive conditions of (re)production—the hyperexploitative conditions responsible for maintenance of the entire system of slavery, especially after the closure of the transatlantic slave trade in 1807. After dispensing with the *Moynihan Report* ("a dastardly ideological weapon designed to impair our capacity for resistance by foisting upon us the ideal of male supremacy" [14]), Davis offers a final appeal to readers (especially "us" black women), to whom she has demonstrated, as had Du Bois before her, that the history of slavery matters in the present and for the future.

While historians rarely cite Davis's article, presumably because they regard it as too undisciplined and politicized, most feminist historians of slavery have nonetheless entered the conversation that Davis initiated. In 1979, for instance, Darlene Clark Hine challenged the then dominant focus of slavery studies, implicitly following Davis in calling for study of the sexual economy of slavery.[26] In her article "Female Slave Resistance: The Economics of Sex," Hine focuses on "black female resistance to slavery" by not only positing enslaved women as insurgent (as had Davis) but also by examining the specific "means through which female slaves expressed their political and economic opposition to the slave system" (123). Delineating three "intimately related forms of resistance"—sexual abstinence, abortion, and infanticide—Hine argues that women's resistance to sexual and reproductive exploitation

contributed to the overthrow of the slave system: when "they resisted
sexual exploitation . . . [when they] reject[ed] their vital economic function as breeders," she observes, female slaves rejected their "role in
the economic advancement of the slave system," effectively undermin-
ing the "master's effort to profit from [female slaves] . . . by exploiting
[them] sexually." Such resistance to sexual and reproductive exploitation, Hine concludes, though private and individualized, had "major
political and economic implications" (126).

Although it is beyond the scope of this essay to treat the numerous
contributions made by black feminist historians in the 1970s, 1980s
and 1990s, suffice it to say that Davis's and Hine's watershed articles are representative of a wide, multivoice black feminist response
to the question of the gender of the general strike that was added to
by Deborah Gray White, Nell Irvin Painter, Paula Giddings, Kathleen
Thompson, and a subsequent generation of scholars that includes
Mia Bay, Stephanie Camp, Sharla Fett, Thavolia Glymph, and Jennifer Morgan, among others. What brings this black feminist work into
dialogue with *Black Reconstruction* is the way it expands upon one of
Du Bois's most unconventional ideas. As Cedric Robinson eloquently
expresses it, in *Black Reconstruction* Du Bois shows us that slaves need
not have been either consciously or collectively organized in the traditional Marxist sense to have made history.[27] Black feminists writing
about women in slavery implicitly concur that slave women's strikes
against sexual and reproductive bondage, though not necessarily consciously or collectively organized, nonetheless possessed profound
revolutionary force. In resisting sexual assault, committing infanticide, and/or aborting unwanted pregnancies, women refused their work
as sex slaves and as breeders and thus refused to participate in the
reproduction of the slave system and in the reproduction of the human
commodities that sustained it. From the vantage point that has been
provided by black feminist historians of slavery, it becomes possible to
comprehend that the "work" performed by "the black worker" of whom
Du Bois wrote involved sexual and in vivo reproductive labor as well
as productive agricultural and domestic labor. And while there may be
no way to empirically verify the extent to which slave women's individual, intimate acts of refusal contributed to the black workers' collective
overthrow of slavery, the existence and persistence of planter counter-
insurgency in the form of rape must itself be recognized as an excellent
index of the impact that slave women's sexual and reproductive insurgency must have continuously exerted.[28]

## The Reproduction of Freedom

Both alongside of and then in the wake of the production of the non-fiction discussed thus far, black feminist writers of fiction pushed at the limits of the conventions of historical narrative, not only to produce counterhistory but also to differently and perhaps more accessibly explore the role of imagination in black feminism's engagement with the past. Creating what some literary critics have come to call "neo-slave narratives," these writers imagined the experience of bondage from the vantage point of slave women, utilizing the latitude offered by fiction to enter the battle over historical "truth" while at the same time sidestepping many of the thorny questions that historians have raised about archive and interpretation. While male authors also participated (and in some accounts of the genre, invented it), black women's contributions arguably comprise the genre's dominant and most distinct formation.[29] On the one hand, black women writers have contested the masculinism of the stories told about slavery by centralizing enslaved women and their children. On the other hand, as they have produced fiction that exposes the sexism of the historiography of slavery and a black male literary canon alike, they have materialized the power of works of creative imagination to inaugurate a new propaganda of history. Improvising on earlier feminist historiographical work, black feminist writers of fiction offered alternative methodological and epistemological responses to the question of the gender of the general strike, thus effectively entering the ongoing dialogue with *Black Reconstruction* in yet another black feminist idiom.

Short stories and especially novels focused on women slavery—including those by Octavia Butler, Lorene Cary, Michelle Cliff, J. California Cooper, Nalo Hopkinson, Gayle Jones, Toni Morrison, Alice Walker, and Sherley Anne Williams, to name some of the most well-known—thematize, *without exception*, the experience of motherhood in bondage, and thus slave women's experiences of sexual and reproductive exploitation, as well as their refusal of their labor as sex slaves and breeders. Daring to imagine—again, *without exception*—what existing archives cannot fully reveal, these writers describe how individual women took sexual and reproductive labor and products out of circulation, and they explore how women and children understood, felt about, and were materially impacted by such actions. As important, insofar as these writers tell stories about women who recode, as they appropriate, sexual and reproductive labor and its products, bestowing on both new meaning, they guide readers toward comprehension of the relationship between the slave past and the present moment of writing—and ultimately toward comprehension of the relationship between slavery and the forms of extraction that characterize the biocapitalist world out of which black feminist writers of neo-slave narratives emerged, in which they wrote, and to which they necessarily if not always self-consciously responded.

Elsewhere I offer close readings of several black feminist neo-slave narratives and in this way fully concretize the present argument.[30] In the space of this short essay, I conclude by offering a provisional sketch of the literary terrain that underscores two of the primary characteristics of black feminist neo-slave narratives: each moves backward into slavery; and each moves forward into the present moment of textual production. In this way each effectively time-travels, animating a bridge between two of the most significant periods in racial capitalist and biocapitalist expansion—those that I argued at the outset of this essay ought to be regarded as the two periods in modern history during which women's in vivo reproductive labor was (and in the case of the present, continues to be) engineered for profit.

In the 1970s Gayl Jones and Octavia Butler presented fictional portraits of black women struggling to interrupt the intergenerational cycles of slavery's reproduction by questioning their own participation in them and, through struggle, shifting if never shattering the hold of the past on the supposedly emancipated present. In Jones's *Corregidora*, a novel published in the wake of the Supreme Court's passage of *Roe v. Wade* and the emergence of a women of color reproductive justice movement, the protagonist, Ursa, wrests control of her reproductive life from the various men who attempt to possess her sexuality and reproduction and, in the process, overdetermine her relationship to her family's slave past. Specifically Ursa's repossession of her body and bodily processes involves her recoding of violently imposed infertility— her transformation of her "barrenness" into an embodied revision of three generations of rape, incest, and forced fecundity as experienced by her female forebears. As Jones details, Ursa's repeated refusal to "make generations" and her repetition, with a difference, of a passed-on story of sexual and reproductive exploitation strengthens as it reworks Ursa's connection to her grandmother and great-grandmother, each of whom had reproduced a girl-child that was subsequently impregnated by her father-master. Straddling the past of slavery and her present through song, Ursa emerges as a phonic time-traveler whose art form replaces childbirth with vocalization. In short, *Corregidora* responds to the question of the gender of the general strike in the form of a manifesto for freedom from reproductive and sexual exploitation that is articulated by Jones and her protagonist in the idiom of the blues.

In Butler's watershed novel, *Kindred*, another time-traveling protagonist, Dana, drives the narrative as she moves between 1970s Los Angeles and a nineteenth-century Maryland plantation on which her ancestors, black and white, reside. Dana appears to be pulled across time by a compulsion to save her slave-owning forefather and, at once, to ensure that he fathers her enslaved foremother. In a story focused on the complexity of obtaining "freedom" in either 1976 (the ironically symbolic year in which the novel opens) or during the height of plantation slavery (when the novel is set), it is imperative to underscore that securing her existence (literally her birth) requires Dana to manipulate the reproductive life of an enslaved woman, Alice, who she believes to be her great-great-grandmother. In this sense, Dana's present "freedom" is predicated on exploitation of an enslaved woman and, more particularly still, on Dana's facilitation of the master's sexual and reproductive (ab)use of her own female kin.

While available scholarship on *Kindred* has mainly focused on Dana, it is imperative to grant her progenitor, Alice, as much if not greater attention. For when we read the novel as a response to the question of the gender of the general strike, it is on Alice's repeated, desperate refusal of enslaved sex and reproduction that we must focus if we hope to understand the space of resistance to slavery that Butler's imagines within the claustrophobic confines of the nineteenth century slave world depicted in her novel.[31] As Butler details, Alice battles to choose her lover (and then she battles against his violent murder by her master); she protests her sexual enslavement by her master; she fights against loss of control over her children; and, finally, she responds to her children's removal by taking her body out of sexual and reproductive use, once and for all, by committing suicide. While we should not naively redeem Alice's suicide as an unmitigated "success," her act of violent refusal must be recognized as an instance of insurgency, one that exists along a continuum of multiple forms of slave women's withdrawal from circulation of their reproductive and sexual labor. Indeed, all of Alice's acts against the sexual and reproductive conditions of work on the plantation on which she resides ought to be understood as expressly gendered contributions to the general strike against slavery.

Significantly, in the year prior to *Kindred*'s publication the successful and healthy birth of the first so-called test-tube baby, Louise Brown, by in vitro fertilization (IVF) was widely reported in the international press. As Butler completed her novel the ethics of biotechnological engineering of human reproduction burst into public consciousness through intensive media coverage of the event—the birth of the "Baby of the Century"—and academic scrutiny. As was clear from the outset, the advent of IVF revolutionized reproductive medicine and opened new lucrative markets. The fertilization of eggs outside the body allowed women to be impregnated with genetic materials to which they were unrelated and it made it possible for women to sell their reproductive labor and thus to work as egg vendors, human incubators, and gestational surrogates. Perhaps unsurprisingly, shortly after Louise Brown's birth the market in surrogate labor took off, as did markets for the array of assisted reproductive technologies that would soon enable gestational surrogates (today the primary type of surrogate laborers) to gestate for payment life comprised of entirely unrelated genetic materials, and thus to (re)produce children thought to "belong" to others. As the celebrated doctors of reproductive medicine, Robert Edwards and Patrick Steptoe, raced to develop the technique that would result in Louise Brown's birth, Butler, alongside other black feminists, catalyzed an outpouring of black feminist fiction about sex and reproduction in bondage that would continue unabated for nearly three decades— the same three decades that have witnessed the rise of the newly (re) formed biocapitalist economy.

By the 1980s, when black women's production of neo-slave narratives reached its apex, public and scholarly outcry over various forms of reproductive exploitation and the emergence of ever-expanding forms of commodification of the human reproductive process, body, and bodily products was loud and insistent. In 1986, when U.S. surrogate mother Mary Beth Whitehead publicly breached contract and refused to turn her baby over to the couple for whom she worked, Whitehead became a household name and the so-called Baby M case an object of academic study. As feminist activists and scholars sought to understand the emergence of a surrogate industry powered by new reproductive technologies, they launched a series of sustained arguments against baby selling, against the commodification of reproductive labor and children, and against the emergence of a racialized class of hyperexploited, impoverished breeders who, they forecast, would increasingly be used to reproduce designer children for those able to pay the price.[32]

For some, surrogacy revealed that reproductive labor is uncannily similar to other forms of productive labor offered for sale.[33] For others surrogacy was thought to be akin not only to other forms of wage slavery but also to the practice of slave breeding and the long history of chattel slavery that it subtended. As Angela Davis observed in an article written in view of the Baby M case, the historical parallels between motherhood in late capitalism and slavery run in two temporal directions:

> The reproductive role imposed upon African slave women bore no relationship to the subjective project of motherhood. . . . Slave women were *birth mothers* or *genetic mothers*—to employ terms rendered possible by the new reproductive technologies—but they possessed no legal rights as mothers, of any kind. Considering the commodification of their children—indeed, of their own persons—their status was similar to that of the contemporary surrogate mother.[34]

According to Davis, surrogacy and the conceptual terminology that it ushered in alter our understanding of the slave past and vice versa: "The term surrogate mother might be invoked as a retroactive description of . . . [slave women's] status because the economic appropriation of their reproductive capacity reflected the inability of the slave economy to produce and reproduce its own laborers" (212). Conversely, Davis concludes, "while the new technological developments have rendered the fragmentation of maternity more obvious [than it has been in the past], the economic system of slavery fundamentally relied upon alienated and fragmented maternities, as women were forced to bear children, whom masters claimed as potentially profitable machines" (213).

Davis's final point is salutary and I wish to expand on it. Surrogacy and the rise of the reproductive economy that it signaled are directly connected to slavery not because contemporary surrogacy is today performed exclusively by black women who are the descendants of slaves, or even because it is performed by women of color located in the Global South (although this is increasingly the case).[35] Rather surrogacy must be understood as inextricably bound up with four hundred years of slave racial capitalism because it is the slave episteme that powered slavery that powers reproductive extraction in the context of contemporary biocapitalism, rendering it conceivable in both senses of that heavily laden term. Put otherwise, surrogacy and slavery must be constellated because the slave episteme enables conceptualization and materialization of reproductive extraction in contemporary biocapitalism.

So many black feminist fictions about reproduction in bondage appeared alongside the growth of the surrogate and reproductive technology industries throughout the 1980s and 1990s that it is possible to engage only the most obvious one here. Crucially, though it is too often forgotten in criticism on Toni Morrison's *Beloved*, the fictionalized story of Margaret Garner's escape with her children from slavery and her subsequent murder of her daughter in her effort to save her from recapture by her master is lifted out of the context of slavery and moved by Morrison into the blurred historical horizon of the novel, which, tellingly, encompasses the Civil War and Reconstruction as well as the present moment of Morrison's writing. As Morrison explains in her retrospective 2004 foreword to a new edition of *Beloved*, her invention of her protagonist, Sethe, as a reincarnation of Garner allowed her to plumb the story for what "was historically true in essence, but not strictly factual in order to relate Garner and her world to contemporary issues about freedom, responsibility and women's 'place.'"[36] As Morrison recalls, Garner's story allowed her to meditate on women's "freedom" in the 1980s and thus, she implies, to meditate on the idea of substantive reproductive freedom which was, at that time, being hotly debated by black feminists mobilized against sterilization abuse and the war on poor black mothers (especially "crack moms"), and involved in the loud feminist outcry against the dispossession of surrogates expressed by feminists across the board. In short, even though most literary critics read *Beloved* as an account of one woman's struggle to free her children from slavery, Morrison gives us ample reason to believe that her novel ought also to be understood as an exploration of women's participation in the general strike against reproductive bondage and as a meditation on the politics of women's withdrawal of sexual and reproductive labor and products from circulation in Morrison's own moment of writing. Underscoring the linkage between the slave past and the present moment in which Morrison wrote, Davis invokes *Beloved* as a relevant antecedent to her discussion of surrogacy (212). Although separated by race and time, Garner and Whitehead are connected by their shared subjection to the logic of reproductive extraction precisely because Morrison's novel offers a philosophy of history that constellates the long histories of racial capitalism and contemporary biocapitalism.

In this essay I have suggested that it is imperative to contextualize black feminism of the 1970s, 1980s, and 1990s in its biocapitalist moment of production, publication, and reception, and to recognize black feminism as a response to this context and thus as constituting the philosophy of history that compels us to consider the relevance of slave women's refusal of reproductive extraction in our biocapitalist times. I have placed black feminism within a long black radical tradition and cast it as a sustained response to a question posed but never answered by Du Bois in *Black Reconstruction*, that of the gender of the general strike. Finally, I have argued that black feminism's imagination of the various forms that slave women's participation in the general strike took constitutes an eloquent freedom dream to which we ought to return if we wish to "tap the well of our own collective imaginations" as we imagine how we might resist reproductive extraction in contemporary biocapitalism and, too, a future in which women might yet reproduce "freedom" rather than commodities.

## Notes

An earlier version of this essay first appeared as "Gendering the General Strike: W. E. B. Du Bois's *Black Reconstruction* and Black Feminism's 'Propaganda of History,'" *South Atlantic Quarterly* 112.3 (Summer 2013). Thanks to Duke University Press for permission to reprint portions of the original article.

1. As I argue elsewhere, reproductive extraction would be unthinkable if it were not for the persistence of *the slave episteme*—a thought system that renders extraction of reproductive labor and products from women's bodies imaginable and thus practicable. See Alys Eve Weinbaum, *The Afterlife of Reproductive Slavery: Biocapitalism and Black Feminism's Philosophy of History* (Durham, NC: Duke University Press, 2019).

2. On biocapital see Kaushik Sunder Rajan, *Biocapital: The Constitution of Postgenomic Life* (Durham, NC: Duke University Press, 2006); Melinda Cooper, *Life as Surplus: Biotechnology and Capitalism in the Neoliberal Era* (Seattle: University of Washington Press, 2008); Catherine Waldby and Robert Mitchell, *Tissue Economies: Blood, Organs, and the Cell Lines in Late Capitalism* (Durham, NC: Duke University Press, 2006); Catherine Waldby and Melinda Cooper, *Clinical Labor: Tissue Donors and Research Subjects in the Global Bioeconomy* (Durham, NC: Duke University Press, 2014). Notably, existing scholarship on biocapitalism has not focused on its epistemic relationship to slavery or on slavery as a biocapitalist formation.

3. Marxist feminist analysis explores how traditional Marxist theory has mistakenly subsumed reproduction within production and thus failed to recognize the specific forms of labor performed by women. When women's reproductive labor is unremunerated—as is often the case with domestic work, care work, and the reproduction of human beings—the exploitation of this labor becomes invisible. Extraction of in vivo reproductive labor has always implicitly been part of the Marxist feminist account of labor, but it is only recently that it has been explicitly theorized. See Waldby and Cooper; Kalindi Vora, *Life Support: Biocapital and the New History of Outsourced Labor* (Minneapolis: University of Minnesota Press, 2015).

4. I elect this term in a nod to Walter Benjamin's account of the distinction between materialism and historicism. See "Theses on the Philosophy of History" (1940), in *Illuminations*, translated by Harry Zohn, edited by Hannah Arendt (New York: Schocken Books, 1968), 253–64.

5. See Robin D. G. Kelley, *Freedom Dreams: The Black Radical Imagination* (Boston: Beacon, 2002), xii.

6. The formulation is Sunder Rajan's.

7. See Kimberly Springer, *Living for the Revolution: Black Feminist Organizations 1968–1980* (Durham, NC: Duke University Press, 2005); Deborah Gray White, *Too Heavy a Load: Black Women in Defense of Themselves, 1894–1994* (New York: Norton, 1999); Paula Giddings, *When and Where I Enter: The Impact of Black Women on Race and Sex in America* (New York: William Morrow, 1984).

8. Jennifer Nelson, *Women of Color and the Reproductive Rights Movement* (New York: New York University Press, 2003); Jill Silliman et al., eds., *Undivided Rights: Women of Color Organize for Reproductive Justice* (Boston: South End Press, 2004); Loretta J. Ross and Rickie Solinger, *Reproductive Justice: An Introduction* (Berkeley: University of California Press, 2017).

9. For instance, Grace Kyungwon Hong, *The Ruptures of American Capital: Women of Color Feminism and the Culture of Immigrant Labor* (Minneapolis: University of Minnesota Press, 2006); Roderick A. Ferguson, *Aberrations in Black: Toward a Queer of Color Critique* (Minneapolis: University of Minnesota Press, 2004).

10. W. E. B. Du Bois, *Black Reconstruction in American 1860–1880* (1935), with an introduction by David Levering Lewis (New York: Free Press, 1992); hereafter cited parenthetically.

11. See David Levering Lewis, *W. E. B Du Bois: The Fight for Equality and the American Century, 1919–1963* (New York: Henry Holt, 2000), 267; chapters by Joy James, Hazel Carby, Michele Elam, and Paul C.

Taylor collected in Susan Gillman and Alys Eve Weinbaum, eds., *Next to the Color Line: Gender, Sexuality, and W. E. B. Du Bois* (Minneapolis: University of Minnesota Press, 2007), quotes 209.

12. Robinson regards this as one of black Marxism's foundational moments. See Cedric Robinson, *Black Marxism* (Chapel Hill: University of North Carolina Press, 1983), 199–203; hereafter cited parenthetically.

13. See Cedric Robinson, "A Critique of W. E. B. Du Bois' *Black Reconstruction*," *Black Scholar* 8.7 (1977): 44–50; Robinson, *Black Marxism*, 185–240.

14. Notably a chapter titled "The White Worker" is wedged between "The Black Worker" and "The Planter." The white worker is of course also a key player in the dynamic between workers and masters that *Black Reconstruction* adumbrates. White workers competed with black slaves; however, as Du Bois points out, many also "fought slavery to save democracy"— that is, until they found themselves situated alongside the black worker as fellow victims of "a new and vaster slavery" (17). The failure to realize an alliance between white and black workers and the import of this failure for the foreclosure of the promise of Reconstruction is beyond the scope of the present essay, though it is my hope that the gender politics of this failure might be taken up by others in future.

15. Du Bois writes, "Child-bearing was a profitable occupation that received every possible encouragement, and there was not only no bar to illegitimacy, but an actual premium put upon it. Indeed, the word was impossible of meaning under the slave system" (*Black Reconstruction*, 44).

16. When Du Bois mentions fugitive women, he further undercuts their role in the war by noting that they "accompanied" husbands. Thanks to Thavolia Glymph for clarifying that from the beginning of the conflict black women and their children fled to Union lines without men. Later the Union Army's enlistment of black men as soldiers left wives especially vulnerable, leading to vast numbers of black women among those whom Du Bois characterized as eagerly "swelling" and "swarming" Union troops.

17. On creation of "counter-history" that "can not be verified" and historical narratives that relate "an impossible story," see Saidiya Hartman, "Venus in Two Acts," *small axe* 26 (June 2008): 12.

18. On the distinction between "fact" and "truth," see Toni Morrison, "The Site of Memory," in *Out There: Marginalization and Contemporary Cultures*, ed. Russell Ferguson et al. (Cambridge, MA: MIT Press, 1990). On the distinction between empirical and historical "truth" see Robinson (*Black Marxism*, 44).

19. This is the black internationalist language of both *Darkwater* and *Dark Princess*. For analysis of the manner in which Du Bois's black internationalism of the 1910s and 1920s is gendered and sexualized see Alys Eve Weinbaum, *Wayward Reproductions: Genealogies of Race and Nation in Transatlantic Modern Thought* (Durham, NC: Duke University Press, 2004), 187–226.

20. In his introduction to *Black Reconstruction*, Lewis designates it "propaganda for the people" (xii), observing that it instantiates slaves and former slaves as agents of their own destiny. Also see David Lemert, "The Race of Time: Du Bois and Reconstruction," *Boundary 2* 27.3 (Fall 2000): 215–48.

21. See Angela Davis, "Reflections on the Black Woman's Role in the Community of Female Slaves," *Black Scholar* 12.6 (November–December, 1971): 2–15; hereafter cited parenthetically. The *Black Scholar* reprinted the article in 1981 as part of an issue on "the black woman," and it was subsequently retooled and redacted in Angela Davis, *Women, Race and Class* (New York: Vintage, 1983), 3–29.

22. Davis singles out E. Franklin Frazier for his support of these ideas in *The Negro Family in the United States* (1939). This appears to be one of a handful of texts Davis had on hand. It is worth recalling that Moynihan built his argument out of Frazier's.

23. Quotations from Du Bois in this essay are from *Darkwater* and *Black Reconstruction*.

24. Davis locates in Aptheker's book an account of black women's role in fugitive and maroon communities, as insurgents within plantation households, and as participants in organized rebellions. She laments that if reigning (male) historians would only interpret their findings correctly they would discover that women were not only "the most daring and committed combatants" but also "the custodian[s] of a house of resistance" ("Reflections," 8, 9).

25. See, among others, Hortense J. Spillers, "Mama's Baby, Papa's Maybe: An American Grammar Book," *Diacritics* 17.2 (Summer 1987): 64–81.

26. Hine cites scholarship by field shapers such as Herbert Aptheker, Eugene Genovese, and Winthrop Jordan. Though she does not cite Davis, the solidarity of their projects is evident. See Darlene C. Hine, "Female Slave Resistance: The Economics of Sex," *Western Journal of Black Studies* 3.2 (Summer 1979): 123–27; hereafter cited parenthetically.

27. I follow Robinson's observation that "the general strike had not been planned or centrally organized. Instead, Du Bois termed as a general strike the total impact on the secessionist South of series of actions circumstantially

related to each other. . . . These events were a consequence of contradictions within Southern society rather than a revolutionary vanguard that
knit these phenomena into a historical force." Robinson continues, "With
respect to class consciousness, Du Bois perceived that official Marxism had
reduced this complex phenomenon to a thin political shell consisting of for-
mulae for the dominance of state and/or part of workers' movements. To
resist this tendency, Du Bois sought to reintroduce the dialectic in its Hegelian form as the cunning of reason. No party could substitute itself for the
revolutionary instrument of history: a people moved to action by the social
and material conditions of its existence" ("A Critique," 48, 50).

28. Hine suggests that acts of refusal such as abortion may have been
collaborative, if not collectively organized in the conventional Marxist
sense ("Female Slave Resistance," 125).

29. Novels by Alex Haley, Ishmael Reed, and Charles Johnson have
been cast as precedent-setting texts within the genre. See Ashraf Rushdy,
*Neo-Slave Narratives* (New York: Oxford University Press, 1999). Though
discussion of the genre is beyond this essay's scope, feminist critics have
noted that inclusion within it can be disabling. See, for example, Angelyn
Mitchell, *The Freedom to Remember: Narrative, Slavery and Gender in Contemporary Black Women's Fiction* (New Brunswick, NJ: Rutgers University
Press, 2002); Jenny Sharpe, *Ghosts of Slavery: A Literary Archeology of
Black Women's Lives* (Minneapolis: University of Minnesota Press, 2003).

30. See Weinbaum, *The Afterlife of Reproductive Slavery*; Alys Eve
Weinbaum, "The Afterlife of Slavery and the Problem of Reproductive
Freedom," *Social Text* 115 (Summer 2013): 49–68.

31. For one especially notable exception see Linh U. Hua, "Reproducing Time, Reproducing History: Love and Black Feminist Sentimentality
in Octavia Butler's *Kindred*," *African American Review* 44.3 (Fall 2011):
391–407.

32. Most famously, Gena Corea and members of the activist group
FINNRAGE called for a moratorium on the use of all reproductive tech-
nologies and all forms of baby selling, surrogacy included. See Corea, *The
Mother Machine: Reproductive Technologies from Artificial Insemination to
Artificial Wombs* (New York: Harper and Row, 1985); Rita Arditti, Renate
Duelli Klein, and Shelley Minden eds., *Test-Tube Women: What Future for
Motherhood?* (London: Pandora, 1984).

33. On surrogacy as (re)productive labor the uniqueness of which
is inscribed in and through the maternal body, see Alys Eve Weinbaum,
"Marx, Irigaray, and the Politics of Reproduction," *Differences* 6.1 (1994):
98–128.

34. Angela Davis, "Surrogates and Outcast Mothers: Racism and Reproductive Politics in the 1990s," in *The Angela Y. Davis Reader*, ed. Joy James
(London: Blackwell, 1998), 212; hereafter cited parenthetically.

35. In the 1980s surrogates received roughly $10,000 for raw materials
(eggs), labor power (gestation and birth), and the contracted release of
their progeny. Prices (if not wages) have gone up substantially, and the map
of distribution has shifted. Today many surrogates, located in the Global
South, reproduce children for export to the Global North. See France
Winddance Twine, *Outsourcing the Womb: Race, Class, and Gestational
Surrogacy in a Global Market* (New York: Routledge, 2011); Amrita Pande,
*Wombs in Labor: Transnational Commercial Surrogacy in India* (New York:
Columbia University Press, 2014); Vora, *Life Support* (2015); Sharmila
Rudrappa, *Discounted Life: The Price of Global Surrogacy in India* (New
York: New York University Press, 2015); Daisy Deomampo, *Transnational
Reproduction: Race, Kinship, and Commercial Surrogacy in India* (New
York: New York University Press, 2016). On the question of the importance
of the present argument about slavery to an understanding of outsourced
or transnational reproduction, especially surrogacy, see Weinbaum, *The
Afterlife of Reproductive Slavery*.

36. See Toni Morrison, *Beloved* (1987; New York: Vintage Books,
2004), xvii.

# W. E. B. Du Bois and Shirley Graham Du Bois

## Personal Memories and Political Reflections

*Bettina Aptheker*

In this essay I share some of my personal memories of the Du Boises and selected correspondence between them. Then I offer some political and feminist reflections about Dr. Du Bois, especially in his last years. The intersecting personal and political pasts presented in this essay highlight the power of living history. Accented with the closing decades of Du Bois's life, it offers a personal portrait of a public scholar and activist and further discloses the place of Shirley Graham Du Bois in the broad scope of black history.

My first very clear memory of Dr. Du Bois and Shirley Graham Du Bois was at their wedding, which took place on February 27, 1951, at Graham's home in St. Albans, Queens. I was six years old. There's a photograph of my parents, Herbert and Fay Aptheker, at the wedding, and I know I was right there with them, but I do not appear in the frame. At the time of the wedding my father, who was a historian, was about to publish the first volume of what was to become his seven-volume *Documentary History of the Negro People in the United States.* Dr. Du Bois wrote the preface for that first volume.

What I remember most about the Du Boises' wedding was the swirl of guests, cigarettes and champagne, flowers seemingly everywhere, and Shirley Graham in a very, very elegant white dress. Dr. Du Bois's daughter, Yolande, served as the matron of honor. I also remember dear David Graham, Shirley Graham's son, who was to become like an older brother to me, an only and lonely child. At the time of their marriage, Dr. Du Bois was eighty-three, and Shirley Graham was fifty-four.

The Du Boises had been officially married ten days earlier at New York's City Hall. They opted for a hastily arranged legal marriage to guarantee that Graham could visit her husband should he be in prison. Unbelievable as this may seem today, the U.S. government had just indicted Dr. Du Bois and accused him of being a foreign agent because he was the chair of the Peace Information Center. Of course, at six I didn't know any of this. I just remember the crush of guests, the sea of reporters, the laughter, and Dr. Du Bois bending down and whispering to me (alone) ever so kindly, ever so gently, as he would do in the years to come.

Another, related memory: In 1957, when I was eleven, my parents received a Thanksgiving dinner invitation from friends in Great Neck, Long Island. They always took me to any such occasions, dressed in whatever finery my mother had managed to fit me into. I was an inveterate tomboy and hated dresses, but I knew that for anything that involved the Du Boises, there was absolutely no point in contesting anything about what I was to wear.

Thanksgiving dinner was at the home of Molly and Irving Cohen. I can clearly see the hostess in my mind's eye; a few years earlier and before she and her family moved to Great Neck, they had resided in Brooklyn and she had been my piano teacher. There were perhaps twenty guests at a long, formally set table. Dr. Du Bois was at the head of the table, and Graham sat to his left, elegant in a maroon silk dress, her hair swept up, and looking radiant. Hired staff served dinner on that occasion. Dr. Du Bois sparkled with laughter and held forth in the middle of a story.

The great Spanish cellist Pablo Casals, then exiled from his homeland to avoid the persecutions of the Franco dictatorship, lived in Puerto Rico at the time. In August of that year, he had married. Casals was eighty, and his bride, Marta Montanez, who was his student, was only twenty. "And I thought I was daring!" Du Bois chortled, referring to the mere forty-year difference in age between himself and Shirley Graham. I don't think I fully understood all of this at the moment; I just remember the words in his joke.

Everyone hooted with laughter, raised their wine glasses, and drank a hearty toast to the long life of Du Bois and Casals; at this moment, I shall refrain from any feminist-inspired commentary! But I will return to the feminist point in a more critical and serious vein.

In my memoir, *Intimate Politics*, I recalled a childhood memory of Dr. Du Bois and Shirley Graham:

I can still see them seated in the back of father's car. He frequently picked them up to bring them to our house for dinner. . . . They would sit in the back seat of the Plymouth holding hands and giggling, sparring with each other, using my father as their straight man. "Now Herbert," Dr. Du Bois would say in his British/Southern lilt, "you know how things are. . . ." Shirley would feign a harrumph. "Herbert, let me tell you what he did . . ." referring to her husband, with her rich, rasping laughter. But they weren't really talking to my father. They were playing with each other, an effervescence of sweet love.[1]

While working at the Schlesinger Library on a research project about Shirley Graham, specifically her career as an operatic composer and playwright (and a little known and amazing career it was), I came across letters from him to her between 1946 and 1948. This is years before they were married, and from these and earlier letters you can surmise that they were lovers from about 1938 on. The letters confirmed exactly that effervescence and carefree, playful loving I so vividly recalled. He was about seventy years old when their courtship began, and she was in her early forties. One typed letter, dated August 4, 1946, Du Bois sent from his holiday at the Cambridge Gun and Rod Club in Litchfield, Maine:

> My darling Shirley: I am here and it is too lovely. I ached for you this morning. I walked alone before breakfast in what I call my secret meadow: green grass, black boulders, and great pines in the golden sunshine and mist, with buzzing things and silence. Behind was the dark, shining lake, with its islands and far-off hills. We had bacon and eggs and griddle cakes for breakfast at ten, and then seven hours later, when we were famished (I had walked, swum, basked in a hammock, meantime) we ate each half of a stuffed baked chicken, with salad, ale and a pint of ice-cream. Then after a session in the hammock, I rowed alone across the lake to a lonesome island and came back facing the setting sun—done in glory! I'm not doing a stitch of work! I love you! W. E. B. D.[2]

Another letter, from Prairie View, Texas, dated March 4, 1947, revealed some of the contradictions in Du Bois's life. During his and Shirley Graham's years of courtship, he was still legally married to Nina

Gomer Du Bois, with whom he had not lived for many years. However, he did provide for her financial support. To Graham, the letter begins, "My darling distracted: I had breakfast at 10—a most reasonable hour—accompanied by panegyrics on my lecture last night, before 1500, subject 'Russia.'" He then referred to Mrs. Du Bois and their daughter, Yolande. Mrs. Du Bois had been ill and hospitalized, and Dr. Du Bois expressed some anxiety over the medical bills. He then asked after Shirley's mother and her son. David was "the Lieutenant"; he was then in the army. He advised Shirley not to worry about him while acknowledging, "Even that is fool advice." Du Bois concluded, "Please sleep, do a movie and hold my hand in spirit (which is, I admit, damned poor gratification, but far better than none at all) and leaving Frederick, devote your affections more and more to Anne Royall."

Dr. Du Bois's comment about Frederick was a reference to Shirley Graham's completion of what was to be her award-winning biography of Frederick Douglass; he urged her to turn her attention instead to the 1830s muckraking journalist and early feminist Anne Royall, the subject of her doctoral dissertation at NYU. His letter concludes, "You are my dear Love and I await your embraces. W. E. B. D."[3]

Finally, I share part of a letter, dated March 6, 1948, from the Palace Hotel in San Francisco:

> My very dear lady:
> . . .
> So far I have had a press conference, a radio broadcast, a lecture in Oakland to 600 persons and a small reception and dinner. Saturday I rest and dine with a son of a Harvard classmate and his family: the Langdon Posts, very companionable people. Most of the people I'm meeting are very human beings. I have decided to resign from the chairmanship of the committee on the Council of African Affairs. The position is impossible. I have no legal power, [Paul] Robeson is away, the Rev. Shelton Bishop won[']t play ball and [Max] Yergan is going to do as he pleases; he has been doing this in the past and I have no way to stop him. The only thing for me to do is to get out. I'm sorry especially for Alpheus [Hunton] and Doxey [Wilkerson]. But I've thought it over carefully and my decision is final. Now I'm off to dinner. I miss you very, very much. Take thoughtful care of yourself and don't stop loving me. . . . Kisses, W. E. B. D.[4]

Then there is this postscript: "Darling! I've lost my Wallace button! Rush me two by air!" Du Bois ardently supported Henry A. Wallace and campaigned vigorously for his presidential bid on the Progressive Party ticket.

Although love and light filled these letters, in the early 1950s, following their marriage, Dr. Du Bois and Shirley Graham Du Bois experienced the magnitude of the political winds sweeping the United States, as the cold war and the anticommunist purges surged forward, gaining unchecked velocity with each passing month. Du Bois and Shirley Graham were in the thick of it. She had been in the Communist Party (or was very close to it) for quite a few years.

Shortly after their marriage, Shirley Graham moved into Dr. Du Bois's home at 31 Grace Court in the Brooklyn Heights section of Brooklyn, New York. It was a beautiful redbrick house with a black iron fence; it was a spacious home of three floors with large rooms. Built in 1899 it had some of the estate charm of those early Brooklyn homes, with a half acre for a spectacularly beautiful garden which Dr. Du Bois frequented, and in which he and I ate lunch every day the summer he employed me to help him sort his papers prior to his departure for Ghana. Du Bois's study was on the lower floor just inside the main entrance to the house, below street level. From the windows in that front room you could see the sidewalk and the ankles of passers-by.

It was here in this house that the Du Boises threw a Christmas Party for Michael and Robby Rosenberg in December 1953, following their parents' execution after their conviction of conspiracy to commit espionage by allegedly giving secret information to the Soviet Union about the construction of an atomic bomb. Their execution, despite appeals to President Eisenhower from millions of people in the United States and the world, including the pope, was one of the great travesties of the anticommunist hysteria of the 1950s. Michael was ten, Robby was six, and I was nine. The party was to raise money for a trust fund for the Rosenberg children, whom Anne and Abel Meeropol had adopted after a considerable custody fight with the U.S. government. They were a Jewish couple, and both were teachers. Abel also went by his pen name, Lewis Allen, as a composer of, among other things, "Strange Fruit," the antilynching song Billie Holiday made famous. Presents for the boys surrounded a floor-to-ceiling Christmas tree festooned with lights and tinsel. It stood by the windows fronting the street.

Jutting out from one wall of this spacious living room was a Steinway grand piano polished to a black sheen. I later played for the Du Boises on this same piano while visiting their home with my parents. Dr.

Du Bois had a beautiful tenor voice and sang along with me as I played, sitting next to me on the piano bench. Sometimes he had to hold his breath rather a long time while I struggled to find my proper notes for whatever melody I was playing! As a child, I naïvely assumed that Dr. Du Bois was the pianist in the family. It was years later that I realized this was Shirley Graham's piano. She was a pianist, singer, and opera composer holding a Master of Fine Arts degree in music from the Oberlin Conservatory.

I don't think I appreciated at the time what an extraordinary experience it was for me to work with Dr. Du Bois in sorting his papers in the summer of 1961. I was a sort of research assistant. He was ninety-three and I was sixteen. He worked at his desk, and I worked at the filing cabinets. He instructed me on the piles of letters, newspaper clippings, and journal articles to make, through which he would later sort. I remember chairs around me on which I placed the various materials and a space on the floor for anything whose category was unclear to me. We started very promptly at 9:00 a.m. He was always formally dressed in a suit, vest, and tie, even at home, in the August heat, although the house was comfortable enough. We broke for lunch exactly at 12 noon, summoned by Shirley Graham, cheerful and always, in my memory, loving. She declined to eat with us even though he always invited her. Lunch was light: perhaps a sandwich, salad, or fruit, something utterly delicious for dessert and always with whipped cream, and iced tea. Invariably we then spent a while talking, relaxed, enjoying the relative cool of the shaded garden and its floral gifts.

Of course, I cannot completely reconstruct those conversations, but I know Dr. Du Bois was very keen on hearing about my own political activities with a youthful socialist organization called Advance, especially our activities in the then nascent days of the civil rights movement. The sit-ins to desegregate the lunch counters in the South had begun in February of that year, and our chapter of Advance had done quite a bit of picketing at the local Woolworth's department store in downtown Brooklyn to encourage a boycott by patrons. I also know that Du Bois had returned from China about a year and half earlier, where he and Shirley Graham had been guests of the state; what he saw there thrilled him. He asked me if I understood that "colored people" were carrying out the Chinese Revolution, and I had to admit that I had never thought about that. He was elated by the elimination of famine in those early years, and of the reconstruction of the country he had seen everywhere. Would that I had had the archival sense to record those conversations! By 1:15, we were back at work, and we stopped at about 4:00 p.m. This was five days a week and lasted until I went back to school in September.

Eventually those papers in their filing cabinets came to my parents' home and lodged in their basement between the laundry and the boiler rooms. They ended up there because no library in the United States dared to take them! Eventually I was to spend many hours on the floor reading those letters. I did have the sense to understand that they were a priceless treasure. There was Woodrow Wilson, Ida B. Wells-Barnett, Mary McLeod Bethune, Langston Hughes, Clarence Darrow, Countee Cullen (who was married for a time to Du Bois's daughter), Claude McKay, Alain Locke, Arthur Schomburg, Mahatma Gandhi, to name just a few of his correspondents. These are the precious letters now archived at the W. E. B. Du Bois Library at the University of Massachusetts, Amherst, and fully digitalized, making them available to the world.

In the years before Dr. Du Bois and Shirley Graham departed for Ghana in 1961, he had become a pariah. Propelled out of the NAACP, then resigning from the Council for African Affairs, arrested as a "foreign agent" by the U.S. government because he was chairman of the Peace Information Center, stripped of his passport, U.S. publishers refused even to consider his manuscripts. At the time, their closest friends were in and around the Communist Party: James and Esther Jackson, Paul and Eslanda Robeson, Beah Richards, Doxey and Yolande Wilkerson, Louis and Dorothy Burnham, Alphaeus and Dorothy Hunton, William L. and Louise Patterson, the artists Elizabeth Catlett and Charles White, my parents, Mark Lane and Martha Schlamme, Bernard Jaffe, and many others I have no doubt omitted.

Just at the end of World War II Du Bois published *Color and Democracy: Colonies and Peace* with Harcourt & Brace, with whom he had a long publishing career, including his epochal study of Reconstruction, released ten years earlier. However, Harcourt & Brace's relationship with Du Bois ended with that 1945 book. Dr. Du Bois could find no publisher willing to consider his trilogy *The Black Flame*. When Du Bois sent Harcourt & Brace an inquiry, they rejected the work out of hand with a standard, preprinted postcard![5] The trilogy, in the words of June Cara Christian, whose critical analysis of it appeared in 2014, is an "unparalleled thirty year study of Atlanta from Black Reconstruction through 1956." It features considerations of racialization, colonization, and globalization as these worked to "dehumanize black education."[6] Focused in some measure upon ordinary southern

black experience from Reconstruction on, the voice of Du Bois's fictional character Manuel Mansart, born in 1876, narrates each of the
three volumes. *The Ordeal of Mansart, Mansart Builds a School,* and
*Worlds of Color* map a world of trauma, struggle, conflict, and disillu-
sionment. The final volume culminates in political intrigue and, in the
words of Henry Louis Gates, "a dark and cynical view of the world," in
contrast to the "black flame" of hope that inspired the trilogy's title. My
father saw to the publication of all three volumes under the auspices
of the Communist Party's publishing company, beginning with volume
1 in 1957. Likewise, through his editorship of the Party's cultural magazine, *Masses & Mainstream,* my father published Du Bois's book *In
Battle for Peace: The Story of my 83rd Birthday,* which told of his arrest
as a foreign agent and the directed acquittal by the judge, who had
finally become aware of who it was he had before him in court. Similarly the Communist Party's International Publishers brought out his
1947 book, *The World and Africa: An Inquiry into the Part Which Africa
Has Played in World History.*[7]

In light of the personal and political history this essay traces out,
why should anyone register surprise at Dr. Du Bois's decision to join
the U.S. Communist Party in October 1961, just before he and Graham Du Bois departed for Ghana? Du Bois had been a serious Marxist
scholar for years. This is perfectly clear, for example, in a careful reading of *Black Reconstruction,* which combines an analysis of race with
that of class. The historian Cedric Robinson gives a complete and
detailed demonstration of this in his book *Black Marxism: The Making
of the Black Radical Tradition.* Du Bois began *Black Reconstruction*
with a discussion of the black worker; the second chapter is titled "The
White Worker," the third "The Planter," and the fourth "The General
Strike." He provides a class analysis of slavery grounded in Marxism
while simultaneously innovating from and transforming Marxist theory. By situating the enslaved as a *worker,* albeit a super-exploited one,
Du Bois, Robinson argues, saw "American slave labor . . . [as] a particular historical development for world capitalism that expropriated the
labor of African workers as primitive accumulation [of capital]. American slavery was a subsystem of world capitalism." Robinson explains
that for Du Bois, "slavery was the specific historical institution through
which the Black worker had been introduced into the modern world
system. However, it was not as slave that one could come to an understanding of the significance these Black men, women, and children had
for American development. It was as labor."[8]

In the fourth chapter of *Black Reconstruction*, having laid a theoretical and historiographic foundation, Du Bois describes the mobile general strike by the formerly enslaved Africans, heralding the collapse of that system as the Union forces advanced. Consider the sheer poetic power of Du Bois's description:

> Every step the Northern armies took meant fugitive slaves. They crossed the Potomac, and the slaves of Northern Virginia began to pour into the army and into Washington. They captured Fortress Monroe, and slaves from Virginia and even North Carolina poured into the army. They captured Port Royal, and the masters ran away, leaving droves of black fugitives in the hands of the Northern army. They moved down the Mississippi Valley, and if the slaves did not rush to the army, the army marched to the slaves. They captured New Orleans, and so captured a great black city and a state full of slaves. . . . The trickling stream of fugitives swelled to a flood. . . . Wherever the army marched and in spite of all obstacles came the rising tide of slaves seeking freedom. . . . Gradually, the fugitives became organized and formed a great labor force for the [Union] army.[9]

At the end of Du Bois's seven-hundred-plus-page history, again we encounter the poetry of the words and the Marxian sway of the language:

> The most magnificent drama in the last thousand years of human history is the transportation of ten million human beings out of the dark beauty of their mother continent into the new-found Eldorado of the West. They descended into Hell; and in the third century they arose from the dead, in the finest effort to achieve democracy for the working millions which this world has ever seen.[10]

I ask again: Why should it have been a surprise to anyone that Du Bois joined the Communist Party? Why are so many biographers dismissive? Why do some think it was evidence of his senility or some other form of dementia, or bitterness? Even David Levering Lewis dismisses Du Bois's decision in one sentence as a "satisfying Homeric nose-thumbing . . . to join a political organization whose membership, FBI agents included, was well under ten thousand."[11] Gerald Horne, in his work on Du Bois's last years, treats his relationship with the Communist Party with something approaching a more appropriate consideration. He devotes a full chapter to "Du Bois and the Communists." He shows the continuity of Du Bois's thought, especially in relationship to a serious study and use of Marxism in his work, and places Du Bois within the context of African American activists who were more sympathetic to the Communist Party relative to other segments of society because of its antiracist agenda.[12]

I am not writing this to defend the Communist Party. However, I was a member of the Party for nineteen years, between 1962 and 1981, and whatever my disagreements with it and assessments of it, I can say that it was a lot more than a decrepit, FBI-ridden organization. It is true that its membership was only several thousand in the 1960s, decimated as it was by the combination of the McCarthy purges, the Smith Act trials, FBI harassment, and Khrushchev's revelations that confirmed Stalin's monstrous crimes. Nevertheless there were legitimate Party members who contributed to the 1950s and 1960s civil rights, peace, and student movements, and others who devoted themselves to efforts to organize workers, especially, for example, the farm workers in California and immigrant women working assembly lines in Silicon Valley's electronics industry. In addition, during the early 1970s the Communist Party's critical efforts saved Angela Davis's life, although this is after Du Bois's time. Dr. Du Bois knew in detail the efforts of the Communist Party in the South in the 1930s to unionize black workers and to end peonage. The Burnhams, the Jacksons, the Pattersons, and my father had all been part of this effort. William L. Patterson had been one of the lawyers in the Scottsboro case and the primary author of the 1951 petition to the United Nations, *We Charge Genocide*, which documented the lynching and murders of African Americans with the active participation and/or collusion of U.S. police authorities. *We Charge Genocide* followed precisely the protocols of the U.N. Convention on Genocide adopted three years earlier by the General Assembly, although not ratified by the U.S. Senate until 1986![13] My father was secretary of the National Anti-Peonage Committee. He and Louis Burnham traveled together in North Carolina helping to unionize tobacco workers. Younger scholars today, like Dayo Gore and Erik McDuffie, have written extensively on African American communists, especially women like Louise Thompson Patterson, Esther Cooper Jackson, Dorothy Hunton, Eslanda Robeson, Shirley

Graham, Audley Moore, and Sallye Bell Davis (Angela Davis's mother) and documented their contributions to the civil rights and early black proto-feminist movements.[14]

What I am saying is that if you look at the anticommunist and anti-Marxist paranoia of the late 1940s and 1950s, if you consider who Dr. Du Bois was and where his investments lay in the anticolonial, national liberation movements, if you consider his experiences in China and the Soviet Union, especially in the Asian Soviet republics, if you consider the formidable political energies and commitments of Shirley Graham for decades, if you consider his knowledge of Communist Party organizers in the South, and if you consider who stood by him, who published him, and who defended him in some of his darkest hours, his decision to join the Communist Party is completely reasonable and, most important, *should in no way detract from a critical reading and appreciation of his later works, the power of his mind, the quality of his writings, and the unwavering commitment of his liberatory vision.* We can be as critical as we wish of the Communist Party, of the often narrowness of its vision, for example, of its undemocratic and bureaucratic structure, of its dogmatic adherence to the Soviet "line," of its homophobic policies until deep into the 1980s, and so forth, but we do not need to so profoundly, condescendingly, and willfully misunderstand Dr. Du Bois's decision in the context of his life and experiences.

It is with much appreciation that I have observed the new and respectful intellectual occupation with Du Bois that began in the last decade of the twentieth century and continues. There are many who are critical of Du Bois for his alleged arrogance, for his apparent elitism, for his idea of "the Talented Tenth." The biographies by Arnold Rampersad, Manning Marable, and Gerald Horne are particularly significant for their critical embrace of Du Bois's later works. And Eric Porter in his study of Du Bois's post–World War II political thought emphasizes his prescience in examining "the antidemocratic practices of the liberal state, the problem of empire, enduring global wars, exclusionary definitions of citizenship status and application of rights . . . that continue to be a source of intractable political problems."[15] Porter also considers Du Bois's new understanding of himself as a "suspect citizen" when the U.S. government indicts him as a foreign agent. Porter suggests that from this, combined with his analysis of the post–World War II national liberation movements in Africa, Du Bois negotiated his way into a new understanding of citizenship itself. "The challenge for Du Bois," Porter suggests,

is to articulate not just a commitment to solidarity across
national boundaries but an intellectual and ethical standpoint rooted in his position as suspect citizen [of the United
States]. . . . Du Bois expresses his loyalty to freedom of thought
and commitment to the truth that stems from responsibilities
of citizenship in the United States *but which is also grounded in
a commitment to global citizenship that transcends and may have
to reject restrictive aspects of national citizenship imposed on or
available to him.*[16]

Porter's analysis offers a profoundly new insight into Du Bois's decision to renounce his U.S. citizenship while residing in Ghana, not so
much as a rejection of the United States as an affirmation of himself
as a citizen of Africa, a reclamation of homeland. Shirley Graham did
the same, but by 1966, when Nkrumah was overthrown, she faced a
life-threatening and profound crisis *sans* passport or citizenship. With
the intervention of her son, David, and her lawyer, Bernard Jaffe, and
a great many public figures she was able to leave Ghana unharmed.
Eventually she settled in Cairo with David.[17]

Porter then puts Du Bois's ideas about citizenship into conversation with the post-9/11 writings of the Trinidadian feminist scholar M.
Jacqui Alexander and her rendition of "suspect citizenship." In doing
this, Porter reveals Du Bois's male supremacist assumptions that
affected so much of his work. Alexander is "interested in the production and function of the 'new citizen patriot.'" But in her insightful
gaze this new post-9/11 citizen patriot is white and hypermasculine.
"This originary citizen is in sharp contradistinction to the (dark) natu-
ralized citizen, the dark immigrant or even the dark citizen of the dark
immigrant whose (latent) 'loyalty' is perennially suspect and therefore
ultimately threatening." As Porter points out, however, in Du Bois's
rendition of suspect citizenship and his "battle for peace," "his critique of Cold War political culture . . . does not include commentary
on ascendant antifeminist, domestic ideologies." Porter argues that
while Du Bois "valuably articulates a powerful critique of national
identity and capitalism and imagines transnational identities and affil-
iations [he] not only subordinates gender as a category of analysis
but also . . . reproduces a masculinist political and intellectual project."[18] This is an unfortunate but consistent, unquestioned intellectual
thread in Du Bois's works, a point Erik McDuffie's essay in this volume
emphasizes.

*The Souls of Black Folk* (1903) and *Black Reconstruction* (1935), for example, have been critically examined for the gendered, masculinist structure of Du Bois's emancipatory vision. I return then to my earlier allusion to propose a more serious feminist commentary. For example, Hazel Carby's *The Souls of Black Men* provides a feminist reading of Du Bois's *Souls*. She writes unequivocally, "Beneath the surface of this apparent desire to become an intellectual and a race leader is a conceptual framework that is gender-specific; not only does it apply exclusively to men, but it encompasses only those men who enact narrowly and rigidly determined codes of masculinity."[19] In a detailed analysis of each of the chapters in *Souls* Carby illustrates these concepts of masculinity, even to the point of showing how Du Bois de-masculinized Booker T. Washington, calling him "unmanly." While acknowledging that "Du Bois advocated equality for women and consistently supported feminist causes in his later life," Carby also asserts that Du Bois's project, in not only *Souls* but also more generally, "suffers from [his] complete failure to imagine black women as intellectuals and race leaders."[20]

Although Carby does not write about her, Du Bois's contemporary, Anna Julia Cooper, forged a black "womanist" intellectual tradition that he chose to ignore. I found Cooper's work in the mid-1970s while doing research for my master's thesis. I was thrilled with her critical readings of white feminists like Anna Howard Shaw and their racism toward Indians, and her critiques of modern theoretical trends like positivism. Likewise I found her discussions of education, race, and gender discrimination eloquent. Cooper, who in 1921 received her doctorate from the Sorbonne and was an extraordinary scholar and teacher, was treated by Du Bois in a formal way in accord with civil etiquette, but at least in his letters he exhibited no warmth toward her. She and Du Bois corresponded in the 1920s and 1930s.[21]

Cooper was an extraordinary intellectual who spent most of her life teaching at the M Street Colored Elementary School in Washington, D.C. Her book *A Voice from the South by a Black Woman of the South* was published in 1892, four years before Du Bois's doctoral dissertation, "The Suppression of the African Slave Trade." The literary scholar Mary Helen Washington described Cooper's book as "an unparalleled articulation of black feminist theory." The *Stanford Encyclopedia of Philosophy* offers an extensive critical appraisal of the work:

> Cooper offers clearly articulated insights about racialized sexism and sexualized racism without ignoring the significance of

class and labor, education and intellectual development, and
conceptions of democracy and citizenship. With an academic
training deeply rooted in the history of Western philosophy and
the classics, Cooper's philosophical significance also lies in her
foundational contributions to feminist philosophy, standpoint
theory, and epistemology, as well as critical philosophy of race
and African-American philosophy (including African American political philosophy). . . . Cooper takes an intersectional
approach to examining the interlocking systems of race, gender,
and class oppression . . . [and because of this,] Cooper argues,
Black women have a unique epistemological standpoint from
which to observe society and its oppressive systems as well as a
unique ethical contribution to make in confronting and
correcting these oppressive systems.[22]

In her doctoral dissertation, "L'attitude de la France à l'égard de l'es-
clavage pendant la révolution," Cooper "succeeds in resituating racial
oppression, colonialism, and slavery as issues central to rather than
tangential to the French and Haitian Revolutions," opines the *Stanford
Encyclopedia*. Charles Lemert, in his introduction to the collected writings of Cooper, considers the theoretical and philosophical acuity of
her work. He writes that Cooper's *Voice* "was the first *systematic* working out of the insistence that no one social category could capture the
reality of the colored woman." Confronted by both the woman question
and the race problem, Cooper focused the terms of debates occurring
today. Many of the concepts of black-feminist and woman-of-color
debates center on the insufficiency of such categories as race and gender, even class, to capture by themselves the complexities of a woman's
social experience. What Susan Bordo calls "gender skepticism," what
Donna Haraway means by "fractured identities," and what Judith Butler views as the "necessary trouble of analytic categories" are all found
in Cooper's late nineteenth- and early twentieth-century works.[23]

Cooper was subjected to a humiliating dismissal from her position
at the M Street Colored School, where she was the principal in 1906.
She was accused in a wholly fabricated sex scandal manufactured by
agents of the Tuskegee Machine, as Booker T. Washington's influence
was called, because she dared to construct a curriculum broader than
the purely vocational training he advocated and because her writings
clearly crossed a forbidden intellectual and political line. Dr. Du Bois
did not come to her defense, although he truly had nothing to lose

given his already fierce and public opposition to Washington articulated in *Souls*. In fact almost no one, not even other prominent black
women like Mary Church Terrell, with whom she had gone to Oberlin,
dared defend her. Terrell's silence was tied to her husband's municipal judgeship in Washington, awarded at Booker T. Washington's
behest.[24]

Consider how remarkable it might have been had Du Bois and Cooper
collaborated! Consider also what a different black intellectual tradition
we might have inherited! Du Bois was a reluctant correspondent with
and supporter of women like Ida B. Wells-Barnett, the architect of the
antilynching movement in the United States, and Mary Church Terrell,
the founding president of the National Association of Colored Women.
Terrell was a highly educated woman holding a master's degree from
Oberlin College and speaking at least four languages, including Latin.
On the other hand, Du Bois unequivocally supported woman suffrage
and women's access to birth control, and argued strenuously for wom-
en's rights to education, professional engagement, and productive labor
in his 1920 essay "The Damnation of Women."[25] He also encouraged
and at times generously supported black women writers and artists,
such as Jessie Fauset, who was the literary editor of *The Crisis* alongside Du Bois, Meta Warrick Fuller, and Augusta Savage, among many
others. He also corresponded with and supported the efforts of the
birth control crusader Margaret Sanger.

In another essay critically assessing Du Bois's *Black Reconstruction*
(and in her chapter in this book) Alys Weinbaum points out that while
Du Bois saw the sexual exploitation of black women as "breeders" to
be foundational to the profitability and durability of slavery, he was
unable to sustain the feminist potential of his analysis. Concerns with a
patriarchal bourgeois morality about "illegitimacy" obscured his insight
and detracted from an analysis of the reproductive *labor* of enslaved
women. By the time he got to his powerful descriptions of the "mobile
general strike" described above, "the gendered and sexualized reproductive contradictions that are constitutive of [Du Bois's] narrative at
the outset go missing from the story of war and Reconstruction that
eventually unfolds." "The unfortunate result," Weinbaum concludes,
"is that the chapter 'The General Strike' . . . is evacuated of the account
of reproductive and sexual work and the account of gendered and sexualized conflict that was initially offered."[26] Presumably all of the black
workers in the general strike are men; women are disappeared from the
rest of the story of the Civil War and Reconstruction. In Marxist terms,

they are no longer "counted," they are no longer black workers, even in the sense of laborers in the fields (which in an earlier essay Du Bois had affirmed), and they are no longer a motive force in history.

Whatever his shortcomings personally and politically, Du Bois was and will remain one of the most significant intellectuals and political activists of the twentieth century. His courage and endurance remain an inspiration. Relative to his African American (male) contemporaries in the late nineteenth and early twentieth centuries (e.g., William Monroe Trotter, Alexander Crummell, and Carter G. Woodson), Du Bois paid more attention to the politics of women's subordination even within his own limitations. My memories of Dr. Du Bois and Shirley Graham Du Bois are strong and loving. Both showed me exceptional kindness and treated me with great love and respect. My reflections, even when engaged with a feminist intellectual project, refract through this archive of feeling.[27]

The last letter I received from Dr. Du Bois, dated February 17, 1963, he wrote only a few months before he died. I had written to him and Shirley Graham to tell them about the founding of a socialist youth organization in which I was involved, named after him, the W. E. B. DuBois Clubs of America; we were deeply engaged in the civil rights movement in the San Francisco Bay Area and in supporting the students in the South. He wrote back with the poetic eloquence so typical of him: "Dear, dear Bettina, Thank you and all members of your Du Bois Club for what you have done to make known the principles for which I have tried to stand. Out of the mist of years I send my love and appreciation and Shirley joins me."

Out of the mist of our years, dear Dr. Du Bois and Shirley Graham Du Bois, we thank you.

## Notes

This is a revised and enhanced version of the W. E. B. Du Bois seventeenth Annual Lecture at the University of Massachusetts Amherst, February 27, 2011.

1. Bettina Aptheker, *Intimate Politics: How I Grew Up Red, Fought for Free Speech and Became a Feminist Rebel* (Berkeley, CA: Seal Press, Perseus Books, 2006).

2. Shirley Graham Du Bois (SGD) Papers, MC476, Box 14, Folder 8, Schlesinger Library, Radcliffe Institute, Harvard University. In a private

conversation David Graham Du Bois told me he had moved his mother's papers from the archives at the University of Massachusetts, Amherst, to the Schlesinger because he felt her work should stand on its own and not be subsumed by the work of Dr. Du Bois.

3. SGD Papers, MC 476, Box 14, Folder 7.

4. SGD Papers, MC 476, Box 14, Folder 8. Shirley Graham Du Bois was awarded the Messner Prize for her historical novel, *There Was Once a Slave: A Life of Frederick Douglass* (1947). She had begun a doctoral program at NYU in 1945. Her dissertation was a biography of Anne Newport Royall (1769–1854), the first professional woman journalist in the United States. Residing in Washington, D.C., and a relentless muckraker, Royall exposed corruption at the highest levels, including land fraud against Native Americans. She opposed slavery, although she was critical of what she saw as the divisiveness of the abolitionist movement. When she took on the Presbyterian Church, she was arrested and tried as a "common scold," a crime reserved exclusively for women who were accused of being a public nuisance. Graham Du Bois was nine units short in her coursework, although the dissertation was completed. She never received her doctorate. SGD Papers, MC 476, Box 3, Folder 9.

5. Dr. Du Bois reported this to me in a private conversation the summer we worked together.

6. June Cara Christian, *Understanding the Black Flame and Multigenerational Education Trauma: Toward a Theory of the Dehumanization of Black Students* (Lanham, MD: Lexington Books, 2014).

7. My knowledge of this comes from private conversations with my father.

8. Cedric Robinson, *Black Marxism: The Making of the Black Radical Tradition* (1983; Chapel Hill: University of North Carolina Press, 2000), 199–200.

9. W. E. Burghardt Du Bois, *Black Reconstruction in America: An Essay toward a History of the Part Which Black Folk Played in the Attempt to Reconstruct Democracy in America, 1860–1880* (New York: Harcourt Brace, 1935; Cleveland, OH: World Publishing, 1962), 62–65.

10. Ibid., 727.

11. David Levering Lewis, *W. E. B. Du Bois: The Fight for Equality and the American Century, 1919–1963* (New York: Henry Holt, 2000), 567.

12. Gerald Horne, *Black and Red: W. E. B. Du Bois and the Afro-American Response to the Cold War, 1944–1963* (Albany: State University of New York Press, 1986). See especially, chapter 20, "Du Bois and the Communists," 288–311.

13. William L. Patterson, ed., *We Charge Genocide: The Historic Petition to the United Nations for Relief from a Crime of the United States Government against the Negro People* (New York: Civil Rights Congress, 1951).

14. See Dayo F. Gore, *Radicalism at the Crossroads: African American Women Activists in the Cold War* (New York: New York University Press, 2011); Erik S. McDuffie, *Sojourning for Freedom: Black Women, American Communism and the Making of Black Left Feminism,* (Durham, NC: Duke University Press, 2011).

15. Eric Porter, *The Problem of the Future World: W. E. B. Du Bois and the Race Concept Midcentury* (Durham, NC: Duke University Press, 2010), 12.

16. Ibid., 166, emphasis added.

17. SGD Papers, MC476, Box 4, Folders 8, 9, 10. SGD held a passport from Ghana issued October 9, 1963, and following the coup and the overthrow of Nkrumah, with whom she worked very closely, she held passports from Guinea, issued September 1966 (renewed October 1970), and Tanzania, issued August 1972. SGD became a resident of Cairo with the Tanzanian passport. Also see Gerald Horne, *Race Woman: The Lives of Shirley Graham Du Bois* (New York: New York University Press, 2000), 202–13. Horne includes a gripping account of SGD's description of the coup that overthrew Nkrumah and her personal terror.

18. Porter, *The Problem of the Future World*, 167. See also M. Jacqui Alexander, *Pedagogies of Crossing: Meditations on Feminism, Sexual Politics and the Sacred* (Durham, NC: Duke University Press, 2005), especially her chapter "Transnationalism, Sexuality, and the State: Modernity's Traditions at the Height of Empire," 181–254.

19. Hazel Carby, *Race Men: The W. E. B. Du Bois Lectures* (Cambridge, MA: Harvard University Press, 1998), 10.

20. Ibid.

21. Search for Anna Julia Cooper in W. E. B. Du Bois Papers, http://credo.library.umass.edu/view/collection/mums312. For example, she wrote to Du Bois on September 10, 1924, inquiring about a possible English translation of a book on Haiti, *Rapport sur les troubles de Saint Domingo* by Garren-Coulon; he responded two days later saying he knew of no English translation and suggesting a translation was unlikely due to the high cost of "book-making." In that same letter Du Bois said he had arranged for her to receive two books and notified her that billing for them would follow. Other letters, for example, one dated September 4, 1923, concern travel arrangements for her to attend a Pan-African conference.

22. https://plato.stanford.edu/entries/anna-julia-cooper/

23. Charles Lemert and Esme Bhan, eds., *The Voice of Anna Julia Cooper, Including "A Voice from the South" and other Important Essays, Papers and Letters* (Lanham, MD: Rowman & Littlefield, 1998), 15–16.

24. Ibid.,11. Cooper was reinstated in 1911 at the M Street School after a teaching stint at Wilberforce College in Ohio. She remained at M Street until her retirement.

25. W. E. B. Du Bois, "The Damnation of Women," in, *Darkwater: Voices from within the Veil* (New York: Harcourt, Brace, and Howe, 1920), 171–92.

26. Alys Weinbaum, "Gendering the General Strike: W. E. B. Du Bois' *Black Reconstruction* and Black Feminism's 'Propaganda of History,'" *South Atlantic Quarterly* 112, no. 3 (Summer 2013): 444.

27. I borrow this phrase from Ann Cvetkovich, *An Archive of Feelings: Trauma, Sexuality, and Lesbian Public Cultures* (Durham, NC: Duke University Press, 2003).

# The Politics of Memory
# and Meaning

# Exile in Brooklyn
## W. E. B. Du Bois's Final Decade

*David Levering Lewis*

William Edward Burghardt Du Bois stood on a pedestal occupied by few Americans, and surely no other person of color in February 1948.[1] He was the senior intellectual of his race and its unexcelled propagandist—idolized or reviled, depending on the region of the United States and the complexion and education of his audience. The celebration of his eightieth birthday at the Hotel Roosevelt sponsored by the New York alumni of Fisk University, Du Bois's first undergraduate college, honored him as a national treasure. NAACP president Arthur Spingarn presided. Celebrated scholars John Hope Franklin, Mark Van Doren, and E. Franklin Frazier spoke. Greetings came from prime ministers Jawaharlal Nehru of India and Norman Manley of Jamaica. Regrets in response to invitations effusively lauded the honoree. Amazed and delighted to see him "carry on," Northwestern University's Melville Herskovits thought Du Bois must be deeply satisfied to realize that "slowly but surely, so many of the things that you have been fighting for are being turned into actuality." John Gunther's massive best-seller published later that year, *Inside U.S.A.*, would quote Du Bois's words in conversation and accord him "a position almost like that of Shaw or Einstein in his field."

His was a fragile eminence nevertheless, hostage not only to the notoriously short attention span of his fellow citizens but subject to the always special conditions that once governed racial preferment in America. Implicit in the celebrity or influence accorded people of color was the requirement of a reciprocated patriotism and gratitude that validated the mythic reality of a land of color-blind opportunity. Although Du Bois would head the *Negro Digest* list "The Big Ten Who Run America" and historian Henry Steele Commager's 1948 list, "Men Who Make

187

Up Our Minds," equating him with Ben Franklin and Thomas Jefferson, his reputation would lay in ruins three years later. His freedom
to work and walk among his compatriots would hang in the balance
of cold war justice. Indeed even as the distinguished cross section of
citizens praised his many achievements, the remarkable octogenarian
signaled his dissent from the emergent geopolitical status quo of post-
war America. Three politically turbulent years after deciding that the
right way to save American democracy was to support the left, Du Bois
became one of the borough of Brooklyn's most distinguished cold war
victims. We might characterize his Brooklyn residency, variously, as the
forgotten decade or the asylum years in Brooklyn Heights. In either
case, he might never have come there by his own free will.

In the spring of 1948, Du Bois decided that the alarming state of
domestic and international unrest compelled him to flout the pro-
hibition of partisan activity imposed by the NAACP, the civil rights
organization he had cofounded nearly forty years prior and to which
he had quite recently returned after a prolific academic career. The
U.S. attorney general's "List of Subversive Organizations" had been
unveiled at the end of 1947, and the trek of suspect individuals to
sessions before the House Committee on Un-American Activities and
Fifth Amendment obloquy had begun in earnest by the spring of 1948.
That March, the *New York Times* identified NAACP research director
Du Bois among the signatories of seven hundred organizations committed to a Henry Wallace run for the presidency. A month earlier he
had shared the stage with Wallace at Harlem's Golden Gate Ballroom
and (for an octogenarian who said his leadership was "largely one of
ideas") delivered a rousing stump speech to five thousand Harlemites.
He carried these convictions to the Progressive Party convention in
Philadelphia that July, where he gratefully declined to give the keynote
address. But his lengthy political meditation in *Masses & Mainstream*
predicted (less than three months before the election) that African
Americans were going to vote for Wallace in November in reaction to
Truman's recent silence on civil rights.

However, nothing had worked for Henry Wallace. What ought to
have been strong points for the candidate—his internationalism, economic democracy, and civil rights courage—turned against the naïve,
principled candidate in a climate of feral hysteria. In June 1948 eleven
members of the Communist Party's national committee received
indictments under the Smith Act for conspiring to overthrow the U.S.
government. A tortured *Time* magazine editor with the look of an

unmade bed, Whittaker Chambers, had identified a former communist cellmate, Alger Hiss, as a Party member. Menaced by the Taft-Hartley Act requiring noncommunist affidavits from union officials on pain of federal decertification, the Congress of Industrial Organizations (CIO) turned upon itself in an orgy of purgation. The November outcome was a rout for the Progressives, a dismal 1,157,172 votes for Wallace—twelve thousand fewer voters than the total amassed by Strom Thurmond's breakaway Dixiecrats. Reflecting on the prominence of communists among the Progressives, Eleanor Roosevelt feared that "Mr. Wallace was deceived."

Du Bois felt himself both pushed and pulled further left in the aftermath of Truman's landslide victory and the wreckage of the Progressive Party. The narrowing parameters of patriotism excluded the internationalism of the recent past advocated by the likes of former GOP presidential candidate Wendell Willkie to such a degree that to advocate disarmament, superpower negotiation, and the existence of legitimate Russian grievances easily solicited a place on the attorney general's subversives list. Other leaders accommodated themselves to the new parameters of cold war civil rights, but Du Bois had profound misgivings about full citizenship for Africans in America if the peoples of Africa and Asia were to become subjects under a Pax Americana maintained for the benefit of the military-industrial complex. Deeply symptomatic of the times, in May 1948 he lost his column in the *Chicago Defender*, the leading black newspaper of the period. Even more telling was the decision of the NAACP board, of which Mrs. Roosevelt was a new member, to terminate Du Bois's services that September. He would be but one victim among the many accused, censured, and convicted, yet the humiliation later visited upon him, as with his friend Paul Robeson, embodied a warning to his people and their leaders—a message that their long struggle for equality must continue to exemplify commendable patience, conventional patriotism, and indifference to radical economic ideas.

Almost simultaneously a new support network formed up quickly around Du Bois toward the end of 1948. Many of the new relationships came through the remarkable dramatist, musicologist, and writer Shirley Graham, whose friendship with communist novelist Howard Fast helped pave her way as a writer of biography and historical fiction. Published that same year, Graham's biography *Paul Robeson: Citizen of the World* received the prestigious Anisfield-Wolfe Award. "Shirley made wonderful gumbo and she never stopped talking," Fast was fond of saying. Neither could Howard Fast. They also shared an admiration for Du Bois. *Freedom Road*, Fast's novel about the post–Civil War period, relied on Du Bois's chef-d'oeuvre, *Black Reconstruction in America*—"relied heavily" on it, Fast said proudly. As Du Bois began to see more of Shirley Graham, he saw more of the people in her progressive circle: Fast, Paul and Essie Robeson, Frieda Diamond, Abbott Simon, and the Jacksons, James and Esther. The editors of the progressive New York–based weekly, *National Guardian*, offered Du Bois an infinitely more appropriate pulpit for his ideas than the *Chicago Defender*. Made aware of Du Bois's salary loss, foreclosed speaking engagements, and writing opportunities, Henry Wallace arranged a meeting in Chicago with Anita McCormick Blaine, daughter of Cyrus McCormick and an angel of progressive causes. Her money had underwritten the startup of the *National Guardian*, run by the socialist triumvirate James Aronson, Cedric Belfrage, and John McManus. Du Bois's discussion with Mrs. Blaine went well enough, though she proved to be slightly absent-minded about remitting checks for Du Bois's five-thousand-dollar research grant.

Du Bois's compulsion to speak truth to power landed him in the forefront of controversial progressive causes in late March 1949. During three memorable days when the Waldorf-Astoria Peace Conference convulsed Manhattan's East Side, he chaired the conference's writers' session. Hundreds of citizens, affiliated and unaffiliated, patrolled the sidewalks hoisting posters bearing a babel of angry messages. Catholic War Veterans picketed. Press and radio had given the conference the advance billing reserved for natural disasters. Sidney Hook, Mary McCarthy, Dwight Macdonald, and a phalanx of Americans for Democratic Action patrolled the hotel hallways to combat communists and Lillian Hellman. Irving Howe, writing for *Partisan Review*, sneered that the conference boasted no "big name" intellectual—no John Dos Passos or Richard Wright or Edmund Wilson, making no mention of Du Bois or that the State Department had denied visas to all Western European applicants (thereby eliminating Picasso and Sartre, among others). Howe ridiculed the writers' session and notably dismissed young panelist Norman Mailer as "a perfect illustration of a politically inexperienced mind." Graham naturally thought that Du Bois's Madison Square Garden speech on the final night was the high point. Centered by spotlight, his clipped diction enhanced by the microphone, eighty-one years seemed to fall away as Du Bois delivered his peroration: "What we all want is a decent world, where . . . sickness and death

are [not] linked to our industrial system. . . . Peace is not an end. It is
the gateway to full and abundant life." Graham claimed that even some
of the police officers in the Garden applauded.

At the beginning of the twentieth century, Du Bois had famously
prophesied that the color line would be the problem of his century.
Now, at midcentury, he believed civilization confronted a problem of
truly existential dimensions: annihilation by atomic warfare. The Soviet
Union tested its first atomic bomb five months after the Waldorf-Astoria
Peace Conference. Chiang Kai-shek's armies surrendered mainland
China to Mao Zedong in early December 1949. The Berlin airlift had
ended successfully in May 1949, followed in June 1950 by war on the
Korean peninsula. Impelled by ideals and a reading of history, Du Bois
enlisted as an officer in the impressive-sounding Peace Information
Center (PIC), whose core group of impassioned progressives was
actively encouraged by Einstein and as actively surveilled by the FBI.
Although Robeson's illustrious career had ended in the United States
only months earlier because he spoke in favor of communism, Du Bois
insisted on decrying the Truman doctrine of overseas communist encir-
clement and nuclear intimidation. Not only did he address thousands
throughout 1950 in Moscow, Prague, Paris, and Mexico as the PIC's
indefatigable spokesperson, but he leant his prestige and improbable
energy to the American Labor Party in order to run for the U.S. Senate
from New York. Senatorial candidate Du Bois campaigned vigorously.
He started at Harlem's Golden Gate Ballroom and climaxed in a powerful delivery on behalf of peace and civil rights in Madison Square
Garden on the night of October 24, 1950. "On the whole I enjoyed this
unique excursion," Du Bois decided, astonishing himself by winning 4
percent of the New York vote and 15 percent of Harlem's for a total of
205,729 votes—impressive totals, but insufficient to benefit the Labor
Party's Vito Marcantonio, whose lone vote against U.S. peacekeeping in
Korea cost him his seat in the House of Representatives.

Meantime, Du Bois's PIC activities roared along to stunning results.
Nineteen days into the Korean War, the PIC issued a *Peacegram* stating
that the so-called Stockholm Peace Appeal had received 1.5 million sig-
natures from forty states, two Nobel laureates, five Protestant bishops,
and (mistakenly) Duke Ellington. Overseas endorsements included
Bernard Shaw, Thomas Mann, Madame Sun Yat-sen, French cardi-
nals and archbishops, and a raft of prominent writers and educators.
*Peacegrams* announced plans for a rally in New York on the scale of
the Paris, Warsaw, and Stockholm peace congresses. On July 12, 1950,

the *New York Times* published a statement headlined across the nation. Secretary of State Dean Acheson warned that the Stockholm petition should be recognized for what it was, "a propaganda trick in the spurious 'peace offensive' of the Soviet Union." Five days later, Du Bois's rejoinder in the *Times* upbraided the secretary's statement as devoid of all "intimation of a desire for peace, or a realization of the horror of another World War or of sympathy with the crippled, impoverished and dead who pay for [the] fighting."

The U.S. Justice Department has rarely invoked the Foreign Agents Registration Act, but on August 11, 1950, the Department informed Du Bois that he was required immediately to register the PIC "as an agent of a foreign principal within the United States." Du Bois and the PIC's attorney, Gloria Agrin (of future Rosenberg case prominence), quickly understood that all appeals for meetings and objections in law were irrelevant. On October 12, in a maneuver intended to moot the registration demand, the PIC board voted to disband the organization. Comedy and tragedy exchanged places rapidly. The Justice Department informed Du Bois on February 2, 1951, that dissolution was unacceptable. It again ordered the now nonexistent PIC to register as an organization representing, in effect, a foreign power. One week later a grand jury in Washington handed down indictments. Arraignment of Du Bois and four PIC officers was set for February 16 in the nation's capital.

Du Bois often joked that at age fifty he had received honor and accolade, but that at seventy-five his death was "practically requested." Coming days before his eighty-third birthday, he suspected his Justice Department indictment was a tantamount request. The gallant old contrarian understandably experienced a bout of depression. Nina Yolande, his wife of fifty years, had died quietly the previous July. "I Bury My Wife," Du Bois's apostrophe, admitted, in effect, that he sacrificed her happiness to his duty to the race. The Philadelphia pediatrician to whom Du Bois dedicated *Black Reconstruction in America*, Virginia Alexander, expired a few months before Nina Yolande. W. E. B. Du Bois was a short man whose impact was a long one on many accomplished women. One was Oberlin College graduate Lola Shirley Graham, twenty-eight years younger than the great man and permanently smitten since first meeting him in her teens. Many of her friends had become his close acquaintances after his NAACP ostracism. Marriage seemed a good thing. The federal indictment occurred as she and he were planning a quiet wedding in late February in Graham's St. Albans home. "Dear,"

Graham informed Du Bois, "this changes our plans. We must be married right away." "By morning I had a plan worked out," she recalled. A somewhat shaken Du Bois accompanied Shirley McCants Graham to the home of a nearby minister on the evening of February 14.

The newlyweds flew to Washington the following morning, where a white and black battery of lawyers awaited them. When the defendants and their attorneys assembled for introductions and preliminary briefings, they realized that they faced the practical problem of accommodations in the segregated capital. The Du Boises had reservations in the Dunbar Hotel, the city's single habitable hostelry available to people of color. The New York attorneys and the three white defendants arrived at the Dunbar not yet realizing the full Jim Crow implications of an extended Washington stay. To continue the battle for peace and justice from two separate and unequal locations would have amounted to a preposterous mockery of principles. In violation of local ordinances, then, the Dunbar management agreed to house the interracial defendants. Released on bail and given a deferred trial date, Du Bois "really felt debased by the whole process," attorney Gloria Agrin, a thin, impatient woman feeling the strain of the Rosenberg defense, recalled later. His statement after the proceedings was appropriate. "It is a curious thing," he wrote, "that today I am called upon to defend myself against criminal charges for openly advocating the one thing all people want—Peace."

In a week Du Bois would reach his eighty-third year. On February 19 the exclusive Essex House hotel informed banquet chair E. Franklin Frazier that it would not honor its commitment. Withdrawals and for-the-record declinations poured in from President Mordecai Johnson of Howard University, Rabbi Abba Hillel Silver of Cleveland, and many more. NAACP president Spingarn washed his hands of the event. Great as was her admiration for the Du Bois of the past, Margaret Mead refused "in any way to have my name associated with [the occasion]," as did Nobel Peace laureate Ralph Bunche. Desperate improvisation at Small's Paradise Restaurant in Harlem turned out to be a splendid solution. "You people always come down to see me when you're in trouble," the amused owner observed. "It was a mad house—if you could get a seat," Louise Patterson, the grand lady of Marxism, remembered. Seven hundred people pressed into the famous nightspot. Frazier presided with gusto. The national head of Alpha Phi Alpha, Belford Lawson, roused the audience with a fighting speech. Paul Robeson spoke with great emotion. Greetings came from Leonard Bernstein,

Maxim Shostakovich, Langston Hughes, Mary Bethune, and Partisans of Peace luminaries. Four days later the Du Boises flew to the Bahamas for a three-week honeymoon. When they returned, Shirley made a point of telling friends that it had been a "real honeymoon." Her husband dispatched roughly identical letters to four disappointed women explaining the logic of his decision to remarry. The new Mrs. Du Bois put her St. Albans house up for sale, moved into her husband's small apartment at 401 Edgecombe Avenue, and began the search for a large residence.

Her indefatigable spouse traveled daily to his office at the Council on African Affairs on West 26th Street. Shortly before leaving for their Bahamas honeymoon, a family acquaintance, Brooklyn lawyer Paul Ross, suggested purchasing a large house with two duplex apartments in the Heights whose owner required more space. Contacting the owner immediately, Shirley Du Bois and Paul Ross arrived for a gracious morning tour of 31 Grace Court by the Millers, Arthur and Mary. They decided the house was perfect as a joint Du Bois–Ross residency, the Du Boises in the lower duplex.

In her vivid memoir of these times, *His Day Is Marching On*, Shirley notes that Arthur Miller dismissed any complications related to the lower duplex. "The Davenports—he's one of Brooklyn's bankers—live there now, but it will suit Dr. Du Bois admirably," Shirley quoted the playwright verbatim. "'But will they move?' I asked." "Oh, yes," Miller assured her, "I've told them I'm selling the place on condition that the entire building be vacated." Preliminary paperwork completed, the Du Boises returned from their honeymoon expecting to share the comfortable house and garden in which *Death of a Salesman* had been finished three years earlier. Securing world peace might be the specialty of great minds, but real estate ventures, as in this case, often present special tribulations. Terminal illness suddenly struck the Rosses' brilliant son and caused them to withdraw, leaving the full purchase price to the Du Boises. The author of sixteen nonfiction books, two large novels, and a hundred opinion pieces in the *National Guardian* despaired. Fortunately, recalled Shirley, "he left the final details to me." With proceeds from her St. Albans home, royalties from two young adult biographies, and her husband's savings, Graham Du Bois disposed of all impediments to occupying the grand house in the Heights, but for one last remaining detail: banker Davenport.

The lower duplex apartment was indispensable to Du Bois's domestic needs. Its formal parlor and French windows were an ideal setting for his cherished five-foot-tall plaster replica of the *Winged Victory of Samothrace* (later inherited, to the despair of his wife, by a Du Bois biographer). But insisting that their lease ran another half dozen years, the Davenports had no plans to leave the morning Shirley explained how unsatisfactory her elderly husband would find the upper duplex. Suddenly the name Du Bois registered with Mr. Davenport. Could she possibly be married to *the* Dr. Du Bois who was at Harvard during the previous century, the Harvard man whose 1895 Ph.D. dissertation is volume 1 of the Harvard Historical Studies? "And, by George, it was hard reading!" Assured that this was the same Du Bois, banker Davenport informed his astonished wife that they would vacate the lower duplex at summer's end. Turning to Shirley, and supposing her husband retired from all activities long ago, he asked, "Is he in good health?" Shirley smiled a simple affirmative and returned to Harlem to undertake the extensive propaganda campaign to build progressive and civil libertarian support for her husband in the time remaining until the PIC trial date, finally set for early November 1951 in Washington.

"The response of Negroes in general was at first slow and not united," Du Bois observed stoically in his memoir of the trial, *In Battle for Peace*. He persevered in a vain quest for the support of civil libertarian and professional organizations. The NAACP board released a statement of correct neutrality. A founder of the American Civil Liberties Union replied that he personally regretted his board's decision not to take up the matter "until *after* the trial." Liberal circles in New York City showed extreme skittishness. On a circuit of the Midwest and the Pacific Coast during June and part of July 1951, Du Bois gave fifteen speeches and Shirley twenty. The United Electrical Workers, the International Fur and Leather Workers, and a number of red CIO unions helped fill auditoriums and churches along the defense fund route. The response in Chicago, Los Angeles, and San Francisco was exceptional. In San Francisco two thousand filled the Civic Auditorium, and a comparable number a large hall in Oakland. The *Chicago Defender* published a Langston Hughes protest distributed in thousands of barbershops and beauty parlors by the Du Bois defense committee. Hughes proclaimed, "If W. E. B. Du Bois goes to jail a wave of wonder will sweep around the world." Nevertheless millions of Americans of all races thought it would be a wonder if Du Bois were acquitted.

In the end, the trial of the PIC defendants before Judge Matthew F. McGuire on the morning of November 8 was a judicial misfire. The Justice Department duly noted the significance of Einstein's agreement to testify on behalf of the accused. The prosecution's argument was based on "parallelism," a variation on the walking-talking-looking-like-a-duck thesis. Ex-Congressman Vito Marcantonio's final two-hour argument for the defense was both theatrical and lucid. Winding down from his ridicule and anger, Marcantonio put the nub of the case to the court: "Unless connection has been shown, there is no relationship of agency and principal." The case was that simple. The judge did not permit the jury to render a verdict. To hand the decision to the jurors would be to "permit them to speculate on a speculation," stated Judge McGuire and, in so saying, dismissed *U.S. v. Peace Information Center* on November 13, 1951. It was a rare courtroom victory in this Red Scare era.

In late November, I. F. Stone and several other sympathizers joined the Du Boises in a small celebration at Grace Court. "The next years were not easy," Shirley remembered. Although he had been acquitted of charges, the State Department confiscated her husband's passport, and the authorities ordered the Council on African Affairs to shut down. "It was a bitter experience," Du Bois said, "and I bowed before the storm. But I did not break." Sustained by Shirley and friends on the left, including Brooklynites Esther and James Jackson, and that Episcopalian lion William Howard Melish of Holy Trinity Church, Du Bois continued speaking, writing, scolding, and infuriating from his book-lined study in Grace Court. He inveighed over and again against Henry Luce's American Century, Joe McCarthy, John Foster Dulles's massive nuclear retaliation policy, the rearming of Germany, and the CIA-orchestrated overthrow of the governments of Iran and Guatemala. Henry Miller, the novelist, never forgot the experience of hearing the proud pariah speak one evening in a New Jersey meeting hall. "The very majesty of the man silenced any would-be demonstration," he wrote afterward. "His words, however, were like cold dynamite."

Social evenings around the grand piano where frequently Lawrence Brown accompanied Paul Robeson in cathartic song and speech marked the Brooklyn decade. The Du Boises hosted memorable Christmas and New Year's parties. Enough so that the FBI embargoed further travel by UN delegates to Brooklyn Heights after the Du Boises entertained Soviet foreign affairs minister Andrei Vishinsky and families from the Russian, Polish, Indian, and Czech UN delegations to a vodka-spirited Christmas party. It was from his and Shirley's foyer that four- and six-year-old Robert and Michael Rosenberg departed after a poignant children's party on Christmas day 1953 with Anne and Abel Meeropol, who were to be the boys' adoptive parents.

Although Du Bois's voice was featured in editorials, speeches, and Smith Act testimonials in the *National Guardian, Daily Worker,* and *Masses & Mainstream*, the African American civil rights establishment played out the hand dealt it by the National Security State: uncritical patriotism in return for incremental race-relations progress. Many of those who kept the political faith in their circle paid with their freedom, and some even with their lives. Arthur Miller's refusal to name names got his passport revoked and risked a contempt citation.

Yet out of this hollow American decade of terror and complacency came *Brown v. Board of Education*, and the old warrior was elated. But the 1954 *Brown* decision also proved illusory, for Du Bois concluded the following year that freedom on the basis of "all deliberate speed" was an oxymoron. The appearance of Martin Luther King Jr. and the Montgomery bus boycott was something of a puzzle for Du Bois. In the Indian journal *Gandhi Marg*, he drew obvious parallels between Gandhi's liberation of India and King's success in Alabama and went on to speculate that the gifted, committed preacher might be the American Gandhi. King wrote a grateful note to Grace Court in response to Du Bois's letter supporting the Montgomery boycott. But nonviolent passive resistance devoid of an economic agenda increasingly disappointed Du Bois, and he finally decided that King was not Gandhi because Gandhi followed "a positive [economic] program to offset his negative refusal to use violence." An eloquent grumpiness seemed to overtake him more often than not as the 1950s ran down, a rutted readiness to pontificate apocalyptically that was due as much to age as to ideology.

A thousand people celebrated Du Bois's ninetieth at New York City's Roosevelt Hotel on the evening of March 2, 1958. Essie Robeson cochaired the grand anniversary dinner. Paul sang, followed by John Hope Franklin, now chair of the Brooklyn College History Department (a racial first) and a Brooklyn Heights neighbor. Salutes arrived from the humble and the prominent. The leading black newspapers issued special biographical supplements. Still, Franklin noted that neither Fisk University nor the NAACP sponsored the occasion and that "numerous so-called 'respectable' people steered clear." A distinguished historian characterized Du Bois as "a lonely and tragic Negro. Once a national audience, black and white, heard his plea for Negro equality. Now few listen, and fewer still heed him." Readers of the *Nation* must have expected a similar verdict from the author of an article titled "W. E. B. Du Bois: Prophet in Limbo." But the biographer Truman

Nelson delivered a judicious message rather different from that suggested by his title. His theme was the redemption of the unappreciated prophet, "arrested—as Thoreau was arrested, and Theodore Parker and Garrison." And Nelson wagered against the present: "Some day the people in this country will demand that their own records be set straight, and alongside the political accidents, the Presidents and Senators, will go the enduring and usable truths of the American Prophets. Among these Prophets will be W. E. B. Du Bois."

A month after the birthday celebration, the Supreme Court, in a 5 to 4 decision, finally handed down an opinion consonant with the First Amendment that denial of passports on political grounds was unconstitutional. His passport restored, Du Bois and Shirley Graham Du Bois sailed away in August 1958 to red-carpet receptions in Eastern Europe, the Soviet Union, and China, mooring in London for a replenishing four weeks in Paul and Essie Robeson's London townhouse before resuming their triumphant progress after appearing on BBC television. They returned home in 1959 on the *Liberte* in time to celebrate July 4th in their Grace Court garden. He returned refreshed but to disappointment. The great contrarian now foretold a dismal future for African Americans. He believed that a militant capitalism now imprisoned African Americans, once the vanguard of the darker world, and cut them off from the progressive trends of the day. "Whither now do we go?" he implored. An answer arrived. On February 15, 1961, a few days shy of his ninety-third birthday, Du Bois received a cable from President Kwame Nkrumah of Ghana informing him that the *Encyclopedia Africana* project, Du Bois's great social science vision, had been "accepted and endorsed by the Ghana Academy of Learning." "Substantial financial support has been voted," the cable iterated. The Du Boises departed for Ghana later that year, four days after Du Bois applied for membership in the U.S. Communist Party on October 1, 1961. "Today, I have reached a firm conclusion: Capitalism cannot reform itself; it is doomed to self-destruction. No universal selfishness can bring social good to all."

With that, he and Shirley were gone from Grace Court. Ghana received the Du Boises with a warmth and material support that surpassed their expectations. The republic of twelve million, with its high rate of literacy and reasonably competent bureaucracy, was the lodestar of a continent appearing to be on its way to prosperity in unity. "We come to witness the last act (or the first?) of a great world drama," Du Bois mused in an unfinished memoir, "Pan-Africa: The Story of a

Dream." Many have seen a great irony of history in Du Bois's death in Ghana two years later, on August 27, 1963, the night before the great March on Washington for Jobs and Freedom. Two hundred fifty thousand Americans gathered around the Reflecting Pool would pause the next morning in silent tribute to a prophet no longer in limbo. Grace Court has a small, pleasant garden, and Shirley, an accomplished gardener, had thought of planting a flowering bush in a corner of it. "You know, Shirley, a tree would be just right for that corner," she relates that Du Bois suggested. "Never mind that I'll not live to sit under its shade. Those who come after me will enjoy it." Today William Edward Burghardt Du Bois's reputation flourishes and his tree grows in Brooklyn.

## Note

1. For relevant bibliographic information presented in this essay, see David Levering Lewis, *W. E. B. Du Bois: The Fight for Equality and the American Century, 1919–1963* (New York: Henry Holt, 2000), chaps. 14–15, pp. 548–67.

# Herbert Aptheker's Struggle to Publish W. E. B. Du Bois

*Gary Murrell*

Dr. Bill Gaboury, my friend and mentor, introduced me to the writing of both W. E. B. Du Bois and Herbert Aptheker when I was an undergraduate at Southern Oregon State College (now Southern Oregon University). For tutorials with Bill I read Du Bois's *The Souls of Black Folk* and *Black Reconstruction in America* and Aptheker's *American Negro Slave Revolts*, *Nat Turner's Slave Rebellion*, and his three-volume *People's History of the United States*. I first heard Herbert speak in 1986, when I attended a Marxist Scholars Conference at the University of Washington with Bill and his daughter Natalie. I don't remember the subject of Herbert's lecture that day, but I recall his being a compelling speaker, his voice rising as his indignation grew, his enunciation precise with his Brooklyn accent, hurtling quotations to support his points, which brought warm, enthusiastic applause from the audience. A few years later Herbert, accompanied by his wife, Fay, spent a week as a scholar in residence at Southern Oregon State. I drove to Ashland from Eugene, where I was working on my master's at the University of Oregon to participate in the events. I attended several of Herbert's presentations that week. I also had the opportunity to have dinner with Herbert and Fay and to engage in lively conversation with them in people's homes. Herbert and Fay both were delightful, warm, open, often funny, and enormously considerate.

In the early 1990s, while working on my doctoral degree at the U of O, I suggested to my adviser that perhaps I should write a biography of Herbert for my dissertation. "Absolutely not," he said. "Aptheker's work can't be trusted." I accepted my adviser's judgment then, but after teaching for a few years I returned in the summer of 1999 to the idea of an Aptheker biography. I contacted Herbert to propose the project, and he agreed to meet with me for a series of interviews which we completed over a ten-day period in August, only two months after Fay's death. Whenever he touched on the subject of Du Bois in those ten days Herbert spoke with veneration bordering on awe. Clearly he loved Du Bois as a son loves a father. Only much later, after Herbert's death, as I organized my research materials to begin writing the biography, did I realize the extent of their mutual admiration and love, the deep devotion, the fierce protectiveness Herbert felt for the memory of Du Bois. "He died in exile," Martin Luther King Jr. said of Du Bois, "praised sparingly and in many circles ignored. . . . He was ignored by a pathetically ignorant America but not by history."[1] That history did not ignore Du Bois is, to a remarkable degree, Herbert Aptheker's fulfillment of a trust placed in him by Du Bois.

Prior to leaving the military at the end of World War II, Aptheker applied for and received a Guggenheim Foundation Fellowship that ran from April 15, 1946, to April 15, 1947. The fellowship required him, during the term of his appointment, "to devote himself . . . to a study of the American Negro in the Second World War."[2] However, between the time he applied for the fellowship and when he actually began work as a fellow, Aptheker had already completed a study of blacks in the armed forces for the U.S. Army. He knew from his work on that study that much of the documentation concerning black troops in World War II that he would need for the work he proposed to the Guggenheim Foundation was not available and would not be available during the tenure of his fellowship. This necessitated a change of topic. After discussion with his friend Philip Foner, he decided to compile a documentary history of black people in the United States.

Once he had settled on the new topic for his research and had the approval of the Guggenheim Foundation, Aptheker made an appointment to meet with W. E. B. Du Bois. Aptheker was thirty-two, Du Bois seventy-seven, and among the left and in the black community in the United States and in the world he held legendary status. He had returned to the National Association for the Advancement of Colored People (NAACP) in the summer of 1944, after being forced out of his position there in 1934. His position amorphous, he became "a sort of minister of foreign affairs, while bearing the title 'Director of Special Research.'"[3]

In the ten years he was away from the NAACP, the organization became a center of power for black Americans' challenge to Jim Crow. "The results astonished me," Du Bois wrote in his *Autobiography*. The executive secretary, Walter White, micromanaged a rigidly top-down organization. White clashed almost immediately with Du Bois's politics. By mid-1946, when Aptheker met with Du Bois, the personal animosity between Du Bois and White had grown to open hostility.[4]

Aptheker laid out for Du Bois his plans for a documentary history of black people. At the end of his presentation, to Aptheker's astonishment, Du Bois asked, "Herbert, would you like to share my office?" Aptheker readily accepted. Du Bois, the "most distinguished representative . . . of the history of Black people . . . whose astonishing memory went back to the 1880's," told Aptheker, "Feel free to ask me questions whenever you wish!" For more than a year Du Bois and Aptheker worked side by side in Du Bois's small NAACP office.[5] How that arrangement passed the scrutiny of the fiercely anticommunist White went unrecorded.

As the bond between Aptheker and Du Bois strengthened through close work on their overlapping projects, Aptheker agreed, at Du Bois's insistence, to edit for publication a collection of Du Bois's correspondence and articles. Anson Phelps Stokes, the director of the Phelps-Stokes Fund, had suggested that Du Bois strongly consider publication of an autobiography and contemplate "leaving your papers to some institution or individual" for future use. "Surely . . . there are some very competent Negro scholars such as Charles H. Thompson, or Alain Locke, or Dr. [Rayford] Logan, or others who could do the work admirably," Stokes wrote. Du Bois responded that Shirley Graham intended to write a biography and that "Herbert Aptheker, a Columbia doctor in philosophy, is going over my letters and articles with view to publication."[6]

Du Bois had tens of thousands of documents in his files that Aptheker began to systematically go through. He placed requests for correspondence in several leftist and black publications as well as the *New York Times Book Review,* and then began actively seeking a publisher. Du Bois warned that the proposed project would likely meet with something less than real cooperation, but Aptheker carried on. He regularly kept Du Bois apprised of his progress. "Let me take this opportunity to assure you that though the need to earn something approximating a livelihood has made it impossible for me recently to actively work on your letters and papers," he wrote in July 1947, "I have continued to seek financial support for that project. I am now in correspondence with Little Brown & Co. concerning this, and will keep at it until it is done."[7] Little, Brown rejected the project, which prompted an acerbic missive to Du Bois the next month. Noting the rejection and his continuing correspondence with Rutgers University,

Aptheker promised to send Du Bois "a detailed account of their rejection, too—pardon the bitterness. As you were good enough to remark to me at one time—I'm just beginning—and bitterness ill becomes a novice."[8] Du Bois responded with words of encouragement and made some suggestions. "What you have got to do in approaching your publishers is to let them know that you are quite aware of what their natural reaction is going to be, but that it is time for them to reappraise the situation and make some venture," he wrote. "Of course even with this argument, you are going to have a hard time to find anybody who will finance the book which you have in mind. . . . I hope you will keep trying."[9] Aptheker corresponded with and sometimes met editors: "All rejected the proposal, some quickly and some belatedly, but all firmly." After a particularly discouraging meeting with a representative of Columbia University Press, he suggested that the difficulty finding a publisher might perhaps be the person Du Bois had chosen as editor. "How much deterring effect . . . is my association with it having?" Aptheker wrote to Du Bois in January 1948. "This troubles me very much," the letter continued. "If you feel for a moment that a somewhat more respectable—and perhaps, more capable—person engaged in this effort might have better luck in accomplishing the main job, please be good enough to indicate that to me." Du Bois dismissed the suggestion out of hand. "I think you are by far the best fitted person to edit my letters," Du Bois responded, "and I hope you will not consider giving up the job, although, as I said before, it is going to be difficult." Just how difficult did not then dawn on Aptheker; intermittently, for the next twenty-five years, even after Du Bois's death, until the University of Massachusetts Press agreed, Aptheker sought, in vain, for a publisher for the Du Bois correspondence.[10]

On February 15, 1961, Ghana's president Kwame Nkrumah notified Du Bois that the Ghana Academy of Learning had endorsed and voted financing for Du Bois's long-standing dream, first enunciated at the beginning of the twentieth century, of compiling an *Encyclopedia Africana*.[11] The Du Boises immediately set plans in motion to move to Ghana. They planned to make the move sometime later in the year or even the next, but at a cocktail party in Washington, D.C., a lawyer whom Shirley knew "very well" warned her that she and Du Bois "must get out of [the country] before October ninth" because on "that day the U.S. Supreme Court is going to hand down an adverse opinion on the Communist Party—and Dr. Du Bois will most certainly be one of the citizens of this country who will be prevented from traveling anywhere."[12] When Shirley related the conversation to Du Bois, "he exploded," she wrote. "Well, they shall not stop me!" he said. "I'll not let them stop this work! I'll not be chained up here! We'll go—we'll go quickly!" After brief discussion, Du Bois asked his wife to "phone Herbert [and] . . . ask him to come and see me in the morning. Let him know it's urgent."[13]

The next morning Du Bois told Aptheker that he would leave the country immediately. He would take some of his correspondence and some papers relating to Africa with him; everything else "I'd like to leave here with you, Herbert, if you have room to keep them. If you can find the time, you can start their classification." Aptheker, Graham Du Bois noted, "was deeply moved. His voice was husky when he said he'd be glad to take care of the files and would consider it an honor to work on them."[14] Aptheker began transferring the files to his house the next morning. "The steel filing cabinets full of his papers ended up in our basement," Aptheker's daughter, Bettina, wrote of the arrangement to house more than 100,000 letters dating from the close of the nineteenth century, "unbelievably in the laundry room under the clothes hanging on the lines to dry." Bettina's recollection of moving Du Bois's archive, and her own participation in the editorial process, as her essay in this volume makes clear, helps to tell the fascinating story of the literal material of his intellectual legacy.[15]

Almost as soon as Du Bois left the country, Aptheker began to receive letters concerning Du Bois's papers. Arna Bontemps, the well-known Harlem Renaissance writer and longtime librarian at Fisk University, to which Du Bois had sold his library for $10,000, wrote to Aptheker telling him that the library had received requests for access to the letters. "Could you tell me what plans you have for them?" he asked.[16] Aptheker told Bontemps that he held the papers and letters for "safekeeping" at Du Bois's request. "I am simply holding them in my home in accordance with the wish expressed by him and his wife. . . . Of course, exactly what disposition is to be made of the papers at any given moment is entirely subject to the will of the Doctor and his wife."[17]

After Du Bois's death in August 1963 the letters to Aptheker from historians eager to mine Du Bois's legacy intensified. Aptheker's replies always indicated that he held custodial powers only, that Shirley Graham Du Bois's desire "has been that they not be opened to other scholars." He and Fay, working as a team, continued to go through the papers. In October 1963 he reported to Graham Du Bois, "I have studied now about 40% with care. The richness is almost unbelievable."[18]

Graham Du Bois responded in December, "Dear, dear Herbert . . .
Obviously, you cannot throw the papers and letters open to other scholars. . . . It is my feeling that they remain for your private use alone. A
lot of people are now 'in the act' of wanting to write on W. E. B.," she
continued, "but as far as possible I think we should <u>choose</u> the people
who write at any length about him. If there is some sincere scholar with
whom you should like to share evenings reading His letters, always feel
free to share them. <u>But this is a personal matter for you</u>."[19] "No one
has seen his letters, though several requests have come in," Aptheker
reported on December 16, 1963. To propel the project for the "Life and
Letters" they had for years planned to publish, Aptheker asked Graham
Du Bois's permission "to actively seek out support for that project. . . .
For instance, I might be able to get a grant from some foundation to
make it possible at least to start the effort in an organized way. Should I
try that? I really don't want to do anything unless you say I should and
whatever I do do, after hearing from you—I want you to know all about
it at every step."[20] A few days later he reported that he had by then read
"page by page and line by line—something like 60% of the collection.
It is simply fabulous and every night as I pore over these pieces of
paper—sacred to me—my admiration and love and incredulity grow.
Good God, there was a man! What inspiration and lessons are in those
papers!"[21]

In January 1964 Graham Du Bois responded to Aptheker's questions
concerning seeking support for publishing the Du Bois collection. "You
are in a better position than I am to judge the <u>timing</u> of this approach,"
she wrote. "From where I sit I can't see the Ford, Carnegie or Rocker-
feller [sic] Foundations giving any assistance to you on this. And it is
essential <u>that the help be given to you</u> and <u>that you have charge of the
project</u>, and <u>do the final editing</u>!" If he could set the plan in motion, she
wrote, "you have my full and unqualified endorsement. But you must
fully consider the snares and pitfalls and deceptions which you will
encounter," she cautioned. "The pure in heart may see God, but they
do not always see their enemies! You, along with W. E. B. are singularly
pure in heart."[22]

As requests for access to the Du Bois papers accumulated and Aptheker's custody came into question, controversy erupted because, posited
the historian Gerald Horne in his biography of Graham Du Bois, "con-
tending forces [sought] to appropriate a historic icon like Du Bois. . . .
A quivering trembler had erupted as a result of the attempt to determine who had standing to claim the immense legacy of Du Bois." By

minimizing the long-standing desires of Du Bois, by ignoring the agreements between and among Aptheker, Du Bois, and Graham Du Bois, Horne in essence dismissed Aptheker's designation as Du Bois's literary executor as if Aptheker was involved in a street brawl. With a simplistic, throwaway one-liner, Horne put the matter to rest: "Aptheker, who would organize Du Bois's papers, felt that this task gave him standing."[23] If Aptheker did not have standing, one wonders who did.

Both the Hoover Institution at Stanford University and the Historical Society of Wisconsin expressed a desire to house the Du Bois papers in 1968 (as did other entities, such as Indiana University Press several years later), but Aptheker's discussions with Harvard University, where Du Bois earned his Ph.D., were the most serious. The director of Harvard University Press, Mark Carroll, contacted Aptheker through the socialist philosopher, radical activist, and Harvard benefactor Corliss Lamont. Although he was not a communist, Lamont and Aptheker maintained a relationship over the years. Carroll asked Aptheker for a proposal that he could discuss with the faculty advisers to the press.[24]

Aptheker proposed two books, inadequate really, given the scope and mass of material in the Du Bois legacy, but such was his desire to get something into print that at that point anything was better than nothing: a one-volume, six- or seven-hundred-page compilation of Du Bois's letters and a collection of his lectures and speeches, both edited with commentary by himself.[25] He met with Ann Orlov, Harvard Press's editor for the behavioral sciences, in August to work out the details of the proposal. He expected, he told Orlov, "that if this were undertaken it should be a definitive edition, and fully to compare with other editions done by Harvard [such] as the Theodore Roosevelt letters and that its scholarship would be as impeccable as possible."[26] Reporting to Graham Du Bois on the meeting, Aptheker noted, "The Press is definitely interested in publishing the Papers." He told Orlov, he wrote to Graham Du Bois, "that it was the Doctor's wish that in no circumstances would anyone else here be in charge of such a project but Dr. Aptheker; that I would be happy to work with other scholars and that I would insist that black men and women have decisive roles in the production of this collection." He said he expected no royalties, that all payments "would have to be made to Mrs. Du Bois." Aptheker said he would move no further in the discussions until he had her agreement.[27]

Graham Du Bois told Aptheker that he was "right in giving [the Harvard offer] serious consideration." The "papers are valuable for the world," she said, "and we would not want to keep them hid away." She thought Du Bois would approve of Harvard "<u>under the conditions laid down by you</u>." She suggested that her lawyer Bernard Jaffe get involved in the discussions. "I'd like for you to call him in for exact legal advice," she wrote. "I trust your scholarship and integrity implicitly, but in a matter of this kind it is well to have a lawyer on hand" since the project involved considerable effort and "all sorts of political considerations," which Aptheker had pointed out earlier, "may arise. We want to be very sure that our interests and the interests of This Sacred Trust are well protected."[28]

In October, having received the written agreement Graham Du Bois and Aptheker had drafted, Orlov let him know that discussions within the university, "with the Harvard Board of Syndics . . . the faculty committee that controls our imprint," were proceeding slowly but they were "getting into position for at least a tentative decision."[29] By November, Aptheker sensed the project fading away. A month earlier he had told Professor Robert S. Cohen, the physicist and philosopher, his cofounder and closest confidant at the American Institute of Marxist Studies, that Harvard seemed to be "really serious" about publishing the Du Bois papers but "problems (mostly me) remain." Orlov, he told Cohen, had been "shocked to learn that some in charge of that press said they would be happy to see the collection burn rather than have my name on a Harvard book. I told her she need not be surprised: The same sort of people burned folks like me in ovens not long ago—gentility and all. I think this shocked her a little."[30] "The Harvard matter still remains in the 'interest' stage," he wrote to Graham Du Bois. "Correspondence continues and possibility remains." He reported that he had also had discussions with the publisher Lippincott that "expresses very real interest in my editing a stout volume of selections of the Doctor's letters. . . . [The] firm's interest is genuine."[31]

While Aptheker was involved in the discussions with Harvard, the historian John Blassingame, then chairman of the Howard University Bibliographic Workshop and assistant editor of the Booker T. Washington Papers, contacted Aptheker with a not so subtle demand that he relinquish his control of Du Bois's papers. The letter was signed by two dozen representatives from colleges and universities around the country: "Scholars and collectors, we think, have a moral obligation to deposit Du Bois's manuscripts in repositories where they can be safely preserved, adequately catalogued and made available for research."[32] Aptheker responded curtly, "I do think your first communication to me might better have been framed in the form of some questions rather than definite suggestions—almost directives. For instance, germane is this: what were the conditions under which my custody was undertaken?" He agreed to meet with any of the signers of the letter "so that the weighty matter you raise can be probed at some length."[33] Blassingame evidently carried a grudge over the matter and exacted his revenge several years later.

Based on the expectation that Harvard or Lippincott or some other publisher would soon publish Du Bois's letters, Herbert and Fay worked feverishly on sorting and typing a manuscript. Aptheker reported to Graham Du Bois in mid-November, "We have selected and Fay has typed—in triplicate—about 650 pages so far and this brings us mid-way into 1923. The first volume I plan to have go through 1934. . . . There may be some battles [over length] but of course I'll quite willingly fight to get the most possible in to this first one."[34] In the end Lippincott did not publish Du Bois's letters, although it did publish Graham Du Bois's memoir of W. E. B., *His Day Is Marching On*, in 1971.[35]

Almost a year after the discussions with Harvard fell apart, Leone Stein, director of the University of Massachusetts Press, contacted Aptheker in October 1969. After some initial telephone conversations, Aptheker proposed "a stout volume" of unpublished Du Bois papers, "not letters," which he would edit. He said he could have the book ready by mid-1971.[36] A month later Aptheker made notes of an additional telephone conversation with Stein. Stein told him that there was "tremendous polarization" among members of the board of UMass. Press. Some board members exhibited both fear of and hatred towards Aptheker, which Stein told Aptheker she had not expected. If the project were to go forward the board would "require . . . two [outside scholars] for surveillance—a word she used—over me in my editing of either the Letters or the Papers." Stein related that the board was interested in expanding Aptheker's proposal to include publication of "the complete letters but with these two people over me." He "explained that I wished to be treated like any other scholar; [that] I would take lessons in honor and integrity from no one on the board of that Press. That I would be the editor and no one else; that I would welcome consultants, scholars who would HELP, who would express opinions as to where my judgment and scholarship might be faulty—etc etc and . . . I would be treated no differently from any other scholar associated with that Press and that I was certain both Du Bois and his widow would not agree to anything else." Stein agreed to present Aptheker's statement to the board. "She added," reads the last sentence of Aptheker's memo of the conversation, "that she was shocked to find such censorship on the board of any university press. I told her I was not."[37]

On November 26, 1969, twenty-three years after Aptheker began searching for a publisher for the papers of Du Bois, Stein wrote that she was "delighted to report that the University of Massachusetts Press Committee has approved publication of a one or two volume selection of the unpublished papers of W. E. B. Du Bois, under your editorship." The press would appoint two "mutually satisfactory scholars" to "assist you in whatever way they can, in checking matters of fact and offering their advice regarding selections." Professor Sidney Kaplan, a leading scholar of black culture and history and founder of the University of Massachusetts African-American Studies Department, had, she reported, "already accepted." The letter stipulated that, with some minor modifications, royalty payments would be apportioned "10% of the list price [to] Mrs Du Bois" and the equivalent of 2½% to Aptheker. Stein ended the letter indicating interest "in a more comprehensive series of publications of the writings of W. E. B. Du Bois, either of the complete correspondence, and/or other unpublished material." The press "would probably have to seek a grant from NEH [National Endowment for the Humanities], which is interested, in principle. . . . I simply wish to make it clear that we do have a genuine interest, at the Press, in further publications."[38] The agreement with the University of Massachusetts proved solid, but the NEH interest "in principle" turned into one of those "political considerations," particularly concerning Aptheker's association with the Communist Party, of which Aptheker had written Graham Du Bois.

While Herbert and Fay proceeded with their work on the two volumes of Du Bois's letters, contracted with Lippincott, he insisted, in his final contract with UMass Press, "that all decisions as to what goes in and what does not go in is made by the Editor. He will turn to the consultants for advice and aid but he will have the decision and the power to make the decision as to what is published."[39] Together Stein and Aptheker wrote a grant to the NEH for additional funding for the project, with Aptheker listed as the principal investigator and Sidney Kaplan and Ernest Kaiser, Schomburg Center archivist and writer, as consulting editors. Initially the NEH questioned Aptheker's status with UMass, so administrators attempted to arrange for Aptheker to receive an appointment of some kind with the History Department. Stein told Aptheker in September that the appointment had gone only as far as the provost but that she was "not optimistic" that the chancellor and trustees would approve of the arrangement.[40]

By mid-December the NEH had rejected Aptheker's grant request. Henry I. Tragle, assistant to the coordinator of research in the Office of the Dean of the UMass Graduate School, wrote Aptheker with suggestions for resubmitting the grant. He mentioned that the Graduate School dean, Mortimer Appley, had begun discussions within the university community for the university to acquire the Du Bois papers. "Although not able to suggest any practical course of action . . . he [Dean Appley] is desirous of having the University become the center for Du Bois scholarship . . . and the possibility of the University of Massachusetts Library becoming the depository for the W. E. B. Du Bois papers." Tragle had visited Dr. William Emerson, head of the Division of Research and Publication of the NEH, in November. Emerson "was frank to indicate his own sympathy for such a publication project and almost equally frank in his reflection that some of the experts (whom he felt he could not identify by name) raised questions which pertained not so much to the desirability of publication per se, but rather to question if your estimate of the quantitative and qualitative value of the papers was an acceptable one." Tragle related to Aptheker his verbal response to Emerson's remarks: "I felt this constituted more of a reflection on [Aptheker's] integrity than a true evaluation of [his] proposed publication and I had the feeling that he agreed with me. He read me some snippets from a voluminous file, presumable [sic] the record of the review procedure."[41]

The confidential "Panel Evaluation" of the proposed NEH grant called the papers of Du Bois "a resource of great value for Black and American history. But merits of making them available overweighed by shortcomings of PI [principal investigator] and weaknesses of plan. Should be supported only if under direction of responsible editorial board with real authority, to ensure editorial objectivity and scholarly access. Panel registered distress that materials of this value remain in possession of private individual in his house; should be deposited for safe-keeping in a university or public library."[42]

The individual reviewer's remarks, which neither Aptheker nor anyone at UMass saw, reveal a group of historians and a professor of English preoccupied with Aptheker's politics. Four of the six reviewers claimed Aptheker's politics would affect negatively the project. Aptheker was "well known for his writing on black history . . . from a Marxist viewpoint," wrote Frank Friedel, a Harvard historian. "Would approve," he wrote, "if PI has editorial board; otherwise would not recommend." Friedel refused to provide a numerical rating, 1–5, for the project. Yale historian John M. Blum, who rated the project a "2," called Aptheker's approach to historical writing "particularly doctrinaire." Blyden Jackson from Southern University, who gave "no numerical rating," feared that Aptheker "may view Du Bois solely from the Marxist angle with real hazard of project becoming too one-sided." Louis Rubin, professor of English at the University of North Carolina, who offered a rating of "3" wrote the most critical report, said Aptheker's "known . . . Marxist bias would wreak havoc with the meaning of Du Bois's life. . . . PI not capable of (any) kind of disinterested, subtle, psychologically-acute inquiry; editor should . . . be a black man. . . . Perhaps it should be done by a team of scholars, black and white." Historian Benjamin Quarles, who gave the project the highest rating, "5," refused the red-baiting. "Potentially a very valuable contribution," he wrote. "PI's qualifications for task . . . unusual and extensive. . . . This is a major project."[43]

Yale historian C. Vann Woodward, with a rating of "4," provided, in retrospect, a fascinating appraisal of Aptheker's proposal. He called the value of the project "potentially very great indeed . . . of first rate importance." He expressed concerns that the plan was not clearly articulated in the proposal, and he questioned whether Aptheker could carry out the project at home. In view of a later controversy at Yale, precipitated by Woodward's adamant assertion that Aptheker's incompetence as a scholar precluded his teaching a seminar on Du Bois at Yale, Woodward's comments as a reviewer on Aptheker's scholarship in the NEH grant reveal a shabby duplicity on Woodward's part: "PI's competence from published work," Woodward wrote as a reviewer for the grant proposal in 1970, "is persuasive."[44] Woodward "wore the mask of a Southern gentleman scholar," historian Jesse Lemisch, a Yale alumnus, recalled. "Woodward's reputation for liberalism was undeserved," he added. "I felt sympathy for Herbert's illusions. Aptheker felt he and Woodward were gentlemen scholars who could get along. Herbert didn't understand that rules of genteel discourse did not apply to him."[45] Nonetheless, in this instance, perhaps for the last time, Woodward did not attempt to sabotage Aptheker's grant applications.

One could understand Aptheker's predictable response when informed of the grant's denial. "The National Endowment for the Humanities has rejected my application for the same reason that the University of Massachusetts has refused my appointment," he wrote Tragle. "What bothered those 'scholars,'" he wrote in the same letter, of another NEH report concerned with the current state of the Du Bois papers, "was the name of the person to whom Dr. Du Bois entrusted his Papers."[46] The NEH turned down two subsequent grant requests from Aptheker and UMass Press.

Aptheker had had infrequent correspondence with Woodward over the years. In January 1971 he wrote Woodward, unaware of Woodward's role as a reviewer for the NEH grant, whom he addressed as "Professor Woodward," asking permission to quote from a 1938 letter Woodward had written to Du Bois. He took the opportunity to tell Woodward that Lippincott would publish the first volume of Aptheker's selected correspondence of Du Bois that covered the period through 1934, when Du Bois left the NAACP the first time. He reported that UMass Press would publish four volumes of the unpublished papers of Du Bois.[47] Woodward's response, beginning "Dear Mr. Aptheker," expressed concern that the first volume of Du Bois's letters would "go all the way down to 1934. I can not believe that this will give you adequate coverage." He reminded Aptheker that the Booker T. Washington letters would cover, probably, ten volumes, "and talk of a new edition of the Douglass papers is in terms of the same scope." Woodward asked "if the original manuscripts down to 1934 may now be made accessible to qualified research students in some good and accessible library? Have any plans been made to find such a library? May I open the question with the Yale Library?" Surely, he wrote Aptheker, "you must be aware of the great need and demand among historians for free access to this material and I am sure you will want to find an appropriate solution." He asked that Aptheker keep him informed about the project without revealing his role as a reviewer for the NEH grant.[48]

In a long response to "Mr. Woodward," Aptheker tried to explain that Lippincott would agree only to a two-volume set of Du Bois letters, "the most significant historical material." The contract allowed the rights to publish "a full and complete edition" later. "No foundation—private or public—has been willing to help me in any way," he told Woodward. "Harvard . . . made it quite clear that it did not want my name associated with its own."[49] Woodward reported that he was relieved, although, he wrote, "you would readily agree that, as useful as these [two volumes] are, they would not be what the scholarly community requires." Again Woodward pressed Aptheker on making the papers available to scholars. "There are many instances . . . where editors of private papers have proceeded with their editions over long periods of years while the manuscripts they are editing are made fully available to qualified scholars, for example the Booker Washington Papers." Couldn't you, Woodward asked, "reach some agreement with a library that would benefit both you and the other members of the scholarly community. . . . I know this must be an embarrassment to you to have a constant request for use . . . and you must regret having to reject legitimate use by others. . . . I might be of some help in finding a solution."[50] No record exists in Aptheker's papers of Woodward assisting in finding a home for the Du Bois papers, but Aptheker indicated agreement with Woodward's suggestions while taking a swipe at the historical profession. "In view of all that the historical profession in the United States has done for me in the past thirty years," he wrote to Woodward in apparent good humor, "it would give me a special satisfaction to be able to help it in the future."[51] Woodward said he "relished the mild irony" of Aptheker's statement, reiterated his interest in taking up the matter with the Yale Library, then suggested that "perhaps the Library of Congress would be best." There, assuring Aptheker that "such an arrangement would take a great burden of responsibility off your shoulders and in no way inhibit your publication plans," the correspondence between Aptheker and Woodward breaks off without a resolution.[52]

Aptheker certainly would have welcomed a serious offer from Yale University Library to house the Du Bois papers. Why did that offer never come? Was Woodward serious? Given his later actions, the offer seems disingenuous at best. Perhaps other calculations were in play. Historian Eugene Genovese thought so. "Woodward was capable of petty jealousy," Genovese said in an interview. "He had a very nasty side. He was jealous about Aptheker having the Du Bois papers and quite likely influenced the National Endowment for the Humanities decisions to deny Aptheker funding for the project."[53] Woodward was not the only person possessed of jealousy. An FBI informant within the Communist Party, in which Aptheker had been a member since 1939, reported in July 1972 that "blacks are envious of [Aptheker] . . . especially [name blacked out—possibly James Jackson?] because he, not [Aptheker], should be the heir of works of W. E. B. Du Bois, Black Historian."[54]

Aptheker delivered the finished manuscript of the Du Bois correspondence to Lippincott in December 1970. Eight months later editors at the firm began asking for written permission from authors to quote from letters to Du Bois. Aptheker began sending out inquiries in September. "You can imagine the problems in terms of locating people," he wrote to Paul M. Wright at UMass Press, "(and Black people at that)

who wrote letters forty or fifty or sixty years ago!" Then he heard nothing from Lippincott until February 1972, when the editor in charge of
the manuscript called, "tremendously excited by the book," and told
Aptheker "that it was then (only then!) going into copy-editing." Two
weeks later, "after it went to the head office in [Philadelphia]," Lippincott informed Shirley Du Bois's attorneys that it was "impossible to
go ahead in terms of permissions!" Clearly, Aptheker wrote, distinctly
disgusted by the whole process, "what was involved here was a top-level
decision by someone in Phila[delphia] based on the well-known politics of the editor of the book."[55] Lippincott canceled its contract with
Aptheker in March 1972. The loss of time infuriated him. Two months
later UMass Press agreed to publish two volumes of Du Bois correspondence, which Aptheker eventually expanded to three.

In 1972 Aptheker and UMass Press, for the third time, applied for a
grant from the NEH that included a recommendation for funding from
Massachusetts Democratic senator Edward Brooke. In June 1972, at
a convention in New Orleans, his "sympathy" for the Du Bois project
having evidently mutated, an enraged William Emerson of the NEH
publicly confronted Leone Stein in a restaurant while she had dinner
with colleagues. Ignoring her companions he asked, "without introduction and in what can hardly be described as a friendly manner, whether
I was from the press involved in the 'Ap-taker' project. . . . Then, without waiting for a response, he proclaimed that it was an 'effrontery'"
that "'America's Number 1 Communist' apply to the National Endowment for a grant. Not only was it an 'effrontery,' it was 'stupidity.'" Stein
reported to Aptheker, in an arresting understatement, that the prospects
for funding from the NEH did not appear encouraging.[56] When Senator Brooke forwarded a copy of the NEH rejection, Aptheker thanked
him for his help and related the substance of Stein's conversation with
Emerson, without mentioning Stein, then told Brook, "I imagine that
the radicalism of Dr. Du Bois himself did not help but I know that my
own dissenting opinions certainly played a major part in the negative
decision."[57]

After agreeing to publish the Du Bois correspondence, in March 1973
UMass Press sought out a board of "distinguished scholars, to advise"
Aptheker on the project, reasoning that the board would strengthen
the odds of a grant from the NEH. The press contacted historians C.
Vann Woodward, Louis R. Harlan, editor of the Booker T. Washington
Papers, Kenneth B. Clark, Charles H. Wesley, and John Hope Franklin.
Both Woodward and Harlan eventually agreed to serve on the board,

and while it is not clear whether Franklin did eventually serve on the board, as he indicated he would "be pleased" to do, he did write "a strong recommendation" for a new NEH application.[58] The University of Massachusetts also reached agreement with Shirley Graham Du Bois to purchase all of the Du Bois papers in Aptheker's custody. In July the university took possession of the papers, which brought a resolution from the Massachusetts State Department of the American Legion condemning the university for purchasing the papers of someone with left-wing tendencies.[59] Later that year the first volume of the Du Bois correspondence went on sale. "I hope you've seen Vol. I of the Correspondence by now," Aptheker wrote Graham Du Bois in December. "Not a word—not a single word—about it in the Times or any other of the free press in the USA."[60] Seven years later, in 1980, when archivists had finally completed their work organizing Du Bois's papers, UMass organized a dedication ceremony at which Aptheker spoke. He lauded UMass Press for having the "grit" to publish the papers of what he called a "dangerous black radical" and his "white notorious editor." He paid homage to Fay, who could not attend, as the one of the two of them who never gave up hope that Du Bois's correspondence would be published. "Can one person make a difference in this world?" he asked the audience toward the conclusion of his remarks. "If you would know, if you would regain confidence in the human, study [Du Bois]. If anything in the world is sacred, it is these papers."[61]

Immediately upon agreeing to serve on the advisory board both Woodward and Harlan began pressing Aptheker to consider more than the three volumes of correspondence that UMass Press had agreed to publish. Aptheker told them both that what stood in the way was money. He told Franklin that the project had received a total of only $4,000 as of late July 1973: $2,000 from the American Council of Learned Societies and $2,000 from the Rabinowitz Fund.[62] By September Aptheker had also raised privately, from friends, about $8,000. Nonetheless, he told Harlan, the two remaining volumes would "include all the significant historical material," which, he wrote, having Harlan's assistance in selecting—"what to include and what to omit—would be very helpful of course, as would reading for accuracy, context, etc."[63] Woodward claimed surprise that the correspondence would not cover ten volumes. "I had assumed when I agreed to serve on your Advisory Board," he wrote Aptheker, "that the correspondence would be the main material included. I hope you will reconsider your plans. . . . I could not in all conscience remain on your Board in support of the present plan."[64]

Aptheker assured Woodward that the correspondence would constitute "three stout volumes of the ten being projected." Seven other
volumes would consist "of his unpublished books . . . his college papers,
some diaries and travel journals . . . and quite a few unpublished essays
on various subjects." Again, Aptheker reported, the problem was money.
"All of the above was projected when all efforts to obtain money from
foundations had failed; I've never expected grants and rarely been disappointed! Of course, if a substantial grant is forthcoming, I would
insist that the Press move to the publication of a fuller collection of his
correspondence."[65]

In early January 1974, one day apart and with similar language unlikely
to have been coincidental, both Woodward and Harlan resigned from
the Advisory Board in what appears to have been an attempt to scuttle
the project. "My main reason," wrote Woodward, "is that I do not agree
with the editor about his policy respecting the selection and editing of
the Du Bois correspondence."[66] In a series of letters lasting through
April to both Woodward and Harlan, Aptheker and Leone Stein and
Malcolm Call at UMass Press attempted to ascertain what disagreements specifically caused the resignations. Both Woodward and Harlan
complained about the content of the first volume of correspondence,
which had appeared in October 1973. Call expressed puzzlement at
Harlan's position. "Your perusal and subsequent endorsement of the
*Correspondence* galleys prior to publication," Call wrote, had, he
thought, precluded any misunderstanding on Harlan's part.[67] Woodward came closest to providing concrete reasons for his resignation,
although he evidently pulled from thin air accusations that Aptheker
had not done the scholarly research necessary for such an undertak-
ing. "The first volume raised doubts about the editorial procedures and
principles of selection," Woodward wrote, about the volume of letters
completed prior to the establishment of the Advisory Board.

> The first volume left me in considerable doubt about the
> thoroughness of the search for Du Bois' correspondence. . . .
> Among collections known to contain Du Bois' letters that
> were apparently not searched for this edition are the papers of
> R. R. Moton . . . George W. Cook . . . Ray Stannard Baker . . .
> Arthur B. Spingarn . . . William S. Braithwaite . . . Charles W.
> Chestnut. . . . Apparently there was no attempt to use the let-
> ters of Du Bois at the American Academy of Arts and Sciences.
> Mr Herman Kahn of the Yale Library tells me that no use was

made of a large collection of Du Bois' letters in the Manuscript
Division. My fear is that the editor placed too much reliance on
the personal collection kept by Du Bois himself and that much
of importance has been overlooked.[68]

Aptheker responded with evident restraint to Woodward's charges of
scholarly inattention. "Search for other Du Bois correspondence was
very considerable," he wrote. He had visited and corresponded with
all of the collections mentioned in Woodward's letter. "There is not a
'large collection' of Du Bois letters in the Yale library;" he corrected
Woodward. "What letters there are were examined by me and again the
very few of any significance were copied by me and are now part of the
collection at Amherst. I do not recall that I was ever asked—or told—
about this in earlier letters," he concluded with obvious frustration.
"Perhaps if Dr. Du Bois had not selected the undersigned to be responsible for the collecting and editing of his unpublished and published
works a force would have been gathered and funded to make that possible. And perhaps the time will come—I think it will—when conditions
will be such . . . that this will actually be undertaken."[69] Neither Woodward nor Harlan withdrew his resignation. In July Stein told Aptheker
she had suggested that the UMass chancellor disband the board since
Woodward and Harlan had resigned.[70]

In July 1975 UMass Press finally received a $69,000 independent
grant to process the Du Bois papers. The grant supported microfilm-
ing and cataloguing the papers but did not apply to the work proposed
or accomplished by Aptheker. Again, in 1976 the press and Aptheker
applied for NEH funding for his work on the unpublished papers.
When the NEH rejection arrived Stein and Professor John Bracey contacted the Endowment for an explanation. George F. Farr responded for
the NEH. He noted that the application "was submitted to a number
of scholars in the field," although he did not name the reviewers. He
claimed that the first volume of the *Du Bois Correspondence* "has come
under significant criticism for its contents; many important items have
been omitted and many unimportant ones included." Farr said that the
"evaluators were concerned" about the Woodward and Harlan resignations from the Advisory Board. He mentioned the previous applications
and said that they had been "unsuccessful because of major questions
raised about the objectivity of the editor's criteria of selection."[71]

Historian Bracey and Stein responded with a fierce defense of
Aptheker. "To fail to provide funding and then to criticize hard, but

rational and objective, decisions dictated by scarce resources is patently unfair," they wrote. They noted Harlan's positive publicity "blurb" for the first volume of the correspondence, then his abrupt withdrawal. "Professor Vann Woodward obviously has some very deep personal and/or political differences with Dr. Aptheker," they asserted. "Professor Vann Woodward has persisted in his criticisms of Dr. Aptheker . . . [and his criticisms] are generally agreed to have exceeded all the bounds of propriety, academic honesty, and common decency. Neither Vann Woodward nor Harlan qualify as objective evaluators of Dr. Aptheker's work." Stein and Bracey then launched an intense criticism of their own on the funding decisions by the NEH. "The issue here seems to be whether or not the era of witch-hunting, red-baiting, and anti-communist hysteria is over. Will the N.E.H. approve a grant to a scholar who is a communist? With two exceptions, the 'scholarly reviews' are overwhelmingly favorable [for the first volume of the *Correspondence*]."

> In short, the reasons offered in your letter do not constitute a satisfactory explanation of why the grant has been rejected. Unless substantive evidence is forthcoming, and you can assure us that no conflict of interest was involved on the part of the panelists or the reviewers, we shall be forced to conclude that personal and/or political considerations determined the decision. If such is the case, we would have little choice but to raise the issue publicly. We can't shake the conviction that if the University of Massachusetts were an elite private institution and Dr. Aptheker were not a communist, then grant support would have been automatic. The latter point is virtually conceded in your letter.[72]

The NEH bristled at the suggestion that its process had been less than objective. "My review of the application file . . . yielded no suggestion whatsoever that the Endowment's evaluations have been influenced by any consideration of Mr. Aptheker's political views," Simone Reagor, director of the Division of Research Grants, wrote emphatically.[73]

Provided with a copy of the letter, Aptheker thanked Stein and Bracey. "I was moved," he wrote them. "Meanwhile, despite hell, high water and Woodwards, the work continues. . . . I think you must be more disappointed than I with the Endowment action—after all I've had forty years experience with academia!"[74] Meanwhile Bracey told Aptheker that Yale historian Blassingame had spread a rumor that

Aptheker "had destroyed & censored . . . the Du Bois Papers. [I] asked
if he could give me names," Aptheker wrote. "[Bracey] mentioned fear;
said he might in [the] future."[75]

Despite the overwhelming agreement on the importance of Du Bois
among scholars and staff at the NEH, Aptheker never did receive a grant
to pursue his scholarly work. "I think the reasons for the lack [of sup-
port] are the same as those which are involved in . . . the censorship of
W. E. B. Du Bois and Paul Robeson," Stein concluded. "And if Du Bois
and Robeson are controversial, certainly Herbert Aptheker is. The support which we did receive . . . was from small foundations which have a
tradition of independent thinking, and a few generous individuals. . . .
Otherwise, the resistance has been massive."[76] Aptheker eventually
edited three volumes of Du Bois's correspondence and four volumes
of unpublished writings for the UMass Press. When the third volume
of Du Bois's correspondence appeared in 1978, historian Eric Foner
reviewed it favorably in the *New York Times Book Review*. "Thank you
for the effort this entailed and for the integrity it displayed," Aptheker
wrote to Foner. "I did not think I'd live to see a thoughtful and favorable review in that paper; and deeply regret that neither Du Bois nor
Shirley Du Bois lived to see that."[77] Kraus International eventually
published thirty-seven volumes of the collected, published writing of
Du Bois edited by Aptheker. "It contains everything that he ever set to
print," Aptheker said in an interview. "Everything. Every review, every
letter to a newspaper, and so on. . . . In 1986 it was finished." He also
published a seven-hundred-page annotated bibliography of Du Bois's
writings, "and that annotates everything he ever wrote. And now the
world is beginning to discover him. They buried him of course, because
he was too radical. . . . So now there's an interest in him here."[78]

Shirley Graham Du Bois demanded, and secured, as a condition
when selling the Du Bois papers to the University of Massachusetts at
Amherst, a professorship for Aptheker in the W. E. B. Du Bois Department of Afro-American Studies. "The state legislature hit the ceiling,"
recalled Bracey, who knew and admired Aptheker for forty years. "Herbert and August Meier," although fierce political and professional
enemies, "were the most knowledgeable white scholars working in Black
History, two of the most important legs on which the field of Black history stands."[79] Even though Aptheker had a legally signed contract for
a professorship, he bargained that position away in return for a guarantee that the Du Bois Department of Afro-American Studies would build
a core faculty for the study of black history. The university created five

positions because of its deal with Aptheker.[80] "He sacrificed . . . a political victory that would have been to his personal advantage for one that benefitted the larger struggle to increase the number of Black people on our campus. I have yet to see such an example of selflessness on the part of the white left of my generation," Bracey wrote in 1987.[81] Aptheker's stature, wrote Eugene Genovese and Elizabeth Fox-Genovese, "as a premier American historian and as the first great white historian of the black experience needs no defense. That stature has been widely recognized throughout the black community, throughout the Left, and even throughout a bourgeois Academy that has disgraced itself by excluding him from a university professorship solely because of his courageous and inspiring political life's work."[82] "Please do not fret," Genovese wrote to Aptheker in the mid-1980s. "Your life's work stands and will stand. . . . Herbert Aptheker will fare very well indeed."[83]

At the dedication of the new multistory W. E. B. Du Bois Library, the University of Massachusetts–Amherst awarded Aptheker an honorary doctorate in February 1996. That same day, as the result of student agitation, the university renamed the Tower Library, built in 1973, the W. E. B. Du Bois Library. That library "houses the world's largest collection of Du Bois works, including more than 130,000 items of correspondence, photographs, manuscripts of published and unpublished writings, audiovisual material and oral history interviews."[84]

Bracey and his colleagues—faculty, staff, and students—said in a statement at Aptheker's New York City memorial in 2003:

> We here at the University of Massachusetts owe Herbert a priceless debt for his acts of friendship, courage and self-sacrifice that enabled our Department to establish itself on a firm foundation during its critical early years. Without his efforts, our successes surely would have been delayed or greatly diminished. We owe him for the presence in our university library of the papers of W. E. B. Du Bois. We owe him for visiting with us from time to time to encourage and enlighten us, and to break bread, to talk and to laugh with us. We will miss him very much. There is much left to do before we live in the world that Herbert dreamed of, and that he devoted his life's work to bringing into fruition. We will continue down the paths he has charted in the study of African American peoples. We will continue the struggles that he waged against the exploitation and oppression in any way, shape or form of one human being by another.[85]

## Notes

Portions of this essay first appeared in Gary Murrell, *"The Most Dangerous Communist in the United States": A Biography of Herbert Aptheker* (Amherst: University of Massachusetts Press, 2015). Thanks to the University of Massachusetts Press for permission to reprint portions of the original material.

1. Martin Luther King Jr., "Honoring Dr. Du Bois," *Freedomways*, Spring 1968, 105.

2. Henry Allen Moe to Herbert Aptheker, April 10, 1946, Box 2, Folder 5, Aptheker Papers, Stanford University.

3. Manning Marable, *W. E. B. Du Bois: Black Radical Democrat* (Boston: Twayne, 1986),144; David Levering Lewis, *W. E. B. Du Bois: The Fight for Equality and the American Century, 1919–1963* (New York: Henry Holt, 2000), 494; Gerald Horne, *Black and Red: W. E. B. Du Bois and the Afro-American Response to the Cold War 1944–1963* (Albany: State University of New York Press, 1986), 24.

4. W. E. B. Du Bois, in Herbert Aptheker, ed., *The Autobiography of W. E. B. Du Bois* (New York: International, 1968), 328, 329; Lewis, *W. E. B. Du Bois*, 520.

5. Herbert Aptheker, interview by Jack Fischer, San Jose, Calif., October 1993, typescript, Box 120, Folders 23, 24, 25, Herbert Aptheker Papers, Department of Special Collections and University Archives, Stanford University Libraries, 232; Herbert Aptheker, "An Unrepentant Rebel," manuscript of an unpublished autobiography. In the Author's possession, 134–35.

6. Anson Phelps Stokes to W. E. B. Du Bois, December 20, 1946; W. E. B. Du Bois to Anson Phelps Stokes, December 31, 1946, in Herbert Aptheker, ed., *The Correspondence of W. E. B. Du Bois*, vol. 3, paperback edition with corrections (Amherst: University of Massachusetts Press, 1997), 130–31.

7. Herbert Aptheker to W. E. B. Du Bois, July 19, 1947, Box 2, Folder 7, Aptheker Papers.

8. Herbert Aptheker to W. E. B. Du Bois, August 5, 1947, Box 2, Folder 8, Aptheker Papers.

9. W. E. B. Du Bois to Herbert Aptheker, August 12, 1947, in Aptheker, *The Correspondence of W. E. B. Du Bois*, 3:176.

10. Aptheker, editorial comment in *The Correspondence of W. E. B. Du Bois*, 175; Herbert Aptheker to W. E. B. Du Bois, January 5, 1948; W. E. B. Du Bois to Herbert Aptheker, January 8, 1948, in Aptheker, *The Correspondence of W. E. B. Du Bois*, 176–77.

11. Lewis, *W. E. B. Du Bois*, 566.

12. Shirley Graham Du Bois, *His Day Is Marching On: A Memior of W. E. B. Du Bois* (New York: Lippincott, 1971), 323.

13. Graham Du Bois, *His Day*, 324.

14. Graham Du Bois, *His Day*, 324–25.

15. Bettina F. Aptheker, *Intimate Politics: How I Grew Up Red, Fought for Free Speech, and Became a Feminist Rebel* (Emeryville, Calif.: Seal Press, 2006), 76-84.

16. Arna Bontemps to Herbert Aptheker, December 20, 1962, Box 8, Folder 18, Aptheker Papers.

17. Herbert Aptheker to Arna Bontemps, December 26, 1962, Box 8, Folder 18, Aptheker Papers.

18. Herbert Aptheker to Shirley Graham Du Bois, October 18, 1963, Box 9, Folder 15, Aptheker Papers.

19. Shirley Graham Du Bois to Herbert Aptheker, December 9, 1963, Box 9, Folder 15, Aptheker Papers, emphasis in the original.

20. Herbert Aptheker to Shirley Graham Du Bois, December 16, 1963, Box 9, Folder 15, Aptheker Papers.

21. Herbert Aptheker to Shirley Graham Du Bois, December 27, 1963, Box 9, Folder 15, Aptheker Papers.

22. Shirley Graham Du Bois to Herbert Aptheker, January 5, 1964, Box 10, Folder 15, Aptheker Papers, emphasis in the original.

23. Gerald Horne, *Race Woman: The Lives of Shirley Graham Du Bois* (New York: New York University Press, 2000), 218, 220.

24. Mark Carroll to Herbert Aptheker, May 21, 1968, Box 28, Folder 6, Aptheker Papers.

25. Herbert Aptheker to Mark Carroll, May 22, 1968, Box 28, Folder 6, Aptheker Papers.

26. Herbert Aptheker to Ann Orlov, October 2, 1968, Box 28, Folder 14, Aptheker Papers.

27. Herbert Aptheker to Shirley Graham Du Bois, August 23, 1968, Box 28, Folder 14, Aptheker Papers.

28. Shirley Graham Du Bois to Herbert Aptheker, September 11, 1968, Box 28, Folder 14, Aptheker Papers, emphasis in the original.

29. Ann Orlov to Herbert Aptheker, August 7, and October 21, 1968, Box 26, Folder 14, Aptheker Papers.

30. Herbert Aptheker to Robert Cohen, October 8, 1968, Box 28, Folder 13, Aptheker Papers.

31. Herbert Aptheker to Shirley Graham Du Bois, November 14, 1968, Aptheker Papers, Box 28, Folder 14.

32. John W. Blassingame to Herbert Aptheker, July 31, 1968, Box 28, Folder 11, Aptheker Papers.

33. Herbert Aptheker to "Ladies and Gentlemen," August 5, 1968, Box 28, Folder 11, Aptheker Papers.

34. Herbert Aptheker to Shirley Graham Du Bois, November 14, 1969, Box 31, Folder 5, Aptheker Papers.

35. Aptheker to Shirley Graham Du Bois, November 14, 1969.

36. Herbert Aptheker to Leone Stein, October 27, 1969, Box 31, Folder 13, Aptheker Papers.

37. Herbert Aptheker, memo of a phone conversation, November 10, 1969, Box 31, Folder 13, Aptheker Papers.

38. Leone Stein to Herbert Aptheker, November 26, 1969, Box 31, Folder 13, Aptheker Papers.

39. Herbert Aptheker to Leone Stein, December 9, 1970, Box 35, Folder 1, Aptheker Papers.

40. Leone Stein to Herbert Aptheker, September 9, 1970, Box 35, Folder 1, Aptheker Papers.

41. Henry Tragle to Herbert Aptheker, December 16, 1970, Box 36, Folder 1, Aptheker Papers.

42. "Application Summary," National Endowment for the Humanities, application H-7708, October 1970, received through a Freedom of Information Act request. The NEH said in response to a Freedom of Information Act request that all of the other applications and reviewer comments had been destroyed.

43. NEH, "Application Summary."

44. NEH, "Application Summary."

45. Jesse Lemisch, interview by Gary Murrell, March 28, 2001, on a train between Boston and New York.

46. Herbert Aptheker to Henry I. Tragle, December 28, 1970 Box 36, Folder 1, Aptheker Papers; "Grant Report from The Association of American University Presses," Grant Number H67-0-111, National Endowment for the Humanities, Box 36, Folder 1, Aptheker Papers.

47. Herbert Aptheker to C. Vann Woodward, January 15, 1971, Box 39, Folder 3, Aptheker Papers.

48. C. Vann Woodward to Herbert Aptheker, January 26, 1971, Box 39, Folder 3, Aptheker Papers.

49. Herbert Aptheker to C. Vann Woodward, February 1, 1971, Box 39, Folder 3, Aptheker Papers.

50. C. Vann Woodward to Herbert Aptheker, February 16, 1971, Box 39, Folder 3, Aptheker Papers.

51. Herbert Aptheker to C. Vann Woodward, February 25, 1971, Box 39, Folder 3, Aptheker Papers.

52. C. Vann Woodward to Herbert Aptheker, March 17, 1971, Box 37, Folder 12, Aptheker Papers.

53. Eugene Genovese, telephone interview by Gary Murrell, September 29, 2001.

54. New York, FBI, memorandum, July 26, 1972, report on Communist Party Central Committee meeting, in the author's possession. Aptheker and Jim Jackson, an old friend of Du Bois, came into increasing conflict over issues within the Party and over Aptheker's role as Du Bois's literary executor. Jackson felt the position should have been his; Du Bois obviously did not.

55. Herbert Aptheker to Paul M. Wright, April 17, 1972, Box 40, Folder 11, Aptheker Papers.

56. Leone Stein to Gary Murrell, email, June 5, 2014; Leone Stein to Alfred Young, December 12, 1972, Box 39, Folder 7, Aptheker Papers.

57. Herbert Aptheker to Edward Brooke, December 4, 1972, Box 39, Folder 7, Aptheker Papers.

58. John Hope Franklin to Malcolm Call, March 15, 1973, Box 43, Folder 9; John Hope Franklin to Herbert Aptheker, July 30, 1973, Box 43, Folder 7, Aptheker Papers.

59. *Springfield (MA) Sunday Republican*, July 15, 1973.

60. Herbert Aptheker to Shirley Graham Du Bois, December 5, 1973, Box 43, Folder 6, Aptheker Papers.

61. David Gillen, "Dedication of the W. E. B. Du Bois Papers," WFCR Radio Broadcast Collection (MS 741), Special Collections and University Archives, University of Massachusetts–Amherst Libraries.

62. Herbert Aptheker to John Hope Franklin, August 1, 1973, Box 43, Folder 7, Aptheker Papers.

63. Herbert Aptheker to Louis R. Harlan, September 25, 1973, Box 43, Folder 10, Aptheker Papers.

64. C. Vann Woodward to Herbert Aptheker, August 21, 1973, Box 44, Folder 8, Aptheker Papers.

65. Herbert Aptheker to C. Vann Woodward, August 28, 1973, Box 44, Folder 8, Aptheker Papers.

66. C. Vann Woodward to Leone Stein, January 28, 1974, Box 46, Folder unidentified, probably 11 or 12, Aptheker Papers.

67. Malcolm Call to Louis R. Harlan, February 15, 1974, Box 46, Folder unidentified, probably 11 or 12, Aptheker Papers.

68. C. Vann Woodward to Herbert Aptheker, February 27, 1974, Box 46, Folder unidentified, probably 11 or 12, Aptheker Papers.

69. Herbert Aptheker to C. Vann Woodward, March 1, 1974, Box 46, Folder unidentified, probably 11 or 12, Aptheker Papers.

70. Leone Stein to Herbert Aptheker, July 31, 1974, Box 46, Folder 13, Aptheker Papers.

71. George F. Farr to Leone Stein and John Bracey, June 30, 1976, Box 51, Folder 3, Aptheker Papers.

72. Leone Stein and John Bracey to George F. Farr, July 12, 1976, Box 51, Folder 3, Aptheker Papers.

73. Simone Reagor to Leone Stein and John Bracey, August 6, 1976, Box 51, Folder 7, Aptheker Papers.

74. Herbert Aptheker to Leone Stein, July 21, 1976, Box 51 Folder 3, Aptheker Papers.

75. Herbert Aptheker, memo to himself, June 7, 1976, Box 49, Folder 25, Aptheker Papers.

76. Leone Stein to Bud Salk, August 30, 1977, Box 54, Folder 14, Aptheker Papers.

77. Herbert Aptheker to Eric Foner, January 5, 1979, Box 57, Folder 10, Aptheker Papers.

78. Herbert Aptheker, interview by James W. Clinton, November 14, 1990, San Jose, California, Box 76, Folder 7, Aptheker Papers.

79. John Bracey, interview by Gary Murrell, March 26, 2004, Boston.

80. Bracey, Murrell interview.

81. John Bracey to editors, *Radical History Review*, February 9, 1987, Box 70, Folder 20, Aptheker Papers.

82. Eugene Genovese and Elizabeth Fox-Genovese to editors, *Radical History Review*, December 15, 1986, Box 70, Folder 1, Aptheker Papers.

83. Eugene Genovese to Herbert Aptheker, December 10, 1986, Box 70, Folder 1, Aptheker Papers.

84. Beth Goldstein, "W. E. B. Du Bois Remembered: Library Formally Dedicated," University of Massachusetts *Chronicle*, February 29, 1996.

85. John Bracey, "Statement for Herbert Aptheker's Memorial Service," March 30, 2003, provided to the author by Bettina Aptheker.

# "A Legacy of Scholarship and Struggle"

## W. E. B. Du Bois's Life after Death

*Phillip Luke Sinitiere*

A bitter ideological struggle is being waged over the name of William Edward Burghardt Du Bois. . . . It is not at all surprising that his name has now and again produced a clash of something like diametrically opposite ideas, and this is perhaps inevitable, considering that his was a personality of many facets and great complexity.
— G. B. Starushenko, *William Du Bois: Scholar, Humanitarian, Freedom Fighter* (1971)

A warm summer day greeted attendees in August 1963 at the March on Washington for Jobs and Freedom. Passionate addresses by A. Philip Randolph, John Lewis, and others made for memorable moments. Moving music by Joan Baez, Pete Seeger, Marian Anderson, and Mahalia Jackson enlivened the spirits of those present. And of course Martin Luther King's stirring speech at the close of the day's program proved both prescient and iconic. It was another speech, however, that stood out for its depiction of W. E. B. Du Bois, who had died in Ghana the day before the March. Marking a moment of profound historical importance, NAACP executive secretary Roy Wilkins announced Du Bois's death by praising his contribution to civil rights with the 1903 publication of *The Souls of Black Folk*. To those gathered at the Washington Mall, Wilkins claimed that it was Du Bois's "voice that [called] to you to gather here today in this cause." However, he lamented that "in his later years Dr. Du Bois chose another path." Wilkins thus referenced Du Bois's vocal advocacy of socialism and communism, political convictions he and others in the NAACP deemed objectionable in a complicated era of cold war civil rights.[1]

But not everyone found agreeable Wilkins's assessment of Du Bois's politics. Black intellectual John Oliver Killens recalled that as he gathered with James Baldwin, Sidney Poitier, and others at the Willard Hotel in Washington, D.C., on the morning of August 28, 1963, someone walked in and announced, "The old man died." According to Killens, no one had to inquire about the old man's identity. "We all knew who the old man was, because he was our old man. He belonged to every one of us. And we belonged to him." Killens fleshed out the feeling of this particular setting: "More than any other single human being, [Du Bois], through the sheer power of his vast and profound intelligence, his tireless scholarship and his fierce dedication to the cause of black liberation, has brought us and the other two hundred and fifty thousand souls to this place, to this moment in time and space." However, Killens also knew that on that August day he was in history's firm grasp. His awareness beamed. "There was a kind of poetic finale that made sense to us," he noted,

> that [Du Bois] should die on the very eve of this historical occasion. He was a man of irony. . . . It was also a bit of poetic justice that he died in a place he loved so dearly, Mother Africa, the land of his forefathers, he, the father of Pan Africanism. . . . He had run a tremendous race, and now it would be up to us, all of us everywhere, to take the torch and carry it forward. He had left us a legacy, of scholarship and struggle.[2]

Two months after the March on Washington, *The Crisis* magazine recognized and commemorated the life of its founding editor. A full-page photograph of a middle-aged Du Bois accompanied a brief summary of his life along with the full text of the NAACP's resolution passed in response to his death. In honor of his towering contribution to the cause of civil rights, *Crisis* editors also included excerpts from Du Bois's "What We Want" statement from the Niagara Movement. Amid the recognition of Du Bois's superlative achievements throughout the course of his ninety-five years, even in death the NAACP maintained a severe distance from its cofounder, not unlike Wilkins's comments at the March on Washington. Reflecting the dominant narrative at the time that only later in life did he take a left turn politically, the summary stated that after his 1948 departure from the NAACP "Dr.

Du Bois became increasingly identified with left-wing and Communist activities. In 1961 at the age of 93 he formally joined the Communist Party."[3]

Even more telling is what the NAACP's resolution on Du Bois's life left out of its summary of his career. It quoted Du Bois's "prophetic announcement" about the color line at the beginning of the twentieth century. It praised his signal role as "the prime inspirer, philosopher and father of the organized Negro protest movement." The resolution also commented on the power of *The Crisis* during Du Bois's editorship. Of Du Bois's publications—a stunning record of production "that no serious research in the Negro field can be done without reference to"—the resolution recognized only the Atlanta sociological studies, his 1896 book on the transatlantic slave trade, *Philadelphia Negro* (1899), and *The Souls of Black Folk* (1903). Despite describing Du Bois's contribution to civil rights and human rights as "imperishable," the NAACP's resolution referenced no book of Du Bois's that appeared after 1903 and praised only the years of his initial stint at the association, from 1910 to 1934. Although the resolution mentioned Du Bois's historical studies and Pan-African activities, absent were references to his professorships, other magazines he founded and edited, his autobiographies, *Black Reconstruction* (1935), his books on Africa, and his novels and plays. Along with not mentioning Du Bois's work with the Council on African Affairs and the Peace Information Center and his federal indictment, the erasures of Du Bois's career in the NAACP resolution speak volumes about the political moment of his cold war passing.[4]

The month following *The Crisis*'s recognition of Du Bois, *Negro Digest* printed a death notice from *Christian Century*, a magazine in which his writing had appeared. The piece glowingly recollected Du Bois's accomplished career but decried his "political deviations," particularly joining the Communist Party. The same issue also printed Eugene Perkins's poem "In Memory of Du Bois." The African American author and playwright began, "Push back the soil! / The Reaper has once again / Extirpated a Titan from our hearts." Using nature imagery Perkins lauded Du Bois's scholarship and activism:

> He who stood tall as pyramids
> Even the rivers sung his deeds.
> He who spoke with elegance
> His words stirred the mountains.

His image gave dignity to black seeds.

. . . . . . . . . . . . . . . . . . . . . . . . . . . . .

Du Bois has fallen asleep.
We must not disquiet his peace
Now he can be free.

Unlike the critical *Century* comments and the erasures in *The Crisis*,
Perkins's poem was much more appreciative of Du Bois's career and
much less critical of his leftist politics.[5]

The cold war political climate that enveloped the March on Washington determined that Du Bois's more recent political trajectory of the
1930s through the early 1960s received a decidedly cooler reception.
His support for Henry Wallace and the Progressive Party in the late
1940s, coupled with his energetic efforts with the Council on African
Affairs and the Peace Information Center, his February 1951 indictment over suspicion that he took orders from Moscow elicited Wilkins's
blazing condemnation. Despite his November 1951 acquittal, numerous black Americans and black institutions stiff-armed Du Bois in the
closing decades of his life because they deemed the aging scholar a
political liability. Content to praise his early twentieth-century achievements, *The Crisis* clearly kept its distance from the more recent political
inflections of the civil rights luminary, even as *Negro Digest* printed
praiseworthy poetry in his honor and courageous black intellectuals
properly contextualized the politics of his nascent historical memory.
Searing criticism of Du Bois's politics—along with spirited defenses of
his political persuasions—would only intensify in the weeks, months,
and years following his death.

An early attempt to honor Du Bois's legacy manifested in 1962 with
the creation of the DuBois Clubs of America, in part spearheaded by
Bettina Aptheker, who believed that invoking Du Bois's name "would
announce our revolutionary intentions without officially tying us to the
Communist Party," a crucial dilemma during the heady days of Berkeley activism and the 1960s student movements. "We felt that with the
DuBois Clubs, we could openly sponsor classes on Marxism and plan
for participation in a burgeoning civil rights movement in an organized and consistent way, rather than only as individuals."[6] Aptheker,
whose father would edit Du Bois's enormous archive, also knew the
black scholar personally. As a high school senior in 1961, she assisted
Du Bois with arranging his papers in the spacious Brooklyn home he
shared with his second wife, Shirley Graham. As Aptheker writes in

her essay in this book, she recalled sitting for hours not only sorting Du Bois's massive collection but also becoming transfixed reading through his correspondence, book and article manuscripts, newspaper articles, and other parts of his personal archive.

Early publications of the DuBois Clubs announced the group's revolutionary intentions. For example, a January 1968 issue of *Spur*, the DuBois Clubs' newsletter, contemplated the utility of student strikes against the Vietnam War and promoted the incorporation of interracial solidarity. That same month an issue of the organization's national magazine, *Insurgent*, included a report from national chair Jarvis Tyner about recent travels to Russia and a reflection on Woodie Guthrie's life along with commentary about communist activism in Greece. Tyner, who would eventually lead the U.S. Communist Party, also authored a tribute to Du Bois. He explained that the origins of the DuBois Clubs lay in Du Bois's own dedication "to the struggle for world peace, for freedom, against racism, colonialism, imperialism and for the day when exploitation of man by man would end." Most important, Tyner continued, "Dr. Du Bois has left the youth of the world many valuable treasures; in his writings and in his struggles."[7]

The DuBois Clubs' focus on young people generated a response from the Catholic Veterans of America, emblematic of the era's rabid anticommunism. A pamphlet the organization produced titled "Target . . . American Youth!," complete with a drawing of a hammer and sickle on the front, listed the names of suspected communists and known communists such as Gus Hall, head of the CPUSA. Deploying conspiratorial language, it described with alarm the DuBois Clubs as a "front" organization of the CPUSA, "a new propaganda tool of the atheistic, totalitarian system dedicated to 'burying' you, the free American." The DuBois Clubs also riled up rabid anticommunists like Richard Nixon. Then chair of the Boys Club of America, in 1966 Nixon made the ludicrous claim that since "Du Bois" rhymed with "Boys," Du Bois Clubs sought to dupe would-be members of Boys Club of America into joining the communist cause.[8]

Another illustration of attempts to mark Du Bois's legacy, a commemorative meeting in his honor took place at New York City's Carnegie Hall in early 1964. Recognizing the anticommunist and antiblack sentiments that animated the times, Du Bois Memorial Committee member Ossie Davis remarked that the event aimed "to secure to the Afro-American consciousness the personality, image and cultural significance of the most illustrious Afro American scholar of our time, and to present to Americans at large a proper sense of Dr. DuBois' intellectual contributions to American life."[9]

History professor John Hope Franklin delivered the keynote. Cognizant of the moment's historical gravity, he observed, "The manner in which the death of W. E. B. Du Bois was reported in some quarters here in the United States is itself a curious commentary on the extent to which the country of his birth was out of touch with him." Conscious of the politicization of Du Bois's memory, Franklin jumped to his defense: "[I] wish I could erase from my memory the picture of Dr. Du Bois at eighty years of age handcuffed like a common thief, accused of being the agent of a foreign power. Even his subsequent exoneration [in 1951] cannot obliterate . . . the impression that, perhaps, will always remain: that he was the victim not merely of the fanaticism that characterized those years, but that he was being punished for what he had represented for more than half a century."[10] Lorraine Hansberry registered explicit support for the politics that Du Bois represented. "In his memory, I mean to say what I mean and mean what I say," she proclaimed. "I think that certainly DuBois' legacy teaches us to look toward and work for a socialist organization of society as the next great and dearly won universal condition of mankind."[11] Similarly, Eslanda Robeson commented, "Dr. DuBois recognized and appreciated the power and success of Socialism, and was convinced that the world—however reluctantly in some places—would have to arrive at some form of Socialism to insure the progress and well-being of the majority of people." "During his last years," she continued, "he recognized that Freedom and Peace are the Number One issues in the world today, and worked consistently toward these goals. . . . In a world context Dr. Du Bois recognized that people everywhere must be free."[12]

These episodes from the 1960s illustrate Russian scholar G. B. Starushenko's 1971 statement in the epigraph about the ideological struggle associated with Du Bois's life and times. This essay, in part, performs a historiographical exercise by historicizing the ideological conflicts that have shaped scholarship on Du Bois in the half-century after his death. As a chapter of intellectual history it also foregrounds the political and cultural contexts that surrounded the rise of Du Bois studies and why and how it matters for considerations of his legacy, scholarship, and struggle.

Critical scholarship on Du Bois commenced during his lifetime. Several master's theses and academic articles along with undergraduate honors theses investigated his work as a literary figure, commented on his political philosophy, and explored his historical thought.[13] However, two scholarly book-length studies that appeared on the eve of Du Bois's passing proved most determinative in orienting Du Bois scholarship away from his late career, a perspective that would last for nearly three decades.

Francis Broderick published *W. E. B. Du Bois: Negro Leader in a Time of Crisis* in 1959, and the following year Elliott Rudwick released *W. E. B. Du Bois: Propagandist of Negro Protest*. Both scholars corresponded with Du Bois during the course of researching their books. Appreciative of Du Bois's career contributions to the black freedom struggle, Broderick's and Rudwick's analyses nevertheless in large measure emphasize his early career. Ultimately, reflecting an anticommunist cold war climate, Broderick and Rudwick dismiss the leftist politics of his late career. Although Broderick contends that Du Bois's "longevity and productivity have given him a quantitative claim hard to match," he seeks to demythologize Du Bois by limiting his ultimate influence to his publications and activism before 1933. Thereafter a firm commitment to Marxist analysis, most particularly in *Black Reconstruction*, "blockaded clarity" in Du Bois's thinking. "Though passable as polemic or melodrama," writes Broderick about Du Bois's 1935 tome, "this was not history." For Broderick a declining scholarly facility led to the "extreme Left woo[ing] Du Bois" that rendered the aging scholar "out of touch, out of sympathy with current Negro planning on domestic matters. . . . Few were listening, for his ideas failed to mesh with his era." Following Du Bois's 1951 trial and acquittal, Broderick writes, Du Bois "cut himself loose from the struggle for Negro equality," after which "the old man sank into the anonymity of retirement."[14]

While less dismissive of Du Bois's later scholarship, Rudwick also questions the radical political orientation of Du Bois's closing years. The defining moment of Du Bois's McCarthy-era persecution led to "this old but very proud man becom[ing] the Communists' ornament," thereby losing his privileged voice. "Hardly anyone was listening on this side of the Iron Curtain," Rudwick maintains. "On the other side, however, Du Bois was regarded as a towering figure to be courted with great attentiveness." As a result, he observes in 1960, Du Bois "is no longer of any influence in the field of contemporary American race relations." Du Bois's leftist political allegiances late in life "shift[ed] at the very time that the status of his race was rapidly rising. . . . But Du Bois had removed himself from old ties. He became a figure of pathos, if not tragedy—talented, even brilliant, but hurt beyond repair after a long life of battling racism."[15]

If Broderick and Rudwick found Du Bois's late career less than impressive and politically unacceptable, the generation of scholars writing about Du Bois in the late 1960s and 1970s were far less dismissive of the iconic civil rights leader. This is attributable to a number of factors. For example, Bobby Seale commented on the influence of Du Bois's *Black Reconstruction* in the initial intellectual and political configurations of the Black Panther Party.[16] Regarding the founding of the Institute of the Black World, theologian and historian Vincent Harding found Du Bois's work particularly noteworthy. "The IBW came into existence as a result of our commitment to the hopes and plans of the dead yet living fathers in the Black intellectual community, most notably W. E. B. DuBois," wrote Harding in the 1970s in the introduction to Lerone Bennett's *The Challenge of Blackness*. "Based as we were in the Atlanta University Center schools," he continued, "it was not difficult for us to remember and recount his work at the beginning of the century toward a research center which would develop a hundred-year study of the Black Experience."[17] Similarly, early participants in the rise of black studies departments listed Du Bois's writings, including publications from his late career, as inspirational in marking out the political shape of their intellectual work.[18] The posthumous appearance of Du Bois's final *Autobiography* in 1968, as well as John Henrik Clarke's 1970 coedited collection of *Freedomways* material, titled *Black Titan*, and Shirley Graham Du Bois's 1971 memoir of her late spouse, *His Day Is Marching On*, provided additional work from which activists and scholars pursued their political and intellectual labors. Also, a steady stream of doctoral dissertations and master's theses commenced during these two decades reflected these developments as graduate students revisited Du Bois's civil rights philosophy, Pan-African thought, leadership strategy, educational theory, and aesthetic conception.[19]

These trends help to contextualize the contents of Table 1, which reveals the appearance of nearly a dozen anthologies of his published work within a decade of his death. However, it was in the 1980s that thirteen Du Bois anthologies appeared, the vast majority edited by Herbert Aptheker. Du Bois anthologies dropped off significantly in the 1990s but witnessed a rebound in the 2000s. Early document readers appeared with leftist presses like International Publishers and Kraus-Thomson; trade presses such as Macmillan and Simon & Schuster, and eventually university presses (e.g., Massachusetts, Oxford, Mississippi), also published Du Bois's writings in the 1970s and thereafter. These primary source collections not only disseminated Du Bois's work for new generations but also signaled substantial growth in Du Bois scholarship across numerous disciplines. In addition to books, from the 1990s to the present scholars have published in journals and books newly discovered Du Bois primary sources such as correspondence, creative writings, and speeches.[20] Very recently, as Robert Williams's essay in this volume details, the digital availability of Du Bois's writings has simultaneously more widely circulated Du Bois's ideas while spawning advances in the field of Du Bois studies.

One of the central figures in the drama of Du Bois scholarship was of course Herbert Aptheker. The Du Bois–Aptheker connection began in the early 1940s, after Du Bois responded to Aptheker's review of *Dusk of Dawn*. The two later shared office space at the NAACP during Du Bois's second stint with the association, and shortly after World War II Du Bois asked Aptheker to edit his massive correspondence and published works. "I considered this charge to be sacred and a great honor," Aptheker gushed. The honor of editing Du Bois's archive proved extremely difficult, as Gary Murrell's essay on Aptheker in this book details. Political and financial obstacles worked in concert against Aptheker's efforts for much of the 1960s and 1970s. As the cold war was ending in the 1980s, the fruit of Aptheker's editorial efforts began to grow. Reflecting on this work in 1997, six years before he died, Aptheker recalled:

> W. E. B. Du Bois has filled my life—first as a teacher, then as a guide, inspiration and father. . . . Happily I devoted much of my life to him and his work in scores of volumes. I had the opportunity and honor of bringing forth his writings, despite the fearful idiocy of the Cold War—highlighted by Washington's effort to actually send Du Bois to prison! . . . Let those who remain emulate Du Bois' courage and persistence and help realize his dream of a decent, equitable, and peaceful world.[21]

A 1998 lecture, "Legacy of W. E. B. Du Bois," at Berkeley's Graduate Theological Union, featured a synopsis of Du Bois's closing decades. Aptheker, perhaps more than any other scholar in recent memory—particularly since Aptheker himself experienced severe persecution for his political views—insisted that academic reflections on Du Bois retain a critical focus on his late career.[22]

While theses and dissertations focused on Du Bois witnessed a marked increase starting in the 1980s, the historical memory of

**Table 1.** Primary Source Anthologies of W. E. B. Du Bois's Work

| Title | Year |
|---|---|
| *An ABC of Color*, ed. W. E. B. Du Bois, introduction by J. O. Killens | 1963, 1970 |
| *W. E. B. Du Bois: A Reader*, edited and introduction by Meyer J. Weinberg | 1970 |
| *Selected Writings of W. E. B. Du Bois*, ed. Walter Wilson, introduction by Stephen J. Wright | 1970 |
| *W. E. B. Du Bois Speaks: Speeches and Addresses, 1890–1919*, ed. Philip S. Foner | 1970 |
| *W. E. B. Du Bois Speaks: Speeches and Addresses, 1920–1963*, ed. Philip S. Foner | 1970 |
| *W. E. B. Du Bois Reader*, ed. Andrew G. Paschal, introduction by Arna Bontemps | 1971, 1993 |
| *Seventh Son: The Thought and Writings of W. E. B. Du Bois*, 2 vols., edited and introduction by Julius Lester | 1971 |
| *W. E. B. Du Bois:* The Crisis *Writings*, edited and introduction by Daniel Walden | 1972 |
| *Emerging Thought of W. E. B. Du Bois:* Crisis, ed. Henry Lee Moon | 1972 |
| *W. E. B. Du Bois*, ed. William M. Tuttle | 1973 |
| *The Education of Black People: Ten Critiques, 1906–1960*, ed. Herbert Aptheker | 1973, 2001 |
| *Writings of W. E. B. Du Bois*, ed. Virginia Hamilton | 1975 |
| *W. E. B. Du Bois on Sociology and the Black Community*, edited and introduction by Dan S. Green and Edwin D. Driver | 1978, 1995 |
| *Selections from* The Brownies' Book, ed. Herbert Aptheker | 1980 |
| *Selections from* Phylon, ed. Herbert Aptheker | 1980 |
| *Prayers for Dark People*, ed. Herbert Aptheker | 1980 |
| *Contributions by W. E. B. Du Bois in Govt Publications & Proceedings*, ed. Herbert Aptheker | 1980 |
| *Writings by W. E. B. Du Bois in Periodicals Edited by Others*, 4 vols., ed. Herbert Aptheker | 1982 |
| *Writings by W. E. B. Du Bois in Non-Periodical Literature Edited by Others*, ed. Herbert Aptheker | 1982 |

| Title | Year |
|---|---|
| *Selections from* The Crisis, 2 vols., ed. Herbert Aptheker | 1983 |
| *Selections from* The Horizon, ed. Herbert Aptheker | 1985 |
| *Creative Writings by W. E. B. Du Bois*, ed. Herbert Aptheker | 1985 |
| *Against Racism: Unpublished Works*, ed. Herbert Aptheker | 1985 |
| *W. E. B. Du Bois, Writings*, ed. Nathan Huggins | 1986 |
| *Pamphlets & Leaflets*, ed. Herbert Aptheker | 1986 |
| *Newspaper Columns*, 2 vols., ed. Herbert Aptheker | 1986 |
| *The World of W. E. B. Du Bois: A Quotation Sourcebook*, ed. Meyer Weinberg, New Intro by John H. Bracey, Jr. | 1992, 2012 |
| *W. E. B. Du Bois: A Reader*, ed. David Levering Lewis | 1995 |
| *Oxford W. E. B. Du Bois Reader*, ed. Eric Sundquist | 1996 |
| *The Best of* The Brownies' Book, ed. Dianne Johnson-Feelings, introduction by Marian Wright Edelman | 1996 |
| *Du Bois on Religion*, ed. Phil Zuckerman | 2000 |
| *Du Bois on Education*, ed. Eugene Provenzo | 2002 |
| *Wisdom of W. E. B. Du Bois*, ed. Aberjhani | 2003 |
| *Social Theory of W. E. B. Du Bois*, ed. Phil Zuckerman | 2004 |
| *W. E. B. Du Bois on Asia*, ed. Bill V. Mullen and Cathryn Watson | 2005 |
| *Du Bois on Reform: Periodical-Based Leadership for African Americans*, ed. Brian Johnson | 2005 |
| *W. E. B. Du Bois and the Sociological Imagination, 1897–1914*, ed. Robert A. Wortham | 2009 |
| *The Sociological Souls of Black Folk*, ed. Robert A. Wortham | 2011 |
| *"Girl, Colored" and Other Stories: A Complete Short Fiction Anthology of African American Women Writers in* The Crisis *Magazine, 1910–2010*, ed. Judith Musser | 2011 |
| *W. E. B. Du Bois on Africa*, ed. Eugene Provenzo and Edmund Abaka | 2012 |
| *W. E. B. DuBois' Exhibit of American Negroes: African Americans at the Beginning of the Twentieth Century*, ed. Eugene Provenzo | 2013 |

**Table 1** (*continued*)

| Title | Year |
|---|---|
| W. E. B. Du Bois: Selections from His Writings, ed. Bob Blaisdell | 2014 |
| Education and Empowerment: The Essential Writings of W. E. B. Du Bois, ed. Randall Westbrook | 2014 |
| The Problem of the Color Line at the Turn of the Twentieth Century: The Essential Early Essays, ed. Nahum Dimitri Chandler | 2015 |
| W. E. B. Du Bois's Data Portraits: Visualizing Black America, ed. Whitney Battle-Baptiste and Britt Rusert | 2018 |

Du Bois's late-career politics remained a liability even as the cold war was ending. Writer and poet Nagueyalti Warren, for example, revealed in her 2011 book on Du Bois and the history of black studies that a potential dissertation adviser in the early 1980s—a World War II veteran—utterly refused to chair her dissertation committee "because Du Bois had been a communist."[23] Despite such stiff resistance, it was toward the end of the cold war in the 1980s that a distinct turn in Du Bois scholarship began to chronicle his later years. Scholars with decidedly leftist political commitments refused to dismiss his socialist convictions. Against the backdrop of the Reagan era, these scholars sought to find in Du Bois's twilight decades a revolutionary philosophy in response to a period of antilabor sentiment, a nascent globalization, and an emerging carceral state buoyed by the War on Drugs and depletion of urban resources.[24]

While not a full analysis of Du Bois's twilight decades, Cedric Robinson's 1983 book, *Black Marxism*, located him as one of America's most important Marxist thinkers. Robinson set the creation of *Black Reconstruction*—a key text from Du Bois's late period—within the historical era of the Great Depression and New Deal (and in the long shadow of World War I) in which it was composed to demonstrate Du Bois's particular conceptualization of Marxist revolutionary theory. He found in *Black Reconstruction* a firm grasp of racial capitalism's obscene arrangements in U.S. history and documented Du Bois's fundamental reconstruction of black freedom's political logic through organized planning and self-determination—in other words, a Marxist framework for black radical historiography.[25]

In the same historical era of the late Cold War, activist and intellectual Tony Monteiro connected Du Bois's Pan-African work to the
immediate context of the historical moment. At the United Nations,
for instance, he linked the anti-apartheid movement in South Africa to
Du Bois's global perspective. "DuBois urged the fighters for liberation
on the African continent, to seek all allies in their struggle," he stated,
"the road to liberation in Africa could not be achieved but in unity
with all of the anti-imperialist forces, and in particular the socialist
community of states." Therefore, he continued, "This fight today is of
particular concern to the peoples of the United States and in particular
the Afro-American people who realize in this struggle against racism a
crucial aspect of their own struggle against racial oppression here in
the United States."[26]

In the same historical moment of the late cold war, Manning
Marable's 1986 biography reimagined Du Bois as a "black radical democrat," an intellectual, social scientist, and popularizer of black history
committed to African American liberation. Marable countered the prevailing anticommunist rendering of Du Bois's later years. "The final
decade of Du Bois's life," he contended, "including his decision in 1961
to become a member of the U.S. Communist Party, cannot honestly
be interpreted as a radical departure or extreme rupture in the earlier
stages of his intellectual evolution."[27] While Marable traced Du Bois's
leftist radicalism across his career, Gerald Horne's equally vital study,
*Black and Red: W. E. B. Du Bois and the Afro-American Response to the
Cold War, 1944–1963*, published the same year as Marable's book, also
vehemently rejected the alienation thesis of Du Bois's closing decades
by focusing specifically on the late period. In concert with Marable,
Horne noted that "the core of Du Bois's thought, his passion for socialism, peace, and equality, remained immutable throughout" his life as "a
fluid and intelligent militant activist with large hopes of changing the
world."[28]

Collectively, Robinson's, Monteiro's, Marable's, and Horne's efforts,
among others, opened a wider angle of analysis for Du Bois's last
decades, proving foundational for studies by political scientists, American Studies specialists, literary scholars, and historians. Additional
work on Du Bois's late career probes the politics of his *Autobiography*,
later novels, democratic theory, educational philosophy, *Black Reconstruction*, global civil rights, and solidarity with Asian nations.[29]

Of particular note in this direction are studies by Eric Porter, Amy
Bass, and Bill Mullen. Shaped by the early twenty-first century's

increasing economic precarity, the extractive shape of neoliberalism, abusive expressions of antiblack police violence, and the intrusive ignobility of the surveillance state, Porter, Bass, and Mullen find Du Bois's life experience and legacy instructive for the contemporary moment.

Bass's unique intervention in *Those about Him Remained Silent: The Battle over W. E. B. Du Bois* contemplates Du Bois's national and international legacy and political heritage in relation to commemorative efforts carried out in his hometown of Great Barrington, Massachusetts. While local activists eventually succeeded in achieving institutional recognition of Du Bois landmarks in western Massachusetts, it took titanic struggles against a meddling FBI, anti–Black power opinion, and a ferocious anticommunism that refused to recognize the black intellectual's cultural significance. "The legacy of disavowal that continues to surround Du Bois in his hometown, in the wake of and regardless of signs and ceremonies," Bass cautions, "ensures that we must continually push to understand how national and global situations continue to be digested and dealt with at the most local of levels."[30]

Porter's *The Problem of the Future World: W. E. B. Du Bois and the Race Concept at Midcentury* underscores Du Bois's cogent analysis of the global color line's persistence through economic inequality coupled with neoliberalism's conceit of color blindness. Porter's rendering of Du Bois as a "suspect citizen" is also instructive; it gives historical shape to the antiblack dimension of the surveillance state's increasing visibility. Notably, whereas Porter suggests that Du Bois dipped into the inarticulations of less nuanced leftist ideology after 1952, Mullen's *Un-American: W. E. B. Du Bois and the Century of World Revolution* resists "commemorative containment" to emphasize the clarity of his theorizing about political revolution, especially in his last decade. Mullen considers Du Bois's global anticolonial thought and explores his theory of economic and political revolution—the achievement of economic democracy and self-determination for both men and women—through his late-career writings, especially an unpublished manuscript from 1950 titled "Russia and America." More explicitly than other scholars of Du Bois's late career, Mullen insists that "the most productive way to read the life and work of Du Bois is backward: as the retrospective fulfillment of a conception of human history best understood as its capacity for world revolution."[31]

Biography is another mode of analysis through which scholars have considered Du Bois's twilight decades. While a number of Du Bois biographies appeared well before the 1980s, as Table 2 indicates,

**Table 2.** Scholarly Biographies of W. E. B. Du Bois

| Title | Publication Date |
| --- | --- |
| *W. E. B. Du Bois: Negro Leader in a Time of Crisis*, Francis L. Broderick | 1959 |
| *W. E. B. Du Bois: A Study in Minority Group Leadership*, Elliott M. Rudwick | 1960, 1968 |
| *Cheer the Lonesome Traveler: The Life of W. E. B. Du Bois*, John Alexander Lacy | 1970 |
| *His Day Is Marching On: A Memoir of W. E. B. Du Bois*, Shirley Graham Du Bois | 1971 |
| *His Was the Voice: The Life of W. E. B. Du Bois*, Emma Gelders Stearn | 1971 |
| *W. E. B. Du Bois: A Biography*, Virginia Hamilton | 1972 |
| *W. E. B. Du Bois: A Pictorial Biography*, Shirley Graham Du Bois | 1978 |
| *W. E. B. Du Bois*, Jack B. Moore | 1981 |
| *Black and Red: W. E. B. Du Bois and the Afro-American Response to the Cold War, 1944–1963*, Gerald Horne | 1986 |
| *W. E. B. Du Bois: Black Radical Democrat*, Manning Marable | 1986 |
| *W. E. B. Du Bois*, James Neyland | 1992 |
| *W. E. B. Du Bois: Biography of a Race*, David Levering Lewis | 1993 |
| *Dark Voices: W. E. B. Du Bois and American Thought, 1880–1903*, Shamoon Zamir | 1995 |
| *W. E. B. Du Bois, 1919–1963: The Fight for Equality and the New American Century*, David Levering Lewis | 2000 |
| *Race Woman: The Lives of Shirley Graham Du Bois*, Gerald Horne | 2000 |
| *W. E. B. Du Bois: American Prophet*, Edward J. Blum | 2007 |
| *W. E. B. Du Bois: A Biography*, David Levering Lewis (condensed volume of two previous biographies) | 2009 |
| *W. E. B. Du Bois: A Biography*, Gerald Horne | 2010 |
| *W. E. B. Du Bois: An American Intellectual and Activist*, Shawn Leigh Alexander | 2015 |
| *W. E. B. Du Bois: Revolutionary across the Color Line*, Bill V. Mullen | 2016 |

historical distance from Du Bois's death, wider availability of his
writings, and the general growth of scholarship on African American
history all contributed to the emergence of a number of scholarly biographies that tackled Du Bois's remarkable career. To mention Du Bois
and biography in the same sentence is to invoke the name David Levering Lewis. Lewis's infinitely detailed biography of Du Bois—published
in two volumes—won two Pulitzer Prizes, a sterling accomplishment.
Although Du Bois's most notable biographer respects his subject's
work as an intellectual, voracious learner, and indefatigable writer,
it is important to note that compared to Marable and Horne, Lewis
appears less supportive of Du Bois's socialism and communism and in
the process gives comparatively slimmer attention to Du Bois's later
career. In an astonishing admission Lewis contended, "Du Bois's pronouncements may ring oddly enough to cause doubt as to his standing
as one of the twentieth century's intellectual heavyweights. Few would
commend the ideological and geographical resting places of his final
years. . . . It should be understood that it is by far the significance of
Du Bois's protest and of his gradual alienation, rather than the solutions
he proposed, that are instructive." Lewis also observed, "An extraordinary mind of color in a racialized century, Du Bois was possessed of
a principled impatience with what he saw as the egregious failings of
American democracy that drove him, decade by decade, to the paradox
of defending totalitarianism in the service of a global ideal of economic
and social justice."[32] While Lewis has little respect for Du Bois's politics in his closing decades, his biographies provide stunning insight
into Du Bois's important life.

While there appeared many important Du Bois biographies in print,
Louis Massiah's 1995 documentary, *W. E. B. Du Bois: A Biography in
Four Voices*, offered a visual, cinematic complement to existing work
and scored a significant contribution to the field. Massiah's production
work on Henry Hampton's *Eyes on the Prize* gave birth to the idea for
a documentary project singularly focused on Du Bois. As a documen-
tarian, Massiah offered a detailed chronology and captivating narrative
to tell the story of Du Bois's nearly one hundred years of life. Rather
than offer the opinions only of scholars, in the film he depended on
the voices of people whose lives intersected with Du Bois's, a style he
termed "witnessed-based" filmmaking, that allowed for Du Bois's contemporaries to "have a more authorial role in the film." Part of this
component included using four separate writers to narrate each section
of the documentary.[33]

The witnessed-based element of Massiah's film proved particularly illuminating in parts 3 and 4, sections that covered the last three
decades of Du Bois's life. Writer Toni Cade Bambara wrote and edited
part 3 of the documentary, "A Second Reconstruction?," which covered the years from 1934 to 1948. It offered a sympathetic portrayal
of Du Bois's emerging Depression-era radicalism and an appreciative
summary of how black internationalism informed his commitment to
socialism. Bambara's presentation rooted Du Bois's intellectual and
social impact in both his writing and his activism, a configuration
that spoke to her own artistic work.[34] Propped up against a piano with
a stack of books close by in order to present a black arts vibe, Amiri
Baraka, narrator of the closing segment of Massiah's documentary,
which covers Du Bois's final years, recalled that the U.S. government's
targeting of Du Bois produced a fidelity to cultivating "consciousness,
humanity, and eventual civilization." This segment displays a fully
global Du Bois whose voice across the world in the service of peace and
economic equality found an international reception during the 1950s.
At the same time, America's attempt to domesticate Du Bois through
his 1951 arrest and trial finds vivid expression through the memories
of contemporaries Carlton Moss, Louis Thompson Patterson, and Bernard Jaffe, among others, along with granddaughter Du Bois Williams
and adopted son David Graham Du Bois. Such witnessed-based filmmaking, most especially in part 4, presented the humanity of the black
radical scholar's ideas, convictions, and commitments through what
Manthia Diawara describes as a "subjective grid." In other words, the
relationship between the primary sources (written, oral, and visual)
used to make the film and the oral history displayed through the memories and voices of those who witnessed Du Bois's life and times offers
a conversational and interpretive conjuncture that produces his long
life "intersubjectively," a "symbolist mode" that traverses Du Bois's existence both at home and abroad. The artistry evident in Massiah's visual
biography in four parts ensures a depiction of Du Bois that narrates his
significance as a black American in light of his identity as a citizen of
the world.[35]

Outside of monographs, document readers, and biographies, it is also
important to mention several additional academic avenues of research
on Du Bois: specialized volumes, juvenile literature, curriculum material, and scholarly essay collections.

Specialized studies comprise a unique assemblage of work related
to Du Bois. A multivolume encyclopedia, *Africana: The Encyclopedia*

*of the African and African American Experience*, edited by Henry Louis
Gates and Kwame Anthony Appiah, is the dream of Du Bois's *Encyclopedia Africana* realized. First published in 1999 (with an accompanying
CD-ROM, Encarta Africana), a second edition followed in 2005. Gates
and Appiah note that, like Du Bois's career-long effort to organize and
published the *Encyclopedia Africana*, their efforts to bring Du Bois's
idea to fruition met with resistance until adequate funding materialized. With the *Encyclopedia*, therefore, the editors and authors could
make the case, again as Du Bois did in much of his work, "that Africa
has never been separate from the rest of the human world."[36] Gerald
Horne and Mary Young's *W. E. B. Du Bois: An Encyclopedia* (2001) is an
equally important resource, the only one of its kind. Characteristically,
the encyclopedia covers nearly all facets of Du Bois's life, and as befits
Horne's scholarship more generally, it connects to the constellation of
black radical networks with which Du Bois had frequent contact, while
it also reflects a decidedly international focus.[37] Herbert Aptheker's *Literary Legacy of W. E. B. Du Bois*, published in 1989, includes all of
the introductions to the Kraus-Thomson Du Bois volumes he edited,
a helpful and appreciative summary of Du Bois's life work. Aptheker
was at least partially right to observe at the end of the volume—and at
the cold war's terminus—that, "as the decades pass, the appreciation of
Du Bois will grow."[38] Also important is the work of Paul G. Partington,
whose bibliographic efforts rival Aptheker's.[39] Meyer Weinberg's *The
World of W. E. B. Du Bois: A Quotation Sourcebook* is a unique compen-
dium of stylish and punchy quotes that usefully document Du Bois's
range of reflection and felicity of opinion. African American studies
scholar John Bracey's new introduction to Weinberg's book helpfully
chronicles the editor's life as an activist and a scholar and recounts the
research that led to the publication of this unique resource. Finally, the
multivolume series published in 2007 as *The Oxford W. E. B. Du Bois*
is the second critical collection of Du Bois's major work available, after
Aptheker's thirty-seven-volume Kraus-Thomson series. While a number of the books in the Oxford series have been published numerous
times (e.g., *The Souls of Black Folk* and *Darkwater*), it is interesting to
observe that Du Bois's later books that are part of the series have not
been reissued since the original publication date. Tables 3 and 4 reflect
the larger orientation to Du Bois's early career; most of Du Bois's late
books, when compared to his earliest studies, have been republished
only a minimal number of times.[40]

Table 3. W. E. B. Du Bois's Publications and Reprints (Numerical Rankings)

| Title | Year Published | Times Republished |
|---|---|---|
| Souls of Black Folk | 1903 | 24 |
| Quest of the Silver Fleece | 1911 | 10 |
| John Brown | 1909 | 7 |
| Suppression of the African Slave Trade | 1896 | 7 |
| Darkwater | 1920 | 7 |
| Black Reconstruction | 1935 | 7 |
| The Negro | 1915 | 6 |
| Philadelphia Negro | 1899 | 5 |
| Dusk of Dawn | 1939 | 5 |
| Gift of Black Folk | 1924 | 5 |
| Dark Princess | 1928 | 3 |
| Black Folk Then and Now | 1939 | 3 |
| The World and Africa | 1947 | 3 |
| The Autobiography | 1968 | 3 |
| Africa, Its Place in Modern History | 1930 | 2 |
| Africa, Its Geography, People, Products | 1930 | 2 |
| Color and Democracy | 1945 | 2 |
| In Battle for Peace | 1952 | 2 |
| Ordeal of Mansart | 1957 | 2 |
| Mansart Builds a School | 1959 | 2 |
| Worlds of Color | 1961 | 2 |

While most scholars are far less impressed with Du Bois's later works due to a stark polemical edge or underdeveloped literary creativity, it is also true that for many Du Bois's later politics remain distasteful. Hence his late work receives minimal exposure. The introductions to each volume of the Oxford Du Bois stand as robust and critical reflections on each book's history and importance. This is especially true for Du Bois's books in the Oxford series that span his life's closing decades.

**Table 4.** W. E. B. Du Bois's Publications and Reprints (Chronological and Longitudinal)

| Title | Year Published | Times Republished |
|---|---|---|
| Souls of Black Folk | 1903 | 24 |
| Quest of the Silver Fleece | 1911 | 10 |
| John Brown | 1909 | 7 |
| Suppression of the African Slave Trade | 1896 | 7 |
| Darkwater | 1920 | 7 |
| Black Reconstruction | 1935 | 7 |
| The Negro | 1915 | 6 |
| Philadelphia Negro | 1899 | 5 |
| Gift of Black Folk | 1924 | 5 |
| Dark Princess | 1928 | 3 |
| Africa, Its Place in Modern History | 1930 | 2 |
| Africa, Its Geography, People, Products | 1930 | 2 |
| Dusk of Dawn | 1939 | 5 |
| Black Folk Then and Now | 1939 | 3 |
| The World and Africa | 1947 | 3 |
| The Autobiography | 1968 | 3 |
| Color and Democracy | 1945 | 2 |
| In Battle for Peace | 1952 | 2 |
| Ordeal of Mansart | 1957 | 2 |
| Mansart Builds a School | 1959 | 2 |
| Worlds of Color | 1961 | 2 |

In his final *Autobiography*, Du Bois expressed the weight of his marginalization by admitting a certain fear and resignation that his work would be lost to future generations—especially young people. Reflecting on his 1951 trial, Du Bois wrote, "From being a person whom every Negro in the nation knew by name at least and hastened always to endorse or praise, churches and Negro conferences refused to mention my past or present existence. . . . I lost the leadership of my race. . . . The colored children ceased to hear my name."[41] Although Jim Crow was to some extent in retreat by the end of Du Bois's life, his worries were not unfounded since anticommunist animus and antiblack sentiment permeated the United States. In reality, as Table 5 illustrates, Du Bois's name and his voice continued to echo, not just for the youth of the DuBois Clubs but also with younger students in the classroom. Much of the juvenile literature forefronts Du Bois's earlier career, but neither does it simply dismiss his later years. This is perhaps due, at least in part, to the fact that the large majority of juvenile titles on Du Bois appeared in the 1990s, after the cold war. In a certain way, Du Bois remained an important race man in his life after death.[42]

Correspondingly, a nascent literature has developed around teaching materials on Du Bois. The education company Cobblestone, based in New Hampshire, publishes primary, intermediate, and secondary curricula, including a magazine called *Cobblestone* that focuses on various historical persons and historical events. In 2000 *Cobblestone* devoted an issue to Du Bois. Bruce Watson's article, "The Lion in Winter," covered his late career rigorously, not dismissively, commenting that Du Bois transformed political difficulties "into a remarkable final chapter of his life."[43] For the Center for History Teaching and Learning at the University of Texas at El Paso, elementary educator Matthew McConnell prepared a very thorough Teacher's Guide for Du Bois in the classroom. To meet curricular standards specific to the state of Texas, McConnell ably covers the span of Du Bois's career, critically assesses biographies of him, and provides a short selection of Du Bois online resources. Commendably, McConnell does not shy away from a robust engagement with Du Bois's closing decades. While the tone of the teaching guide is not entirely sympathetic regarding Du Bois's later politics, it does not decry his leftist orientation.[44] Du Bois's debate with Booker T. Washington is the subject of additional pedagogical analysis, as are the subjects of sociology and religion.[45]

Table 6 displays scholarly essay collections devoted to Du Bois's life and work. Several observations stand out immediately. First, the wide-ranging topics that Du Bois's publications encompassed not only reflect his acquaintance with numerous disciplinary fields but show that critical study of Du Bois necessitates a vast collection of specialties that can find expression only in collaborative enterprises. These anthologies make it clear that Du Bois's work has a significant bearing for gender theory, sexuality studies, psychology, literature, critical social theory, religion, and print culture, among other topics. Second, scholarly anthologies on Du Bois remained relatively sparse until the

**Table 5.** Juvenile Literature on W. E. B. Du Bois

| Title | Publication Date |
|---|---|
| *Lift Every Voice*, Dorothy Sterling and Benjamin Quarles | 1965 |
| *Cheer the Lonesome Traveler: The Life of W. E. B. Du Bois*, John Alexander Lacy | 1970 |
| *W. E. B. Du Bois: A Biography*, Virginia Hamilton | 1972 |
| *W. E. B. Du Bois*, Mark Stafford | 1989 |
| *W. E. B. Du Bois*, Patricia and Frederick McKissack | 1990 |
| *W. E. B. Du Bois: Crusader for Peace*, Kathryn T. Cryan-Hicks | 1991 |
| *W. E. B. Du Bois and Racial Relations*, Seamus Cavan | 1993 |
| *W. E. B. Du Bois: Civil Rights Leader*, Nathaniel Moss | 1996 |
| *W. E. B. Du Bois: Champion of Civil Rights*, Mark Rowh | 1999, 2015 |
| *W. E. B. Du Bois*, Don Troy | 1999, 2009 |
| *W. E. B. Du Bois: Scholar and Civil Rights Activist*, Melissa McDaniel | 1999 |
| *W. E. B. Du Bois: Scholar and Activist*, Mark Stafford with additional text by John Davenport | 2005 |
| *Stranger in My Own House: The Story of W. E. B. Du Bois*, Bonnie Hinman | 2005 |
| *W. E. B. Du Bois: The Fight for Civil Rights*, Ryan P. Randolph | 2005 |
| *W. E. B. Du Bois*, Jennifer Blizin Gillis | 2006 |
| *W. E. B. Du Bois: A Twentieth-Century Life*, Tonya Bolden | 2008 |
| *W. E. B. Du Bois: Civil Rights Activist, Author, Historian*, Jim Whiting | 2010 |
| *W. E. B. Du Bois*, Jeni Wittrock | 2015 |
| *W. E. B. Du Bois*, Hillary Lochte | 2016 |
| *W. E. B. Du Bois: Co-founder of the NAACP*, Meghan M. Engsberg Cunningham | 2017 |

Table 6. Scholarly Anthologies on W. E. B. Du Bois

| Title | Publication Date |
|---|---|
| *Black Titan: W. E. B. Du Bois*, ed. John Henrick Clarke et al. | 1970 |
| *William Du Bois: Scholar, Humanitarian, Freedom Fighter*, ed. G. B. Starushenko et al. | 1971 |
| *W. E. B. Du Bois: A Profile*, ed. Rayford Logan | 1971 |
| *Critical Essays on W. E. B. Du Bois*, ed. William L. Andrews | 1985 |
| *W. E. B. Du Bois: His Contribution to Pan-Africanism*, ed. Kwadwo O. Pobi-Asamani and Daryl F. Mallett | 1994 |
| *W. E. B. Du Bois on Race and Culture*, ed. Bernard W. Bell, Emily R. Grosholz, and James B. Stewart | 1996 |
| *W. E. B. Du Bois, Race, and the City:* The Philadelphia Negro *and Its Legacy*, ed. Michael B. Katz and Thomas J. Sugrue | 1998 |
| *W. E. B. Du Bois and Race: Essays Celebrating the Centennial Publication of* The Souls of Black Folk, ed. by Chester J. Fontenot Jr. and Mary Alice Morgan, with Sarah Gardner | 2001 |
| *W. E. B. Du Bois*, ed. Harold Bloom | 2001 |
| *Reconsidering* The Souls of Black Folk, ed. Stanley Crouch and Playthell Benjamin | 2002 |
| The Souls of Black Folk: *One Hundred Years Later*, edited and introduction by Dolan Hubbard | 2003 |
| The Souls of Black Folk: *Centennial Reflections*, ed. Tamara Brown, Ida Jones, and Yohuru Williams | 2004 |
| *The Souls of W. E. B. Du Bois*, ed. Alford A. Young Jr. | 2007 |
| *Next to the Color Line: Gender, Sexuality, and W. E. B. Du Bois*, ed. Susan Gillman and Alys Eve Weinbaum | 2007 |
| *Re-cognizing W. E. B. Du Bois in the Twenty-First Century: Essays on W. E. B. Du Bois*, ed. Mary Keller and Chester J. Fontenot Jr. | 2007 |
| *The Cambridge Companion to W. E. B. Du Bois*, ed. Shamoon Zamir | 2008 |

Table 6 (continued)

| Title | Publication Date |
|---|---|
| The Souls of W. E. B. Du Bois: New Essays and Reflections, ed. Edward J. Blum and Jason R. Young | 2009 |
| W. E. B. Du Bois, ed. Reiland Rabaka | 2010 |
| Protest and Propaganda: W. E. B. Du Bois, The Crisis, and American History, ed. Amy Helene Kirschke and Phillip Luke Sinitiere | 2014 |
| A Political Companion to W. E. B. Du Bois, ed. Nick Bromell | 2018 |
| W. E. B. Du Bois and the Africana Rhetoric of Dealienation, ed. Monique Leslie Akassi | 2018 |

dawn of the twenty-first century. On the one hand, it took some years for Du Bois scholarship to develop, particularly once his papers were available for research and once Aptheker commenced publication of Du Bois's works during the mid-1970s. Yet at the same time, it is undeniable that the shadow of the cold war continued to place limitations on scholarly analysis of Du Bois. While only four anthologies appeared between 1985 and 1998, the explosion of Du Bois anthologies in the twenty-first century mostly appeared as commemorations of *The Souls of Black Folk*'s centenary—not an unworthy endeavor—but the anthological focus on *Souls* portended subsequent essay collections that remain mostly confined to moments and texts that defined Du Bois's early career.

In recent times, scholars conscious of Du Bois's relevance have staged commemorative acknowledgments of several of his key contributions to American history. Some of this work, especially in sociology and philosophy, prizes his early career, whereas publications in literature and art history consider his intellectual output from the 1930s onward.

In 2000, for example, *The Annals of the American Academy of Political and Social Science* published the special issue "The Study of African American Problems: W. E. B. Du Bois's Agenda, Then and Now." Focused largely on sociology and political science, articles also surfaced Du Bois's thought in relation to religion and literature. The essays collectively acknowledged his intellectual contributions to a broad program of studying African Americans and provided avenues to think about the continuing relevance of Du Bois's work to the study of race, culture, and society. Not directly focused on his late publications, the appearance of this *Annals* issue reflected a pressing desire to contemplate the necessity of Du Bois's intellectual legacy for today and preceded developments in Du Bois studies during the past two decades. Under the editorship of Manning Marable, a 2005 issue of *Souls: A Critical Journal of Black Politics, Culture, and Society* devoted an issue to "Critical Perspectives on W. E. B. Du Bois." Similarly, to honor the sesquicentennial of Du Bois's birth in 2018, several print and online outlets, including *Socialism and Democracy*, *Black Perspectives*, and *Sounding Out!*, produced scholarly pieces that reflected on Du Bois's legacy, some of which centered his late career.[46]

One development has been in the field of sociology. For example, in 2005 the online journal *Sociation Today* featured a series of articles devoted to Du Bois's social science, which anticipated fuller analysis of Du Bois's sociology from Earl Wright II, Robert Wortham, Reiland Rabaka, and Aldon Morris.[47] In literary and cultural studies, under Nahum Dimitri Chandler's editorship the *New Centennial Review* published three issues devoted to Du Bois which prefigured Chandler's subsequent Du Bois books. Similarly, recent works by Stephanie Shaw, Rebecka Rutledge Fisher, Robert Gooding-Williams, Carol Anderson, Robeson Taj Frazier, and Vaughn Rasberry, among many others, produced new and innovative perspectives on Du Bois's long career, especially his closing decades.[48] Turning attention to Du Bois's later decades, Duke University hosted a 2010 symposium to honor *Black Reconstruction*'s seventy-fifth anniversary. Several years later *South Atlantic Quarterly* published the conference proceedings; from that issue Alys Eve Weinbaum's examination of gender and *Black Reconstruction* appears in revised form in this volume.

The year 2013 marked the fiftieth anniversary of Du Bois's death, an occasion for additional commemorative work in light of the need to press new analysis forward. Universities held conferences, produced scholarship, and staged art instillations. In journalistic forums and popular venues, writers considered Du Bois's history and legacy in relation to today's bedeviling problems and potential for revolutionary change.

With this memory in mind, Keith Feldman's *Al Jazeera* article "A Haunting Echo: W. E. B. Du Bois in a Time of Permanent War" called for contemporary application of Du Bois's commitments to peace. "We turn to Du Bois to plumb the thick emancipatory dreams persistently articulated by and for the world's darker peoples, to draw on their searing legacies and insights," Feldman argued. "We need Du Bois today, perhaps more than ever." A writer in *Political Affairs* (when it still appeared as an online publication) drew attention to Du Bois's legacy in the form of late-career scholarship and the ways that it offered an international perspective on global politics, questioned the gospel of capitalism, and inspired interracial alliances for justice. In addition, a 2013 reunion of former DuBois Clubs members demanded a reassertion of principles that guided the movement in order to address current inflections of class conflict and working-class activism. Finally, sparked by reflections on the fifty-year anniversary of the March on Washington and a connection between Du Bois and Martin Luther King, Werner Lange commended a re-visioning of Du Bois's later decades. "It is high time for the roaring silence and/or gross distortions regarding DuBois to end," he stated, "Fifty years after his death, let his prophetic voice be heard once again."[49]

Clark Atlanta University hosted a four-day gathering, W. E. B. Du Bois and the Wings of Atlanta 50th Anniversary Commemorative Conference. The meeting staged a comprehensive consideration of nearly all facets of Du Bois's work, from literature and philosophy to religion and political science. A large contingent of recognized Du Bois scholars presented research, while other sessions provided forums for students and even some of Du Bois's descendants to engage his intellectual production and legacy. Amiri Baraka keynoted the conference's final session, where he read from his play *The Most Dangerous Man in America*, a project focused on Du Bois's 1951 trial. Baraka passed away in early 2014, not long before the play premiered at New York City's New Federal Theatre under the direction of Woody King Jr. In addition, artist Ayokunle Odeleye created a commissioned Du Bois bust for Clark Atlanta University that conference organizers dedicated during a ceremony on February 23, Du Bois's birthday. Rich symbolism of the Clark Atlanta festivities marked a new day and potential future for Du Bois studies in the twenty-first century.[50] Importantly, the conference mobilized in 2014 the return of one of Du Bois's important late-career intellectual projects, *Phylon*. While the new journal's early issues reprinted some of Du Bois's *Phylon* writings and featured articles about Du Bois specifically, its broader vision of "carrying memory forward to an ever-wider world" articulates Du Bois's intellectual legacy.[51]

At the University of Massachusetts–Amherst, visual artists, scholars, and activists collectively staged "Du Bois in Our Time." As a conversation designed to probe the present in light of the past, artists and

scholars creatively captured Du Bois's notions of double consciousness, his writings in *Darkwater*, as well as his engagements with African
history and black feminism, among other subjects. Loretta Yarlow,
director of UMass's University Museum of Contemporary Art, framed
the exhibit around the following questions: "Can we examine the legacy of W. E. B. Du Bois and his relevance in the twenty-first century
through the lens of contemporary art? Can we commission artists to
create works of art to help provide a broader understanding of Du Bois,
who has been viewed too narrowly as a sociologist and historian rather
than as a thinker and a humanist in the richest sense of these words?"[52]
Conference presenter and Africana studies scholar Reiland Rabaka
echoes Yarlow's point on bifurcation of Du Bois's thought and legacy.
"Many of Du Bois's critics have heretofore downplayed and diminished
the real brilliance and brawn of his work by failing to grasp its antino-
mies and have, therefore, put forward a divided and distorted Du Bois,"
he contends, work that "falls shamefully short of capturing the complex
and chameleonic character of Du Bois's discourse and the difficulties
involved in interpreting it using one-sided, single-subject theory and/or
monodisciplinary devices."[53]

While Rabaka's comments refer to the full scope of Du Bois's days,
one artist in particular used Du Bois's late career to grapple with antin-
omies, complexities, and contradictions in his life. New York–based
artist Anne Messner created *DuBois: The FBI Files* to spotlight both
hypocrisy in America and Du Bois's radical insistence on freedom of
expression. She curried 447 feet of Du Bois's massive FBI file, some
of which rested on top of (or beside) a 22-foot table on which a list of
songs and speeches played through speakers fixed to the table. John
Coltrane's "Alabama" was part of the playlist, as was "Strange Fruit"
and the words of Malcolm X, Angela Davis, James Baldwin, and John
Carlos, among others. Combining visual and aural records to document a particular moment in cold war history, Messner designed the
exhibit for viewers to listen and look. As the audio looped, viewers witnessed Messner's provocative exhibit: she excised the redacted black
lines from printed copies of Du Bois's FBI file. "What is removed forms
a tale of its own of elegiac proportion, evidence of persisting secrets and
forbidden truths," she comments. "My resolute *removal of the removal*,
the cutting out to cancel, to void the space of redaction, perhaps an act
of futility, nevertheless stands as a small gesture, a nod in recognition
of what we lose when we do not allow the space for dissent, when we
condemn to silence what is different." A visual and sonic commentary

informed by the surveillance state in contemporary times, Messner's instillation powerfully surfaced U.S. government attempts to sabotage Du Bois's freedom, especially in his final three decades, even as he attempted to lift up his voice and work on behalf of colored people across the globe.[54]

The "Du Bois in Our Time" exhibit also coincided with another landmark of contemporary Du Bois scholarship: the digitization of Du Bois's UMass archive. In 2009 a $200,000 grant from the Verizon Foundation initialized the digitization of the Du Bois papers at UMass. Two years later the National Endowment for the Humanities contributed funds to assist with the project's completion, which made available in 2014 the nearly 100,000 items in the Du Bois collection.[55] Through a searchable online platform called Credo—the name adopted from Du Bois's own personal statement of his life's philosophy—Du Bois's letters, books, poems, newspaper writings, and a host of other documents are publicly available. The symbolic importance of using the word "Credo" for the collection also extends to the matter of wider accessibility of his work. Since "Du Bois fit that intersection between academia and public action," stated UMass Special Collections director Robert Cox, "people who use the collection often do the same."[56] On the point of next-generation academic research in the Du Bois collection, Henry Louis Gates observed, "Digitizing these works will lead to a renaissance in scholarship about the greatest thinking of African descent in history."[57]

While scholars noted the potential for new research and the promise that a fully searchable archive holds for the future of Du Bois studies, technical aspects of the digitization process also speak to particularities of Du Bois's work and intellectual legacy. A platform like Credo that allows researchers to peer into different parts of his life and career both at home and abroad also makes discoverable new networks of understanding among his many interlocutors and across his various publications. Cox considers this symbolic of Du Bois's intrepid internationalism since his work was "never confined to place or time. . . . [It] intended to help people see the interconnectedness. He was speaking to a world audience about the issues he saw across borders."[58] For Aaron Rubinstein, the university and digital archivist at UMass who managed the digitization project, the sense of Du Bois's interconnection cut two ways. As a Massachusetts native, Rubinstein knew basic facts about the black scholar from the state's history curriculum. However, after working with thousands of Du Bois documents over the several years the digitization process took—after reading his published, public works as well as his private thoughts in correspondence—Rubinstein obtained "a certain level of intimacy" with Du Bois that contrasted substantially from his grandparents' era, when the nation reviled the Great Barrington native as a communist traitor to the United States. In other words, Rubinstein's own positive relationship to Du Bois through working with the digital and physical archives augmented his initial exposure to the black intellectual, a hostile rendering of Du Bois that extended from the black radical politics of his later decades.[59]

Whereas the story behind UMass receiving Du Bois's papers involved loud anticommunist outcry and stiff antiblack resistance, the digitization project proceeded with far fewer political obstacles and with considerably less fanfare over funding. However, carrying out the digital complexities for a manageable, accessible, and user-friendly platform was no less ambitious than attempts to house Du Bois's archive at the university. There is rich irony in the stirring and important accomplishment of making Du Bois's papers more widely accessible. For example, in the 1970s the NEH balked at funding early projects that proposed to put some of Du Bois's archive into print—a story Gary Murrell recounts in this volume—while half a century later it provided the capital to complete the project. Perhaps there is a sense of poetic justice in the reality that the same U.S. government that targeted and arrested Du Bois funded the digital delivery of his papers, some of which offer his critical commentary on federal harassment of black radicals.

If there is any semblance of poetic justice, it is also of interest to note that the Verizon Foundation's seed money launched the project. As documents in the Edward Snowden archive revealed, the modern manifestation of the surveillance state that eyed Du Bois—which, with more bemoaning irony, grew in size and power during the administration of the nation's first black president and under the gaze of a black attorney general—extended its reach with the assistance of modern communications corporations like Verizon. Journalist Glenn Greenwald broke the story in 2013, when he reported that Verizon provided telephone data of its customers daily to the National Security Agency, which the FBI had also received access to through a FISA court order.[60] While with one hand Verizon's funding made more widely available the historical records of Du Bois's dissent, with the other hand it assisted the extension of the surveillance state, whose history of stifling resistance portends a future in which Du Bois's black radicalism will remain vital for both scholarship and political resistance.[61]

The history of Du Bois's twilight years, like the man himself, has been wide-ranging and has reflected numerous disciplinary perspectives. While there was wide availability of his writings within a dozen years of his death, scholarly production on Du Bois steadily gained momentum starting in the 1970s and 1980s, and at present in the early twenty-first century shows little sign of fatigue. However, in the years ahead, in the context of increasing economic inequality and political conflict and as assessments of the Obama era appear in light of Donald Trump's election, there remains a tremendous amount of work to do, most especially analysis that propels our understanding of Du Bois's closing decades—a fitting tribute to his legacy of scholarship and struggle.

## Notes

A portion of this essay appeared previously in ""A Legacy of Scholarship and Struggle": W. E. B. Du Bois and the Political Affairs of His Twilight Years," *Poitical Affairs*, August 26, 2013. Thanks to editor Joe Sims and the CPUSA for permission to include the earlier portions in this expanded essay. I also thank Gerald Horne and Bettina Aptheker for comments on an earlier draft.

1. Charles Euchener, *Nobody Turn Me Around: A People's History of the 1963 March on Washington* (Boston: Beacon, 2011), 182–84; David Levering Lewis, *W. E. B. Du Bois: A Biography* (New York: Henry Holt, 2009), 1–4; Carol Anderson, *Bourgeois Radicals: The NAACP and the Struggle for Colonial Liberation, 1941–1960* (New York: Cambridge University Press, 2015), 1–9.

2. John Oliver Killens, introduction to W. E. B. Du Bois, *An ABC of Color* (New York: International Publishers, 1968), 9–10.

3. "William Edward Burghardt Du Bois," *The Crisis*, October 1963, 469–70.

4. "NAACP Mourns Passing of Dr. Du Bois, A Founder," *The Crisis*, October 1963, 472–73; Manning Marable, *W. E. B. Du Bois: Black Radical Democrat* (Boulder, CO: Paradigm, 2005), 214.

5. Eugene Perkins, "In Memory of Du Bois" and "William Edward Burghardt Du Bois," *Negro Digest* 13.1 (November 1963): 64–65.

6. Bettina Aptheker, *Intimate Politics: How I Grew Up Red, Fought for Free Speech, and Became a Feminist Rebel* (Emeryville, CA: Seal Press, 2006), 93–94.

7. W. E. B. DuBois Clubs' publications included *Spur* (January 3, 1968) and Jarvis Tyner, "Dr. W. E. B. Du Bois," *Insurgent*, January–March

1968, 25–26, Billy James Hargis Papers, Box 56, Folder 48, University of Arkansas.

8. "Target . . . American Youth!," Church League of America Collection, Box 33, Folder 10, Tamiment Library, New York University; Douglas Robinson, "Du Bois 'Duplicity' Decried by Nixon," *New York Times*, March 9, 1966, http://www.nytimes.com/books/00/11/05/specials/dubois-nixon .html; cf. *W. E. B. Du Bois*, ed. William M. Tuttle, Jr. (Englewood Cliffs, NJ: Prentice-Hall, 1973), 1-2.

9. "Souvenir Program in Memory of Dr. William E. Burghardt Du Bois, February 23, 1964," W. E. B. Du Bois Papers Digital Archive, mums312-b156-i191.

10. John Hope Franklin, "William Edward Burghart DuBois," Communist Party of the United States of America Records, Box 112, Folder 96, Tamiment Library, New York University; cf. John Hope Franklin, "W. E. B. Du Bois: A Personal Memoir," *Massachusetts Review* 31.3 (Autumn 1990): 409–28.

11. Lorraine Hansberry, "Remarks by Lorraine Hansberry at the Memorial Meeting for W. E. B. Du Bois," Communist Party of the United States of America Records, Box 112, Folder 96, Tamiment Library, New York University.

12. Eslanda Robeson, "Tribute to Dr. W. E. B. DuBois," Abbott Simon Papers, Box 1, Folder 31, Tamiment Library, New York University.

13. Theses completed during Du Bois's lifetime include Mary Means Drake, "W. E. B. Du Bois as a Man of Letters," MA thesis, Fisk University, 1934; Hobart Sidney Jarrett, "The American Problems of Racial Democracy as Seen in the Works of William E. Burghardt Du Bois," MA thesis, Wiley College, 1936; Emmett Wilfort Bashful, "W. E. B. Du Bois and Booker T. Washington: A Study of Techniques in Race Relations," MA thesis, University of Illinois at Urbana-Champaign, 1947; George H. Weldon, "W. E. B. Du Bois: The Sorrow Singer," MA thesis, University of Denver, 1949; Gladys Noel Bates, "The Marginal Man: An Interpretation of W. E. B. Du Bois," MA thesis, West Virginia University, 1952; William Henry Chafe, "The Emergence of Racialism: W. E. B. Du Bois and the Two World Wars," AB Honors Thesis, History, Harvard University, 1962; Kathryn D. Emmet, "W. E. B. Du Bois: A Biographical Study," AB Honors Thesis, Psychology, Harvard University, 1966. Academic articles during Du Bois's lifetime include Herbert Aptheker, "W. E. B. Du Bois: The First Eighty Years," *Phylon* 9.1, first quarter (1948): 59–62; Elliot M. Rudwick, "W. E. B. Du Bois in the Role of *Crisis* Editor," *Journal of Negro History* 43.3 (July 1958): 214–40; Jessie P. Guzman, "W. E. B. Du Bois—The Historian," *Journal of Negro Education* 30.4 (Autumn 1961): 377–85; Daniel

Walden, "W. E. B. Du Bois: Black Reconstruction Historian," *Negro History Bulletin* 26.5 (February 1963): 159–60, 164.

14. Francis L. Broderick, *W. E. B. Du Bois: Negro Leader in a Time of Crisis* (Stanford, CA: Stanford University Press, 1959), 183, 185, 190–91, 211, 219, 225, 229.

15. Elliott M. Rudwick, *Propagandist of the Negro Protest*, 2nd edition (Philadelphia: University of Pennsylvania Press, 1968), 289, 293, 314.

16. Stephen Shames and Bobby Seale, *Power to the People: The World of the Black Panthers* (New York: Abrams), 204. In interviews I've heard Bobby Seale comment on the influence of Du Bois's thought, including his opening remarks at a Black Panther Party anniversary dinner in Houston I attended in 2014. Historian Gerald Horne delivered the keynote lecture for this event, "Audacity Personified: The Black Panther Party Reconsidered," in author's possession. See "Happenings in Houston," *Houston Defender*, November 6, 2014, https://issuu.com/defendermediagroup/docs/11.06.2014_e-full.

17. Vincent Harding, introduction to Lerone Bennett, *The Challenge of Blackness*, Black Paper No. 1 (Atlanta, GA: Institute of the Black World, 1970), iii, Printed Ephemera Collection on Organizations, Box 41, Tamiment Library, New York University; cf. Marable, *W. E. B. Du Bois*, xv–xvi; Manning Marable, *Living Black History: How Reimagining the African-American Past Can Remake America's Racial Future* (New York: Basic, 2006), 98–119; Derrick E. White, *The Challenge of Blackness: The Institute of the Black World and Political Activism in the 1970s* (Tallahassee: University Press of Florida, 2011).

18. See the March 2012 theme issue of the *Journal of African American Studies*, "Expanding the History of the Black Studies Movement." Also helpful on the black studies movement are Nagueyalti Warren, *W. E. B. Du Bois: Grandfather of Black Studies* (Trenton, NJ: Africa World Press, 2011); James B. Stewart, "The Legacy of W. E. B. Du Bois for Contemporary Black Studies," *Journal of Negro Education* 53.3 (Summer 1984): 296–311; James Turner and C. Steven McGann, "Black Studies as an Integral Tradition in African-American Intellectual History," *Issue: A Journal of Opinion* 6.2–3 (Summer–Autumn 1976): 73–78. See also the 1966 issue from the *Journal of Human Relations* devoted to W. E. B. Du Bois, as well as volume 1 of *The Black Scholar* in 1970. Manning Marable helpfully historicizes various applications of Du Bois's thought during this point in U.S. history; see Marable, *W. E. B. Du Bois*, xiv–xviii.

19. John Henrik Clarke et al., *Black Titan: W. E. B. Du Bois* (Boston: Beacon, 1970); Shirley Graham Du Bois, *His Day Is Marching On: A Memoir of W. E. B. Du Bois* (Philadelphia: J. B. Lippincott, 1971). A WorldCat

search of graduate student work on Du Bois in the 1960s and 1970s populates nearly three dozen theses and dissertations.

20. See, for example, Kenneth M. Glazier, "W. E. B. Du Bois' Impressions of Woodrow Wilson," *Journal of Negro History* 58.4 (October 1973): 452-59; William M. Tuttle, "W. E. B. Du Bois' Confrontation with White Liberalism During the Progressive Era: A *Phylon* Document," *Phylon* 35.3 (3rd Qtr., 1974): 241-58; Mark D. Higbee, "A Letter from W. E. B. DuBois to his Daughter Yolande, Dated "Moscow, December, 10, 1958,"" *Journal of African American History* 78.3 (1993): 188-95; Kenneth Barkin, "W. E. B. Du Bois and the Kaiserreich," *Central European History* 31.3 (1998): 155-96; Robert W. Williams, ""The Sacred Unity in All the Diversity": The Text and a Thematic Analysis of W.E.B. Du Bois' "The Individual and Social Conscience" (1905)," *Journal of African American Studies* 16 (2012): 456-97; Nahum Dimitri Chandler, "The Meaning of Japan," *CR: The New Centennial Review* 12.1 (2012): 233-56; Nahum Dimitri Chandler, "Chapter 16—Jones in Japan," *CR: The New Centennial Review* 12.1 (2012): 257-74; Nahum Dimitri Chandler, "Chapter 17—Jones Looks Back on China," *CR: The New Centennial Review* 12.1 (2012): 275-90; Adrienne Brown and Britt Rusert, "The Princess Steel," *PMLA* 130.3 (2015): 819-29; Nagueyalti Warren, "A. D. 2150," *African American Review* 49/1 (Spring 2016): 53-57; Phillip Luke Sinitiere, ""Outline of Report on Economic Condition of the Negroes in the State of Texas": W. E. B. Du Bois' 1935 Speech at Prairie View State College," *Phylon* 54.1 (Summer 2017): 3-24; W. E. B. Du Bois, *The Fantasy Worlds of W. E. B. Du Bois*, eds. Britt Rusert and Adrienne Brown (New York: Penguin, forthcoming). For autobiographical reflections on researching and editing Du Bois manuscripts see Nahum Dimitri Chandler, "Introduction. Toward a New History of the Centuries: On the Early Writings of W. E. B. Du Bois," in W. E. B. Du Bois, *The Problem of the Color Line at the Turn of the Twentieth Century: The Essential Early Essays*, ed. Nahum Dimitri Chandler (New York: Fordham University Press, 2015), 1-32 and Phillip Luke Sinitiere, "Making Material Memories: Transformative Moments in W. E. B. Du Bois's Archive," *The Activist History Review*, December 27, 2018, https://activisthistory.com/2018/12/27/making-material-memories-transformative-moments-in-w-e-b-du-boiss-archive/.

21. Herbert Aptheker, "Personal Recollections: Woodson, Wesley, Robeson and Du Bois," *Black Scholar* 27.2 (Summer 1997): 42–45.

22. Herbert Aptheker, "The Legacy of W. E. B. Du Bois," February 13, 1998, Graduate Theological Union, Berkeley, California, Herbert Aptheker Papers, Series 2, Box 124, Folder 7, Stanford University. In addition to

Murrell's essay in this volume, on Aptheker and Du Bois, see Robin D. G. Kelley, "Interview of Herbert Aptheker," *Journal of American History* 87.1 (June 2000): 151–67; Herbert Aptheker, "Vindication in Speaking Truth to Power," in *Against the Odds: Scholars Who Challenged Racism in the Twentieth Century*, ed. Benjamin P. Bowser and Louis Kushnick with Paul Grant (Amherst: University of Massachusetts Press, 2002), 216–19; Eric Foner, Jesse Lemisch, and Manning Marable, "Epilogue: The Historical Scholarship of Herbert Aptheker," in *Herbert Aptheker on Race and Democracy: A Reader*, ed. Eric Foner and Manning Marable (Urbana: University of Illinois Press, 2006), 246–57; Gary Murrell, "Herbert Aptheker's Unity of Theory and Practice in the Communist Party USA," *Science & Society* 70.1 (June 2006); 98–118; Herbert Shapiro, ed., *African American History and Radical Historiography: Essays in Honor of Herbert Aptheker* (Minneapolis: Marxist Educational Press, 1998), part 1; Herbert Aptheker, "Du Bois: The Final Years," *Journal of Human Relations* 14 (1966): 149–55; Gary Murrell, "On Herbert Aptheker and His Side of History: An Interview with Eric Foner," *Radical History Review* 78 (2000): 6–26.

23. Warren, *W. E. B. Du Bois*, xvii.

24. A WorldCat search of graduate student work on Du Bois from the 1980s to the present populates over one hundred English-language theses and dissertations.

25. Cedric Robinson, *Black Marxism: The Making of the Black Radical Tradition* (Chapel Hill: University of North Carolina Press, 2000), 185–240.

26. See Monteiro's UN testimony in John Henrik Clarke, ed., *Pan-Africanism and the Liberation of Southern Africa: International Tribute to William E. B. DuBois* (New York: United Nations Centre against *Apartheid*, 1978), 56-57. Relatedly, see Tony Monteiro, "W. E. B. Du Bois: the 'logic of life' leads to socialism," *People's World Weekly* (February 19, 1994): 12-13, where he states, "The modern civil rights movement and African liberation movements own more to him than any other single person" (12), Communist Party of the United States of America Records, Box 112, Folder 96, Tamiment Library, New York University, and Tony Monteiro, "The Scientific & Revolutionary Legacy of W. E. B. Du Bois," April 21, 1994 UMass Amherst lecture flyer, W. E. B. Du Bois Papers, Box 290, Folder 20, University of Massachusetts Amherst Special Collections. Monteiro's subsequent scholarship built upon these earlier observations in which he advocated for an Africana-centered consideration of Du Bois's intellectual and political work. See, for example, Anthony Monteiro, "Being an African in the World: The Du Boisian Epistemology," *The Annals*

*of the American Academy of Political and Social Science* 568 (March 2000): 220-34; Anthony Monteiro, "Race and the Racialized State: A Du Boisian Interrogation," *Socialism and Democracy* 17 (2003): 77-97; Anthony Monteiro, "Race and Empire: W. E. B. Du Bois and the US State," *The Black Scholar* 37.2 (Summer 2007): 35-52; Anthony Monteiro, "W. E. B. Du Bois and the Study of Black Humanity," *Journal of Black Studies* 38.4 (March 2008): 600-21; Anthony Monteiro, "The Epistemic Crisis of African American Studies: A Du Boisian Resolution," *Socialism and Democracy* 25.1 (March 2011): 192-210. I thank Josh Myers and Ife Flannery for helpful discussion about Monteiro's scholarship.

27. Marable, *W. E. B. Du Bois*, xiii.

28. Gerald Horne, *Black and Red: W. E. B. Du Bois and the Afro-American Response to the Cold War, 1944–1963* (Albany: State University of New York Press, 1986), 8–10.

29. See, for example, William Cain, "From Liberalism to Communism: The Political Thought of W. E. B. Du Bois," in *Cultures of United States Imperialism*, ed. Amy Kaplan and Donald E. Pease (Durham, NC: Duke University Press, 1993), 456–73; Werner Sollers, "W. E. B. Du Bois in Nazi Germany, 1936," *Amerikastudien/American Studies* 44.2 (1999): 207–22; Harold Brackman, "'A Calamity Almost Beyond Comprehension': Nazi Anti-Semitism and the Holocaust in the Thought of W. E. B. Du Bois," *American Jewish History* 88.1 (March 2000): 53–93; Michael Rothberg, "W. E. B. Du Bois in Warsaw: Holocaust Memory and the Color Line, 1949–1952," *Yale Journal of Criticism* 14.1 (2001): 169–89; Kate Baldwin, *Beyond the Color Line and the Iron Curtin: Reading Encounters between Black and Red, 1922–1963* (Durham, NC: Duke University Press, 2002); George Bornstein. "W. E. B. Du Bois and the Jews: Ethics, Editing, and *The Souls of Black Folk*," *Textual Cultures* 1.1 (2006): 64–74; Lawrie Balfour, *Democracy's Reconstruction: Thinking Politically with W. E. B. Du Bois* (New York: Oxford University Press, 2011); Eve Darian-Smith, "Re-reading W. E. B. Du Bois: The Global Dimensions of the U.S. Civil Rights Struggle," *Journal of Global History* 7.3 (November 2012): 483–505; Jodi Melamed, "W. E. B. Du Bois's UnAmerican End," *African American Review* 40.3 (Fall 2006): 533–50; Claire Parfait, "Rewriting History: The Publication of W. E. B. Du Bois's *Black Reconstruction*," *Book History* 12 (2009): 266–94; Nahum Dimitri Chandler, "A Persistent Parallax: On the Writings of W. E. Burghardt Du Bois on Japan and China, 1936–1937," *CR: The New Centennial Review* 12.1 (2012): 291–316; Gao, "W. E. B. Du Bois and Shirley Graham Du Bois in Maoist China," *Du Bois Review* 10.1 (2013), 59–85; Brent Hayes Edwards, "Late Romance," in *Next to the*

*Color Line: Gender, Sexuality, and W. E. B. Du Bois*, ed. Susan Gillman and Alys Eve Weinbaum (Minneapolis: University of Minnesota Press, 2007), 124–49; Derrick P. Alridge, *The Educational Thought of W. E. B. Du Bois: An Intellectual History* (New York: Teachers College Press, 2008),122–36; Yuichiro Onishi, *Transpacific Antiracism: Afro-Asian Solidarity in 20th Century Black America, Japan, and Okinawa* (New York: New York University Press, 2013), 1–15, 54–93; Phillip Luke Sinitiere, "Leadership for Democracy and Peace: W. E. B. Du Bois's Legacy as a Pan-African Intellectual," in *Leadership in Colonial Africa: Disruption of Traditional Frameworks and Patterns*, ed. Baba J. Jallow (London: Palgrave Macmillan, 2014), 202–39.

30. Amy Bass, *Those about Him Remained Silent: The Battle over W. E. B. Du Bois* (Minneapolis: University of Minnesota Press, 2009), 159. Bass's study notes the range of opinion about Du Bois in western Massachusetts that on balance improved after the 1960s. For example, in 2018, the sesquicentennial of Du Bois's birth, local Great Barrington artists produced murals in honor of his life. By contrast, shortly after the mural dedications controversy erupted again in Great Barrington over the proposal of a Du Bois statue in town; veterans decried the idea of dedicating a statue to a radical communist. On the murals, see Whitney Battle-Baptiste, "Bringing W. E. B. Du Bois Home Again," *Black Perspectives*, February 23, 2018, https://www.aaihs.org/bringing-w-e-b-du-bois -home-again/. On the Du Bois statue, see Terry Cowgill, "Veterans Protest Statue to Memorialize 'Communist' Du Bois," *Berkshire Edge*, June 15, 2018, https://theberkshireedge.com/war-veterans-protest-statue-to -memorialize-communist-du-bois/.

31. Eric Porter, *The Problem of the Future World: W. E. B. Du Bois and the Race Concept at Midcentury* (Durham, NC: Duke University Press, 2010); Bill Mullen, *Un-American: W. E. B. Du Bois and the Century of World Revolution* (Philadelphia: Temple University Press, 2015), 13, 201.

32. Lewis, *W. E. B. Du Bois*, 713.

33. Author phone interview with Louis Massiah, August 22, 2014; see also Elizabeth Amelia Hartley, "*Eyes on the Prize*: Reclaiming Black Images, Culture, and History," in *Struggles for Representation: African American Documentary Film and Video*, ed. Phyllis R. Klotman and Janet K. Cutler (Bloomington: Indiana University Press, 1999), 99–123.

34. Jonathan Scott Holloway, "The Soul of W. E. B. Du Bois," *American Quarterly* 49.3 (September 1997): 609.

35. Manthia Diawara, "The 'I' Narrator in Black Diaspora Documentary," in Klotman and Cutler, *Struggles for Representation*, 315–28.

36. Henry Louis Gates Jr. and Kwame Anthony Appiah, *Africana: The Encyclopedia of the African and African American Experience*, 2nd edition (New York: Oxford University Press, 2005), xv.

37. Gerald Horne and Mary Young, eds., *W. E. B. Du Bois: An Encyclopedia* (Westport, CT: Greenwood, 2001).

38. Herbert Aptheker, *The Literary Legacy of W. E. B. Du Bois* (White Plains, NY: Kraus-Thomson, 1989), 354.

39. Paul G. Partington, *W. E. B. Du Bois: A Bibliography of His Published Writings* (Whittier, CA: Partington, 1984); Paul G. Partington, The Moon Illustrated Weekly: *Black America's First Weekly Magazine* (Whittier, CA: Partington, 1986); Robert W. McDonnell and Paul G. Partington, *W. E. B. Du Bois: A Bibliography of Writings About Him* (Whittier, CA: Partington, 1989).

40. Meyer Weinberg, *The World of W. E. B. Du Bois: A Quotation Sourcebook* (1992), new introduction by John H. Bracey Jr. (Amherst: University of Massachusetts Press, 2013).

41. W. E. B. Du Bois, *The Autobiography of W. E. B. Du Bois: A Soliloquy on Viewing My Life from the Last Decade of Its First Century*, ed. Henry Louis Gates Jr. (1968; New York: Oxford University Press, 2007), 255.

42. Of the juvenile literature that devotes considerable space to Du Bois's late career in substantial if not sympathetic detail, see Mark Rowh, *W. E. B. Du Bois: Champion of Civil Rights* (Berkeley Heights, NJ: Enslow, 1999), 85–111; Nathaniel Moss, *W. E. B. Du Bois: Civil Rights Leader* (New York: Chelsea House, 1996), 63–74.

43. Nancy I. Colamussi prepared the teacher's guide for the *Cobblestone* issue, available online at http://www.cobblestonepub.com/resources /cob0002t.html. See Bruce Watson, "The Lion in Winter," *Cobblestone*, February 2000, 36–39.

44. Matthew McConnell, "W. E. B. Du Bois: A Teacher's Guide," http:// academics.utep.edu/Portals/1719/Publications/DuBois.pdf.

45. Phillip Luke Sinitiere, "Of Faith and Fiction: Teaching W. E. B. Du Bois and Religion," *History Teacher* 45.3 (May 2012): 421–36; Leo J. Alilunas, "What Our Schools Teach about Booker T. Washington and W. E. B. Du Bois," *Journal of Negro Education* 42.2 (Spring 1973): 176–86; Susan Searles Giroux, "Reconstructing the Future: Du Bois, Racial Pedagogy and the Post–Civil Rights Era," *Social Identities* 9.4 (2003): 563–98; Earl Wright II, "Why, Where and How to Infuse the Atlanta Sociological Laboratory into the Sociology Curriculum," *Teaching Sociology* 40 (2012): 257–70.

46. For more on *Annals*, and similar projects, see Porter, *The Problem of the Future World*, 181–82n22. For a summary of commemorations in 2018 that marked the 150th anniversary of Du Bois's birth, see Phillip Luke Sinitiere, Gerald Horne, and Edward Carson, ""If we neglect to mark this history, it may be distorted or forgotten": Socialism and Democracy in W. E. B. Du Bois's Life, Thought, and Legacy," *Socialism and Democracy* (forthcoming).

47. W. E. B. Du Bois, *W. E. B. Du Bois and the Sociological Imagination: A Reader, 1897–1914*, ed. Robert Wortham (Waco, TX: Baylor University Press, 2009); Reiland Rabaka, *Against Epistemic Apartheid: W. E. B. Du Bois and the Disciplinary Decadence of Sociology* (Lanham, MD: Lexington, 2010); Aldon Morris, *The Scholar Denied: W. E. B. Du Bois and the Birth of Modern Sociology* (Berkeley: University of California Press, 2015); Earl Wright II, *The First American School of Sociology: W. E. B. Du Bois and the Atlanta Sociological Laboratory* (New York: Routledge, 2016).

48. The *New Centennial Review* issues include "W. E. B. Du Bois and the Question of Another World" (6.3, 2006); "Toward a New Parallax: Or, Japan in Another Traversal of the Pacific" (12.2, 2012); "W. E. B. Du Bois and the Question of Another World, II (Or, Another Poetics and Another Writing—Of History and the Future)" (15.2, 2015). See also Nahum Dimitri Chandler, *Toward an African Future—Of the Limit of the World* (London: Living Commons Collective, 2013); Nahum Dimitri Chandler, *X—The Problem of the Negro as a Problem for Thought* (New York: Fordham University Press, 2014); W. E. B. Du Bois, *The Problem of the Color Line at the Turn of the Twentieth Century: The Essential Early Essays*, ed. Nahum Dimitri Chandler; Stephanie J. Shaw, *W. E. B. Du Bois and* The Souls of Black Folk (Chapel Hill: University of North Carolina Press, 2013); Rebecka Rutledge Fisher, *Habitations of the Veil: Metaphor and the Poetics of Black Being in African American Literature* (Albany: State University of New York Press, 2015); Robert Gooding-Williams, *In the Shadow of Du Bois: Afro-Modern Political Thought in America* (Cambridge, MA: Harvard University Press, 2011); Anderson, *Bourgeois Radicals*; Vaughn Rasberry, *Race and the Totalitarian Century: Geopolitics in the Black Literary Imagination* (Cambridge, MA: Harvard University Press, 2015); Robeson Taj Frazier, *The East Is Black: Cold War China in the Black Radical Imagination* (Durham, NC: Duke University Press, 2014).

49. Keith Feldman, "A Haunting Echo: W. E. B. Du Bois in a Time of Permanent War," *Al Jazeera*, February 10, 2013, http://www.aljazeera.com /indepth/opinion/2013/02/20132772031503974.html; Phillip Luke Sinitiere, ""A Legacy of Scholarship and Struggle": W. E. B. Du Bois and the

Political Affairs of His Twilight Years," *Political Affairs*, August 26, 2013, http://politicalaffairs.net/a-legacy-of-scholarship-and-struggle-w-e-b-du -bois-and-the-political-affairs-of-his-twilight-years-2/ (link active as of 2013, until *Political Affairs* ceased its online publication); Tim Wheeler, "DuBois Clubs Reunion: Memories, Battles Yet to Be Fought and Won!," *Peoples World*, June 18, 2013, http://peoplesworld.org/dubois-clubs -reunion-memories-battles-yet-to-be-fought-and-won/; Werner Lange, "On the Passing of W. E. B. Du Bois, and the Torch, 50 Years Ago," *Cleveland. com*, August 25, 2013, http://www.cleveland.com/opinion/index.ssf/2013 /08/on_the_passing_of_web_dubois_a.html.

50. See the conference website, http://cauduboislegacy.net/Home_Page .html, which includes photos and videos of selected conference sessions, including Baraka's presentation and reading.

51. Stephanie Y. Evans, "Sankofa: The Deed of Memory," *Phylon* 51.1 (Fall 2014): vii.

52. Loretta Yarlow, "Reflections on *Du Bois in Our Time*," in *Ten Contemporary Artists Explore the Legacy of W. E. B. Du Bois in Our Time*, ed. Radcliffe Bailey et al. (Amherst: University of Massachusetts Press, 2014), 9.

53. Reiland Rabaka, "'To Make a Name in Science, to Make a Name in Literature, and Thus Raise My Race': Du Bois in Our Time, in His Time, and in the Future," in Bailey et al., *Ten Contemporary Artists Explore the Legacy of W. E. B. Du Bois in Our Time*, 49.

54. Anne Messner, "DuBois: The FBI Files," in Bailey et al., *Ten Contemporary Artists Explore the Legacy of W. E. B. Du Bois in Our Time*, 104–11, 146–47.

55. Diane Lederman, "Website Extends Influence of W. E. B. Du Bois Writings," *Masslive*, July 15, 2011, https://www.masslive.com/news/index .ssf/2011/07/website_extends_influence_of_w.html; Joshua Sternfeld, "W. E. B. Du Bois in Cyberspace," National Endowment for the Humanities, February 12, 2015, https://www.neh.gov/divisions/preservation /featured-project/web-du-bois-in-cyberspace. See also Cynthia Yeldell, "Du Bois Collection Digitized," *The Crisis* 116.3 (Summer 2009): 10.

56. Cox quoted in Melissa Trujillo, "UMass to Put Papers of Du Bois Online," *Network Journal*, April 6, 2009, http://www.tnj.com/umass-to-put -papers-of-web-du-bois-online.

57. Gates quoted in ibid.

58. Quoted in Lederman, "Website Extends Influence of W. E. B. Du Bois Writings."

59. Author interview with Aaron Rubinstein, University of Massachusetts–Amherst Special Collections, August 6, 2014.

60. Glenn Greenwald, "NSA Collecting Phone Records of Millions of Verizon Customers Daily," *The Guardian*, June 6, 2013, https://www .theguardian.com/world/2013/jun/06/nsa-phone-records-verizon-court -order; "'A Massive Surveillance State': Glenn Greenwald Exposes Covert NSA Program Collecting Calls, Emails," *Democracy Now!*, June 7, 2013, https://www.democracynow.org/2013/6/7/a_massive_surveillance_state _glenn_greenwald.

61. Andrew Lanham, "When W. E. B. Du Bois Was Un-American," *Boston Review*, January 13, 2017, http://bostonreview.net/race-politics/andrew -lanham-when-w-e-b-du-bois-was-un-american; Gary Wilder, "If You Want to Build an Alternative to Trumpism, You Need to Read Black Freedom Fighter W. E. B. Du Bois," *Open Democracy*, May 6, 2017, https:// www.opendemocracy.net/gary-wilder/if-you-want-to-build-alternative-to -trumpism-you-need-to-read-black-freedom-fighter-web-.

# The Digital Legacy of W. E. B. Du Bois in the Internet Age

*Robert W. Williams*

## Introduction

A person's legacy is at once retrospective and prospective. A legacy commemorates past actions and works that convey the official or unofficial significance of that person for how things became as they are. It also evokes inspiration and even exhortation to others for future action, perhaps to live up to the ideals enshrined and celebrated in the legacy. Monuments and songs materialize a legacy, as do narratives in official and unofficial realms, in education and in popular and academic presses.

Although often supportive of a social and political status quo, a legacy does not necessarily reinforce uncritically the received wisdom of a community or nation. A legacy carries with it the seeds that can also prompt us to reexamine a person's thoughts and deeds from the perspective of a new age and a new generation. Consequently there is no finality about a legacy; rather it is provisional, albeit within the boundaries of evidence advanced and intellectual approaches used. Future generations will interpret and reinterpret the evidence, whether new, old, symbolic, or imagined.

Marble and granite sculptures do not embody a legacy, and this is all the more evident in a digital era. In an age of electronic books, a digital legacy extends the idea and practice of scholarship by providing new opportunities to conduct and distribute research and insights. It also brings to critical light new connections among the words and deeds of one person or between one and many, including individuals, organizations, groups, societies, and cultures.

This essay centers on the importance and relevance of a digital legacy for W. E. B. Du Bois in the era of the internet. Or, to paraphrase

Walter Benjamin, this essay examines the work of Du Bois in an age of digital (re)production and distribution.[1] New opportunities to make Du Bois more accessible and to provide information, insights, interactions, and inspiration to new generations counterbalance the loss of the aura of singular, illuminated manuscripts and the loss of the physicality of mass-produced books.

I will highlight some, but not all, of the various manifestations of Du Bois's digital legacy in the twenty-first century. Accordingly I will present a range of websites that offer relevant primary (and sometimes secondary) sources. This is not an exhaustive list. Then I will examine the general advantages of a digital Du Bois for purposes of education and academic scholarship. I will individualize the topic of his digital heritage by focusing on my academic website, WEBDuBois.org. The creation and maintenance of WEBDuBois.org provides a personal case study illustrating one online implementation of Du Bois's digital legacy. In that discussion I will sketch some of the difficulties encountered in the construction of a site, including technical and other challenges. I conclude the essay by briefly discussing several social dimensions of a digital Du Bois: the digital divide of the wired haves vis-à-vis the have-nots; the epistemic implications of the knowledge produced by archival creation and by websites presenting links to other sites (such as mine); and the scholarly necessity, but ultimate uncertainty, of compiling an exhaustive digital corpus of Du Bois's works.

I must stipulate several caveats and disclaimers. First, I will mention numerous institutional and archival websites and resources where materials are available online and freely accessible. Mostly due to space limitations in a print publication, I will not be able to mention all of those resources that might be useful or applicable. In addition, given the vast reaches of an expanding cyberspace, it is likely that I have missed some web-based resources. It is also possible that any particular text or specific repository or website is no longer available or is no longer free to access. Such is the digital, often ephemeral world of the internet. Second, I am concentrating on Du Bois's digital legacy in terms of primary sources. Although I am not delving into it due to space restrictions, another valuable part of a digital legacy is the varied types of online networks and communities that discuss Du Bois, among other topics. Third, as a disclaimer, my WEBDuBois.org site is sometimes included on the sites mentioned herein.

I will make one final note about the textual referencing of websites and web pages. Because the sites mentioned often have long and intricate URL addresses, I have cited them within the essay by the website name. The full URL to which I refer appears in the appendix "Websites Referenced."

## W. E. B. Du Bois's Digital Legacy

The increasing use of electronic media and digital sources for educational purposes and academic scholarship provides us with the opportunity to support a digital legacy for Du Bois. Academically oriented websites have proliferated over the past decade. They range from scholars' personal web pages and social media, including blogs, Facebook, Twitter, and related sites, to online intellectual communities, such as H-Afro-Am, *Black Perspectives*, the African American Intellectual History Society's blog, and the U.S. Intellectual History blog, among many others. Examples of academically oriented online repositories include the Women Writers Project, the Valley of the Shadow, Malcolm X: A Research Site, the Digital Schomburg African American Women Writers of the 19th Century, and the Dickinson Electronic Archive. Also available are sites for learning about research techniques and tools, such as NINES (Networked Infrastructure for Nineteenth Century Electronic Scholarship) and the Roy Rosenzweig Center for History and New Media at George Mason University. In addition, we can find varied sites listing digital tools (e.g., DiRT repository) and sites inviting online analysis of texts (e.g., Voyant tools and TAPoR 3, or Text Analysis Portal for Research). Although all such sites occupy a part of the environment of Du Bois's digital legacy, I will concentrate on the places that host primary sources online.

Some online repositories present the documents in text-based formats—which facilitate many computational analyses—while other sites also include page facsimiles. Such image files are also crucial to understanding an author and his or her process of creation and composition. Page images allow us to view the primary source, possibly with the revisions and emendations made by the author or under the author's direction. Accordingly we can better understand the development of the document itself.[2]

Du Bois's digital legacy offers us several distinct advantages in the twenty-first century. I will discuss (1) what is available online, such as the types of repositories of freely accessible primary sources by Du Bois and also the tools by which to search for them, and (2) how such online

270    ROBERT W. WILLIAMS

resources might be utilized to understand and illuminate Du Bois in new ways.

### Resources Available Online

Repositories of primary and secondary sources are a popular tool for research and education. Online repositories of primary materials often contain unpublished manuscripts and typescripts. They are not necessarily copies of published items in print format. Books Du Bois published after 1923 typically are not freely accessible online, although most, if not all, reside behind a paywall (see below). In sequence, I will outline the following types of repositories, as well as the online tools to locate source materials:

- Du Bois–specific repositories
- Topical and thematic collections (especially as relates to Africana studies)
- Institutionally focused collections
- General repositories
- U.S. government repositories
- Search and metasearch engines
- For-profit collections
- Human-organized directories.

### Du Bois–Specific Collections

Several institutionally based repositories—often libraries—permit online access to Du Bois's primary sources and sometimes to relevant secondary sources. They have become vital research and educational tools in the internet age.

The largest online Du Bois–specific collection is the Credo online repository located at the Special Collections and University Archives at the University of Massachusetts–Amherst Library. It contains mostly unpublished materials written by Du Bois, including drafts of published works as well as correspondence to and from him. Notable too are the many photographs of Du Bois throughout the years and a few audio recordings and movies. Hence this collection contains important works spanning his entire life, making it an especially valuable resource for the thought and activism of his later years. The Credo archive provides a finding aid online. Moreover the archive includes photographs of Du Bois and his second wife, Shirley Graham Du Bois, in various places around the world (e.g., China, Soviet Union, Ghana, USA, European countries) and in the company of numerous world leaders, such as Mao Zedong, Kwame Nkrumah, and Nikita Khrushchev. There are wedding photos as well as photos of Graham Du Bois without her husband in various world cities. The archive also contains the material from which Herbert Aptheker, Du Bois's literary executor, compiled and edited the three volumes of Du Bois's correspondence, the anthologies *The Education of Black People* and *Prayers for Dark People*, and the many volumes of the collected published writings released by the Kraus-Thomson publishing house.[3] An alternate way to access the Credo repository is via the Digital Commonwealth, Massachusetts Collections Online. This metasearch engine locates items among various archives in Massachusetts and returns the results.

The Beinecke Rare Book and Manuscript Library at the Yale University Library houses another collection of primary materials by Du Bois. The archive is smaller in size than the Credo repository but contains some important primary sources. The online finding aid lists the holdings, but only some can be viewed online, such as the incomplete drafts of his *Dusk of Dawn* and *The World and Africa*. Significantly, one can access the page facsimiles of Du Bois's undergraduate paper "The Renaissance of Ethics," which was written for a philosophy class conducted by William James. (The professor's handwritten notes are legible in the margins.) One can search for "Du Bois" in the "Digital Collections" and then focus the filters on Du Bois himself or on Carl van Vechten (for his portrait-style photographs of the elder Du Bois and of Graham Du Bois, but not together).[4]

The Encyclopaedia Africana Project, located in Accra, Ghana, offers a few essays by Du Bois describing the project. Related sources also located on the website originate from President Kwame Nkrumah as well as others associated with the project.

Several other important archives of Du Boisian primary materials are not accessible online. Fisk University library has a major archival collection of materials, especially drafts of manuscripts, written by Du Bois and other texts accumulated by him. Only the finding aid is viewable online, not the items themselves. At the New York Public Library, in the Archives and Manuscripts section, we find "W. E. B. Du Bois Papers, 1906–1966 [bulk 1942–1948]." The Du Bois collection is somewhat small. It is housed at the Schomburg Center for

Research in Black Culture, Manuscripts and Rare Books Division. This
archive does not provide a detailed finding aid, only an overview of
the materials. The overview lists Du Bois's correspondence with Arthur
Schomburg, a typescript of the first two chapters of *Dusk of Dawn*,
and various speeches (e.g., on Gandhi and Franklin D. Roosevelt). The
W. E. B. DuBois Centre for Pan-African Culture, situated in Accra,
possesses Du Bois's personal library. Many of the books contain handwritten comments by Du Bois himself; such marginalia would interest
many Du Bois scholars.[5] There is no finding aid online.

*Topical and Thematic Collections*
The internet has various topical archives containing items relevant to
Africana or African American matters, persons, or communities. The
following sites contain primary sources by Du Bois. One may need to
use the search function to locate the Du Boisian materials. First is
the University of North Carolina's Documenting the American South.
It contains collections of works divided into several categories spanning North Carolina history, culture, and literature over time. It also
includes a few early texts written or edited by Du Bois, such as the
Atlanta University studies and *The Souls of Black Folk*.[6] Second, the
Black Past, as stated on its home page, is "the Online Reference Guide
to African American History." It provides a small number of Du Bois's
primary texts presented in HTML as web pages. Of significance for
the study of the later Du Bois, we find the texts of "The Negro Nation
within the Nation" (1934), "Behold the Land" (1946), and "An Appeal
to the World: A Statement of Denial of Human Rights to Minorities
in the Case of the Citizens of Negro Descent in the United States of
America and an Appeal to the United Nations for Redress" (Summary
ca. 1946).[7] One can locate those works via a site search for "Du Bois."
Third (but not an Africana-oriented site), the Marxist.org site provides
an online text written by Du Bois for the 1945 Pan-African Congress;
he entitled it "The Pan-African Movement."[8]

The Modernist Journals Project, organized by Brown University and
the University of Tulsa, provides a range of periodicals relevant to the
study of modernism, including *The Crisis* (at least those issues in the
public domain, from 1910 to 1922). Du Bois edited *The Crisis* for many
years and it published numerous editorials and other works by him and
various important activists of the first half of the twentieth century.
In addition, Du Bois utilized fictional works in the pursuit of racial

equality. The Poetry Foundation posts several poems by Du Bois on separate web pages, including "Ghana Calls" (1962).

Newspapers are an important resource, providing information and views on Du Bois, but also at times quoting him and thereby offering a type of primary source revealed through the medium of journalism. At the Black Press Research Collective the resources page links to various repositories of digital newspapers, although some are behind paywalls and require subscriptions or memberships. I will discuss the Library of Congress's website Chronicling America: Historic American Newspapers below, under "U.S. Government Repositories."

*Institutionally Focused Collections*
These encompass collections of materials centered on an institution or individuals associated with it. Such collections can contain useful secondary sources on Du Bois, and sometimes his primary sources. The Digital Collection of the Robert W. Woodruff Library at the Atlanta University Center holds the valuable *Bulletin of Atlanta University*, the periodical that contains much information on Du Bois's activities while he was a professor there and the coordinator of the *Atlanta University Studies*. The University of California's Bancroft Library houses an interview Julie Shearer conducted with the journalist Sidney Roger as part of International Longshoremen's and Warehousemen's Union Oral History Series. Roger discusses Du Bois, among numerous other social matters. Roger's interview transcript contains a transcript of Du Bois talking about race issues of the 1950s, which comes from an interview Roger conducted with Du Bois in 1956. The Digital Library of Georgia at the University of Georgia Libraries contains all but one of the first twenty "Atlanta University Publications"—which includes most of the studies that Du Bois edited or coedited. The Smithsonian Folkways collection lists two recordings of Du Bois: his speech at the Wisconsin Socialist Club in 1960 and Moses Asch's interview of him in 1961. The site makes the transcripts available (as PDF files) and offers the option to purchase the recordings. The *Jewish Currents* site contains items associated with that periodical, including articles published when it was called *Jewish Life*. We find two primary sources by the later Du Bois there: an excerpt of a 1948 *Chicago Defender* newspaper column (published in 1972 as "W. E. B. Du Bois on the Jews") and the article "Two Hundred Years of Segregated Schools" (1955).[9]

*General Repositories*

A few internet-based collections are not specifically or solely focused on Du Bois but do contain publicly accessible materials by and about him. Several such repositories come quickly to mind: Google Books, the HathiTrust Digital Library, the Internet Archive, and the grandparent of them all, Project Gutenberg. Such broad-based collections may require searching with terms such as "W. E. B. Du Bois" or "W. E. B. DuBois" (or some variant) in order to locate his primary items or relevant secondary sources. We often find that archival records and repositories catalogue Du Bois materials under his last name, both with and without a space. Sometimes a search with his full name, William Edward Burghardt Du Bois, yields some success. Other search terms (such as book or article titles or place names) will probably facilitate one's search. Typically the many pages of search results that ensue necessitate careful perusing. Another useful, generalized repository, with an emphasis on American periodicals, is unz.org. The site contains PDFs of articles in numerous periodicals within the public domain. It will present tables of content for those periodicals still under copyright. One will find other publications listed, such as books. Searching for Du Bois at unz.org returns various primary and secondary sources.

*U.S. Government Repositories*

The institutions of the U.S. government have tracked Du Bois on suspicion of being an agent of the USSR and also offer us resources to learn more about him as a civil rights activist. The Federal Bureau of Investigation surveilled Du Bois for many years, and its website provides redacted PDFs of its files on him. The Library of Congress created the site Chronicling America: Historic American Newspapers, which contains newspapers in the public domain. One can search for Du Bois across all newspapers in the archive or else filter the search by state and/or by what the site labels "ethnicity" (which includes the category "African American"). In addition, the Library of Congress offers a web guide, "W. E. B. Du Bois: Online Resources." It lists external links as well as internal links to a small number of primary sources archived at the Library, notably the "African American Photographs Assembled for the 1900 Paris Exposition." Du Bois incorporated those photographs into his award-winning exhibit at the exposition. Embracing what came to be called "respectability politics," the photos demonstrated to the white exposition attendees that African Americans should not be stereotyped in negative ways.[10]

## Search and Metasearch Engines

The well-known search engines Google, Yahoo, and Bing often return results listing the contents of the archives mentioned so far. Metasearch engines such as Dogpile and DuckDuckGo compile results based on the top search hits from other search engines. At least two metasearch engines pertain to Du Bois research directly. The Digital Public Library of America is a metasearch engine that finds materials housed at various libraries, including the New York Public Library. Umbra Search focuses specifically on African American history. It searches the Digital Public Library, the Credo repository, the collection at Yale's Beinecke Library, and many others. When entering the search string, Umbra Search will offer names and keywords that relate to the letters being typed. Overall, metasearch engines are useful, but in my experience they do not completely replace a targeted search of the individual repositories.

## For-Profit Collections

Profit-oriented companies offer access both to public domain works as well as to works still under copyright protection. In the case of Du Bois, this means that his works published after 1923 typically are not freely accessible in the public domain.[11] Small subsets of a copyrighted text might be viewable at Google Books and Amazon.com. Google Books provides free access to public domain texts and offers snippets or a small number of pages for those under copyright protection (and potentially available as merchandise). While the Modernist Journals project referenced above contains the full run of *Crisis* issues through part of 1922, in Google Books researchers can access selected issues of the magazine from 1922 through 1933, when Du Bois left his NAACP position as *Crisis* editor. Likewise, Amazon.com is a commercial site that sometimes allows potential customers to view a small subset of pages inside a book. In my experience, one company provides access to the full text of copyrighted Du Bois works. Paying subscribers to the collections available at Alexander Street Press can read many of Du Bois's primary sources, both books and articles, including those under copyright. Pacifica Radio Archives sells several audio recordings by Du Bois: "World Peace and Revolt in Africa," a 1953 interview, as well as the two recordings also listed at the Smithsonian Folkways collection (see above). One will need to search the archives with both "Du Bois" and "DuBois." Pacifica Radio Archives also has radio broadcasts about Du Bois delivered by scholars, such as Herbert Aptheker and Gerald Horne. Unlike the Smithsonian Folkways collection, Pacifica does not provide written transcripts of the speeches.

## Human-Organized Directories

Individual curation of a directory that points to external sites can be time-consuming to those involved but very useful to the end-user, especially if the curators are diligent. Two such human-curated sites are noteworthy. The Online Books Page is a very extensive links-site and regularly updates the free texts available on the internet via the "New Listings" page. Du Bois has his own author's page. In addition, the Voice of the Shuttle is a well-established directory that provides external links to humanities-based sites. It allows browsing according to academic disciplines and by resource type (e.g., teaching, reference, listservs, conferences, and so forth).

## The Significance of Du Bois's Digital Legacy

Certainly, many persons still use and may even prefer hard-copy texts. Digital works nonetheless facilitate their own portability because many can be contained within the storage of a laptop, tablet, or smartphone. They also facilitate easier searching if the document type possesses machine-readable text (e.g., as with word processors) or else text layers in graphically oriented page facsimiles (e.g., of which PDF or DJVU formats are capable). This subsection discusses two important dimensions of Du Bois's digital heritage: the potential for cross-referencing via hypertext structures and the possibility of applying computational approaches to the study of Du Bois. I will also sketch the theoretical implications of cross-referencing and computational research.

Digital works can permit the cross-referencing of ideas, allusions, and themes, whether between primary sources and secondary sources or between primary sources and those sources that authors mentioned or to which they alluded but did not explicitly cite. This is especially important for Du Bois's works, because he did not always specifically name those whom he referenced via quoted passages or else via non-specific nouns. Hypertext protocols allow for any given text to link to others. This facilitates our understanding of Du Bois with his other works and within his intellectual context, and thereby makes it possible to grasp more clearly similarities and differences among his works and between his texts and others. New insights expand our understanding of Du Bois and accordingly expand his legacy for a new millennium.

Cross-referencing texts is not new, of course. Concordances have long been useful for print publications. Nevertheless in the internet era cross-references via hypertextual techniques allow for new levels of interactivity between one text and others. We can trace new paths through the texts, paths that are not preestablished by the typically linear structure of print. As a theoretical consequence, multiple interpretations are possible, all of which emerge from the text itself or on variants of the text.[12]

The digitization of books, or ebooks, also offers the promise of new discoveries. With hypertext embedded within the digital work, new information—other digital works, like audio or video—can be incorporated so the initial material is elaborated upon or clarified in intellectually and pedagogically important ways. As a case of the former, Richard Cullen Rath created a hypertext version of *The Souls of Black Folk*. He linked the musical scores that preceded each of the book's chapters to web pages where one can read the associated lyrics and listen to a sample of the music.[13]

Another significance of the legacy of Du Bois emerges in the digital age. With the digitalization of texts comes the possibility of computer-assisted analysis, whether via online applications or downloadable software. Digital humanities (DH) as an interdisciplinary field involves the application of computational approaches to the study of human artifacts, such as texts, music, and art works.[14] DH includes curating online resources, a task we have been documenting through this essay for Du Bois. Such resources can encompass exhibitions spotlighting a person, group, theme, or time period, among other topics. Very common is a mapping component, which geographically contextualizes the cultural and historical information (e.g., Digital Harlem, which also contains data on Du Bois as a resident). Also, DH performs a variety of qualitative and quantitative analyses on works, whether as collections (corpora) or as an individual work. Numerous materials on DH can be found, especially, as one might imagine, on the internet (e.g., DHCommons.org).[15]

An internet search for "Du Bois" and "digital humanities" reveals a range of search results. A few completed DH projects, not already considered as primary source repositories, include "The Ward: Race and Class in Du Bois' Seventh Ward." This digital history project examines the area studied by Du Bois in his 1899 book, *The Philadelphia Negro*,[16] both in terms of Du Bois's era and the present-day residents. Du Bois also figures significantly in "disruptive" DH: he is the "virtual" embodiment of a critical-theoretical framework that analyzes both the paucity of archives that recover the works of persons of color and the dearth of scholars of color in the digital humanities.[17]

As regards the application of DH to the computational analysis of Du Bois's works, internet searches for "Du Bois" and "digital humanities" (at the time of writing this essay) yield only the "Retextualizer" project that I created. The project is a browser-based Javascript application that randomly rearranges the sentences of several of Du Bois's shorter essays. The methodological basis of the project derives from McGann and Samuels, who argue for what they call the deformation of texts as a way to gain new interpretive insights.[18] Given the present scarcity of DH-themed computational analyses of Du Bois, future research probably will benefit from the creation of a more extensive digital corpus of his works—a topic addressed below.

As this section has indicated, Du Bois's post-1923 works face the restraints of U.S. copyright law. Hence we typically do not find those works available as free online materials. Such works will become a part of the public domain sixty-five years after they were first published. Nevertheless the repositories discussed herein remain quite important today for the study of the later Du Bois because they offer us ways to better understand the development of his thought. In this regard, for example, the Beinecke and Credo repositories contain drafts of some of Du Bois's published works, including the ones secured by copyright. While we wait for copyright to expire, Uzoma Miller argues for another importance of the archived sources already accessible to us.[19] As the archivist who helped to catalogue Fisk University's Du Bois collection, Miller suggests that students can learn much from archival materials, such as letters and draft manuscripts, because such items are tangible evidence of a person once alive. Those items are not the unfamiliar vistas portrayed in a textbook or the distant abstractions conveyed in a theory. As a consequence, students might be more inspired to engage with the archival materials than with conventional teaching documents.

## A Case Study of WEBDuBois.org:
## Personal Observations

In order to illustrate Du Bois's digital legacy I will focus on one case: my academic website at WEBDuBois.org. This section examines the factors that have conditioned—in terms of both opportunities and limitations—the creation of a site that links to resources by and about Du Bois. I address this from the standpoint of freely accessible, legally available, academically useful materials. Three questions inform the discussion of the conditions underpinning the creation of WEBDu-Bois.org:

- What occasioned the creation of WEBDuBois.org?
- How have I located and organized resources on the website?
- What challenges have I experienced creating the website?

## What Occasioned the Creation of WEBDuBois.org?

After completing research on environmental justice, I began to research Du Bois in the summer of 2003 for what became my first essay on Du Bois. At that point I had not decided whether I would pursue my Du Bois studies further because I was working on several other non–Du Bois projects, such as cyberpolitics. However, my long-standing interest in the philosophy of social science coupled with the social justice aspects of my academic education and my environmental studies prompted me to inquire further in Du Bois's engaged scholarship for social and racial justice. During fall 2004 I commenced in earnest and soon discovered that, as with so many other research topics, materials were often plentiful but were scattered across the Web. I thought that creating some way to list the internet resources on Du Bois, and then be able to view them anywhere via web browser, would prove useful to me as I progressed in my research.

Hence WEBDuBois.org arose as a means to preserve and enhance a digital Du Bois. The website exists at the intersection of a vast, expanding cyberspace of sites and the search engines that crawl the Web. Ultimately it functions as a clearinghouse through which I evaluate and present material useful to the academic study of Du Bois.

An obvious name for an internet site on Du Bois might include the initials by which we know him. A quick look at whois.net indicated that the highly appropriate name—at least for the Net—of "WEBDuBois. org" was not yet registered. I registered it and started site construction in late November 2004. My previous experiences with website creation helped me in this new endeavor. I am self-taught in HTML, CSS (Cascading Style Sheets), and Javascript, all of which typically undergird web pages, including mine at the site. I do consult the expertise, examples, and coding solutions found on the Web.

## How Are the Resources Located and Organized on WEBDuBois.org?

The process by which I create and maintain the website directly involves locating internet resources and then attempting to organize them in a logical and user-friendly way. Search engines prove their inestimable value in a cyberspatial environment of numerous, loosely linked websites with Du Bois materials, assuming of course that the search engines have indexed the relevant web pages. I regularly use Google and Bing to search the internet, as well as metasearch engines, including Dogpile and more recently DuckDuckGo. This is a time-consuming task, not least because of the numerous results that populate the search findings. When displaying search results, the search engines may list academically useful sites farther down the page or on subsequent pages. I typically will read through hundreds of search results, page after page, skipping past listings for commercially based sites in order to find free items relevant to academic purposes.

Adding more terms in the search request helps to focus my inquiry, such as specific names and titles. Searching is also labor-intensive because I have found it useful, even necessary, to search using various combinations of his full name, as well as variant spellings of his name. I am not referring to "Du Bois" and "DuBois," both of which seem to yield the same results. Rather I refer to some combination of "William Edward Burghardt Du Bois," with and without initials substituting for some of his names. In addition, there are various renderings of "Burghardt" (e.g., "Burkhardt"), all of which researchers should query. To Du Bois's name one may add "Atlanta University" or "*The Crisis*" or even a book or article title. This may yield some relevant hits. We cannot exclude serendipity, of course, to which my own experience attests. With good fortune and persistence one may locate interesting, even relatively unknown and understudied primary sources.

The WEBDuBois.org site has a straightforward organizational structure. I established a web page for primary sources to which I was linking, with separate pages oriented to specific books and to individual stand-alone essays. I add the entries to the appropriate web page as part of one HTML file, but a server-side database would function more effectively as I list more entries. In addition to a "Sources" page I have other general pages, including an "About" page, which is subdivided into several categories pertinent to Du Bois's life and to the numerous secondary sources about him and his work.

I dedicate a separate page to Du Bois's books that are available and free within the public domain. Such book pages contain external links to the text located at one or more repositories around the web. Each page typically contains book reviews and notices, as well as contemporary and later secondary sources. Such secondary works help us to understand the text and its context.

The website provides a few individual essays by Du Bois, each on its own web page with the full text of the primary source. In addition, I have created web pages for a few pertinent essays written by other thinkers, such as Frantz Boas and Henry Lyman Morehouse. I typically add notes that provide some commentary by contemporaries as well as some contextual information. I usually cross-reference some aspects of the Du Bois text to provide more insights. The "Sources" page, the "Research" page, and the site map allow visitors to access the individual Du Bois essays.

Of relevance to the study of the later Du Bois, WEBDuBois.org includes the text and also editorial annotations for the following primary sources:

- "The Superior Race (An Essay)" (1923)
- "Criteria of Negro Art" (1926)
- "Douglass, Frederick" (1930)
- "The Negro Citizen" (1930)
- "The Church and Religion" (1933)
- "Jacob and Esau" (1944)
- "My Evolving Program for Negro Freedom" (1944).[20]

Site navigation occurs via the navigation links located in each page's header and footer. There is also a site search page that uses Google search to locate items on any or all relevant pages. A site map lists all available pages; this is available directly via URL or will display if a 404 error ("Page not found") occurs. The "Research" page also lists the available Du Bois essays on the site. A table of contents on the home page details a current list of updates on the individual pages within the site.

## Challenges to the Creation and Maintenance of WEBDuBois.org

The challenges I have experienced creating and maintaining the website are not unique to me; they highlight many of the general aspects of creating a repository or links website. Below I discuss five challenges:

- The technical requirements of digital projects (including web-based projects)
- Website ephemerality
- The expanding internet (i.e., the increasing number of websites and pages)
- Project institutionalization
- Copyright protections.

There are many technical requirements of such a project, often necessitating skills not part of traditional academic humanities or social science degrees. Indeed such technical skills were not necessary for my graduate education. The servers and associated software constitute the "back end" of web-based projects. At the front end is the web design of the site, involving interface and content. All involve some degree of coding and programming. My Internet Service Provider handles the server-side matters, although I could become involved in some aspects of this. I directly create the website structure via coding in HTML and CSS, as well as via programming with Javascript. The challenge lies in creating user-friendly interfaces and in managing content (i.e., the updating of pages with links to primary and secondary sources). A server-side database would be of great help here, but this is a task for the future, as I indicate below in the institutionalization challenge.

Another technical challenge involves the digitalization of the sources presented on the website itself. Digitalization can generate certain problems, such as introducing errors when creating searchable texts via optical character recognition. OCR technology has significantly advanced in the past few years, but errors can still occur during the conversion from image files to machine-readable text. Hence OCR still requires human oversight and double-checking. Certainly digitalization projects may create page facsimiles via book scanning and omit the OCR process that creates searchable text layers for end-users. Repositories utilize human curators to write metadata describing via keywords the page facsimiles in the collection. By so doing, searches are limited to the attendant—and valuable—metadata that were written later to describe the works themselves. Nonetheless being able to search the texts themselves can offer opportunities to discover new dimensions of the text not described by the metadata.

Websites and pages can be ephemeral, especially for noninstitutionalized sites. Sometimes without warning or notification, digitized texts and web pages can disappear. As a consequence, links are unstable and may not point to an extant web page or site. Site managers need to monitor the availability of their external links and update them. For their part, end-users might be able to locate such broken links and lost content by searching the Wayback Machine website, which archives many, if not all, web pages and sites. Thus the ephemeral aspects of websites emphasize the need to institutionalize digital projects so that they persist beyond the career of one or a few individuals.

Juxtaposed rather glaringly with the ephemerality of websites is the phenomenon of the increasing number of websites and web pages. The tendency of cyberspace denizens to add new sites and materials illuminates the key role of search engines that index the internet and the need to allocate more time to seek those new items. Search engines "crawl" the web to develop a massive collection of links. Yet search engines can only find web pages that link to one another. Web pages not so linked may not be included in a search engine's cache of crawled pages and thus may not populate a search query. This has significance for content: unless someone directly cites a page, it will be invisible to others. Hence researchers may not find some materials.

Sustaining a digital legacy for Du Bois will involve institutionalizing the process.[21] Monetary resources and technical expertise figure prominently on the list. A trained staff can help in various ways, from digitizing and proofing documents to searching for and adding cross-references and contextual information to the works. In addition, technical knowledge, such as creating database structures, would make for better searching and for greater expansion of a site. All of these limitations can be erased or moderated with some sort of institutional support, whether as part of an organization or as a recipient of funds from a granting agency. Such assistance would also help to perpetuate any given Du Bois site beyond the career or time of any one person.

Copyright restrictions seriously constrain the creation of a freely available digital collection of Du Bois's works. Following copyright law, free primary and secondary sources are typically limited to those legally found in the public domain.[22] Hence there tends to be a bias toward the works of Du Bois published prior to 1923. The legal constraints on the online availability of the author's works can result in an emphasis, perhaps overemphasis, on texts in the public domain. Excluded from free perusal and downloading on the internet would be most of Du Bois's published later works. Consequently their significance for his legacy remains bound to digital paywalls and to the hard-copy realm of libraries and booksellers.

## In Closing

This essay has focused on the examples that point to a digital heritage of Du Bois in the twenty-first century. I wish to close by sketching three dimensions that mediate any understanding of Du Bois's legacy in the internet age:

- The digital divide
- The epistemic implications of the content of a website
- The incomplete corpus factor as regards Du Bois's works.

A point that the later Du Bois would no doubt mention is the material base upon which the whole discussion of a digital legacy of Du Bois is predicated. In particular, I refer to the digital divide, which is the split between those with and without computers and internet access. The digital divide has decreased in some general respects over the past few years. However, as with such generalizations there are still gaps between those with access to the internet and those without. Poorer households, rural communities, and black and Hispanic households still face disparities compared with richer households, urban areas, and white households. Moreover broadband connectivity has become a component of the digital divide.[23] Because a digital divide still exists within the USA and across the globe, many people will not possess the interconnectivity that has become an integral part of a globalizing world. Accordingly, access to the internet and to archival sources, such as a digital Du Bois, will tend to be more demographically limited than it should be. Scholars such as Ernest James Wilson III research such inequalities in the digital age (see his website at www.digitaldubois.net).

The second dimension that mediates our understanding of Du Bois's digital legacy involves the production of knowledge. To archive items and to select items for reporting is as much about the conditions for producing knowledge as it is about making information accessible.[24] Each archive and links-site faces the epistemic implications of the curators' choices. We can ponder such implications in the following question: Whose work is archived or linked and whose is not? And what type of knowledge can be produced from the materials housed at and linked from a website? I will address the epistemic implications with reference to WEBDuBois.org.

The overall scope of my academic research tends to influence the content of the materials presented on the site. Specifically, I am interested in Du Bois and his intellectual context, with emphases on philosophical issues and on the relationship between social research and activism. I consider my site an academic clearinghouse of links to freely accessible online materials that will help and inform academic research. Of course, my definitions of academic research and the materials useful for scholarly study are not the only possible definitions. I emphasize academics (scholars and/or professional educators, regardless of ideological orientation), as well as those who cover academic topics, which would encompass other professionals (e.g., journalists). Such criteria will also include related organizations and institutions, such as academically related professional associations or societies and the Library of Congress. Obviously, other persons in addition to academic scholars and other professionals may very well have something to contribute to our understanding of Du Bois, his context, and his relevance. I recognize that such nonprofessional commentators can create works and responses that are themselves worthy of study. This, however, is not my line of research, and thus the knowledge base represented by WEBDuBois.org typically does not list them.

The third dimension that mediates our understanding of Du Bois's digital legacy I call the "incomplete corpus factor." We have repositories but no single corpus of the works of Du Bois. That is to say, we have no comprehensive set of Du Bois's published and unpublished works (including drafts, notes, and marginalia). Umbra Search and Digital Commonwealth have taken steps to create search pathways across repositories, but this is not the same as one single assemblage of Du Boisian primary sources. One single corpus—indeed the striving toward the ideal of one exhaustive corpus—would be doubly important. More comprehensive studies of the development of Du Bois's thinking could be pursued across the many and varied works, and the computational approaches of digital humanities might be used to analyze at one time and as one group the entirety of all of Du Bois's works, or at least all works so far recovered.[25]

We do not even know the full extent of Du Bois's primary sources that might be available. Extant bibliographies are useful but do not include everything.[26] This I can attest based on my personal research and my regular updating of WEBDuBois.org. For an interesting case study illustrating my claim, see my web page on Du Bois's "The Individual and Social Conscience," a primary source once unknown to Du Bois scholars.[27] Because new materials might be recovered in the future from an even more expanded set of digital resources, any corpus that we can create would be uncertain, even if it is the best available at one point in time.

Although a digital corpus of Du Bois's works might never be exhaustive, that could remain a vital goal in the project of promoting Du Bois's digital legacy, a legacy through which he might add his voice to the analyses of abiding oppression and share his ideals of equality and democracy in the struggles toward justice. For such a goal and such a project, perhaps it would not be too bold of us to imagine the support of W. E. B. Du Bois.

## Appendix: Websites Referenced

### Du Bois-Specific Collections

Credo online repository at the Special Collections and University Archive at the University of Massachusetts–Amherst Library (finding aid with links to online items), http://credo.library.umass.edu/view/collection/mums312

Digital Commonwealth, Massachusetts Collections Online, https://www.digitalcommonwealth.org/collections/commonwealth-oai:z603r1187

Beinecke Rare Book and Manuscript Library at the Yale University Library, http://beinecke.library.yale.edu

Beinecke Rare Book and Manuscript Library, Yale University (Du Bois's items online), http://brbl-dl.library.yale.edu/vufind/Search/Results?lookfor=JWJ_MSS_8&type=CallNumber

Beinecke Rare Book and Manuscript Library (finding aid for Du Bois collection), http://drs.library.yale.edu/HLTransformer/HLTransServlet?stylename=yul.ead2002.xhtml.xsl&pid=beinecke:dubois&clear-stylesheet-cache=yes

The Encyclopaedia Africana Project (Accra, Ghana), http://www.endarkenment.com/eap/legacy/scholars/index.htm

Special Collections and Archives, Fisk University (no online access to the Du Bois materials), www.fisk.edu/academics/library/special-collections-and-archives (the finding aid for the Du Bois manuscripts is accessed from this page)

New York Public Library, Archives and Manuscripts (Schomburg Center), "W. E. B. Du Bois Papers, 1906–1966 [bulk 1942–1948]," http://archives.nypl.org/scm/20716

W. E. B. DuBois Memorial Centre for Pan African Culture, Accra, Ghana, https://www.facebook.com/WEB-Du-Bois-Memorial-Centre-for

-Pan-African-Culture-256159387785989/; http://webduboiscentreaccra
.ghana-net.com. (The latter URL is not the official site of the Du Bois
Centre; it is as part of Ghana-Net.com. This notice is located at the bottom of the home page for the site. No name or date is listed.)

### Topical and Thematic Collections

Documenting the American South is maintained by the University of North
 Carolina, http://docsouth.unc.edu/browse/collections.html; http://docsouth
 .unc.edu/browse/author/d.html
The Black Past: The Online Reference Guide to African American History
 (Quintard Taylor), https://blackpast.org
Marxists.org, https://www.marxists.org/archive/padmore/1947/pan-african
 -congress/ch05.htm
Black Press Research Collective, http://blackpressresearchcollective.org
 /resources/scholarship-archives
Modernist Journals Project, http://www.modjourn.org/render.php?view=
 mjp_object&id=crisiscollection
The Poetry Foundation, https://www.poetryfoundation.org/bio/w-e-b-du
 -bois

### Institutionally Focused Collections

Digital Collection of the Robert W. Woodruff Library at the Atlanta University Center, http://hbcudigitallibrary.auctr.edu/cdm/landingpage
 /collection/rwwl (*Bulletin of Atlanta University*)
Roger, Sidney. 1998. "A Liberal Journalist on the Air and on the Water-
 front: Labor and Political Issues, 1932–1990," an oral history
 conducted in 1989 and 1990 by Julie Shearer, International Longshoremen's and Warehousemen's Union Oral History Series, Regional Oral
 History Office, Bancroft Library, University of California. Transcript:
 Online Archive of California, http://www.oac.cdlib.org/view?docId=
 kt1000013q&brand=oac4&doc.view=enitre_text
Online Archive of California, http://www.oac.cdlib.org
The Digital Library of Georgia at the University of Georgia Libraries, "Atlanta
 University Publications," http://fax.libs.uga.edu/E185x5xA881p/; http://
 fax.libs.uga.edu/E185x5xA881p/aupmenu.html
Smithsonian Folkways, www.folkways.si.edu
Du Bois's speech at the Wisconsin Socialist Club, 1960, https://www
 .folkways.si.edu/search/?query=Du+Bois+socialism

Moses Asch's 1961 interview of Du Bois, https://www.folkways.si.edu
/albumdetails.aspx?itemid=1031;    https://www.folkways.si.edu/search/
?query=Du+Bois+Asch
*Jewish Currents,* https://jewishcurrents.org; http://archive.jewishcurrents
.org/sid-resnick-historical-archive/; http://archive.jewishcurrents.org/wp
-content/uploads/2016/10/jcarchive016-1.pdf

### General Repositories

Google Books, https://books.google.com
HathiTrust Digital Library, https://www.hathitrust.org
Internet Archive, https://archive.org
Project Gutenberg, http://www.gutenberg.org
"Du Bois, W. E. B. (William Edward Burghardt)," http://www.gutenberg
.org/ebooks/author/226
Unz.org (Ron Unz), http://www.unz.org

### U.S. Government Repositories

F.B.I. Records, The Vault (surveillance files on Du Bois), https://vault.fbi
.gov/E.%20B.%20(William)%20Dubois
Library of Congress, Web guide entitled "W. E. B. Du Bois: Online
Resources" (compiled by Angela McMillian), https://www.loc.gov/rr
/program/bib/dubois/
Library of Congress, "Chronicling America: Historic American Newspapers," https://chroniclingamerica.loc.gov

### For-Profit Collections

Alexander Street Press, https://alexanderstreet.com; https://alexanderstreet
.com/products/black-thought-and-culture
Pacifica Radio Archives, https://www.pacificaradioarchives.org

### Search and Metasearch Engines

Dogpile, www.dogpile.com
DuckDuckGo, https://duckduckgo.com
The Digital Public Library of America, https://dp.la
Umbra Search, www.umbrasearch.org

## Human-Organized Directories

The Online Books Page (Mark Ockerbloom), http://onlinebooks.library
.upenn.edu

Voice of the Shuttle (Alan Liu), http://vos.ucsb.edu

## Other Sites Mentioned in the Essay

African American Intellectual History Society, www.aaihs.org

Black Perspectives, https://www.aaihs.org/black-perspectives/

DHCommons.org: A Collaboration Hub, http://www.dhcommons.org

Dickinson Electronic Archive, http://www.emilydickinson.org

Digital Du Bois: Considering W. E. B., Communities & the Information Age
(Ernest James Wilson III), www.digitaldubois.net; www.ernestjwilson
.com

Digital Harlem: Everyday Life 1915–1930, http://digitalharlem.org

"Digital Schomburg African American Women Writers of the 19th Century," http://digital.nypl.org/schomburg/writers_aa19/

DiRT Directory, https://dirtdirectory.org

H-Afro-Am, http://networks.h-net.org/h-afro-am

Malcolm X: A Research Site (Abdul Alkalimat), http://www.brothermalcolm
.net

NINES (Networked Infrastructure for Nineteenth Century Electronic
Scholarship), http://www.nines.org

Retextualizer: Digital Humanities Project by Robert W. Williams, http://
www.webdubois.org/dhp/rwdhp.html

Roy Rosenzweig Center for History and New Media, George Mason University, https://rrchnm.org/

U.S. Intellectual History, https://s-usih.org

TAPoR 3 (Text Analysis Portal for Research), http://tapor.ca/home

The Valley of the Shadow, http://valley.vcdh.virginia.edu

Voyant tools, https://voyant-tools.org/

The Ward: Race and Class in Du Bois' Seventh Ward (Amy Hillier), http://
www.dubois-theward.org

Wayback Machine, https://archive.org/web/

Women Writers Project, https://wwp.northeastern.edu/

## Notes

I wish to thank Phillip Luke Sinitiere for very helpful comments and suggestions in the drafting process of this essay.

1. Walter Benjamin, "The Work of Art in the Age of Mechanical Reproduction," in *Illuminations*, ed. Hannah Arendt, trans. Harry Zohn (New York: Schocken Books, 1968).

2. Martha Nell Smith, "Computing: What's American Literary Study Got to Do with IT,?" *American Literature* 74:4 (2002): 833–57, at 839.

3. W. E. B. Du Bois, *The Education of Black People: Ten Critiques, 1906–1960*, ed. Herbert Aptheker (Amherst: University of Massachusetts Press, 1973); W. E. B. Du Bois, *The Correspondence of W. E. B. Du Bois*, vol. 1: *Selections, 1877–1934*, ed. Herbert Aptheker (Amherst: University of Massachusetts Press, 1973); W. E. B. Du Bois, *The Correspondence of W. E. B. Du Bois*, vol. 2: *Selections, 1934–1944*, ed. Herbert Aptheker (Amherst: University of Massachusetts Press, 1976); W. E. B. Du Bois, *The Correspondence of W. E. B. Du Bois*, vol. 3: *Selections, 1944–1963*, ed. Herbert Aptheker (Amherst: University of Massachusetts Press, 1978); W. E. B. Du Bois, *Prayers for Dark People*, ed. Herbert Aptheker (Amherst: University of Massachusetts Press, 1980); W. E. B. Du Bois, *Against Racism: Unpublished Essays, Papers, Addresses, 1887–1961*, ed. Herbert Aptheker (Amherst: University of Massachusetts Press, 1985).

4. W. E. B. Du Bois, "The Renaissance of Ethics: A Critical Comparison of Scholastic and Modern Ethics" (1889), W. E. B. Du Bois Collection, JWJ MSS 8, Box 3, Folder 57, Beinecke Rare Book & Manuscript Library, Yale University; W. E. B. Du Bois, *Dusk of Dawn: As Essay toward an Autobiography of a Race Concept* (New York: Harcourt, Brace, 1940); W. E. B. Du Bois, *The World and Africa* (1947; Millwood, NY: Kraus-Thomson, 1976).

5. Ed Madison, "WEB Du Bois Center—Ghana West Africa—Personal Library," YouTube, September 1, 2013, https://youtube.com/watch?v=qCzSKHkCkXs.

6. W. E. B. Du Bois, *The Souls of Black Folk* (Chicago: A. C. McClurg, 1903); W. E. B. Du Bois, ed., *Atlanta University Publications* [Various titles] (Atlanta, GA: Atlanta University Press, 1898–1916).

7. W. E. B. Du Bois, "The Negro Nation within the Nation," *Current History* 42 (June 1935): 265–70; W. E. B. Du Bois, "Behold the Land," *Freedomways* 4 (Winter 1946): 9–15; W. E. B. Du Bois, Summary of "An Appeal to the World: A Statement of Denial of Human Rights to Minorities in the Case of the Citizens of Negro Descent in the United States of America and an Appeal to the United Nations for Redress" (ca. 1946), W. E. B.

Du Bois Papers, Special Collections & University Archives, University of Massachusetts–Amherst Library, accessed January 14, 2019, http://credo .library.umass.edu/view/full/mums312-b229-i021.

8. W. E. B. Du Bois, "The Pan-African Movement," in *Colonial and Coloured Unity: A Programme of Action. History of the Pan-African Congress*, ed. George Padmore (London: Hammersmith Bookshop, 1947), accessed: January 14, 2019, http://www.marxists.org/archive/padmore /1947/pan-african-congress/ch05.htm.

9. W. E. B. Du Bois, "Two Hundred Years of Segregated Schools," *Jewish Life*, February 1955, accessed January 14, 2019, http://archive .jewishcurrents.org/wp-content/uploads/2016/10/jcarchive016-1.pdf .

10. Allison Meier, "W. E. B. Du Bois's Modernist Data Visualizations of Black Life," *Hyperallergic*, July 4, 2016, https://hyperallergic.com /306559/w-e-b-du-boiss-modernist-data-visualizations-of-black-life/. On data portraits, see http://www.loc.gov/pictures/collection/anedub/. See also Whitney Battle-Baptiste and Britt Rusert, eds., *W. E. B. Du Bois's Data Portraits: Visualizing Black America* (Princeton: Princeton Architectural Press, 2018).

11. Peter B. Hirtle, "When Is 1923 Going to Arrive and Other Complications of the U.S. Public Domain," *Searcher* 20:6 (September 2012), http://www.infotoday.com/searcher/Sep12/Hirtle--When-Is-1923-Going-to -Arrive-and-Other-Complications-of-the-U.S.-Public-Domain.shtml.

12. Martha Nell Smith, "The Human Touch Software of the Highest Order: Revisiting Editing as Interpretation," *Textual Cultures: Texts, Contexts, Interpretations* 2:1 (Spring 2007): 1–15.

13. Richard Cullen Rath, "W. E. B. Du Bois, *Souls of Black Folk*, Musical Hypertext Edition," accessed January 14, 2019, http://way.net /SoulsOfBlackFolk/.

14. Allan Liu, "The Meaning of the Digital Humanities," *PMLA: Proceedings of the Modern Language Association* 128:2 (2013): 409–23, https://escholarship.org/uc/item/5gc857tw.

15. Matthew K. Gold and Lauren F. Klein, eds., *Debates in the Digital Humanities, 2016 Ed.* (Minneapolis: University of Minnesota Press, 2016), http://dhdebates.gc.cuny.edu/debates?id=2; Kenneth M. Price and Ray Siemens, *Literary Studies in the Digital Age: An Evolving Anthology, 2013–2015*, accessed January 14, 2019, https://dlsanthology.mla .hcommons.org/. Susan Schreibman, Ray Siemens, and John Unsworth, eds., *A Companion to Digital Humanities* (Oxford: Blackwell, 2004), http:// www.digitalhumanities.org/companion/.

16. W. E. B. Du Bois, *The Philadelphia Negro: A Social Study* (Philadelphia: Ginn, 1899).

17. For example, Dorothy Kim and Jesse Stommel, eds., *Disrupting the Digital Humanities*, accessed January 19, 2019, www.disruptingdh.com /position-papers/; Roopika Risam, "On Disruption, Race, and the Digital Humanities," *Disrupting the Digital Humanities*, digital edition, January 5, 2015, www.disruptingdh.com/on-disruption-race-and-the-digital -humanities.

18. Jerome McGann and Lisa Samuels, "Deformance and Interpretation," *New Literary History* 30:1 (Winter 1999): 25–56.

19. Uzoma O. Miller, "Talented 10th Revisited: Contextualized Knowing and Transdisciplinary Implications Associated with the Processing of the W. E. B. Du Bois Collection, 1867 to 1963," Fisk University, *2011 Monograph Series* conference proceedings, 1293–311, National Association of African American Studies, 19th Annual Conference, February 14–19, 2011, https://www.naaas.org/wp-content/uploads/2014/10 /2011monograph.pdf.

20. W. E. B. Du Bois, "The Superior Race (An Essay)," *Smart Set: A Magazine of Cleverness* 70:4 (April 1923): 55–60, http://www.webdubois.org /dbSuperiorRace.html; W. E. B. Du Bois, "Criteria of Negro Art," *The Crisis* 32 (October 1926): 290–97, http://www.webdubois.org/dbCriteriaNArt .html; W. E. B. Du Bois, "Douglass, Frederick," *Dictionary of American Biography: Cushman—Eberle*, vol. 5, ed. Allen Johnson and Dumas Malone (London: Humphrey Milford, Oxford University Press, 1930), http://www .webdubois.org/dbDouglass1930.html; W. E. B. Du Bois, "The Negro Citizen," in *The Negro in Civilization*, ed. Charles S. Johnson (New York: Henry Holt, 1930), 461–70, http://www.webdubois.org/dbTNCitizen.html; W. E. B. Du Bois, "The Church and Religion," *The Crisis* 40.10 (October 1933): 236–37, http://www.webdubois.org/dbChurchAndReligion .html; W. E. B. Du Bois, "Jacob and Esau," *The Talladegan* 62.1 (November 1944): 1–6, http://www.webdubois.org/dbJacobEsau.html; W. E. B. Du Bois, "My Evolving Program for Negro Freedom," in *What the Negro Wants*, ed. Rayford W. Logan (Chapel Hill: University of North Carolina Press, 1944), 31–70, http://www.webdubois.org/dbMyEvolvingPrgm.html.

21. Ashley Reed, "Managing an Established Digital Humanities Project: Principles and Practices from the Twentieth Year of the William Black Archive," *Digital Humanities Quarterly* 8.1 (2014), http://www .digitalhumanities.org/dhq/vol/8/1/000174/000174.html.

22. Rich Stim, "The Public Domain," Copyright and Fair Use, Stanford University Libraries, accessed January 14, 2019, https://fairuse.stanford .edu/overview/public-domain/welcome; U.S. Copyright Law, December 2011, http://www.copyright.gov/title17.

23. Council of Economic Advisers, "Mapping the Digital Divide," *Council of Economic Advisers Issue Brief, July 2015*, accessed January 14, 2019, https://obamawhitehouse.archives.gov/sites/default/files/wh_digital_divide_issue_brief.pdf; Lee Raine, "Digital Divides 2016," Pew Research Center: Internet, Science & Technology (2016), accessed January 14, 2019, http://www.pewinternet.org/2016/07/14/digital-divides-2016/.

24. Adeline Koh, "Addressing Archival Silence on 19th Century Colonialism—Part 1: The Power of the Archive," blog post, March 4, 2012, http://www.rogerwhitson.net/?p=1509.

25. For example, Franco Moretti, *Distant Reading* (London: Verso Books, 2013).

26. For example, Herbert Aptheker, ed., *Annotated Bibliography of the Published Writings of W. E. B. Du Bois* (Millwood, NY: Kraus-Thomson, 1973); Joan Nordquist, ed., *W. E. B. Du Bois: A Bibliography* (Santa Cruz, CA: Reference and Research Services, 2002); Paul G. Partington, compiler, *W. E. B. Du Bois, 1883–1922: The First Four Decades of His Published Writings—A Collected Edition of His Shorter Works*, Los Angeles Microfilm Company of California (Whittier, CA: Paul G. Partington, 1979); Paul G. Partington, compiler, *W. E. B. Du Bois: A Bibliography of His Published Writings*, revised Edition (Whittier, CA: Paul G. Partington, 1979).

27. Robert W. Williams, "W. E. B. Du Bois's 'The Individual and Social Conscience' (1905): The Primary Source and Its Interpretation," revised May 1, 2018, http://www.webdubois.org/wdb-iasc.html.

# Afterword

## Gerald Horne

Those who publish often inflate the importance of their work. It would be difficult for those who have contributed to this worthy volume to engage in this typical academic puffery, for from the title on the cover to the last sentence, hundreds of pages later, this book has vaulted to the forefront not only of the already capacious field of Du Bois studies but, as well, it establishes a new interpretive framework for African American studies. That is to say, Robert Williams's innovative sketching of the "digital Du Bois" is the pathfinder pointing scholars toward the future of scholarship, which—inevitably though not *exclusively*—must encompass cyberspace.

However, it is the title of this volume that is illuminating. Because of the horrid oppression endured by peoples of African descent in North America, we have been compelled to engage forces beyond these shores (not to mention Native American polities within these borders), be they in Spain or Britain or Haiti or Mexico or Japan or the Soviet Union or China—not to mention a rising Africa and the Caribbean. In short, Du Bois as a "citizen of the world" was both emulating and leading what Yuichiro Onishi and Toru Shinoda—citing the father of Pan-Africanism himself—refer to as "a Negro nation within the nation." Indeed the direct (dialectical) implication of this stimulating book is that a black nationalist perforce must be a black internationalist.

This concept, simple and anodyne at first blush, actually sheds light on some of the more controversial aspects of Du Bois's legacy. For nations since time immemorial have often felt constrained to enter into global alliances that cosseted scholars then interpret out of context.

Thus few—even within the U.S. ruling elite—take issue with the pro-Moscow alliance brokered by Washington in 1941–45. During this conflictual era, in aid of this desperately needed relationship, the White House importuned Hollywood to produce pro-Soviet movies.[1] The most telling of this celluloid onslaught, *Mission to Moscow*, portrays the

Soviet leader Josef Stalin as a benevolent generalissimo much beloved by his compatriots, and echoes the Georgian's position with regard to the internal opposition he faced from the likes of Leon Trotsky. Of course, this film was hardly sui generis but echoed a consensus in the mass media and elite circles generally, as the U.S. thought it was in a pitiless struggle for survival against formidable foes in Berlin and Tokyo particularly.

Strikingly, those who reproach Du Bois for taking a similar pro-Moscow view before 1941 and after 1945 have not been vocal about critiquing Washington for adopting a similar stance, though the "Negro nation"—subject to lynching, mass murder, systematic deprivation, and worse—also found itself in a pitiless struggle for survival. I take it that there is one set of rules for a superpower and another for a persecuted minority.

A corresponding viewpoint is illuminating in, for example, scrutinizing Du Bois's lack of sympathy for those who were seeking to overthrow the pro-communist regime in Budapest in 1956. Just recently, George Soros, the Hungarian American billionaire, characterized today's Hungarian regime as a "Mafia State" and extended his reproach to neighboring Poland.[2] These current regimes followed the much-beleaguered communist parties, and a fair characterization renders them lineal descendants of those who sought strenuously and successfully during the cold war to attain power. Whereas the predecessor regimes during Du Bois's lifetime—often at the eminent scholar's behest—sought to educate young Africans seeking to escape the torpor of colonialism, the current regimes of late have made a fetish of expelling Africans escaping the misery of neocolonialism[3] and have revived the coruscating specter of racism and anti-Semitism that, it was thought, had been extirpated.

It is well past time to compare the deposed regimes not to the idealized fantasies that prevailed among some in 1989 but to those that supplanted them. It is quite illuminative that the man accused of assassinating Chris Hani in 1993, the man thought widely to be Nelson Mandela's logical successor and who would spearhead the next stage of South Africa's evolution—radical economic redistribution, given his articulate predilections as leader of the South African Communist Party—was an anticommunist refugee from socialist Poland, Janusz Walus.[4]

Similarly, it is now notorious—though rarely acknowledged—that Washington overdetermined Moscow during the cold war and forged alliances with religious zealots and China, precisely the two forces that will be dogging this republic for decades to come. (Before he died, Richard Nixon—the supposedly savvy architect of the new tie to Beijing—confessed in embarrassment, "We may have created a Frankenstein" in the untrammeled zeal to destabilize Moscow by bolstering Beijing.)[5] And even with the excessive focus on regime change in Moscow during the cold war, today's relations with Russia have eventuated in a relationship that in some ways is worse than that which operated during the tensest cold war days.[6] In sum, even the U.S. ruling elite may have benefited from emulating Du Bois and toning down its zealous anticommunism and anti-Sovietism, which now have backfired and boomeranged with consequences too ghastly to contemplate.

In other words, nations—including the "Negro nation"—make choices based upon the realities with which they are faced and not necessarily upon nonexistent idealized fantasies. This is precisely what Du Bois—and his comrades—did during their tumultuous lifetimes, when they leaned toward now deposed governments in Eastern Europe. As some of the work I have produced in recent decades—which has been cited generously within these pages—tends to suggest, radicals like Du Bois were sacrificial lambs whose cold war sacrifice helped to engender a retreat from the more egregious aspects of Jim Crow; however, the condition precedent for this Copernican change was the alliance with the global left embodied in the person of Du Bois.

Just as it can be argued fairly that the Haitian Revolution engendered a general crisis of the entire slave system that could be resolved only with the collapse of this edifice of iniquity,[7] it is also fair to suggest that it was the Scottsboro case, a cause dramatized by pro-Moscow communists at home and abroad, that forged a global movement against Jim Crow—not unlike that which beset apartheid in the 1980s—that led ultimately to the collapse of this successor edifice of iniquity: U.S. apartheid.[8] The price paid for this "concession" was the marginalizing of those like Du Bois, which has handicapped African Americans in the present conjuncture and makes our future quite dicey. Du Bois, a man whose roots reached into Hispaniola and who boldly epitomized the honored status as "citizen of the world," thus becomes an embodiment of this still besieged minority: his life carries many lessons that this valuable book reflects.

Tellingly, once these so-called pro-Moscow Negroes were isolated, it led to the rise of those who adopted a pro-Tokyo posture in previous decades—for example, the Nation of Islam—and the ultimate triumph of those who had walked in the footsteps of M. K. Gandhi, such as the pro-Delhi Negroes.[9] (Interestingly, Islam too is a transnational movement.)

The Negro as a "nation within a nation" is also a useful lens through which to view Du Bois's much-scrutinized advocacy of cooperatives in the 1930s. When Washington pursues an explicit policy of apartheid, depriving a significant percentage of its citizenry of employment and a simple livelihood, one can assuredly seek to break down these walls of oppression. On the other hand, just as radical political parties globally not only struggle against capitalism but also develop enterprises—be they journals or publishing houses or travel agencies or mutual aid agencies and the like—it surely made sense then (as now) for African Americans to act in a like manner.

In sum, self-determination, which has been a pivotal ethos among Africans on this continent since the 1600s,[10] is not simply an expression of nationality which then requires diplomatic relations with other nations (particularly those who are at odds with your primary antagonist), but also this concept is a matter of hardheaded defense in the face of merciless oppressors.

What this also suggests is that the currently operative frameworks for understanding African American history are deficient. "From slavery to freedom" shrouds more than it reveals,[11] while making our odyssey seem like fraternity hazing before "crossing the burning sands": this trope simultaneously obscures the all-important global factor. "From plantation to ghetto" is conversely much too downbeat,[12] while similarly concealing—once more—the global factor. This veiling may not be accidental, for the pursuance of global allies by African Americans often brings this group into conflict with Washington and—as ever—potentially compromises both U.S. sovereignty and national security alike. A more accurate—and helpful—framework should incorporate a contrasting trope: "from counterrevolution to revolution," that is, from the revolt against abolition in 1776[13] through the Haitian Revolution to the Bolshevik Revolution and considering in between the Mexican Revolution,[14] the Cuban Revolution,[15] and so on. This is the most explanatory framework for contemplating our history.

Yet, for my purposes here, this worthy volume illustrates decisively that why we continue to celebrate Du Bois a century and a half since his birth is precisely because his internationalism embodies the central lesson of our often difficult history: today more than ever we need many more to exemplify Du Bois, a true "citizen of the world."

# Notes

1. See, e.g., Gerald Horne, *Class Struggle in Hollywood, 1930–1950: Moguls, Mobsters, Stars, Reds, and Trade Unionists* (Austin: University of Texas Press, 2001).

2. Palko Karasz, "Soros Sees 'Mafia State' under Hungary's Leader," *New York Times*, June 1, 2017. See also Lili Bayer and Larry Cohler-Esses, "The Two Jews in Viktor Orban's Life," *Forward* (New York City), June 2, 2017: the anticommunist regime in Budapest "has been waging an increasingly shrill campaign against . . . George Soros, often using classical anti-Semitic imagery." One of the regime's close allies is Arthur Finkelstein, a former aide to Jim Crow senators Jesse Helms and J. Strom Thurmond. Ironically, Soros financed Orban during the cold war era, as the billionaire's class interests surpassed other considerations. Intriguingly, this is one of the risks African Americans endure today, as those with elite class interests often speak for the entire community—whose interests often are inconsistent with those of the elite. Contradictorily, many who hail the 1956 anti-Soviet revolt in Budapest simultaneously are critical of the current government in Washington, D.C., which too has been sympathetic to this uprising. See, e.g., Lili Bayer, "Gorka Backed Formation of Anti-Semitic Militia," *Forward*, April 14, 2017: a key foreign policy adviser to the current government in Washington, Sebastian Gorka, not only "publicly supported" a "violent racist" grouping in the land of his birth, Hungary, but hails from a prominent anticommunist family there. See also the editorial "The EU Must Act against Illiberal Forces Within,' *Financial Times*, May 25, 2017: here "authoritarianism" in Poland is condemned unreservedly.

3. Mabel Berezin, *Illiberal Politics in Neo-Liberal Times: Culture, Security and Populism in the New Europe* (New York: Cambridge University Press, 2009); Paul Lendvai, *Hungary: Between Democracy and Authoritarianism* (London: Hurst, 2012).

4. John Pomfret, "Alleged S. African Assassin Is Called Anti-Communist," *Washington Post*, April 13, 1993; George Fetherling, *The Book of Assassins* (New York: Random House, 2001).

5. Graham Allison, *Destined for War: Can America and China Escape Thucydides's Trap?* (Boston: Houghton Mifflin, 2017), 215–16.

6. Gerald Horne, *Blows against the Empire: U.S. Imperialism in Crisis* (New York: International, 2008).

7. Gerald Horne, *Confronting Black Jacobins: The U.S., the Haitian Revolution, and the Origins of the Dominican Republic* (New York: Monthly Review Press, 2016).

8. Gerald Horne, *Black Revolutionary: William Patterson and the Globalization of the African American Freedom Struggle* (Urbana: University of Illinois Press, 2013).

9. Gerald Horne, "Race for the Planet: African Americans and U.S. Foreign Policy Reconsidered," *Diplomatic History* 19 (1995): 159–65.

10. V. P. Franklin, *Black Self-Determination: A Cultural History of African-American Resistance* (Brooklyn, NY: Lawrence Hill, 1992).

11. John Hope Franklin et al., *From Slavery to Freedom: A History of African Americans* (New York: McGraw Hill, 2011).

12. August Meier and Elliott Rudwick, *From Plantation to Ghetto* (New York: Hill and Wang, 1976).

13. Gerald Horne, *The Counter-Revolution of 1776: Slave Resistance and the Origins of the United States of America* (New York: New York University Press, 2014).

14. Gerald Horne, *Black and Brown: African Americans and the Mexican Revolution, 1910–1920* (New York: New York University Press, 2005).

15. Gerald Horne, *Race to Revolution: The U.S. and Cuba during Slavery and Jim Crow* (New York: Monthly Review Press, 2014).

# CONTRIBUTORS

**Lauren Louise Anderson**, an artist and author, holds a PhD in American history from Michigan State University. After a postdoctoral fellowship at the University of Kentucky, she taught African American history at Luther College in Iowa. She has recently shifted from academic history to art creation. She uses the knowledge and insights she gained as a historian to visually represent race, gender, and sexuality in diverse, real, and beautiful ways. She also created digital exhibits to showcase the extraordinary holdings of Smith College Special Collections. Her recent work can be seen at whimsandwhimsy.wordpress.com and sophia.smith .edu/ssw100-history.

**Bettina Aptheker** is Distinguished Professor Emerita in the Department of Feminist Studies at the University of California, Santa Cruz. She holds the Peggy and Jack Baskin Foundation Presidential Chair for Feminist Studies for 2017–20. She has published seven books, including a memoir, *Intimate Politics: How I Grew Up Red, Fought for Free Speech, and Became a Feminist Rebel* (2006), and *The Morning Breaks: The Trial of Angela Davis* (2nd ed., 1999). She has published many scholarly articles, including "The Passion and Pageantry of Shirley Graham's Opera *Tom-Tom*" (2016) and "Queer Dialectics/Feminist Interventions: Harry Hay and the Quest for a Revolutionary Politics" (2015). An activist for peace and social justice since the early 1960s and a major architect of the Feminist Studies Department at UCSC over a nearly forty-year career, she is now working on a book project, "Queering the History of the Communist Left in the United States," based on extensive archival research and interviews. Her father, Herbert, was the literary executor of the W. E. B. Du Bois papers.

**Derek Charles Catsam** is a professor of history and the Kathlyn Cosper Dunagan Professor in the Humanities at the University of Texas of the Permian Basin and is a senior research associate at Rhodes University in Grahamstown, South Africa, where he spent 2016 as the Hugh Le May Fellow in the Humanities. He is the author of three books: *Freedom's Main Line: The Journey of Reconciliation and the Freedom Rides*

(2009), *Beyond the Pitch: The Spirit, Culture, and Politics of Brazil's 2014 World Cup* (2014), and *Bleeding Red: A Red Sox Fan's Diary of the 2004 Season* (2005). He is currently working on books about bus boycotts in the United States and South Africa in the 1940s and 1950s and on the 1981 Springbok rugby tour to the United States. He has written widely on American and African politics and sports in both scholarly and popular outlets.

**Gerald Horne** holds the John J. and Rebecca Moores Chair of History and African American Studies at the University of Houston. His research addresses racism, labor, white supremacy, black radicalism, black internationalism, civil rights, and film. He is the author of more than thirty books, including *Negro Comrades of the Crown: African-Americans and the British Empire Fight the U.S. before Emancipation* (2012), *Black Revolutionary: William Patterson and the Globalization of the African American Freedom Struggle* (2013), *The Counter-Revolution of 1776: Slave Resistance and the Origins of the United States of America* (2014), *Paul Robeson: The Artist as Revolutionary* (2016), and *The Rise and Fall of the Associated Negro Press: Claude Barnett's Pan-African News and the Jim Crow Paradox* (2017).

**David Levering Lewis** is the Julius Silver University Professor Emeritus at New York University. A renowned historian, he received a 2009 National Humanities Medal. He is the author of books about Martin Luther King Jr. and the Harlem Renaissance, among many other subjects in the history of U.S. and European politics and culture. Lewis won the Bancroft Prize and two Pulitzer Prizes for his two-volume biography *W. E. B. Du Bois: Biography of a Race, 1868–1919* (1993) and *W. E. B. Du Bois, 1919–1963: The Fight for Equality and the New American Century* (2000). He has also written numerous articles on Du Bois, as well as editorial introductions to editions of *Black Reconstruction in America* and an essay about Du Bois's 1900 Paris Exhibition in *A Small Nation of People: W. E. B. Du Bois and African American Portraits of Progress* (2003).

**Erik S. McDuffie** is an associate professor of African American studies and history at the University of Illinois at Urbana-Champaign. He is author of the award-winning book *Sojourning for Freedom: Black Women, American Communism, and the Making of Black Left Feminism* (2011). Currently he is completing a book tentatively titled "Garveyism in the Diasporic Midwest: The American Heartland and Global Black Freedom, 1920–1980." Drawing on extensive original research conducted in Canada, Ghana, Grenada, Jamaica, Liberia, South Africa, Trinidad and

Tobago, the United Kingdom, and the United States, the book establishes the importance of the U.S. Midwest to twentieth-century global black history and demonstrates the vibrant political exchanges between the heartland and the African world through Garveyism. He is the recipient of fellowships from both National Endowment for the Humanities and the American Council for Learned Societies.

**Bill V. Mullen** is a professor of English and American studies at Purdue University. His books include *Un-American: W. E. B. Du Bois and the Century of World Revolution* (2015); *W. E. B. Du Bois: Revolutionary across the Color Line* (2016); *Afro-Orientalism* (2004), a study of interethnic antiracist alliance between Asian Americans and African Americans; and *Popular Fronts: Chicago and African American Cultural Politics 1935–1946* (1999). He has edited five other books in collaboration with Sherry Lee Linkon, James Smethurst, and Fred Ho. He has been a Fulbright lecturer at Wuhan University in the People's Republic of China. He is a faculty adviser to Students for Justice in Palestine at Purdue and a member of the organizing collective for the United States Campaign for the Academic and Cultural Boycott of Israel (USACB). His articles have appeared in *Social Text, African-American Review, American Quarterly, Modern Fiction Studies, Electronic Intifada, Truthout, Mondoweiss, Jacobin,* and elsewhere. He teaches courses in African American literature and culture, American studies, working-class literature, cultural studies, and postcolonial literature. He is currently working on a biography of James Baldwin titled "James Baldwin: Living in Fire," focusing on Baldwin's radical and queer politics.

**Gary Murrell** is an emeritus professor of history at Grays Harbor College in Washington state. He is the author of *The Most Dangerous Communist in The United States: A Biography of Herbert Aptheker* (2015) and *Iron Pants: Oregon's Anti–New Deal Governor, Charles Henry Martin* (2000). He is a regular contributor to *Works in Progress,* the radical monthly newspaper of Olympia, Washington.

**Yuichiro Onishi** is an associate professor of African American and African studies and Asian American studies at the University of Minnesota, Twin Cities. He is the author of *Transpacific Antiracism: Afro-Asian Solidarity in Twentieth-Century Black America, Japan, and Okinawa* (2013). His work also appears in several edited volumes, including *The Routledge Handbook of Asian American Studies* (2017) and *Traveling Texts and the Work of Afro-Japanese Cultural Production: Two Haiku and a Microphone* (2015). He is also the co-editor of the anthology titled *Transpacific Correspondence: Dispatches from Japan's Black Studies* (with Fumiko Sakashita of Ritsumeikan University in Kyoto), which will be published by Palgrave Macmillan.

**Toru Shinoda** is a professor of comparative labor studies in the School of Social Sciences at Waseda University in Tokyo. His numerous publications in Japanese and international periodicals range widely, from topics on U.S. labor history to those focusing on Japan. He has served as a columnist for *Rengo*, the organ of the Japan Trade Union Confederation, Japan's largest labor organization. Currently he is dean of the Center for International Education at Waseda University.

**Phillip Luke Sinitiere** is a professor of history at the College of Biblical Studies, a predominately African American college located in Houston's Mahatma Gandhi District. In 2018–19 he was a W. E. B. Du Bois Visiting Scholar at the University of Massachusetts–Amherst. A scholar of American religious history and African American studies, his books include *Christians and the Color Line: Race and Religion after* Divided by Faith (2013), *Protest and Propaganda: W. E. B. Du Bois,* The Crisis, *and American History* (2014), and *Salvation with a Smile: Joel Osteen, Lakewood Church, and American Christianity* (2015). His research addresses contemporary racial justice issues, including "Religion and the Black Freedom Struggle for Sandra Bland" (2018) and "The Aesthetic Insurgency of Sandra Bland's Afterlife" (2018). Sinitiere's Du Bois scholarship includes the essays "Of Faith and Fiction: Teaching W. E. B. Du Bois and Religion" (2012), "Leadership for Democracy and Peace: W. E. B. Du Bois's Legacy as a Pan-African Intellectual" (2014), "'Outline of Report on Economic Condition of the Negroes in the State of Texas': W. E. B. Du Bois' 1935 Speech at Prairie View State College" (2017), and ""There must be no idle mourning": W. E. B. Du Bois's Legacy as a Black Radical Intellectual" (2018).

**Alys Eve Weinbaum** is Professor of English at the University of Washington, Seattle. She teaches feminist studies, black studies, Marxist theory, and transatlantic literature and culture. She is the author of *The Afterlife of Reproductive Slavery: Biocapitalism and Black Feminism's Philosophy of History* (2019) and *Wayward Reproductions: Genealogies of Race and Nation in Transatlantic Modern Thought* (2004). She is coauthor (with the Modern Girl Around the World Research Group) of *The Modern Girl around the World: Consumption, Modernity, and Globalization* (2008) and a coeditor (with Susan Gillman) of *Next to the Color Line: Gender, Sexuality, and W. E. B. Du Bois* (2007). She is currently at work on two projects. One focuses on dystopian literary and filmic representation as historiography. The second expands on her ongoing study of the relationships among slave racial capitalism, biocapitalism and social reproduction.

**Robert W. Williams** is an associate professor of political science at Bennett College in Greensboro, North Carolina. He teaches courses on politics and government, political theory, African American political thought, and the writings of W. E. B. Du Bois. Other scholarly interests include environmental justice and the spatiality of politics. His current projects focus on the philosophical dimensions of Du Bois's thinking, especially as they pertain to his research and activism. He also works on Du Bois through digital humanities by using collation analysis and algorithmic textual displacement. Williams created and maintains a website devoted to W. E. B. Du Bois, http://www.webdubois.org, which contains primary and secondary sources available on the internet.

310